Japan Decides 2024

Kenneth M. McElwain · Robert J. Pekkanen ·
Daniel M. Smith
Editors

Japan Decides 2024

The Japanese General Election

Editors
Kenneth M. McElwain
University of Tokyo
Institute of Social Science
Tokyo, Japan

Robert J. Pekkanen
University of Washington
Seattle, WA, USA

Daniel M. Smith
University of Pennsylvania
Philadelphia, MA, USA

ISBN 978-3-031-98796-0   ISBN 978-3-031-98797-7 (eBook)
https://doi.org/10.1007/978-3-031-98797-7

© The Editor(s) (if applicable) and The Author(s), under exclusive license to Springer Nature Switzerland AG 2025

This work is subject to copyright. All rights are solely and exclusively licensed by the Publisher, whether the whole or part of the material is concerned, specifically the rights of translation, reprinting, reuse of illustrations, recitation, broadcasting, reproduction on microfilms or in any other physical way, and transmission or information storage and retrieval, electronic adaptation, computer software, or by similar or dissimilar methodology now known or hereafter developed.
The use of general descriptive names, registered names, trademarks, service marks, etc. in this publication does not imply, even in the absence of a specific statement, that such names are exempt from the relevant protective laws and regulations and therefore free for general use.
The publisher, the authors and the editors are safe to assume that the advice and information in this book are believed to be true and accurate at the date of publication. Neither the publisher nor the authors or the editors give a warranty, expressed or implied, with respect to the material contained herein or for any errors or omissions that may have been made. The publisher remains neutral with regard to jurisdictional claims in published maps and institutional affiliations.

Cover credit: Jon Hicks | Getty Images

This Palgrave Macmillan imprint is published by the registered company Springer Nature Switzerland AG
The registered company address is: Gewerbestrasse 11, 6330 Cham, Switzerland

If disposing of this product, please recycle the paper.

To Tomoka.
—*from Kenneth M. McElwain*

I dedicate this book to my friend, Erik Bleich, for his courage.
—*from Robert J. Pekkanen*

To John.
—*from Daniel M. Smith*

Acknowledgements

We are delighted to present the fifth volume in our series of high-quality analyses of general elections to Japan's House of Representatives, following *Japan Decides 2012, 2014, 2017,* and *2021*. This election saw Japan's perpetually dominant Liberal Democratic Party (LDP) post its second-worst showing ever, leaving it to eventually form a minority government. The chapters in this volume unpack the reasons behind this historical result. We wish to express our thanks once again to our wonderful editor, Ambra Finotello. We also welcomed on board a new editorial team member, Kenneth Mori McElwain. Thanks to Kenneth's efforts, this volume features many contributions from outstanding new Japan-based authors, further strengthening the volume in your hand and cementing its status as the premier venue for English-language analyses of Japanese elections. This is the first of the *Japan Decides* volumes not to feature Steven R. Reed as co-editor. The current editors salute Steve and thank him for his work to establish this series. It would not have been possible without him. Kenneth thanks his extended family in Japan and Ireland for their encouragement and inspiration. Robert thanks his family for their support. Dan thanks Kenneth and Robert for shouldering most of the hard parts of being an editor while still letting him join in on the fun parts.

CONTENTS

Part I Introduction

1 Introduction: LDP Dominance on the Edge 3
Kenneth M. McElwain, Robert J. Pekkanen,
and Daniel M. Smith

2 The 2024 Election Results: A Political Earthquake 17
Ko Maeda

Part II Political Parties

3 Reasons Behind the LDP's Loss in the 2024 Election 37
Kuniaki Nemoto

4 The CDP in 2024: The Legacy of the Electoral
Coalition with the JCP 57
Fumi Ikeda

5 A Costly Coalition: Kōmeitō's Enduring Partnership
with the LDP 75
Axel Klein and Levi McLaughlin

6 Why Did Public Support for the Japan Innovation
Party Decline in the 2024 HR Election? 91
Masahiro Zenkyo

Part III The Campaign

7 Electoral Campaigns in Japan's 2024 HR Election: Emerging Signs of Transformation   109
Michio Umeda

8 Policy Positions of the Candidates   127
Masaki Taniguchi, Taka-aki Asano, Shōko Ōmori, and Shūsuke Takamiya

9 How Party Manifestos Framed Political Distrust in the 2024 Election   145
Tomoko Matsumoto

10 Public Opinion and Scandals in Economic Hard Times   165
Yukio Maeda

11 Social Media in the 2024 General Election   183
Robert A. Fahey

12 Partisanship and Turnout in the 2024 General Election   199
Tetsuya Matsubayashi

Part IV Issues

13 Scandals During the Kishida Administration   219
Matthew M. Carlson

14 Perennial Fears, Novel Responses: The Unification Church in Japan after the Abe Assassination   237
Levi McLaughlin

15 Increase in Women's Representation and Candidates' Positions on Gender Equality Issues   257
Yuki Tsuji

16 LGBTQ+ Rights Issues and the 2024 Japanese Election   275
Kazuyoshi Kawasaka

17 Childcare Policy in the 2024 Election: Who Resonated with the Public Amid an Unprecedented Birthrate Decline?   295
Reiko Arami

18 Election Under Inflation: LDP's Choice
    of Macroeconomic Policy   319
    Kenya Amano and Saori N. Katada

19 Japan Decides Its Role in the Global Economy: Trade
    and Economic Security in the 2024 Election   335
    Kristin Vekasi

20 Conclusion: The LDP Loses Trust and the Illusion
    of Invincibility   349
    Kenneth M. McElwain, Robert J. Pekkanen,
    and Daniel M. Smith

Index   361

List of Figures

Fig. 2.1	Winning % of the LDP's SMD candidates	23
Fig. 2.2	LDP's PR vote change, 2021–2024	26
Fig. 2.3	Ishin candidates' votes in SMDs	28
Fig. 2.4	Ishin's PR votes by prefecture	29
Fig. 2.5	PR vote percentages, 2003–2024 (selected parties)	31
Fig. 3.1	Approval and disapproval rates of the cabinet	39
Fig. 4.1	Visits by prominent CDP party officials	64
Fig. 4.2	The percentage of votes obtained by major parties in PR tier	69
Fig. 5.1	Kōmeitō PR & SMD seats, 2000–2024	86
Fig. 5.2	Komeito PR votes in general elections, 2000–2024	86
Fig. 5.3	SMD results for Kōmeitō in Osaka	87
Fig. 6.1	The changes in support rates for Ishin in 2024	96
Fig. 6.2	Evaluations of Baba and support for both Ishin and Osaka Ishin	99
Fig. 6.3	Evaluations of Ishin's competence and voting shifts in the 2024 election	102
Fig. 8.1	Average values by political party for foreign policy and security issues	129
Fig. 8.2	Average values by political party for economic issues	130
Fig. 8.3	Average values by political party for social issues	131
Fig. 8.4	Average values by political party for corporate and group donations and factions	132
Fig. 8.5	The ideological positions of the candidates in the 2021 and 2024 elections	137

Fig. 8.6	Emotional temperature between political parties	141
Fig. 9.1	How parties mentioned political distrust in their manifestos	152
Fig. 9.2	Political distrust among younger voters	156
Fig. 10.1	Approval ratings of the Kishida cabinet, October 2021–August 2024	167
Fig. 10.2	Primary reason for cabinet approval, November 2021–August 2024	170
Fig. 10.3	Primary reason for disapproval, November 2021–August 2024	171
Fig. 10.4	Consumer price index and expectation for Kishida's economic policy	172
Fig. 10.5	Who is suited to be the next prime minister?	174
Fig. 11.1	Types of media used for political information, by party supported	193
Fig. 12.1	The probability of voting in 2022 and 2024 by party support	203
Fig. 12.2	Voter turnout in 2024 by party support and Kishida cabinet support	207
Fig. 12.3	Voter turnout in 2024 by party support and age	208
Fig. 12.4	Ideological difference between own position and party position by party support	210
Fig. 12.5	Evaluation of own party leader by party support	211
Fig. 12.6	Turnout and absolute party vote share	213
Fig. 15.1	Number of female candidates and winners by party in 2021 and 2024	262
Fig. 15.2	Shifts in issue positions of the LDP candidates on the dual surname legislation between 2021 and 2024 by gender	269
Fig. 17.1	Percentage of candidates who selected "Education and Childcare" as the policy they consider most important in this election (UTAS)	299
Fig. 17.2	Average percentage of candidates who selected the following policies as top-three priorities (UTAS)	300
Fig. 17.3	Childcare and education policy emphasis and vote share: regression coefficient estimates with 95% CIs	313
Fig. 17.4	Predicted vote share by "children and education emphasis (Yes = 1)"	313
Fig. 18.1	Inflation and currency	322

List of Tables

Table 2.1	Votes and seats in the 2021 and 2024 general elections	20
Table 2.2	Determinants of LDP candidates' vote change	24
Table 3.1	Factional affiliations, Unification Church ties, and *Uragane* involvement of LDP presidential candidates' endorsers	46
Table 3.2	Regression analysis on LDP candidates' vote share	50
Table 4.1	Districts where the CDP nominated no candidates	63
Table 4.2	Constituencies visited by major party officials	66
Table 4.3	The party that won in the 1st district	70
Table 4.4	Electoral outcomes of constituencies with political funding scandals	71
Table 6.1	Changes in Ishin's PR vote share in the 2021 and 2024 elections	92
Table 7.1	The 2024 HR election PR vote preference by age group	115
Table 7.2	The 2024 HR election daily projections of party seat counts in majoritarian tier	121
Table 8.1	OLS estimations of ideological positions of the candidates in 2024	139
Table 8.2	Effects of running only in SMD on the electoral strategies of LDP candidates	140
Table 9.1	Campaign slogans and mentions of political funding in the 2024 election manifestos	151
Table 10.1	The next prime minister by partisanship	175
Table 10.2	What is most important for you in your voting decision for this election? Please select two from the ten listed	178

Table 11.1	X (Twitter) follower counts for candidates and party leaders	187
Table 13.1	Results of the LDP survey on contacts with Unification Church	225
Table 15.1	Number and percentage of female candidates and winners by party	260
Table 15.2	Winning rates among candidates by party and gender	263
Table 15.3	Winning rates of newcomer candidates by party, gender, and constituency	264
Table 15.4	Classification of careers of female newcomer candidates in the five parties	266
Table 17.1	Key measures of Acceleration Plan and implementation schedule for childcare policies	303
Table 17.2	Childcare and education policy: descriptive statistics and variable definitions	312
Table 18.1	Key economic policy differences of leading candidates	325
Table 18.2	Key economic policy differences of political parties	329

NOTES ON CONTRIBUTORS

Kenya Amano is an independent scholar. Previously, he was a Postdoctoral Research Fellow at Harvard's Program on U.S.-Japan Relations. He holds a Ph.D. in Political Science from the University of Washington.

Reiko Arami is a Professor of Political Science in the Department of Law at Nagoya University (Japan). She was previously an Assistant Professor at the University of Tokyo, and was also a visiting scholar at the Massachusetts Institute of Technology. Her research focuses primarily on social policies and local governance, with recent studies on how family models shape the efficacy of policy enforcement in local government. Her research has appeared in *Political Behavior*, *Urban Studies*, and *Social Science and Medicine*, among other outlets. Additionally, she serves as a committee member on various governmental bodies, providing valuable insights and advice on policy matters.

Taka-aki Asano is an Associate Professor of Political Science in the Department of Law at Kansai University (Japan). He completed his Ph.D. at the University of Tokyo in 2022. His research mainly focuses on political communication, public opinion, and electoral politics. He has earned several awards, including The University of Tokyo's President's Award and Best Presentation Award from the Japanese Association of Electoral Studies. He is the author of *Supporters, Tolerators, and Fence-sitters: Responses to the LDP Government in the 2010s* (Yuhikaku 2024). He has also published in numerous journals, including *Political Behavior*,

Social Science Japan Journal, and *Journal of Elections, Public Opinion and Parties*.

Matthew M. Carlson is a Professor of Political Science at the University of Vermont, USA. He is the author of *Money Politics in Japan* (2007) and co-author of *Political Corruption and Scandals in Japan* with Steven R. Reed (2018). His work has been published in numerous political science journals, including *Political Studies Review, Democratization, Party Politics, Asian Survey*, and *Public Administration and Policy*.

Robert A. Fahey is an Assistant Professor at the Waseda Institute for Advanced Study (WIAS) at Waseda University (Japan). He previously held a visiting scholar position at the University of Milan. His research focuses on populism and polarization, with a particular focus on the influence of conspiracy theories and social networks on political behavior. He is the author of a chapter in *The Oxford Handbook of Japanese Politics*, and his research has appeared in the *International Journal of Information Management, Social Science and Medicine*, and *PLOS One*, among other journals.

Fumi Ikeda is an Associate Professor at Ehime University (Japan). Previously, she was an Assistant Professor at Waseda University. She obtained her M.Sc. in Japanese Studies from Oxford University (Wolfson College) and her Ph.D. in Policy Studies from Chuo University. Her research interests lie in comparative politics and Japanese politics, with a particular focus on political institutions, including organizational votes and distributive politics. Her research has been published in *Social Science Japan Journal* and *Journal of East Asian Studies*, among other journals.

Saori N. Katada is a Professor of International Relations and the director of the Center for International Studies at the University of Southern California (USA). Her research focus is geoeconomy, Japanese foreign policy, international political economy, and regionalism. Her book *Japan's New Regional Reality: Geoeconomic Strategy in the Asia-Pacific* was published by Columbia University Press in July 2020. She has also co-authored two recent books: *The BRICS and Collective Financial Statecraft* (Oxford University Press, 2017), and *Taming Japan's Deflation: The Debate over Unconventional Monetary Policy* (Cornell University Press, 2018). She obtained her Ph.D. from the University of North Carolina at Chapel Hill (Political Science) and her B.A. from Hitotsubashi University (Tokyo). Before joining USC, she served as a researcher at the World Bank in

Washington D.C., and as International Program Officer at the UNDP in Mexico City.

Kazuyoshi Kawasaka is a Lecturer at the Organization for Global Japanese Studies, the Graduate School of Arts and Science, University of Tokyo (Japan). He was the principal investigator of the DFG-funded project "Sexual Diversity and Human Rights in 21st Century Japan: LGBTIQ Activisms and Resistance from a Transnational Perspective" at the Institute for Modern Japanese Studies, Heinrich Heine University Düsseldorf (Germany), from 2020 to 2024. His research interests include nationalism and queer politics in Japan, globalization of LGBTIQ politics, and transnational anti-gender/LGBTIQ movements. He is a co-editor of *Beyond Diversity: Queer Politics, Activism, and Representation in Contemporary Japan* (Düsseldorf University Press, 2024).

Axel Klein is a Professor of Japanese Politics at the Institute of East Asian Studies at the University of Duisburg-Essen (Germany). Previously, he was a Senior Research Fellow at Bonn University (1998–2007) and at the German Institute for Japanese Studies in Tokyo (2007–2011). His research focus is election campaigning, demographic change, and the relationship of politics and organized religion in Japan. He has also produced a documentary film on Japanese elections (*Pictures at an Election*, 2008), conducted extensive field research in the country, and is an expert on the political party Kōmeitō. In 2020, he started the *Populism in East Asian Democracies* project.

Ko Maeda is a Professor in the Department of Political Science at the University of North Texas (USA). He obtained his Ph.D. from Michigan State University in 2005. His research focus is Comparative Politics, with particular interests in political institutions, political parties, and elections. His work has appeared in numerous journals, including the *Journal of Politics*, *British Journal of Political Science*, *Comparative Political Studies*, *Electoral Studies*, and the *Journal of Theoretical Politics*.

Yukio Maeda is a Professor of Political Science at the Institute of Social Science at the University of Tokyo (Japan). He completed his Ph.D. at the University of Michigan (Ann Arbor). His research focuses on the relationship between mass media and politics, party politics, and voting behavior. His research has appeared in numerous journals including *Social Science Japan Journal* and *Journal of Social Science*. He is also the author of a chapter in *The Oxford Handbook of Japanese Politics* (2021).

Tetsuya Matsubayashi is a Professor in the Osaka School of International Public Policy at Osaka University (Japan). Previously, he was an Assistant Professor at the University of North Texas, after earning his Ph.D. from Texas A&M University. His research primarily focuses on understanding the mechanisms and outcomes of the democratic process. His works have been published in various esteemed journals such as the *American Journal of Political Science* and *American Political Science Review*. He is also co-author of a book, *Economic Analysis of Suicide Prevention* (Springer, 2017).

Tomoko Matsumoto is an Associate Professor of Political Science at Tokyo University of Science (Japan). She received her Ph.D. from the University of Tokyo in 2016. Her research focuses on public opinion, elections, and redistribution. Her research has appeared in the *European Journal of Political Economy*, *The British Journal of Sociology*, *Japanese Journal of Political Science*, and *Electoral Studies*, among others. Before joining Tokyo University of Science, she was a visiting scholar at New York University.

Kenneth M. McElwain is a Professor of Comparative Politics at the Institute of Social Science, University of Tokyo. His research focuses on comparative political institutions, most recently on the politics of constitutional design. He received his B.A. in public policy from Princeton University and Ph.D. in political science from Stanford University. He has published more than fifty journal articles and book chapters in both English and Japanese, and his recent book, *The Universality and Originality of the Japanese Constitution in Quantitative Perspective* (Chikura Shobō, 2022), won the 44th Ishibashi Tanzan Book Award and the 34th Asia-Pacific Award Special Prize. He also serves as Editor-in-Chief of *Social Science Japan Journal*.

Levi McLaughlin is a Professor in the Department of Philosophy and Religious Studies at North Carolina State University (USA). He received his Ph.D. from Princeton University after previous study at the University of Tokyo. His research focuses primarily on religion in modern and contemporary Japan, and his book, *Sōka Gakkai: Buddhism and Romantic Heroism in Modern Japan*, was published by University of Hawai'i Press in 2019. He is also the co-editor of *Kōmeitō: Politics and Religion in Japan* (Berkeley, 2014), and the author of numerous journal articles.

Kuniaki Nemoto is a Professor of political science in the Department of Economics at Musashi University (Japan). He received his Ph.D. from the University of California, San Diego in 2009. As a postdoctoral fellow, he was affiliated with Waseda University, the Department of Political Science at the University of British Columbia, and the Korea Institute at Harvard University. His research interests lie in party politics, legislative behavior, and electoral systems in the Asia-Pacific (Japan, South Korea, and New Zealand). His works have been published in *Comparative Political Studies*, *British Journal of Political Science*, and *Party Politics*, among others.

Shōko Ōmori is an Associate Professor in the Department of Media and Communication Studies at Hosei University (Japan). She received her Ph.D. from the University of Tokyo in 2021. Her research interests center on the media and its influence on political behavior. Her work has recently been published in *Journal of Elections, Public Opinion, and Parties*. Her monograph on political communication in the internet age was recently published by Keisō Shobō (2023).

Robert J. Pekkanen is a Professor at the Henry M. Jackson School of International Studies, University of Washington (USA). He received his Ph.D. in political science from Harvard University in 2002. His research interests lie in electoral systems, political parties, and civil society. He has published articles in political science journals such as the *American Political Science Review*, *British Journal of Political Science*, and *Comparative Political Studies*, as well as Asian studies journals including the *Journal of Asian Studies* and *The Journal of Japanese Studies*. He has published over a dozen books on American nonprofit advocacy, electoral systems, Japanese civil society, and Japanese elections and political parties.

Daniel M. Smith is an Associate Professor of Political Science at the University of Pennsylvania (USA). His research interests cover a range of topics in comparative politics, political economy, and political behavior, with a core focus on political institutions and democratic representation. He has regional expertise in both Western Europe and Japan. He is the author of *Dynasties and Democracy* (Stanford University Press, 2018), and articles appearing in the *American Political Science Review*, *American Journal of Political Science*, *The Journal of Politics*, *Comparative Political Studies*, and *Political Analysis*, among other journals and edited volumes. He holds a Ph.D. (2012) and M.A. (2009) in political science from the

University of California, San Diego, and a B.A. (2005) in political science and Italian from the University of California, Los Angeles.

Shūsuke Takamiya is an Assistant Professor in the Faculty of Political Science and Economics at Takushoku University (Japan). He obtained his Ph.D. from the University of Tokyo in 2021. His research interests lie in party politics and local governance, with a particular emphasis on Japan. His work has recently been published in the *Journal of Elections, Public Opinion, and Parties*. Additionally, he has been honored with the Best Dissertation Award from the University of Tokyo.

Masaki Taniguchi is a Professor in the Graduate Schools for Law and Politics at the University of Tokyo (Japan). His research focuses on electoral studies and political communication. He is the author of *Representative Democracy in Japan* (University of Tokyo Press, 2020) and *Politics and Mass Media* (University of Tokyo Press, 2015). His research has also been published in various journals including *International Political Science Review*, *Political Communication*, *Electoral Studies*, and *Journal of Elections, Public Opinion and Parties*. Additionally, he has served as a commissioner of the National Commission for the Management of Political Funds, nominated by the Japanese Diet.

Yuki Tsuji is a Professor of Political Science and Economics at Tokai University (Japan). She obtained her Ph.D. from Kyoto University. Her research focuses on political representation, gender politics, family politics, and welfare regimes. Her work has appeared in *Social Science Japan Journal* and *The Annals of the Japanese Political Science Association*, among others.

Michio Umeda is a Professor of Political Science at Komazawa University (Japan). He obtained his Ph.D. from the University of Michigan (Ann Arbor), and subsequently worked as Research Fellow at the European University Institute. His recent research mainly focuses on dyadic representation, and voting behavior. His work has been published in numerous journals, including *Political Behavior*, *Electoral Studies*, *Japanese Journal of Political Science*, and *International Journal of Forecasting*.

Kristin Vekasi is the Mansfield Chair of Japanese and Indo-Pacific Affairs and an Associate Professor in the Department of Political Science at the University of Montana. Her research focuses on economic security and the political risk management of supply chains. She specializes in

Northeast Asia and the political economy of critical minerals and their downstream technologies.

Masahiro Zenkyo is a Professor in the School of Law and Politics at Kwansei Gakuin University (Japan). Previously, he was a visiting researcher in the Jack W. Peltason Center for the Study of Democracy at the University of California, Irvine. His research interests lie in political behavior, political psychology, and survey methodology. His work has been published in *Party Politics, Journal of Public Policy Studies, Annals of the Japanese Political Science Association,* and *Japanese Journal of Electoral Studies.* He is also the author of numerous books published in Japanese, including *Support for the Ishin: A Consequence of Populism or Rational Choice?* which was awarded the Suntory Prize for Social Sciences and Humanities.

Abbreviations

Political Parties

CDP	Constitutional Democratic Party of Japan (Rikken Minshutō)
CPJ	Conservative Party of Japan (Nippon Hoshutō)
DPJ	Democratic Party of Japan (Minshutō)
DPP	Democratic Party for the People (Kokumin Minshutō)
Ishin	Japan Ishin no Kai (Nippon Ishin no Kai; Japan Innovation Party)
JCP	Japanese Communist Party (Nihon Kyōsantō)
Kōmeitō	Kōmeitō (Clean Government Party)
LDP	Liberal Democratic Party (LDP) (Jiyu Minshutō)
NHKP	NHK Party (Various names in Japanese)
Reiwa	Reiwa Shinsengumi
SDP	Social Democratic Party (Shakai Minshutō)

Other abbreviations

CPTPP	Comprehensive and Progressive Agreement for Trans-Pacific Partnership
FPTP	First-past-the-post
HC	House of Councillors
HR	House of Representatives
MP	Member of Parliament, or Diet Member (also "DM")

PR	Proportional Representation
SDF	Self-Defense Force
SMD	Single-Member District
TPP	Trans-Pacific Partnership
UC	Unification Church

PART I

Introduction

CHAPTER 1

Introduction: LDP Dominance on the Edge

Kenneth M. McElwain, Robert J. Pekkanen, and Daniel M. Smith

This book brings together top experts of Japanese politics to analyze the political context, central policy issues, party strategies, and voter behavior in the 50th General Election for Japan's House of Representatives (HR), the more important chamber of the bicameral National Diet, held on October 27, 2024. This is the fifth volume of the *Japan Decides* series, following our analyses of the general elections of 2012, 2014, 2017, and 2021 (Pekkanen et al. 2013, 2016, 2018, 2023), and we believe it is among the most important to date.

K. M. McElwain
University of Tokyo, Tokyo, Japan
e-mail: mcelwain@iss.u-tokyo.ac.jp

R. J. Pekkanen (✉)
University of Washington, Seattle, USA
e-mail: robert.pekkanen@gmail.com

D. M. Smith
University of Pennsylvania, Philadelphia, USA
e-mail: dms2323@sas.upenn.edu

© The Author(s), under exclusive license to Springer Nature Switzerland AG 2025
K. M. McElwain et al. (eds.), *Japan Decides 2024*,
https://doi.org/10.1007/978-3-031-98797-7_1

The 2012 general election marked the triumphant return to power of the Liberal Democratic Party (LDP), in coalition with Kōmeitō, after 3 years in opposition. In each subsequent general election, the LDP–Kōmeitō coalition continued to dominate a divided opposition, winning commanding majorities of seats. Between 2012 and 2020, the government was led by Abe Shinzō, Japan's longest-serving prime minister, who leveraged his electoral strength to advance ambitious economic and foreign/security policies (Funabashi and Ikenberry 2020; Harris 2023; Funabashi and Nakakita 2024) and steer the country in a more conservative direction (Oguma and Higuchi 2020). Abe's immediate successors as prime minister, Suga Yoshihide and then Kishida Fumio, largely maintained the stability of the Abe era through the 2021 general election, even as they dealt with the COVID-19 pandemic and its aftermath (Pekkanen et al. 2023).

In contrast, the headline of the 2024 general election was the dramatic rebuke of the governing parties by voters. The LDP–Kōmeitō coalition lost a combined 76 seats and fell short of a majority in the HR. The LDP's loss of 68 seats marked its second-worst defeat in its 70-year history, exceeded only by the 2009 general election that briefly sent it into opposition. With no majority and a fragmented but emboldened opposition, Prime Minister Ishiba Shigeru was forced to limp forward under a precarious minority government, relying on policy concessions to the Democratic Party for the People (DPP) and Nippon Ishin no Kai (Ishin) in exchange for legislative votes. The main opposition Constitutional Democratic Party (CDP) achieved its best result since its formation in 2017 and stepped up its criticism of the ruling coalition.

Why did the LDP fare so poorly? Did the opposition win as much as the LDP lost? And what do the results reveal about the future trajectory of Japanese electoral politics, including whether the LDP can recover its governing dominance, whether the persistent fragmentation of the opposition will continue, and how the dynamics of voter outreach will evolve in an increasingly digital and generationally segmented electorate?

In this introduction, we begin with a brief narrative of political developments between the 2021 and 2024 general elections to set the stage for the volume. We then provide an overview of the chapters, each of which examines an important aspect of the 2024 election, and which collectively offer a coherent picture of its significance. The concluding chapter synthesizes these analyses, offering our interpretation of the election and reflecting on what may lie ahead for Japanese politics.

Japanese Politics Between 2021 and 2024

It is worth remembering that the previous HR general election in 2021 took place during the COVID-19 pandemic (Smith et al. 2023). Although the pandemic played little direct role in the 2024 campaign, several major events in the intervening years significantly altered the political context. Chief among these was Russia's invasion of Ukraine on February 24, 2022, which unsettled many in Japan and raised concerns about regional security in Northeast Asia. In response, Prime Minister Kishida adopted a robust diplomatic stance, implementing strong sanctions on Russia and aligning Japan firmly with Ukraine and the broader democratic alliance.

Perhaps even more consequential domestically was the assassination of former Prime Minister Abe on July 8, 2022, just 2 days before the House of Councillors (HC) election. Abe was shot at close range during a campaign stop in Nara Prefecture by a former member of the Self-Defense Forces, who targeted Abe for his ties to the Unification Church (UC)—a group he claimed had ruined his family through excessive financial demands on his mother, who was a member of the group. Despite the shocking nature of the attack, the LDP did not appear to suffer immediate political consequences. The HC election proceeded as scheduled on July 10, and the ruling coalition performed well: the LDP gained five seats to reach 118, and together with Kōmeitō, the coalition retained a comfortable 59% majority in the 248-member chamber. Public sympathy and national shock likely shielded the party from any near-term fallout.

Following the HC election, Prime Minister Kishida initially appeared to be on relatively stable footing. In the months that followed, however, the LDP's ties to the UC came under growing scrutiny. As discussed in this volume by McLaughlin (2025), the assassination triggered intense media and parliamentary investigations into the relationship between the LDP and the UC, raising broader concerns about the role of religious organizations in Japanese politics. Although the government eventually revoked the UC's legal status as a religious corporation, the controversy continued to haunt the LDP and played a central role in shaping the political context of the 2024 election.

The backlash intensified after Kishida announced a state funeral for Abe, a decision that generated significant public opposition. Although the funeral itself was not politically catastrophic, it reinforced perceptions of tone-deafness within the ruling party. Further discontent arose in 2023 with the rollout of the *My Number* identification card system (Maeda 2025). Initially introduced in 2016 as a voluntary tool for accessing health, tax, and pension services, the system was effectively made mandatory, despite earlier assurances to the contrary. Administrative errors and the mishandling of personal data further eroded public trust in the government.

The most serious blow, however, came with the emergence of a "money and politics" scandal in late 2023 (Carlson 2025). Multiple LDP factions were found to have failed to report income from fundraising events, in violation of campaign finance laws. Some also engaged in a kickback scheme, where politicians received funds from their faction if they exceeded ticket sales quotas—practices that, while not necessarily illegal in themselves, were required to be disclosed. This slush fund (*uragane*) scandal led to the resignation of four cabinet ministers and severely damaged the party's credibility. As Nemoto (2025) details, the scandal also prompted the formal dissolution of several factions, including Kishida's own, signaling a potentially transformative shift in the internal organization of the LDP. As the story unfolded, it became increasingly clear that Kishida would not be able to weather the storm. On August 14, 2024, he announced that he would not run in the upcoming LDP presidential election, effectively stepping down as party leader and prime minister.

Kishida's resignation set the stage for a wide-open leadership contest within the LDP, held on September 27, 2024. Nine candidates entered the race, reflecting both the absence of a clear successor and the weakened role of factions, which had traditionally coordinated leadership bids in advance. Among the early frontrunners were Ishiba, Koizumi Shinjirō, and Takaichi Sanae. Takaichi, widely regarded as the most conservative of the leading candidates, secured the highest number of votes in the first round. However, concerns about her polarizing image and limited appeal to swing voters prompted a consolidation of support around Ishiba in the second round. Ultimately, Ishiba emerged as the winner, offering a more moderate profile at a time when the party sought to regain public trust.

Ishiba formally assumed the office of prime minister on October 1, 2024. Seeking to project momentum, he moved quickly to dissolve the HR and called a general election for October 27—exactly one month after his leadership victory. Yet the political fallout from the slush fund scandal continued to shadow the party. As part of its effort to demonstrate accountability, the LDP denied formal nominations to twelve candidates in single-member districts (SMDs) and prohibited another thirty-seven from running jointly in both the SMD and proportional representation (PR) tiers of the electoral system.

Despite these gestures, public skepticism remained high. Just 4 days before the election, it was revealed that the party had transferred identical sums of money to each of its local branches, including those led by disqualified or sidelined candidates. The move contradicted the LDP's reform messaging and gave the strong impression that it intended to preserve existing patronage practices. This so-called "October surprise" reinforced perceptions that the LDP remained resistant to structural change, further undermining its credibility with voters.

For many members of the electorate, particularly those already disillusioned by economic stagnation and political scandal, this episode confirmed their doubts about the LDP's willingness to reform. Some chose to abstain; others shifted their support to opposition or peripheral parties. The incident shaped the closing days of the campaign and arguably played a key role in the LDP's substantial electoral losses. It was the straw that broke the camel's back for many voters, crystallizing the 2024 general election as a referendum not only on policy performance but also on the integrity and accountability of the ruling party.

Overview of the Volume

The electoral dynamics and controversies just outlined provide the backdrop for the analyses that follow. As with previous volumes in the *Japan Decides* series, the chapters in this edition are organized thematically, each addressing a key aspect of the 2024 general election—from party strategies and candidate behavior to voter attitudes and institutional developments.

In the next chapter, Ko Maeda provides the core analysis of the election results, showing that the LDP's losses were particularly severe in SMDs, where it faced centrist opposition candidates and lost 55 contests. The CDP's seat gains resulted more from LDP vote losses than from any surge in its own support, while the DPP made significant inroads among younger voters by leveraging social media and running a campaign focused on raising take-home pay. Despite Ishin's momentum in previous elections, the party's growth stalled, and it was the DPP that emerged as the most popular opposition party among voters under 40.

The several chapters that follow examine developments within and between the major political parties. In Chapter 3, Kuniaki Nemoto takes a closer look at the reasons behind the LDP's major loss in seats. He attributes the LDP's poor showing to two scandals—the UC revelations and the *uragane* (slush fund) affair—which eroded public trust and were poorly managed by party leadership. Despite calls for reform, the party's responses were limited and ad hoc, with scandal-tainted candidates often avoiding meaningful punishment. Ishiba's attempts at damage control came too late and lacked credibility, fueling voter backlash. The chapter argues that this failure to restore public confidence contributed to the LDP's poor showing.

In Chapter 4, Fumi Ikeda analyzes the CDP's strategic positioning from 2021 to 2024, focusing on the party's complex relationship with the Japanese Communist Party (JCP). Although the CDP increased its seat count, it fell short of leading a change in government, in part because of internal concerns about how close alignment with the far-left JCP might be perceived by centrist voters. To broaden its appeal, the CDP limited visible cooperation with the JCP and concentrated its campaign efforts in urban areas while avoiding competition with the DPP. The chapter illustrates how the CDP's balancing act between coalition politics and electoral pragmatism shaped its mixed performance.

Axel Klein and Levi McLaughlin turn to the LDP's longtime coalition partner, Kōmeitō, in Chapter 5. The party suffered a significant electoral decline in 2024, which Klein and McLaughlin attribute to both internal and external pressures. Internally, the party struggled with the aging of its core base in Sōka Gakkai and the loss of its spiritual leader, Ikeda Daisaku. Externally, its alliance with the scandal-plagued LDP diminished its credibility and strained the coalition's coordination. Yet, despite its losses, Kōmeitō remains a pivotal actor in Japanese politics due to its organized support and potential influence in a fragmented Diet.

Finally, in Chapter 6, Masahiro Zenkyo uses survey data to examine the sharp decline in support for Ishin in the 2024 election. His findings indicate that evaluations of party leader Baba Nobuyuki and perceptions of the party's administrative competence played crucial roles in voters' decisions. Although there were no significant policy shifts, inconsistent behavior during legislative debates, particularly regarding political funding reform, tarnished the party's reputation. The chapter concludes that voter doubts about competence, more than ideology, accounted for Ishin's electoral setbacks.

The next several chapters of the volume dive into various aspects of the campaign, public opinion, and voting behavior. Michio Umeda sets the stage for these analyses in Chapter 7, with a general overview of the campaign in historical context. Umeda situates the 2024 election at the intersection of structural continuity and demographic and technological change. While familiar features have persisted, such as the short official campaign period and rural-focused messaging, generational shifts and redistricting have given more weight to urban voters. Newer parties like the DPP and Reiwa Shinsengumi (Reiwa) engaged younger electorates effectively using digital platforms, contrasting with stagnation among traditional parties. Strategic missteps by Ishiba, including neglecting urban voters and mishandling scandals, contributed to the ruling coalition's decline.

In Chapter 8, Masaki Taniguchi, Taka-aki Asano, Shōko Ōmori, and Shūsuke Takamiya provide a comprehensive analysis of candidates' policy preferences, drawing from the 2024 joint survey of the University of Tokyo and *Asahi Shinbun* (UTAS). The authors map the policy preferences of election candidates across key issue areas, including constitutional revision, economic management, and social policy. Political reform emerged as the foremost issue among candidates, fueled by public backlash against the LDP's funding scandal. While ideological divides persist—especially on security and constitutional issues—there is also growing polarization on economic policy, with smaller populist parties gaining traction. The DPP stood out as a pragmatic centrist force, while the overall landscape exhibited signs of both realignment and rising fragmentation.

Tomoko Matsumoto in Chapter 9 analyzes how political parties addressed political distrust in their 2024 election manifestos, revealing clear contrasts between the LDP and opposition parties. The LDP framed distrust as a transparency issue, proposing superficial reforms without questioning systemic problems. In contrast, opposition parties, particularly those on the left, emphasized actual corruption, money politics, and plutocratic influence. The chapter also notes how younger voters were courted through promises of economic relief, with the DPP distinguishing itself by focusing on tax cuts and youth-oriented messaging.

Yukio Maeda argues in Chapter 10 that the LDP's loss of its HR majority in 2024 was driven by a combination of political scandal and economic dissatisfaction. While scandals involving the UC and slush funds damaged public trust, rising consumer prices since 2022 deepened voter frustration. Despite initial approval following Abe's death, Kishida's failure to distance himself from Abe's faction and respond decisively to misconduct eroded his support. The chapter demonstrates how economic anxiety amplified the effects of the scandals, culminating in the electoral punishment of the ruling coalition.

In Chapter 11, Robert A. Fahey explores how challenger parties like the DPP, the Conservative Party of Japan (CPJ), and right-wing Sanseitō capitalized on a fragmented media environment and declining trust in traditional news to deliver polarizing messages during the 2024 election. In contrast, mainstream parties largely adhered to passive forms of social media campaigning, failing to adapt to evolving digital trends. The chapter warns of an emerging "information cleavage" between voters who rely on social media and those who trust conventional media, with growing implications for political alignment. This digital gap was evident not only in the general election but also in other 2024 contests, signaling a shift in how political influence is cultivated.

Tetsuya Matsubayashi rounds out this set of chapters on the campaign and voting behavior in Chapter 12, with an analysis of voter turnout. He shows that partisanship strongly shaped turnout in 2024, contributing to significant shifts in vote share. Disenchanted LDP supporters were demobilized by their party's scandals, while energized DPP supporters—particularly younger and middle-aged voters—turned out in larger numbers. Large-scale survey and municipal-level election data reveal that declines in turnout harmed the LDP, while turnout surges benefited the DPP. The chapter underscores the importance of emotional attachment and perceived policy alignment in motivating voter participation.

As with previous editions of *Japan Decides*, the next several chapters focus on specific issues of importance to contemporary Japanese politics, including those that played a major role in the campaign. Arguably, the biggest issue of all was that of "money and politics" and political finance reform.

In Chapter 13, Matthew M. Carlson explores how overlapping scandals under Kishida—most notably the LDP's ties to the UC and the *uragane* slush fund affair—reflected deeper features of Japan's "influence market" political system. These scandals, exacerbated by Abe's assassination in 2022, exposed widespread collusion between politicians and interest groups. The LDP's reluctance to confront these relationships seriously undermined public confidence and contributed to its 2024 electoral losses. The chapter frames these events as a convergence of moral panic, institutional failure, and systemic vulnerabilities.

In Chapter 14, Levi McLaughlin traces the aftermath of Abe's assassination and the legal and political campaign that culminated in the dissolution of the Unification Church in 2025. McLaughlin situates the government's unprecedented legal action within Japan's long history of moral panics targeting minority religions. While the move garnered broad public support, it also revealed the political risks of entanglement between religious organizations and state power. The chapter ends by highlighting the social and emotional burden now borne by female UC parishioners at the local level.

Yuki Tsuji in Chapter 15 documents a record increase in women elected to the HR in 2024, with many winning through SMDs backed by strong local or professional credentials. The rise was facilitated by a larger pool of female candidates, especially from opposition parties like the CDP and DPP. While PR list placements still revealed party differences in prioritizing gender equality, a modest shift among LDP female candidates toward support for separate surnames for married couples suggests evolving norms. The chapter underscores both progress and continued limitations in Japan's gender representation.

While previous volumes in the series have tracked developments in gender representation, the question of LGBTQ + rights has not featured prominently in Japanese elections. This began to change in the 2021 general election, when parties took positions on same-sex marriage. Chapter 16, by Kazuyoshi Kawasaki, explores how LGBTQ + rights became a politically divisive issue in the 2024 election, with manifestos revealing a general conservative shift. While the CDP remained vocally supportive of LGBTQ + rights, other major parties—including the LDP—moved away from inclusive policies, reflecting a broader backlash and religious conservative influence. The chapter also highlights how LGBTQ + rights were "weaponized" by opponents to galvanize their base. Despite growing public support for diversity, the political narrative grew more cautious and less LGBTQ + -friendly.

In Chapter 17, Reiko Arami examines how childcare policy featured in the 2024 general election amid Japan's deepening demographic crisis. While nearly all parties proposed expanding childcare and education benefits, the DPP and Reiwa stood out for offering more comprehensive redistribution plans. However, the limited electoral gains for candidates whose campaigns prioritized childcare suggest weak incentives for parties to continue emphasizing this issue. The chapter argues that without addressing deeper structural challenges—such as workplace norms and gender inequality—childcare policy alone is unlikely to generate lasting political or demographic impact, particularly as the number of households raising children continues to decline.

Inflation was a major political issue in elections across many democracies in 2024, and Japan was not an exception. In Chapter 18, Kenya Amano and Saori N. Katada argue that the LDP's decision to prioritize fiscal discipline during a period of inflation narrowed its policy space and exposed it to electoral backlash. In the 2024 LDP leadership race, Ishiba's support for budgetary conservatism prevailed over alternative candidates' calls for more distributional spending. However, this stance left the party vulnerable to rivals like the DPP, which gained support by proposing more expansionary economic policies. The authors frame this outcome as a consequence of both electoral pressures and internal party tensions in navigating Japan's economic policy trilemma.

Moving to Japan's economic policy vis-à-vis the international arena, Kristin Vekasi shows in Chapter 19 how economic security, rather than traditional trade issues, became a dominant framework for international economic policy in the 2024 election. While not a major campaign issue overall, the mainstream parties converged on strengthening domestic capacity in strategic sectors like semiconductors and critical materials. The LDP emphasized sovereignty and resilience, while opposition parties offered variations in focus and execution. Despite critiques from smaller parties, the election reaffirmed broad support for Japan's dual approach of global engagement and economic security.

In the concluding chapter, we return as editors of the volume to provide our synthesis of what we see as the major takeaway lessons of the 2024 general election, as well as an assessment of where Japanese politics may be headed.

What the 2024 Election Tells Us About the State of Japanese Politics

The 2024 general election marked a pivotal moment in Japanese politics. The LDP lost its majority in the HR for only the third time in its postwar history, prompting widespread reflection on the causes of its decline and the future of Japan's political landscape. While some observers interpreted the result as part of a broader "anti-incumbent wave" seen across advanced democracies in 2024, Japan's case was shaped by specific domestic dynamics.

Economic dissatisfaction provided the structural backdrop for voter discontent. Inflation returned for the first time in over two decades, while real wages remained stagnant. Although economic underperformance is not new, the LDP had historically mitigated its effects through redistributive spending and rural development. In 2024, this strategy faltered. Fiscal restraint and internal divisions limited the party's flexibility, and initiatives like *chihō sōsei* (regional revitalization) gained little traction.

At the same time, while the LDP has long held an advantage over the opposition in terms of non-policy (valence) characteristics such as a reputation for competence and stability (Kuriwaki et al. 2025), this valence advantage collapsed in 2024 under the weight of political scandal. Revelations of deep ties between LDP lawmakers and the UC, coupled with the factional slush fund scandal, undermined public trust in the party's integrity. While political reform emerged as a prominent campaign issue, the LDP's leadership candidates offered no credible proposals. Opposition parties framed the scandals as evidence of systemic corruption, while the LDP's messaging focused on technical compliance. Many traditional LDP supporters, disillusioned by the party's response, chose to stay home rather than vote, further weakening the party's position.

Although the opposition did not present a unified front, the election highlighted important shifts in the competitive landscape. The CDP gained seats but did not expand its vote share, in part due to its move toward the political center. Smaller parties such as the DPP and Reiwa, by contrast, were more effective in mobilizing younger and disaffected voters. Their policy platforms were concrete and redistributive, and their campaigns made strategic use of digital media to engage segments of the electorate that more established parties often struggle to reach.

These trends also reflect broader transformations in electoral mobilization. Traditional methods such as street-level oratory sessions and organized group endorsements appear to be declining in effectiveness, especially among younger voters. Kōmeitō's poor performance—driven by internal challenges and backlash for its alliance with the LDP—underscores this shift. Meanwhile, newer and more ideologically distinct parties gained attention by challenging mainstream consensus and offering outsider appeals.

Taken together, we argue that the 2024 election signals growing volatility in Japanese politics. The LDP's losses stemmed not only from short-term discontent but also from deeper fractures in its political brand. Whether the party—and Japan's broader political system—can adapt to a more fragmented, issue-driven, and digitally mediated political environment remains uncertain.

References

Carlson, Matthew M. 2025. "Scandals During the Kishida Administration." In *Japan Decides 2024: The Japanese General Election*, edited by Kenneth M. McElwain, Robert J. Pekkanen, and Daniel M. Smith, 217–233. Palgrave Macmillan.

Funabashi, Yoichi, and G. John Ikenberry (eds.). 2020. *The Crisis of Liberal Internationalism: Japan and the World Order*. Brookings Institution Press.

Funabashi, Yoichi, and Koji Nakakita (eds.). 2024. *Critical Review of the Abe Administration: Politics of Conservatism and Realism*. Routledge.

Harris, Tobias. 2023. "Abe's Legacy." In *Japan Decides 2021: The Japanese General Election*, edited by Robert J. Pekkanen, Steven R. Reed, and Daniel M. Smith, 87–102. Palgrave Macmillan.

Kuriwaki, Shiro, Yusaku Horiuchi, and Daniel M. Smith. 2025. "Winning Elections with Unpopular Policies: Valence Advantage and Single-Party Dominance in Japan." *Quarterly Journal of Political Science*, 20 (4): 439–476.

Maeda, Yukio. 2025. "Public Opinion and Scandals in Economic Hard Times." In *Japan Decides 2024: The Japanese General Election*, edited by Kenneth M. McElwain, Robert J. Pekkanen, and Daniel M. Smith, 163–179. Palgrave Macmillan.

McLaughlin, Levi. 2025. "Perennial Fears, Novel Responses: The Unification Church in Japan after the Abe Assassination." In *Japan Decides 2024: The Japanese General Election*, edited by Kenneth M. McElwain, Robert J. Pekkanen, and Daniel M. Smith, 235–253. Palgrave Macmillan.

Nemoto, Kuniaki. 2025. "Reasons Behind the LDP's Loss in the 2024 Election." In *Japan Decides 2024: The Japanese General Election*, edited by Kenneth M. McElwain, Robert J. Pekkanen, and Daniel M. Smith, 37–55. Palgrave Macmillan.

Oguma, Eiji, and Naoto Higuchi (eds.). 2020. *Nihon wa Ukeika Shitanoka*. Keio University Press.

Pekkanen, Robert, Steven R. Reed, and Ethan Scheiner (eds.). 2013. *Japan Decides 2012: The Japanese General Election*. Palgrave Macmillan.

Pekkanen, Robert J., Steven R. Reed, and Ethan Scheiner (eds.). 2016. *Japan Decides 2014: The Japanese General Election*. Palgrave Macmillan.

Pekkanen, Robert J., Steven R. Reed, Ethan Scheiner, and Daniel M. Smith (eds.). 2018. *Japan Decides 2017: The Japanese General Election*. Palgrave Macmillan.

Pekkanen, Robert J., Steven R. Reed, and Daniel M. Smith (eds.). 2023. *Japan Decides 2021: The Japanese General Election*. Palgrave Macmillan.

Smith, Daniel M., Steven R. Reed, and Robert J. Pekkanen. 2023. "Conclusion: Voters Choose Competence in Japan's Coronavirus Election." In *Japan Decides 2021: The Japanese General Election*, edited by Robert J. Pekkanen, Steven R. Reed, and Daniel M. Smith, 387–396. Palgrave Macmillan.

CHAPTER 2

The 2024 Election Results: A Political Earthquake

Ko Maeda

INTRODUCTION

Ishiba Shigeru became Japan's 102nd Prime Minister on October 1, 2024, and dissolved the House of Representatives (HR) on October 9, setting the election date for October 27. This closely mirrors the actions of his predecessor, Kishida Fumio, who became prime minister on October 4, 2021, and dissolved the HR 10 days later. New prime ministers often enjoy relatively high initial approval ratings, making an early election a sensible strategy. Ishiba apparently sought to replicate Kishida's approach but failed to match his predecessor's 2021 electoral success.

This was the 10th HR election since the 1994 electoral system reform introduced the mixed-member majoritarian electoral system. Currently, 289 of the total 465 seats of the chamber are elected through the single-member district (SMD) tier, and the remaining 176 seats are elected through the proportional representation (PR) tier. Each voter has two ballots and casts one vote for each tier.

K. Maeda (✉)
University of North Texas, Denton, US
e-mail: Ko.Maeda@unt.edu

© The Author(s), under exclusive license to Springer Nature Switzerland AG 2025
K. M. McElwain et al. (eds.), *Japan Decides 2024*,
https://doi.org/10.1007/978-3-031-98797-7_2

As has always been the case since 2003, the ruling coalition of the Liberal Democratic Party (LDP) and Kōmeitō coordinated candidate nominations in SMDs to ensure their candidates do not compete against each other in the same district. The LDP ran candidates in 266 SMDs, down from 277 in the previous election. It did not nominate 11 incumbents involved in a slush fund scandal that surfaced in 2023 (see Carlson 2025 and Nemoto 2025); 9 ran as independent candidates, while 2 did not run (*Yomiuri*, October 9, 2024, online edition). Unlike Koizumi Junichiro's approach in the 2005 election against LDP-turned-independent candidates (see, e.g., Maeda 2006), Ishiba's LDP did not nominate rival candidates to the former LDP incumbents who ran as independents. Kōmeitō ran 11 SMD candidates, up from nine in 2021, with the increase occurring in Saitama and Aichi, where the number of SMDs rose by one due to the 2022 redistricting.

On the opposition side, many parties fielded more candidates than in 2021. The six largest opposition parties—the Constitutional Democratic Party (CDP), Nippon Ishin no Kai (hereafter referred to simply as "Ishin"; also known as the Japan Innovation Party), the Democratic Party for the People (DPP), the Japanese Communist Party (JCP), the Social Democratic Party (SDP), and Reiwa Shinsengumi (hereafter "Reiwa")—ran a total of 455 SMD candidates in 2021, but this increased to 653 this time. In 2021, the CDP, the JCP, the SDP, and Reiwa made an agreement on policy principles before the election and tried to coordinate candidate nominations to avoid splitting votes (Rehmert 2022). However, in this election, the CDP did not seek such an alliance (see Ikeda 2025), prompting the JCP to field more than twice as many candidates as in 2021. Ishin and the DPP, two opposition parties that did not join the alliance in 2021, also increased their SMD candidates.

Further, two new opposition parties entered the general election. Sanseitō is a new party founded in 2020 by some right-wing political activists. The party's website has an English version but does not list the party's English name.[1] The word "Sansei" means political participation, and "tō" means political party. Sanseitō's positions include anti-global capitalism, naturalism, and right-wing conspiracy theories (Toriumi et al. 2024). Its founding leader, Kamiya Sōhei, according to his website, previously served on a city council from 2007 to 2012 and unsuccessfully ran

---

[1] https://www.sanseito.jp/, accessed on December 25, 2024.

for a seat in the HR as an LDP candidate in 2012.[2] The party won one seat in the 2022 House of Councillors (HC) election. Another new party is the Conservative Party of Japan (CPJ), founded in 2023 by Hyakuta Naoki, a best-seller author known for far-right views. The party's slogan, "Make Japan Richer and Stronger," is featured on its website, alongside policies favoring immigration restrictions and preserving traditional Japanese culture.[3]

The Ishiba cabinet's approval rating, according to a Jiji Tsushin survey conducted on October 11–14, was 28.0%. Although it was an improvement over Kishida's final rating of 18.7%, it was the lowest initial cabinet approval rating since 2000 (*Jiji*, October 17, 2024, online edition). Right before the 2021 election, Kishida's approval rating was 40.3%.[4]

Election results are presented in Table 2.1, with the 2021 result included for comparison.[5] The LDP-Kōmeitō coalition, which had maintained 63%–69% of total seats since returning to power in 2012, suffered a clear defeat, losing its majority. Even if all 12 conservative-leaning independent legislators cooperated with the coalition, it was still 12 seats short of a simple majority of the 465-seat HR. The largest opposition party, the CDP, won 148 seats, a major gain from 96 in 2021, largely due to its success in the SMD tier. Ishin gained seats in SMDs, but it won fewer seats in PR, reducing its overall share. The DPP more than doubled its seats, from 11 to 28, with its PR vote share more than tripling compared to the last election. The JCP lost two seats and was surpassed by Reiwa, which became the fourth-largest opposition party. The two new right-wing parties, Sanseitō and the CPJ, each won three seats.

Voter turnout was 53.9%, according to the official report by the Ministry of Internal Affairs and Communications, which is the third-lowest in the country's post-war history. The number of female HR members rose significantly, from 45 (9.7% of total seats) in 2021 to

---

[2] https://www.kamiyasohei.jp/, accessed on December 25, 2024.

[3] https://hoshuto.jp/, accessed on December 25, 2024.

[4] https://www.crs.or.jp/backno/No769/7690.htm, accessed on December 24, 2024.

[5] The election results data used in this chapter are based on the government's official publications and various newspaper reports, part of which were compiled and provided by Yuki Yanai.

Table 2.1 Votes and seats in the 2021 and 2024 general elections

		LDP	Kōmeitō	CDP	Ishin	DPP	JCP	SDP	Reiwa	Other/Indep	Total
SMD (2021)	Candidates	277	9	214	94	21	105	9	12	116	857
	Total votes	27,626,235	872,931	17,215,621	4,802,793	1,246,812	2,639,631	313,193	248,280	2,491,536	57,457,033
	Average vote %	50.2%	48.8%	40.5%	25.7%	29.9%	12.6%	17.5%	10.4%	10.8%	
	Seats	187	9	57	16	6	1	1	0	12	289
PR (2021)	Total votes	19,914,883	7,114,282	11,492,095	8,050,830	2,593,396	4,166,076	1,018,588	2,215,648	900,181	57,465,979
	Vote %	34.7%	12.4%	20.0%	14.0%	4.5%	7.2%	1.8%	3.9%	1.6%	100%
	Seats	72	23	39	25	5	9	0	3	0	176
Total (2021)	Seats	259	32	96	41	11	10	1	3	12	465
	Seat %	55.7%	6.9%	20.6%	8.8%	2.4%	2.2%	0.2%	0.6%	2.6%	100%

		LDP	Kōmeitō	CDP	Ishin	DPP	JCP	SDP	Reiwa	Sanseitō	CPJ	Other/Indep	Total
SMD (2024)	Candidates	266	11	207	163	41	213	10	19	85	1	97	1113
	Total votes	20,867,762	730,401	15,740,860	6,048,104	2,349,685	4,807,283	283,287	425,445	1,357,189	95,613	2,667,825	54,261,878
	Average vote %	41.8%	35.4%	40.5%	19.8%	30.5%	9.2%	15.1%	11.9%	8.5%	50.9%	14.6%	
	Seats	132	4	104	23	11	1	1	0	0	1	12	289
PR (2024)	Total votes	14,582,690	5,964,415	11,565,123	5,105,127	6,171,533	3,362,966	934,598	3,805,060	1,870,347	1,145,622	42,239	54,549,720

	LDP	Kōmeitō	CDP	Ishin	DPP	JCP	SDP	Reiwa	Sanseitō	CPJ	Other/Indep	Total
Vote %	26.7%	10.9%	21.2%	9.4%	11.3%	6.2%	1.7%	7.0%	3.4%	2.1%	0.1%	100%
Seats	59	20	44	15	17	7	0	9	3	2	0	176
Total (2024) Seats	191	24	148	38	28	8	1	9	3	3	12	465
Seat %	41.1%	5.2%	31.8%	8.2%	6.0%	1.7%	0.2%	1.9%	0.6%	0.6%	2.6%	100%

Source Ministry of Internal Affairs and Communications (MIC)

Notes The number of single-member district (SMD) candidates for the parties is officially nominated candidates. They do not include independent candidates implicitly affiliated with a party. The LDP's seats in 2021 were 261 if two candidates who obtained an ex-post nomination are included

The official result by the MIC classifies Kawamura Takashi of the CPJ who won in the Aichi-1st district as an "other" candidate for a technical reason. He is counted as a CPJ candidate in this table

Party abbreviations: LDP ~ Liberal Democratic Party; CDP ~ Constitutional Democratic Party; Ishin ~ Nippon Ishin no Kai; JCP ~ Japanese Communist Party; SDP ~ Social Democratic Party; DPP ~ Democratic Party for the People; Reiwa ~ Reiwa Shinsengumi; CPJ ~ Conservative Party of Japan

73 (15.7%). The percentage of women was higher among PR winners (21.4%) than SMD winners (12.1%).[6]

Although the LDP-Kōmeitō coalition lost its majority, the framework of the ruling cabinet remained intact. No opposition party was willing to join the coalition, forcing the LDP and Kōmeitō to form a minority coalition cabinet. A special Diet session was convened on November 11 to elect the new prime minister, and the HR elected Ishiba after members of Ishin, the DPP, and a few other opposition parties cast invalid votes in the runoff round (*Mainichi*, November 11, 2024, online edition).

Where Did the LDP Lose Votes?

The biggest story of this election was the LDP's loss, although it was an expected outcome given the party's struggles with declining popularity over the past year and heavy criticism following the slush fund scandal. For the first time since returning to power in 2012, the LDP failed to secure a single-party majority. As Table 2.1 indicates, while the party lost votes in both the SMD and PR tiers, its performance was significantly worse in SMDs, where it lost 55 seats. With the exception of the 2009 election, the LDP had consistently won more than half of the SMDs under the current electoral system. This time, it won only 132 out of 289 SMDs. The average vote share of LDP candidates in SMDs fell from 50.2% in 2021 to 41.8% in 2024.

The LDP's poor showing in SMDs in this election is ironic because, as discussed earlier, opposition parties nominated far more SMD candidates than they did in 2021. Before the election, opposition politicians and supporters expressed concern that having many opposition candidates in each district might benefit the LDP by splitting the anti-government votes (*Yomiuri*, October 1, 2024, online edition). It turned out, however, that the LDP fared much worse than in the last election.

Where did LDP candidates lose votes? Fig. 2.1 displays the winning percentages of LDP candidates in SMDs since 2012, broken down into three levels of urbanization. Urbanization is measured in the same way as in Maeda (2022).[7] The figure clearly indicates that the LDP victory rates declined across all levels, with similar magnitudes of decline in all three

---

[6] See Tsuji (2025) for more on gender issues.

[7] The SMDs where more than 90% of residents reside in the census-designated "densely inhabited districts" are considered "urban" SMDs. Between 90 and 50% are "middle,"

groups. Unlike the 2021 election, where the party's decline was primarily an urban phenomenon, the 2024 results indicate a nationwide pattern.

Among the 212 LDP candidates who ran in the SMD tier in both the 2021 and 2024 elections, 198 (93.4%) experienced a decline in their vote share percentages. On average, these candidates saw a drop of 8.5 percentage points, with a standard deviation of 7.0.

A series of regression analyses were performed to examine the factors influencing the SMD vote percentage changes among those 212 LDP candidates. Table 2.2 presents the results. Model 1 is the basic model with three independent variables: the candidate's vote share in 2021; the district's level of urbanization; and the candidates' number of previous terms served. The 2021 vote share has a negative coefficient and is statistically significant, which is expected because candidates with a higher vote share in the previous election have more votes to lose. Urbanization is also negative and significant, although its coefficient is very close to zero. The number of terms is statistically insignificant.

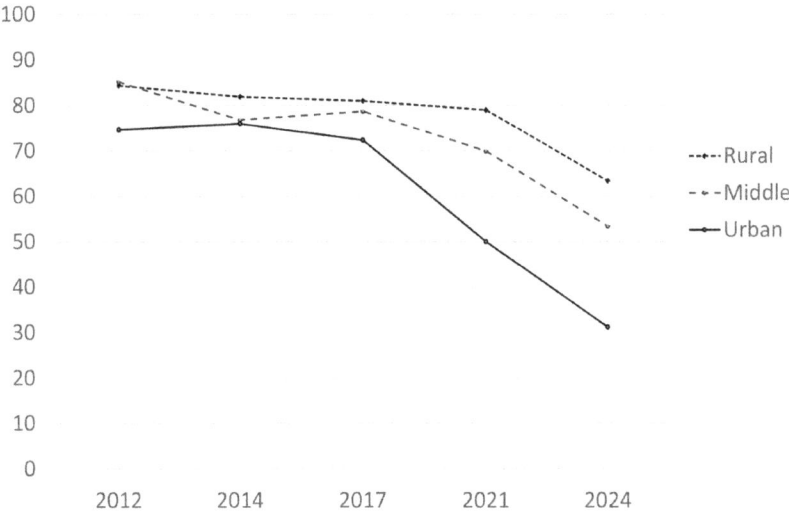

Fig. 2.1 Winning % of the LDP's SMD candidates

and below 50% are "rural." The three categories contain roughly the same number of SMDs.

Table 2.2 Determinants of LDP candidates' vote change

	(1)	(2)	(3)
Vote share in 2021	−0.238**	−0.187**	−0.216**
	(0.060)	(0.055)	(0.055)
Urbanization	−0.054*	−0.018	−0.012
	(0.021)	(0.020)	(0.020)
Previous terms	0.082	0.065	0.110
	(0.201)	(0.150)	(0.153)
Another conservative		−12.752**	−13.376**
		(3.862)	(3.699)
# Opposition candidates		−2.625**	−2.009**
		(0.437)	(0.442)
CDP but no Ishin or DPP			−0.307
			(1.029)
CDP plus Ishin and/or DPP			−3.395**
			(1.089)
Intercept	7.080	4.565	6.297
	(3.749)	(3.570)	(3.552)
# Observations	212	212	212
R-squared	0.114	0.318	0.355

Dependent variable: LDP candidates' vote share change from 2021 to 2024
Robust standard errors in parentheses. ** $p < 0.01$, * $p < 0.05$

Model 2 adds two independent variables. Some LDP candidates had an independent candidate in the same district known to be conservative and LDP-leaning, and such candidates are expected to steal votes from LDP co-partisans. The *Another Conservative* variable takes the value of 1 if there was such a candidate in 2024 and not in 2021. The value of −1 is assigned if there was no such candidate in 2024, but there was in 2021. All other observations have the value of 0.[8] As expected, this variable has a negative and significant coefficient. The # *Opposition Candidates* variable is the change in the number of opposition candidates from 2021 to 2024. Only the candidates of the parties listed in Table 2.1 were counted. As discussed earlier, opposition parties ran more SMD candidates in 2024. The average of this variable is 0.9, and both the median and mode are 1, which means that a typical SMD had about one additional opposition

---

[8] Conservative independent candidates who won less than 10% of votes were ignored in the coding of this variable.

candidate in 2024 than in 2021. This variable is statistically significant, and the coefficient is −2.625, indicating that each additional opposition candidate reduced the LDP candidate's vote share by an average of 2.625 percentage points, other factors being equal.

Model 3 investigates one of the central questions about this election. The CDP has been the largest opposition party since 2017 and has been agonizing over its ideological position (see Ikeda 2025 and Matsumoto 2025). It has often been argued that it may be too leftist to attract centrist voters (see Maeda 2022). In this election, when the LDP was unpopular and lost support, were Ishin and the DPP—the two parties positioned to the right of the CDP—recipients of anti-incumbent votes because they are not left-wing? Two dummy variables are added in Model 3. The *CDP but No Ishin or DPP* variable takes the value of 1 if there was a CDP candidate and no Ishin or DPP candidate in this election, and 0 otherwise. The *CDP plus Ishin and/or DPP* variable takes 1 if there was a CDP candidate as well as an Ishin and/or DPP candidate, and 0 otherwise. Cases where there was no CDP candidate are the reference category. As Table 2.2 shows, the former variable is statistically insignificant with a near-zero coefficient, while the latter variable is significant with a coefficient of −3.395. This result indicates that while there is no evidence that an LDP candidate lost votes when facing a CDP opponent but not an Ishin or DPP opponent, an LDP candidate who competed against a CDP candidate as well as an Ishin and/or DPP candidate experienced, on average, a 3.395 percentage point decline in vote share, other factors being equal. This suggests that the presence of an Ishin or DPP candidate promoted anti-incumbent voting by providing a non-left alternative to voters who previously voted for the LDP but sought to punish it this time.

In the PR tier, Fig. 2.2 shows the prefectural-level change in the LDP's PR vote share from 2021 to 2024, plotted against the urbanization levels of the prefectures (see footnote 7). Clearly, the LDP's vote share declined in most parts of the country. In fact, Tottori prefecture, which includes Ishiba's district, was the only one that saw an improvement in the LDP's vote share. In the rest of the country, it went down with an average decrease of 7.9 percentage points. The magnitude of the change was quite uniform—about two-thirds of the prefectures saw a 5 to 10 percentage point decrease. This pattern confirms the notion that the LDP's decline in this election was a nationwide phenomenon that occurred across all regions of the country and at all levels of urbanization.

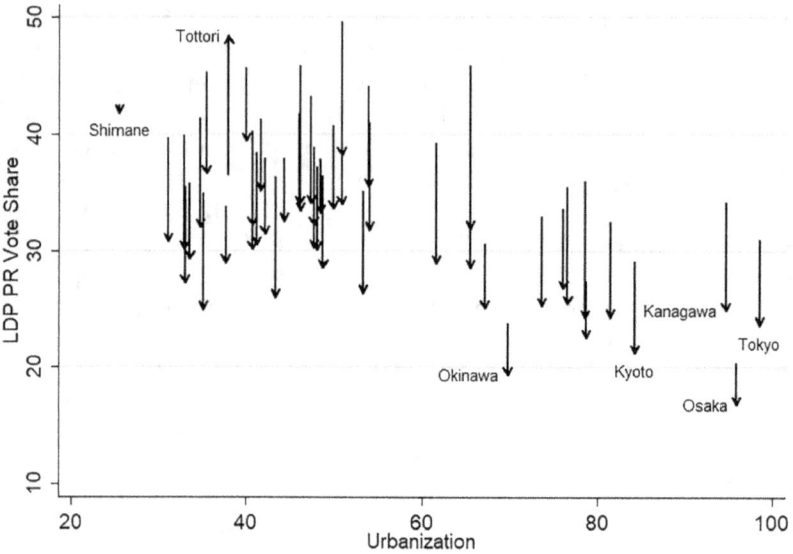

Fig. 2.2 LDP's PR vote change, 2021–2024

Ishin's Fall

The biggest winner in the 2021 election was Ishin, which more than tripled its seats compared to the 2017 election. Following this success, Ishin was on an upward trajectory and made surpassing the CDP its goal (*Sankei*, March 24, 2024, online edition). Ishin was originally a regional party based in Osaka (Reed 2013), but as the party became more popular, its leaders tried to transform it into a national party. As a symbolic move, Ishin had Otokita Shun, a young and well-known incumbent HC member, resign from the HC and run for the Tokyo-1st district in this HR election (*Yomiuri*, September 6, 2024, online edition). Considering that the Tokyo-1st district already had veteran LDP and CDP candidates, Ishin's leaders must have been very confident in the party's momentum.

However, as shown in Table 2.1, the number of Ishin's HR seats declined from 41 to 38, and its PR vote share, which reflects the party's overall popularity, also dropped from 14.0% to 9.4%. Exit polls show that while 21% of voters who considered themselves independents voted for Ishin in 2021, the percentage fell to 11% in 2024 (*Mainichi*, October

31, 2021, online edition; *Mainichi*, October 28, 2024, online edition). A media report suggests that Ishin's decline in popularity can be attributed to multiple factors, including concerns over the ever-expanding costs of the 2025 Osaka World Expo, widely seen as Ishin's pet project, and alleged workplace bullying involving the governor of Hyogo prefecture, whom Ishin supported during his initial election (*Yomiuri*, August 6, 2024, online edition). Zenkyo (2025), in this volume, argues that these problems worsened voters' perceptions of Ishin's policy competence, as well as the image of its leader, Baba Nobuyuki.

Although Ishin's SMD seats increased from 16 to 23, this should not be interpreted as a sign that Ishin performed better than in the last election in the SMD tier. Out of the 23 SMDs Ishin won, 19 are in Osaka, Ishin's stronghold. Until the last election, Ishin did not field candidates in four Osaka SMDs where Kōmeitō also ran its candidates, in an apparent effort to avoid direct confrontation with Kōmeitō, which boasts significant strength in Osaka. That is why Ishin won 15 SMDs in Osaka in 2021, even though every one of Ishin's Osaka candidates won. However, Ishin changed its course for this election and fielded candidates in all 19 Osaka SMDs, sweeping them. While it is true that Ishin remains the dominant party in Osaka, it should be noted that, out of the 15 SMDs where Ishin had a candidate in both 2021 and 2024, 11 saw a drop in the vote share for Ishin candidates. Furthermore, among the four remaining SMDs where Ishin candidates' vote share improved, three were districts where the CDP did not field a candidate, thereby helping Ishin attract anti-incumbent votes.

Ishin's SMD candidates outside Osaka performed worse. Figure 2.3 plots the vote shares of Ishin's SMD candidates (y-axis) against the distance from Osaka (x-axis).[9] Circles represent candidates who were elected in their districts, and X's are those who did not win. The circles aligned at the far-left side of the graph are the 19 Ishin candidates in Osaka. The graph indicates that most Ishin candidates outside Osaka and its adjacent areas earned less than 20% of the votes and were thus not competitive in their districts (Otokita in the Tokyo-1st district mentioned above finished 3rd in his district with 16.3% of the votes). Four Ishin candidates outside Osaka won their races, shown as circles in the graph (Kyoto—2nd, Shiga—1st, Hiroshima—4th, and Fukuoka—11th), but

---

[9] The distance was not to the districts but to the prefectural capitals. The data were obtained from https://home.hiroshima-u.ac.jp/tomozawa/Matrix%20of%20distances.xlsx.

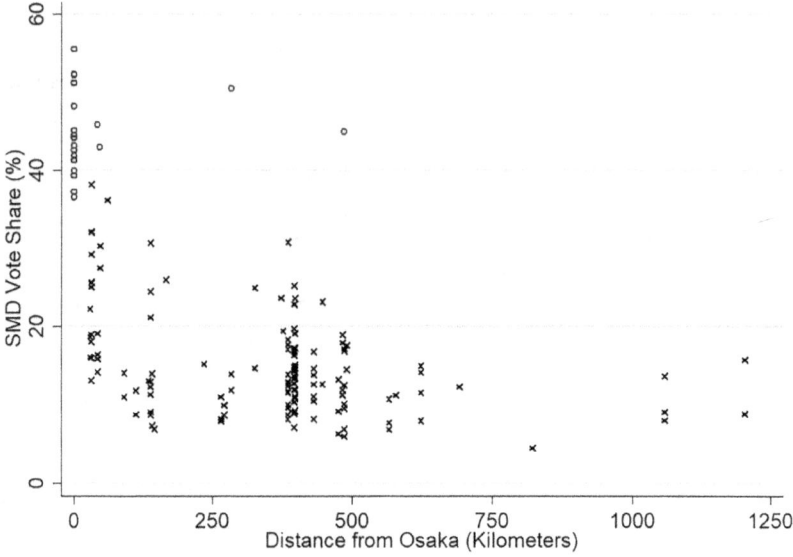

Fig. 2.3 Ishin candidates' votes in SMDs

none of these districts had a CDP candidate, which undoubtedly helped their campaigns.

The arrows in Fig. 2.4 show Ishin's PR vote share change by prefecture from 2021 to 2024, again plotted against the distance from Osaka. Ishin's PR vote share decreased in 46 of the 47 prefectures, and the size of the drop was especially large where Ishin performed well in 2021. In summary, while the 2021 election results suggested that Ishin might develop into a third pillar in Japan's party politics—alongside the LDP-Kōmeitō duo and the CDP-led opposition parties—forming a structure of trilateral competition (Maeda 2022), Ishin's momentum has clearly halted.

The DPP's Surge

Although the DPP is the fourth-largest party in size, much attention was paid to it after this election because of its sudden growth. This party held only 7 HR seats before this election but won 28. In fact, the DPP was entitled to three more seats but had to forfeit them to other parties

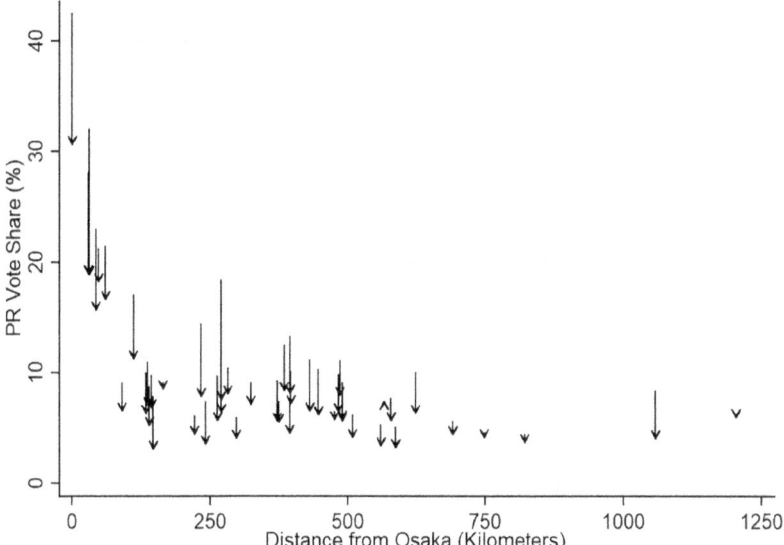

Fig. 2.4 Ishin's PR votes by prefecture

because it did not include enough candidates on its PR lists (*Nikkei*, October 28, 2024, online edition). This anecdote suggests that even the DPP's leaders did not anticipate the scale of their victory.

The DPP's origin can be traced back to the Democratic Party of Japan (DPJ), which was the main rival to the LDP for many years and was in power from 2009 to 2012. The DPP was originally established in May 2018 after the Party of Hope disintegrated. In September 2020, most of its members joined the CDP, and the remaining members created the current DPP, a new party in a legal sense while retaining the same name (Pekkanen and Reed 2022). Four DPP legislators defected from the party in November 2023, making the party even smaller (*Asahi*, November 30, 2023, online edition). Tamaki Yūichirō, the party leader since 2018, has been using the slogan "Solution rather than confrontation" (*Taiketsu yori kaiketsu*, in Japanese) and has cooperated with the government on some policy issues in an effort to increase the visibility of his small party in the political scene (*Jiji*, January 9, 2024, online edition).

During the electoral campaign, the DPP appealed to relatively younger voters with the tagline "We'll raise your take-home pay," advocating for tax and economic policies that would benefit younger generations while effectively utilizing social media platforms (*Japan Times*, November 1, 2024, online edition). An exit poll suggests that the DPP received more PR votes than any other party from voters in their 20 s and was the most popular opposition party among all age groups under 40 (*Asahi*, October 28, 2024, online edition). The DPP's support was much lower among older generations, making a stark contrast to the CDP, whose popularity was higher among the elderly.

The CDP—The Bitter Winner

The largest opposition CDP earned 148 seats—52 more than in the last election. This marked the first time any non-LDP party had won triple-digit seats since 2009. The seat differential between the LDP and the CDP is 43, which is the narrowest gap between the top two parties under the current electoral system. However, the CDP can hardly be considered a winner of this election.

As discussed earlier, the CDP entered the 2021 HR election with a cooperative relationship with the JCP and two other parties but failed to perform well. Consequently, the party's founding leader, Edano Yukio, resigned, and Izumi Kenta succeeded him as the CDP leader. Reflecting on the party's experience in the 2021 HR election, Izumi chose not to cooperate with the JCP in the 2022 HC election (see Ikeda 2025). However, the party lost seats in that election as well. Ultimately, Izumi lost his bid to secure reelection as the party leader, and Noda Yoshihiko took over the CDP leadership in September 2024 (see Ikeda 2025).

Noda, who served as the DPJ leader and prime minister from 2011 to 2012, is widely regarded as a right-leaning politician within the CDP. Upon assuming the party leadership, he toned down the party's leftist policies and declined to collaborate with the JCP—a move interpreted as an effort to broaden the party's appeal among moderate and conservative voters (*Tokyo Shinbun*, September 24, 2024, online edition).

As shown in Table 2.1, while the CDP's total seats increased, its average SMD vote share remained steady at 40.5%, and its PR vote share improved only slightly, from 20.0% to 21.2%. The significant increase in SMD seats despite no change in the average vote share suggests that many CDP candidates won due to the LDP's declining popularity rather than the CDP's own appeal. Perhaps more concerning for the CDP is the fact that its total PR votes increased by only 73 thousand while the LDP-Kōmeitō duo's combined PR votes plummeted by as much as 6.5 million. Clearly, despite being the largest opposition party since 2017, the CDP failed to become the primary recipient of anti-incumbent votes in the 2024 election.

Figure 2.5 shows selected parties' PR vote percentages since the 2003 election. The CDP's PR votes have remained mostly steady at around 20% since its foundation in 2017, which is nowhere near the level achieved by the DPJ during the 2003–2009 period. Even in 2005, when the LDP won a massive victory under Koizumi Junichiro, the DPJ managed to secure slightly above 30%. Between 2003 and 2009, no parties other than the LDP, the DPJ, and Kōmeitō surpassed 10% in their PR votes. However, after 2012, the opposition side became fragmented with the advent of Ishin in 2012 and the split of the DPJ in 2017. While the CDP has won the most PR votes among opposition parties in the last three elections, a party positioned to the right of the CDP has consistently earned a significant share of votes: Hope in 2017, Ishin in 2021, and the DPP in 2024. The CDP's struggle to attract centrist votes, even with Noda as party leader and his deliberate efforts to moderate the party's position, underscores the severity of the CDP's challenges.

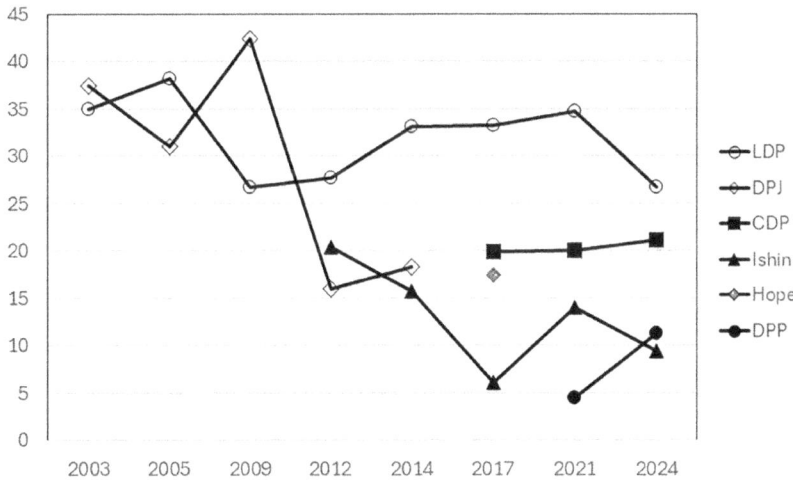

Fig. 2.5 PR vote percentages, 2003–2024 (selected parties)

After the election, as the ruling coalition lost its majority, the government entered policy negotiations with the DPP and Ishin to secure support for a supplementary budget proposal. These negotiations and the DPP's sudden rise in the election shifted post-election media attention away from the CDP. The DPP's party approval rating, which had been hovering below 3% before the election, rose above 10% in some December surveys, surpassing the CDP to become the highest-rated opposition party (*Yomiuri*, December 16, 2024, online edition; *Asahi*, December 16, 2024, online edition). Despite gaining the largest increase in seats compared to the last election, the CDP's visibility and popularity have diminished.

Conclusion

The 2024 general election delivered a political earthquake. The LDP-Kōmeitō coalition, which returned to power in 2012, had since appeared invincible—enacting major legislation while retaining a comfortable parliamentary majority. However, the slush fund scandal that came to light in late 2023 completely altered the political landscape, leading to the end of Kishida's tenure and then resulting in the first hung parliament since 1993.

Ishiba's new minority cabinet will face significant challenges in governing and will need to make policy concessions to opposition parties to pass annual budgets. Opposition parties, particularly the DPP, will claim credit for partially achieving the policy promises they made during the campaign. Positioned as a small party between the two major parties, the DPP has at times oscillated between aligning with the CDP and cooperating with the government. However, following its major triumph in this election—achieved without partnering with a larger party—it will most likely continue on its current path. Although the Japanese Trade Union Confederation (*Rengo*), the country's largest labor organization, has urged the CDP and the DPP to cooperate closely or even merge into a single party, the prospects for such a scenario now appear slim.

As paradoxical as it may sound, the party that made the largest seat gains compared to the last election, the CDP, is the one that has been cornered into a difficult position as a result of this election. As explained above, its gains in the SMD tier were primarily a consequence of the LDP's decline rather than an increase in support for the CDP. Moreover, the party struggled to increase its PR votes despite the ruling coalition's significant loss of votes. What makes this outcome even more concerning for the CDP is that a non-leftist leader, who took over just before this election, attempted to attract centrist voters with moderated policies but failed to become the primary recipient of anti-incumbent votes.

For three consecutive elections, a party positioned to the right of the CDP has captured a significant share of votes, depriving the CDP of an opportunity for victory. If the CDP wants to break out of its current position and compete for power, it will need to broaden its appeal by winning centrist votes while maintaining its existing base. However, given that the DPP is receiving considerable post-election attention and rising in popularity, the CDP's prospects for attracting centrist votes seem slim. With both the LDP and the CDP struggling, Japan's party system does not appear to be converging toward a stable structure of party competition.

References

Carlson, Matthew M. 2025. "Scandals During the Kishida Administration." In *Japan Decides 2024: The Japanese General Election*, edited by Kenneth M. McElwain, Robert J. Pekkanen, and Daniel M. Smith, 217–233. Palgrave Macmillan.

Ikeda, Fumi. 2025. "The CDP in 2024: The Legacy of the Electoral Coalition with the JCP." In *Japan Decides 2024: The Japanese General Election*, edited by Kenneth M. McElwain, Robert J. Pekkanen, and Daniel M. Smith, 57–74. Palgrave Macmillan.

Maeda, Ko. 2006. "The General Election in Japan, September 2005" *Electoral Studies* 25(3): 621–627.

Maeda, Ko. 2022. "The 2021 Election Results." In *Japan Decides 2021: The Japanese General Election*, edited by Robert J. Pekkanen, Steven R. Reed, and Daniel M. Smith, 23–39. Palgrave Macmillan.

Matsumoto, Tomoko. 2025. "How Party Manifestos Framed Political Distrust in the 2024 Election". In *Japan Decides 2024: The Japanese General Election*, edited by Kenneth M. McElwain, Robert J. Pekkanen, and Daniel M. Smith, 143–161. Palgrave Macmillan.

Nemoto, Kuniaki. 2025. "Reasons Behind the LDP's Loss in the 2024 Election." In *Japan Decides 2024: The Japanese General Election*, edited by Kenneth M. McElwain, Robert J. Pekkanen, and Daniel M. Smith, 37–55. Palgrave Macmillan.

Pekkanen, Robert J., and Steven R. Reed. 2022. "The Opposition in 2021: A Second Party and a Third Force." In *Japan Decides 2021: The Japanese General Election*, edited by Robert J. Pekkanen, Steven R. Reed, and Daniel M. Smith, 59–69. New York: Palgrave Macmillan.

Reed, Steven R. 2013. "Challenging the Two-Party System: Third Force Parties in the 2012 Election." In *Japan Decides 2012: The Japanese General Election*, edited by Robert J. Pekkanen, Steven R. Reed, and Ethan Scheiner, 72–83. New York: Palgrave Macmillan.

Rehmert, Jochen. 2022. "Candidate Selection for the 2021 General Election." In *Japan Decides 2021: The Japanese General Election*, edited by Robert J. Pekkanen, Steven R. Reed, and Daniel M. Smith, 59–69. New York: Palgrave Macmillan.

Toriumi, Fujio, Takeshi Sakaki, Tetsuro Kobayashi, and Mitsuo Yoshida. 2024. "Anti-vaccine rabbit hole leads to political representation: the case of Twitter in Japan." *Journal of Computational Social Science* 7(1): 405–423.

Tsuji, Yuki. 2025. "Increase in Women's Representation and Candidates' Positions on Gender Equality Issues." In *Japan Decides 2024: The Japanese General Election*, edited by Kenneth M. McElwain, Robert J. Pekkanen, and Daniel M. Smith, 255–271. Palgrave Macmillan.

Zenkyo, Masahiro. 2025. "Why Did Public Support for the Japan Innovation Party Decline in the 2024 HR Election?" In *Japan Decides 2024: The Japanese General Election*, edited by Kenneth M. McElwain, Robert J. Pekkanen, and Daniel M. Smith, 91–105. Palgrave Macmillan.

PART II

Political Parties

CHAPTER 3

Reasons Behind the LDP's Loss in the 2024 Election

Kuniaki Nemoto

The election for the House of Representatives (HR) on October 27, 2024 was historical in several ways. First, it resulted in a major defeat of the coalition of the Liberal Democratic Party (LDP) and the Kōmeitō. Although the LDP-Kōmeitō coalition has been so successful in winning national-level elections since its comeback to power in 2012, for the first time in 12 years, the coalition was unable to maintain its majority in the HR. Second, since the LDP's leader, Ishiba Shigeru, could not win a majority of the votes in the first round of the Prime Ministerial nomination, the nomination process went on to the final majority run-off round for the first time in 30 years. Although Noda Yoshihiko, the recently selected leader of the major opposition Constitutional Democratic Party of Japan (CDP), had some chance to win the nomination, thanks to some opposition parties that decided to cast invalid votes in the final round, Ishiba won the nomination and became the Prime Minister.

K. Nemoto (✉)
Musashi University, Tokyo, Japan
e-mail: knemoto@cc.musashi.ac.jp

© The Author(s), under exclusive license to Springer Nature Switzerland AG 2025
K. M. McElwain et al. (eds.), *Japan Decides 2024*,
https://doi.org/10.1007/978-3-031-98797-7_3

This chapter explores why the LDP lost badly. To jump to the conclusion, there seem to be three major reasons: (1) the assassination of Abe Shinzō in 2022 eventually revealed collusive ties between many LDP members and the highly controversial Unification Church; (2) the *Uragane* (Slush Fund) scandal found LDP members received illegal kickbacks from their factions; and (3) none of the candidates in the leadership race in September 2024, including Ishiba, expressed support for additional measures for these scandals.

The chapter, therefore, consists of four sections. The first and second sections chronologically describe the two scandals and the LDP's reactions. There was much the same pattern: the LDP tried to ignore the scandals at first, but as the public's discontent mounted, the party decided to take some countermeasures that turned out to be largely ineffective. The third section focuses on the LDP's party organization and its effects on the leadership selection. Since factions disbanded and as many as nine candidates ran, the race became very unpredictable, forcing candidates to keep silent as to how to deal with scandal-tainted members. In the fourth section, a simple regression analysis shows that LDP members received fewer votes if they had had some ties to the Unification Church and if they had received kickbacks. A brief conclusion follows.

The Unification Church

Abe Shinzō, the longest-serving Prime Minister of Japan, was assassinated on July 8, 2022, in his campaign rally for the House of Councillors (HC) election. This shocking event to Japan and the rest of the world soon took an unpredictable turn. Police investigations against the assailant revealed that his mother was a member of the Unification Church (UC hereafter), which allegedly made his family go bankrupt (*Nikkei*, July 12, 2022). According to further investigations, the assailant decided to assassinate Abe, when he developed his conviction that Abe had close ties with the UC and its leaders. Reportedly, he watched Abe's video message delivered at an event sponsored by a UC-affiliated organization (*Nikkei*, July 15, 2022).

The UC is a controversial religious organization, to say the least (see McLaughlin 2025).[1] It faced accusations of forcing its members to donate

---

[1] There is very little scholarly work on the UC and Japanese politics. A few exceptions include Kingston (2023), McLaughlin (2023, 2025), and Saitō (2024).

huge sums of money through what is called "spiritual sales" (*reikan shōhō*)—the practice of using spiritual fear to fraudulently cajole people into buying potteries and other goods at extremely high prices (*Nikkei*, July 15, 2022). Although the UC claimed that it had focused on legal compliance since 2009, the National Network of Lawyers Against Spiritual Sales reported approximately 30,000 compensation claims totaling at 123.7 billion yen between 1987 and 2021 (*Nikkei*, August 10, 2022). Politicians like Abe were used by the UC as an implicit endorsement for its activities to expand members and mobilize donations (*Nikkei*, September 2, 2022).

What ensued was the spiral of growing discontent among the public, as seen in the declining cabinet approval rating in Fig. 3.1. In early August 2022, then Secretary-General Motegi Toshimitsu denied any organizational relationship between the party and the UC and only stated that "each member should be accountable for their own political activities" (*Nikkei*, August 3, 2022), implying that the party would not conduct any systematic investigation about the issue. However, opinion polls showed that the government's decision to hold a state funeral for Abe was not favorable among citizens. Thus, the Prime Minister decided to reshuffle his cabinet and sack cabinet ministers tied to the UC (*Nikkei*, August 6, 2022). This reshuffle was only half-hearted, though, since as many as five of the ministers in the cabinet reshuffled on August 10 were found to have some ties to the UC (*Nikkei*, August 11, 2022).

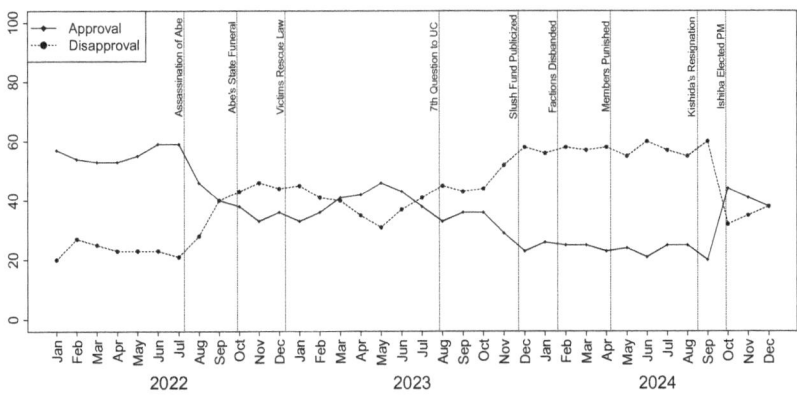

Fig. 3.1 Approval and disapproval rates of the cabinet. *Source* NHK (2025)

With the disapproval rate surpassing the approval rate in September 2022, as shown in Fig. 3.1, the LDP decided to introduce a new governance code in the same month (*Nikkei*, August 26, 2022), under which its members were to strictly refrain from having contacts with socially problematic organizations. In addition, the LDP also asked all of its 379 members questions, including: (1) if they gave a greeting at an event sponsored by a UC-affiliated group; (2) if they gave a speech at an event sponsored by a UC-affiliated group; (3) if they participated in an event sponsored by the UC itself; (4) if they expensed some fees for a UC-sponsored event; (5) if they received donations from the UC; (6) if they received voluntary campaign support from the UC; and (7) if they requested and received organizational campaign support from the UC. It shockingly revealed that 179 members had had some kind of contact with the Church. The party decided to publicize through major newspaper outlets the list of 121 members who said yes to any of the seven questions above (*Nikkei*, September 9, 2022). Despite these measures, the public disapproved of the way the LDP conducted its self-investigation, since members only voluntarily reported their ties to the UC (*Nikkei*, September 28, 2022b), and other LDP members later admitted one after another that they had some ties with the UC (*Nikkei*, October 1, 2022). While the state funeral for Abe was held, citizens organized protests against it in front of the National Diet (*Nikkei*, September 28, 2022a).

The LDP finally decided to change gears by responding to the mounting discontent among the public with two measures. The first is the revised Consumer Contract Act, which allows consumers to rescind contracts if they are signed under unfair conditions. The revision made in December 2022, more commonly known as the Law to Rescue Victims (*Higaisha Kyūsai Hō*), was to enlarge the scope of consumer contracts to religious donations and ban organizations from soliciting donations through spiritual fear. Consumers would also be able to cancel their donations up to ten years after they entered their contracts (*Nikkei*, December 11, 2022).

As the second measure, the government started in November its investigations into the UC, with an eye toward an eventual 2023 dissolution request. In conducting investigations, the government used its right to question a religious organization for the first time in history (*Nikkei*, November 22, 2022). The government's questions were delivered to the UC seven times in total between November 2022 and July 2023, covering a wide range of issues including the UC's assets and finance, organization structure, and transnational remittance of money (*Nikkei*, September 7, 2023). But as the UC declined to answer more than 100 questions, the government decided to seek an administrative penalty fine from the UC (*Nikkei*, September 7, 2023). In October 2023, the government submitted a request to the court seeking the dissolution of the UC, contending that the UC had inflicted considerable harm upon numerous individuals in its pursuit of wealth and had substantially deviated from the legitimate purposes of a religious organization (*Nikkei*, October 13, 2023).

With the countermeasure to rescue victims and the tough measure to request the dissolution of the UC, the government's approval somehow stabilized in 2023. However, questions remained. Beyond publicizing the list of those who voluntarily admitted their contacts with the UC, the LDP did not make any efforts to systematically and comprehensively investigate its relationship with the UC. LDP members were only discouraged from refraining from having contact with the UC, with no disciplinary measures ever taken. *Asahi* later scooped the fact that in 2013 then Prime Minister Abe met with UC leaders at the President's Reception Room in the LDP Headquarters (*Asahi*, September 17, 2024) and asked them to offer campaign support for the upcoming HC election, casting some doubts on the party's claim that there was no organizational relationship between the party and the UC.

THE URAGANE SCANDAL

The second scandal is what is called the *Uragane* (Slush Fund) scandal, as discussed in depth in Carlson (2025). When the scandal was first scooped in November 2022 by *Akahata*, a daily newspaper run by the Japanese Communist Party (JCP), the media's attention was not so high. However, as Kamiwaki Hiroshi, a constitutional law scholar who also works on corruption and political funds, filed a criminal complaint with the Tokyo District Public Prosecutors Office about the case, the Office opened a probe by forming a special investigation team. Then, major newspapers like *Asahi* started to cover the scandal in late 2023, and the public's attention became very high (Kamiwaki 2024a, 2024b).

Prosecutors' and journalists' investigations gradually brought to light the very opaque money flows between LDP factions and their members. The first allegation was that factions inside the LDP might have violated the Political Funds Control Act, since they under-reported monetary donations in their fund-raising parties. Given that the Act prohibits organizations other than political parties from receiving donations, factions frequently held fund-raising parties, which were allowed under the Act. The Act still required that when a certain group donated 200,000 yen or more to a fund-raising party, the group's name and the amount of the donation should be reported. The failure to do so was a criminal offense (*Nikkei*, November 19, 2023). The second allegation was that LDP members also might have violated the Act, since they received the under-reported donations from factions as kickbacks, and many of them inappropriately reported their income. The Act provided that failure to report income and misstatement of income were both illegal (*Nikkei*, December 2, 2023).

When the scandal was first publicized by major newspapers, then Prime Minister Kishida only stated that factions had made appropriate revisions to their financial reports and there was no *uragane* (*Nikkei*, November 22, 2023). However, prosecutors' investigations revealed that the involvement of the Abe and Nikai factions was extraordinary. The Abe faction allegedly distributed to members kickbacks of approximately 500 million yen over the period of 2018–2022. The faction also ordered its members not to report those kickbacks in their financial reports, suggesting that the faction organizationally and systematically continued this practice over many years (*Nikkei*, December 13, 2023). The Nikai faction seemed to have used much the same scheme to distribute approximately 100 million yen over the same period (*Nikkei*, December 15, 2023). Other factions—the Asō faction, the Motegi faction, and the Kishida faction—reportedly engaged in a similar practice, although the amount involved was much smaller.

The most important question in investigating these illegal money transfers was who was responsible for the establishment and implementation of this very complex mechanism. If a politician colluded with the treasurer in distributing the kickbacks, it should be an illegal act worthy of indictment. However, prosecutors concluded that there was not enough evidence that the Abe faction's leaders colluded with the treasurer to distribute the *uragane* (*Nikkei*, January 8, 2024). When they completed their investigations in January 2024, they indicted only the treasurers for the Abe and Nikai factions and three LDP members who received more than 40 million yen as kickbacks. This means that the faction leaders were able to evade criminal charges by shifting the blame from themselves, but their moral responsibilities remained unresolved.

As Fig. 3.1 shows, the cabinet's approval rate dropped to a low of 23% in December 2023, forcing the LDP to take several actions. The first of them was attacks on and eventual dissolution of factions. Kishida decided to replace the Abe faction's leaders from the cabinet and the LDP leadership (*Nikkei*, December 15, 2023). Kishida further announced in January 2024 that he would disband his own faction (*Nikkei*, January 19, 2024a). Although some other factions complained at first (*Nikkei*, January 19, 2024b), the Abe and Nikai factions decided to follow suit (*Nikkei*, January 20, 2024). As the factions that had little to do with the scandal, such as the Moriyama faction and the Tanigaki group, also decided to disband, 70% of the LDP members were now not affiliated with any of the factions (*Nikkei*, January 26, 2024).

Second, following requests from the opposition, some LDP members, including Kishida, chose to appear in the Diet's Deliberative Council on Political Ethics (*Seiji Rinri Shinsakai*), a body to examine whether a Diet member has violated the code of conduct. The Council is very weak, though, since it does not have any formal power to punish Diet members and participation is voluntary. Thus, even though the opposition requested more than 50 members to participate and explain their scandals, many refused to appear (*Nikkei*, February 23, 2024). In total, only 10 members appeared in the Council in February and March, and Kishida in the Council could not give a clear answer to the question of how and when the *uragane* mechanism started (*Nikkei*, March 1, 2024).

Third, the LDP leadership also launched its in-house investigations, such as interviews with members, and took disciplinary actions aimed at scandal-tainted members. The interviews conducted by the leadership revealed the lack of compliance awareness: even though they were concerned about the kickbacks they received, many members did not correct their financial reports (*Nikkei*, February 16, 2024). Based on its investigations, the party's Party Ethics Committee (*Tōki Iinkai*) announced in April its decision to punish scandal-tainted members. No member was expelled. Two leaders of the Abe faction ended up with the second most severe of the party's eight punishments, that is, a recommendation to leave the party. Three members received the third most severe punishment of suspension from party membership for six to twelve months. Meanwhile, the 17 members who failed to report less than 10 million were given only a reprimand, and no punishment was given to more than 50 members whose kickbacks were less than five million yen (*Nikkei*, April 5, 2024a), meaning that nearly 70 members were able to escape any substantive punishments. Nikai Toshihiro, the leader of the Nikai faction, was exempt too, since he had already announced that he would not seek his reelection.

Fourth, the Diet also revised, in June, the Political Funds Control Act. In order to prevent under-reporting of donations, the newly revised Act now requires that a politician's financial report should disclose those who purchased more than 50,000 yen worth of fund-raising party tickets. In addition, to clarify a politician's accountability, he or she now needs to submit a written document to confirm that a financial report has been appropriately prepared. However, according to the criticisms from the opposition, the very hastily made revision contained some loopholes. For instance, even though the threshold was lowered from 200,000 yen to 50,000 yen, no limit was introduced to the number of fund-raising parties (*Nikkei*, June 20, 2024). In addition, the LDP ignored the opposition's demand for a ban on donations from corporations and organizations (*Nikkei*, May 30, 2024).

As can be seen in Fig. 3.1, the public's reaction to the LDP's measures was lukewarm, since the approval rate never recovered until Kishida announced his resignation (see also Maeda 2025). Even though the *Uragane* scandal revealed that many members inside the LDP had received illegal kickbacks from their factions, only a handful of members were indicted, while many others were able to avoid any criminal charge, with moral responsibilities remaining unfulfilled. The media's attention now shifted to the LDP presidential selection, as Kishida's two-year term would terminate at the end of September.

LDP Party Organization, Presidential Election, and Campaign

As mentioned above, almost all the factions in the LDP decided to disband. As I have argued elsewhere (Nemoto 2021), factions in their heyday used to play important roles in providing their members with money, nominations, and posts, while the introduction of the new, party-centered electoral system in 1993–1994 significantly weakened these functions of factions. Although as of writing, it may be premature to reach a definitive conclusion, the *Uragane* scandal seemingly helped accelerate the transformation of the LDP to a centralized party.

First, the dissolution of factions would mean that LDP members' financial dependence on the party should further increase. In 2022, the six

LDP factions mobilized 1.18 billion yen in total, which was considerably smaller than the LDP's revenue of 24.86 billion yen. Before the 2022 HC election, the LDP leadership provided at least 15 million yen to many local branches facing reelection and 50 million yen to a candidate in a very competitive district (*Nikkei*, November 25, 2023). In contrast, according to a member from the Asō faction, he used to receive six million yen every year from the faction (*Nikkei*, April 19, 2024). Now that factions were gone and fund-raising parties became difficult to hold, members would have to rely on their own financial sources or the party's.

Second, the leadership's control over members' training and promotion was further strengthened. For instance, the LDP announced a new plan to introduce a centralized database system to manage members' specialties and achievements in allocating cabinet portfolios while scrapping the traditional method of receiving recommendations from factions (*Nikkei*, February 7, 2024). In addition, whereas in the past, senior members provided training to junior members within factions, now the party held seminars and study groups in the Central Institute of Politics (*Chūō Seiji Daigakuin*) to train relatively junior members with basic political philosophy (*Nikkei*, April 5, 2024b).

Third, the dissolution of factions most significantly affected the LDP's presidential selection process, since it enabled many more candidates to run than in the past and made the race very unpredictable. As it seemed to be very unlikely that the approval rate would recover, Prime Minister Kishida announced on August 14 that he would not seek reelection in the upcoming LDP presidential race, saying that he would like to take responsibility for the *Uragane* scandal (*Nikkei*, August 15, 2024). Under the most recent rule for presidential selection, an LDP member would require 20 endorsers from his or her colleagues in the Diet to run. The race would have two rounds. In the first round, each of the LDP's 368 members in the HR and the HC would have one vote. In addition, more than one million grassroots party members across the country would have 368 votes, which would be proportionally allocated to candidates based on the d'Hondt method. If the first round ended with no candidate winning a majority of these 736 votes, there would be a second majority run-off round, in which two top candidates would compete over a total of 415 votes: the LDP's 368 members in the Diet and each of the 47 prefectural branches.

The dissolution of factions made the race unprecedented in a couple of ways. First, compared to the past, when usually two to five candidates competed, more than ten candidates were interested in running in the race at first (*Nikkei*, August 21, 2024). This is because in the past, a candidate would need his or her faction's backing, while now anyone could run, as long as he or she could secure 20 endorsements (Table 3.1).

Second and relatedly, as seen in Table 3.1, many candidates were able to secure endorsements from a wide array of (former) factions. In particular, nearly three-quarters of Koizumi Shinjirō's and Ishiba Shigeru's endorsers were non-faction members, suggesting that it is now indeed possible to run and win the presidential selection race without any factional help. In addition, none of the (former) factions seems to give support *en masse* to one specific candidate any longer. For instance, even though many members from the Asō faction endorsed its candidate, Kōno Taro, other members from the Asō faction endorsed other candidates.

When the candidacy registration was closed on September 12, as many as nine candidates ran in total. Given that there would be no coalition bargaining between factions or no factional headcount calculation, the

Table 3.1 Factional affiliations, Unification Church ties, and *Uragane* involvement of LDP presidential candidates' endorsers

	Abe	Asō	Kishida	Motegi	Nikai	Moriyama	Non-faction	UC Contacts	Uragane
Takaichi Sanae	14	2	0	0	2	0	2	9	13
Kobayashi Takayuki	4	4	1	0	5	2	4	11	0
Hayashi Yoshimasa	1	0	15	0	0	0	4	6	0
Koizumi Shinjirō	1	1	2	2	0	0	14	6	1
Kamikawa Yōko	2	9	5	1	2	0	1	6	1
Katō Katsunobu	4	1	6	0	4	1	4	2	4
Kōno Taro	0	18	0	1	1	0	0	7	0
Ishiba Shigeru	0	0	0	1	4	1	14	5	0
Motegi Toshimitu	3	2	0	14	0	0	1	9	2

Source Nikkei, September 13, 2024; *Nikkei*, September 9, 2022; *Yomiuri*, February 14, 2024
Note The first seven columns denote votes from each faction (referred to by the name of the former faction leader) to each presidential candidate (rows). The two right-most columns are subsets of LDP politicians with ties to the two scandals

race was seen as very unpredictable. In addition, since it was very unlikely that a single candidate would win a majority of the votes in the first round, candidates would need to appeal to Diet members with an eye toward the second run-off round, where 88.7% of the votes would come from Diet members. As a result, many of the candidates set aside the two scandals that caused the termination of the Kishida cabinet and appealed to scandal-tainted members. None of the nine candidates gave clear answers to whether they would be interested in re-investigating LDP members' ties to the UC (*Asahi*, September 19, 2024). Some of them also kept silent on re-investigations into the *Uragane* scandal (*Nikkei*, September 13, 2024). As Table 3.1 shows, all nine candidates were in fact endorsed by those who had some ties to the UC, who under-reported kickbacks from their factions, or both.

The presidential selection on September 27 picked Ishiba Shigeru. In the first round, none of the candidates won a majority as expected. Somehow surprising was that popular Koizumi ended up in third place, while Takaichi Sanae, known for her hawkish security policy stance, won the most votes in the first round. The second run-off round was fought between Ishiba and Takaichi, with the former winning more votes from Diet members and prefectural branches. When Ishiba was nominated by the Diet as the new Prime Minister and a new cabinet was formed a couple of days later, the approval rate jumped up by 24 percentage points, as shown in Fig. 3.1. Just as Kishida did three years ago (Nemoto 2023), Ishiba decided to ride the wave of rising popularity and set October 9 as the date for HR dissolution.

But the LDP's own in-house surveys reportedly predicted that in many districts, especially where scandal-tainted incumbents were running, the party's candidates were losing. Therefore, Ishiba came to realize that some additional punishments for scandal-tainted members would be necessary (*Nikkei*, October 8, 2024a). Eventually, twelve members were not given nominations from the LDP in their single-member districts, based on fairly arbitrary criteria: (1) if their party membership was suspended in April; (2) if their party positions were suspended in April and they did not appear in the Diet's Deliberative Council on Political Ethics in February and March; or (3) if they were hopeless in their districts according to the surveys (*Nikkei*, October 8, 2024b). Nine of the twelve ran as independents, while three of them decided not to run. In addition, other 37 scandal-tainted members were banned from running on the proportional representation tier. This means that they would have to win in their single-member districts without proportional representation as a safety net (*Nikkei*, October 10, 2024). Ishiba also decided not to nominate three incumbents who ran only on the proportional representation tier in the 2021 election, so two of them gave up running this time, while one ran as an independent.

In order to assess how harsh these measures were, it might be useful to compare 2005 and 2024. In 2005, then Prime Minister Koizumi Junichirō dissolved the HR and called for a snap election when his pet policy of postal privatization was voted down (Nemoto et al. 2008). He denied nominations to 37 LDP incumbents who defected from the party line, so many of them had to run as independents or launch new parties. Almost all of these defectors had to face in their districts the LDP's officially nominated candidates, while none of them was able to receive endorsements from the coalition partner, the Kōmeitō. In contrast, none of the ten independents in the 2024 election faced LDP candidates in their districts, while two of them received endorsements from the Kōmeitō. In addition, *Akahata* scooped that right after the official campaign period started, the LDP sent 20 million yen to all the local party branches, including the ones headed by the non-nominated candidates (*Nikkei*, October 24, 2024). Although Ishiba stated that the money should be used only for expanding the party base and not for campaign expenses, opposition leaders criticized the move since the heads of local party branches were candidates themselves (*Nikkei*, October 25, 2024; also see Umeda 2025).

In sum, the newly elected leader Ishiba could have taken advantage of the popularity surge he enjoyed to reform the party, but in reality, he was unable to do so. During his campaign for the LDP's presidential selection race, Ishiba kept ambivalent about additional punishments, since he needed as many votes as possible from the LDP's Diet members in the race. As soon as the LDP's electoral loss loomed large, he finally made decisions to deny nominations to and ban dual candidacy for scandal-tainted members in an ad hoc manner. However, these measures were hardly comparable to those found in the 2005 election, and endorsements from the Kōmeitō and the distribution of 20 million yen might have looked to the eyes of voters as if they were covert campaign support.

A Simple Regression Analysis

Based on the descriptions above, this section analyzes the determinants of LDP candidates' electoral performance in their single-member districts in the 2024 election. The sample covers 282 candidates who could be broadly categorized as LDP candidates. They include 266 candidates who got nominations and 10 candidates who were denied nominations due to the *Uragane* scandal. The remaining six candidates are what Reed (2009) calls Liberal Democratic Independents, as they once belonged to the LDP but ran as independents this time: for instance, Izumida Hirohiko was denied a nomination because of redistricting, but decided to run at any rate.

The dependent variable is a candidate's vote share. The first independent variable is *Ties to the Unification Church*. As explained above, the LDP disclosed the list of its members who had some ties to the UC under seven different categories (*Nikkei*, September 9, 2022). *Ties to the Unification Church* is simply a sum of positive answers to these seven different questions. The second independent variable is *Uragane*, a dummy variable coded 1 if a candidate was found to under-report his or her factional kickbacks. The list of such LDP members is widely available (*Yomiuri*, February 14, 2024).

The model includes several controls. The first of them is *No Nomination from the LDP*, a dummy variable coded 1 if a candidate had to run as an independent. The second is *Kōmeitō's PR Vote Share*, calculated as the Kōmeitō's vote share on the proportional representation tier in a single-member district. Other controls include: *Number of Terms* (how many terms in the Diet served by a candidate previously); *Incumbent Minister* (a dummy variable coded 1 if a candidate was an incumbent minister); *District Incumbent* (a dummy variable coded 1 if a candidate was elected on a single-member district in the 2021 election); and *Age* (the age of a candidate).

The model below uses the ordinary least squares method without any additional assumptions for the sake of simplicity. Admittedly, there could be some biases in the model, such as endogeneity; for instance, it might be the case that electorally vulnerable members approached the UC, not the other way around. Still the model below should be helpful in understanding associations between the scandals and candidates' electoral performance (Table 3.2).

Table 3.2 Regression analysis on LDP candidates' vote share

Ties to the Unification Church	−0.017**
	(0.007)
Uragane	−0.033**
	(0.016)
No Nomination from LDP	−0.066***
	(0.026)
Kōmeitō's PR Vote Share	0.938***
	(0.211)
Number of Terms	0.008***
	(0.003)
Incumbent Minister	0.078***
	(0.027)
District Incumbent	0.111***
	(0.013)
Age	−0.001*
	(0.001)
Constant	0.290***
	(0.039)
N	282
adj. R^2	0.447

Standard errors in parentheses.
* $p < 0.10$, ** $p < 0.05$, *** $p < 0.01$.

The results, as shown in Table 3.2, confirm the hypotheses. That is, ties to the UC and under-reporting kickbacks have significantly negative associations with candidates' vote shares. First, a candidate with the deepest tie to the UC had the vote share 6.8 percentage points lower than those without any ties. Second, a candidate who under-reported his or her kickback also had the vote share 3.3 percentage points lower than others.

Some other variables are worth mentioning. Ishiba's punishment of non-nomination seemed to have some impact, since the vote share of a non-nominated candidate was 6.5 percentage points lower. This suggests that, indeed, the party label matters, and independent candidates are now significantly disadvantaged in Japan. In line with the literature (Liff and Maeda 2018; Thies 2022), the Kōmeitō's electoral endorsement also seems to be very important. The size of the coefficient for *Kōmeitō's PR Vote Share* (0.938) suggests that almost all the Kōmeitō voters voted for LDP candidates on single-member districts. Assuming that 93.8% of the

Kōmeitō voters voted for LDP candidates, a very rough estimate suggests that 50 of the 137 winners in the LDP camp were saved by the Kōmeitō.[2]

In sum, a very simple regression analysis in this section confirms the argument that Japanese voters, enraged by the two scandals, punished the LDP in the 2024 HR election. Candidates' vote shares were significantly lower if they had ties to the UC and they under-reported their kickbacks from factions. Still, the LDP was able to maintain its largest party status thanks to its electoral alliance partner, the Kōmeitō.

CONCLUSION

This chapter investigated why the LDP lost in the 2024 HR election. It argued that the two scandals—the Unification Church scandal and the *Uragane* scandal—intensified the public's discontent with the party. In addition, the LDP and its new leader, Ishiba, could not regain enraged voters' trust since their countermeasures were ineffective. LDP members with some ties to the UC were not met with any disciplinary actions at all. Most of those who received illegal kickbacks were able to evade any criminal charges, with some punishments given in an ad hoc manner just right before the official campaign period began. As a result, enraged voters electorally punished LDP candidates by using their ballots.

This chapter does not argue that the LDP was destined to lose. Not at all. In fact, the LDP had some chances. First, the party could have conducted comprehensive and thorough investigations into its relationship with the UC. Even though very little is known, investigative journalists argue that the relationship could be traced back to the 1960s (Arita 2024). The party could have tried to clarify suspicions against the party and its former leaders, including Abe. Second, the party could have also realized that violations of the Political Funds Control Act, such as failure to report income in financial reports, could lead to criminal charges. Traditionally, the norm inside the LDP was that, whenever some problems arose, members responded only by modifying their reports and shifting the blame to financial accountants. But they could have questioned its moral appropriateness and considered much harsher measures.

---

[2] This rough estimate is based on the following calculations: (1) a LDP candidate's baseline votes are calculated by subtracting 93.8% of the Kōmeitō's PR votes in his or her district from his or her district votes; and then (2) these baseline votes are compared with the best loser's votes.

Third, the leadership could have learned lessons from Koizumi. Koizumi won the 2005 election because his pet policy was unfavorable within his party but popular among the general public. What was required this time was not covert campaign support for scandal-tainted candidates, but rather the implementation of bold party reform to win trust among the general public.

References

Arita, Yoshifu. 2024. *Dare mo Kakanakatta Tōitsu Kyōkai* [The Unification Church Nobody Had Written]. Tokyo: Shūeisha.

Asahi Shinbun. September 17, 2024. "Abe-shi, Kyū Tōitsu Kyōkai Kaichō to Mendan ka [Abe Met with Former Unification Church Leaders]." p. 1.

Asahi Shinbun. September 19, 2024. "Kyōdan to no Kankei Zen Kōho Mukaitō [All Candidates Didn't Respond to the Question about the Unification Church]." p. 25.

Carlson, Matthew. 2025. "Scandals During the Kishida Administration." In *Japan Decides 2024: The Japanese General Election*, edited by Kenneth M. McElwain, Robert J. Pekkanen, and Daniel M. Smith, 217–233. New York: Palgrave Macmillan.

Kamiwaki, Hiroshi. 2024a. *Jimintō 'Uragane' Jiken* [LDP's "Uragane" Scandal]. Osaka: Nihon Kikanshi Shuppan Sentā.

Kamiwaki, Hiroshi. 2024b. *Kenshō: Seiji to Kane* [Analysis: Politics and Money]. Tokyo: Iwanami Shoten.

Kingston, Jeff. 2023. "Bad Karma? Abe's Assassination and the Moonies." *The Asia-Pacific Journal: Japan Focus* 21: 1–19.

Liff, Adam P., and Ko Maeda. 2018. "Electoral Incentives, Policy Compromise, and Coalition Durability: Japan's LDP–Komeito Government in a Mixed Electoral System." *Japanese Journal of Political Science* 20: 53–73.

Maeda, Yukio 2025. "Public Opinion and Scandals in Economic Hard Times." In *Japan Decides 2024: The Japanese General Election*, edited by Kenneth M. McElwain, Robert J. Pekkanen, and Daniel M. Smith, 163–179. New York: Palgrave Macmillan.

McLaughlin, Levi. 2023. "The Abe Assassination and Japan's Nexus of Religion and Politics." *Current History* 122: 209–216.

McLaughlin, Levi. 2025. "Perennial Fears, Novel Responses: The Unification Church in Japan after the Abe Assassination." In *Japan Decides 2024: The Japanese General Election*, edited by Kenneth M. McElwain, Robert J. Pekkanen, and Daniel M. Smith, 235–253. New York: Palgrave Macmillan.

Nemoto, Kuniaki. 2021. "Japan's Liberal Democratic Party: Changes in Party Organization under Shinzō Abe." In *The Oxford Handbook of Japanese Politics*, edited by Robert J. Pekkanen and Saadia M. Pekkanen, 161–181. Oxford: Oxford University Press.

Nemoto, Kuniaki. 2023. "How the Liberal Democratic Party Avoided a Loss in 2021." In *Japan Decides 2021: The Japanese General Election*, ed. Robert J. Pekkanen, Steven R. Reed, and Daniel M. Smith, 43–58. New York: Palgrave Macmillan.

Nemoto, Kuniaki, Ellis S. Krauss, and Robert Pekkanen. 2008. "Policy Dissension and Party Discipline: The July 2005 Vote on Postal Privatization in Japan." *British Journal of Political Science* 38: 499–525.

NHK. 2025. "Naikaku Shijiritsu." https://www.nhk.or.jp/senkyo/shijiritsu/

Nikkei Shinbun. July 12, 2022. "Abe-shi Jūgeki Tsuyomaru Keikakusei [Well-planned Shooting of Abe]." p. 39.

Nikkei Shinbun. July 15, 2022. "Haha Kenkin 1-oku En Kyōkō Hottan ka [Mother's Donation of 100 Million Yen Triggered the Assassination?]." p. 39.

Nikkei Shinbun. August 3, 2022. "Kyū Tōitsu Kyōkai to no Kakawari Tou [Questioning the Relationships with the Former Unification Church]." p. 4.

Nikkei Shinbun. August 6, 2022. "Seiken Unei no Hidane Osaekomi [Extinguish Issues that Could Set the Administration on Fire]." p. 4.

Nikkei Shinbun. August 10, 2022. "Kyū Tōitsu Kyōkai Meguru Sōdan Kyūzō [Surge in Consultations about the Former Unification Church]." p. 42.

Nikkei Shinbun. August 11, 2022. "Habatsu Yūsen Sukeru Shusei [Priority to Factions Shows Defensiveness]." p. 3.

Nikkei Shinbun. August 26, 2022. "Mondai no Aru Dantai Jimin Kankei Danzetsu he [LDP to Cut Ties with Problematic Organizations]." p. 4.

Nikkei Shinbun. September 2, 2022. "Kyū Tōitsu Kyōkai to Seiji 3 [The Former Unification Church and Politics 3]." p. 2.

Nikkei Shinbun. September 9, 2022. "Kyū Tōitsu Kyōkai Meguru Jimintō no Chōsa Yōshi [A Summary of LDP's Survey about the Former Unification Church]." p. 4.

Nikkei Shinbun. September 28, 2022a. "Abe-shi Kokusō, Saikō Reberu no Keibi Taisei [Highest Level of Security for Abe's State Funeral]." p. 41.

Nikkei Shinbun. September 28, 2022b. "Wareta Sanpi Shiji Teika Maneku [Divided Opinion Leads to a Decline in Support]." p. 4.

Nikkei Shinbun. October 1, 2022. "Kyū Tōitsu Kyōkai Setten wo Tsuika Hōkoku Shita Giin [Additional LDP Members Who Reported Their Contacts with the Former Unification Church]." p. 4.

Nikkei Shinbun. November 22, 2022. "Kyū Tōitsu Kyōkai he no Shitsumon Ken Kōshi Ryōshō [Right to Question the Former Unification Church Approved]." p. 47.

Nikkei Shinbun. December 11, 2022. "Higaisha Kyūsai Shinpō Ihan ni ha Bassoku [New Law to Rescue Victims, Penalties for Violations]." p. 3.
Nikkei Shinbun. September 7, 2023. "Chōsa 10-kagetsu, Kaisan Seikyū Shiya [10-month Investigation with an Eye toward Dissolution Request]." p. 3.
Nikkei Shinbun. October 13, 2023. "Kyū Tōitsu Kyōkai no Kaisan Seikyū he [Government Moves forward Dissolution Request for the Former Unification Church]." p. 1.
Nikkei Shinbun. November 19, 2023. "Shūnyū 4,000-man En Fukisai ka [Income of 40 Million Yen Not Reported?]." p. 27.
Nikkei Shinbun. November 22, 2023. "Jmin Habatsu Aitsugu Shūsei [LDP Factions Made a Series of Amendments]." p. 4.
Nikkei Shinbun. November 25, 2023. "22-nen Seiji Shikin Shūshi Hōkokusho [2022 Financial Reports on Political Funds]." p. 9.
Nikkei Shinbun. December 2, 2023. "Abe-ha 'Uragane' wo Jūten Sōsa [Investigation of Abe Faction's 'Slush Fund']." p. 27.
Nikkei Shinbun. December 13, 2023. "'Uragane' Habatsu Shudō Irokoku [Slush Fund Driven by Factions]." p. 47.
Nikkei Shinbun. December 15, 2023. "Hayashi Kanbō Chōkan Ra 4 Kakuryō Shūnin [4 Ministers Including Cabinet Secretary Hayashi Newly Appointed]." p. 1.
Nikkei Shinbun. January 8, 2024. "Abe-ha, Saranaru Dageki [Another Blow to the Abe Faction]." p. 2.
Nikkei Shinbun. January 19, 2024a. "Kishida-ha Kaisan wo Shushō Hyōmei [Prime Minister Announces Dissolution of Kishida Faction]." p. 1.
Nikkei Shinbun. January 19, 2024b. "Shushō, Kiban Yurugasu Kake [Prime Minister's Gamble Could Shake His Own Base]." p. 3.
Nikkei Shinbun. January 20, 2024. "Abe-ha Nikai-ha Kaisan he [Abe and Nikai Factions to Disband]." p. 1.
Nikkei Shinbun. January 26, 2024. "Moriyama-ha Tanigaki G mo Kaisan Kettei [Moriyama Faction and Tanigaki Group Also Decided to Disband]." p. 4.
Nikkei Shinbun. February 7, 2024. "Jimin Jinji, Honbu de Ichigen Kanri [LDP to Centralize Personnel Management at Headquarters]." p. 4.
Nikkei Shinbun. February 16, 2024. "Jimin, Toboshii 'Junpō Ishiki' [LDP Members Lack 'Compliance Awareness']." p. 4.
Nikkei Shinbun. February 23, 2024. "Jimin, Hikōkai no Seirinshin Teian [LDP to Propose Closed Meetings for Deliberative Council on Political Ethics]." p. 1.
Nikkei Shinbun. March 1, 2024. "Fushōji Taiō Minkan to Sa [LDP's Responses to Scandals Differ from Private Companies]." p. 2.
Nikkei Shinbun. April 5, 2024a. "Jimin Shobun Makuhiki ha Tōku [LDP's Disciplinary Actions Far from Ending the Scandal]." p. 3.

Nikkei Shinbun. April 5, 2024b. "Datsu Habatsu, Shinjin Giin no Sodate Kata [How to Train Junior Members after Factions]." Evening ed. p. 2.
Nikkei Shinbun. April 19, 2024. "Todaeta Shien Futokoro Kibishiku [Discontinued Financial Support Strains Politicians' Purses]." p. 4.
Nikkei Shinbun. May 30, 2024. "Yatō 'Jimin An, Zero Kaitō' [Opposition Receives 'Zero Response' from LDP]." p. 4.
Nikkei Shinbun. June 20, 2024. "Seiji Shikin Tōmeika Tōku [Far from Transparent Political Funds]." p. 3.
Nikkei Shinbun. August 15, 2024. "Kishida Shushō Taijin he [Prime Minister Kishida to Resign]." p. 1.
Nikkei Shinbun. August 21, 2024. "Habatsu Kasumi Saguri Ai [Factions Fading, Candidates Probing]." p. 3.
Nikkei Shinbun. September 13, 2024. "Jimin Sōsaisen 2024 [LDP Presidential Selection 2024]." p. 4.
Nikkei Shinbun. October 8, 2024a. "'Hikōnin' Yureta Ishiba Shikkōbu [Ishiba Leadership Shaken by 'Non-endorsement']." p. 4.
Nikkei Shinbun. October 8, 2024b. "Seiji Shikin Fukisai 'Senhiki' no Uchimaku [Scenes behind How to Draw the Line for Those Who Under-reported Political Funds]." p. 4.
Nikkei Shinbun. October 10, 2024. "Jimin 'Kiretsu' Kakae Senkyosen [LDP to Enter the Race with a 'Crack']." p. 3.
Nikkei Shinbun. October 24, 2024. "Jimin, Hikōnin Kōho ni Katsudōhi [LDP Distributes Funds to Non-nominated Candidates]." p. 4.
Nikkei Shinbun. October 25, 2024. "Jimin, Hikōnin Kōho ni 2,000-man En [LDP Distributes 20 Million Yen to Non-nominated Candidates]." p. 4.
Reed, Steven R. 2009. "Party Strategy or Candidate Strategy: How Does the LDP Run the Right Number of Candidates in Japan's Multi-Member Districts?" *Party Politics* 15: 295–314.
Saitō, Masami. 2024. "The Abe Assassination, the Unification Church, and Local Media: A Case Study of Journalism in Toyama Prefecture." *The Asia-Pacific Journal: Japan Focus* 22: 1–22.
Thies, Michael F. 2022. "The Era of Coalition Government in Japan: The Institutional Logic of Surplus Majorities and Strange Bedfellows." In *The Oxford Handbook of Japanese Politics*, edited by Robert J. Pekkanen and Saadia M. Pekkanen, 182–200. Oxford: Oxford University Press.
Umeda, Michio. 2025. "Electoral Campaigns in Japan's 2024 General Election: Emerging Signs of Transformation." In *Japan Decides 2024: The Japanese General Election*, edited by Kenneth M. McElwain, Robert J. Pekkanen, and Daniel M. Smith, 109–124. New York: Palgrave Macmillan.
Yomiuri Shinbun. February 14, 2024. "Seiji Shikin Shūshi Hōkokusho [Financial Reports for Political Funds]." p. 4.

CHAPTER 4

The CDP in 2024: The Legacy of the Electoral Coalition with the JCP

Fumi Ikeda

The 2024 general election was held under similar circumstances to the 2009 general election, in which the former Democratic Party of Japan (DPJ), the largest opposition party at the time, defeated the ruling party, the Liberal Democratic Party (LDP). In the 2009 general election, the DPJ won a landslide victory primarily because the public had become distrustful of the LDP. The 2024 general election was held amid a similar loss of public confidence. Leading up to the 2024 general election, the LDP was associated with multiple scandals, including the Unification Church and political finance issues (see Carlson 2025; Nemoto 2025; McLaughlin 2025). For the Constitutional Democratic Party of Japan (CDP), the 2024 election was a potential step toward a change in government, like that in 2009, by gaining voters critical of the LDP. The CDP, citing the need to restore trust in politics as a challenge, adopted the slogan "regime change is the greatest political reform" as its goal (CDP, October 15, 2024).

F. Ikeda (✉)
Ehime University, Matsuyama, Japan
e-mail: ikeda.fumi.bi@ehime-u.ac.jp

In the 3-year period from the 2021 and 2024 general elections, the CDP sought an electoral coalition among opposition parties (*Yatō-Kyōtō*). However, electoral cooperation with the Japanese Communist Party (JCP) was a controversial issue. The CDP allied with the JCP in 2021 under Edano Yukio, the party leader at that time, but the result was a crushing defeat (Pekkanen and Reed 2022). This experience with the JCP in 2021 left a negative legacy on the subsequent management of the CDP.

In a summary of the 2021 general election released by the CDP, the party stated that gaining support from independent voters by unifying candidates through an electoral coalition of opposition parties would be challenging and that a major revision of strategy was necessary (*Asahi*, January 26, 2022). The difficulty of aligning with the JCP was also mentioned, as more than 30% of voters in close districts and 5% of voters in proportional blocs changed their votes from the CDP candidate to another because of their affiliation with the JCP (*Asahi*, January 26, 2022). Despite negative opinions toward the electoral coalition with the JCP, the CDP faced the dilemma of weighing the CDP's party image against the JCP's regionally rooted electoral base and the unification of candidates.

This chapter examines the party management of the CDP for approximately 3 years, from the last general election in 2021 to the 2024 general election, especially from the perspective of its electoral coalition with the JCP. It then analyzes the CDP's candidate nominations, election strategies, and election results in the 2024 general election.

The CDP Under Izumi's Leadership

After the 2021 general election, there were growing calls from party representatives for Edano's resignation. Edano subsequently announced his resignation on November 2, 2021, following which a presidential election was held on November 30, 2021. Four candidates—Izumi Kenta, Ōsaka Seiji, Ogawa Junya, and Nishimura Chinami—filed their candidacies. One of the issues in the 2021 leadership election was the electoral coalition among opposition parties, especially with the JCP. None of the four candidates expressed a positive attitude toward continuing the electoral cooperation with the JCP. Ogawa, Izumi, and Nishimura stated that they would seek collaboration with the Democratic Party for the People (DPP) because it promoted policies similar to the CDP (*Asahi*, November

23, 2021). During this leadership election period, Yoshino Tomoko, president of the Japanese Trade Union Confederation (JTUC) (*Rengō*), the largest support group for the CDP, expressed a negative view of electoral cooperation with the JCP (*Asahi*, November 30, 2021). In the first round of voting, Izumi received the most votes at 189 votes, followed by Ōsaka at 148 votes, Ogawa, and Nishimura. Izumi won the second round of voting, with 205 votes to 128 for Ōsaka.

At his first press conference after assuming the leadership, Izumi expressed his intention to review the electoral coalition with the JCP, stating that it would not be a simple continuation (CDP, November 30, 2021). While there was dissatisfaction within the party, negative opinions from the JTUC and the need to review electoral cooperation with the JCP for the House of Councillors election in 2022 troubled Izumi.

The first electoral alliance with the JCP in the House of Representatives election occurred in 2021 (*Asahi*, October 20, 2021). However, in the House of Councillors, the electoral alliance began in 2016 (*Mainichi*, July 11, 2022). The impetus for the electoral coalition came in the 2013 House of Councillors election when opposition candidates ran wild in single-seat constituencies and were trounced by the LDP, winning 2 of 31 seats (*Asahi*, December 1, 2021). Owing to subsequent electoral coalitions, the opposition's seat gains in the single-seat constituencies increased to 11 of 32 seats in 2016 and 10 of 32 seats in 2019 (*Asahi*, December 1, 2021). Some CDP members who would be up for re-election in 2022 also won seats in the 2016 Upper House election through electoral cooperation with the JCP. Therefore, no easy conclusion has been reached regarding electoral alliances with the JCP.

In this context, the JTUC announced its policy for the House of Councillors election in February 2022. The JTUC implied that an electoral coalition with the JCP would be unacceptable (*Asahi*, February 18, 2022). The policy was unusual for national elections in that it stated that it could not support candidates who would align or cooperate with parties with substantially different objectives and basic policies, and that it would not specify which parties it would support in the former DPJ-affiliated parties whose movements were not yet clear. In response to the JTUC's policy, Izumi met with Yoshino to discuss measures for the House of Councillors election and confirmed the plan to unify opposition party candidates, including those from the JCP (*Asahi*, February 26, 2022). The JTUC and CDP confirmed that "candidate coordination" (*kōhosha chōsei*) was the chosen direction. They reiterated that they would not engage in electoral alliances, including policy agreements with the JCP, and would only coordinate their candidates.

In May 2022, the CDP and JCP confirmed that they would proceed with candidate coordination in the 32 single-seat constituencies nationwide, prioritizing constituencies where opposition candidates were expected to win. However, they decided not to reach a "policy agreement" in the form of a signature by the leader of each party (*Asahi*, May 10, 2022). Ultimately, only 11 constituencies could coordinate candidates among the opposition parties, including the JCP (*Asahi*, July 26, 2022). The CDP was defeated in the 2022 House of Councillors election. It won only 17 seats, six seats less than its pre-election tally.

Even after the 2022 House of Councillors election, the issue of electoral cooperation with the JCP remained unresolved. This issue arose again in the July 2024 Tokyo gubernatorial election, which the CDP chose to contest by forming an alliance with the JCP (*Yomiuri*, June 2, 2024). Renhō, a former CDP member of the House of Councillors, ran as a CDP candidate but fought the election as an independent candidate because of an electoral coalition with the JCP. Subsequently, the incumbent, Koike Yuriko, won the election, and Renhō came in third, falling behind former Akitakata City Mayor Ishimaru Shinji.

In the wake of Renho's dismal defeat, there were harsh calls from within the CDP and DPP to reconsider the electoral coalition with the JCP. Ozawa Ichirō, a member of the CDP, said that the CDP's reliance on the JCP was apparent. Regarding the party's leadership election scheduled for September 2024, Ozawa said, "It is necessary to have an executive committee that builds a system of electoral coalition among the opposition parties in order to take power" (NHK, July 9, 2024).

Electing a New Leader in 2024

The election for a new party president was held on September 23, 2024. The objective was to choose the "face of the party" (*seitō no kao*) for the coming general election. In addition to Izumi, Edano (Izumi's predecessor), Noda Yoshihiko (who served as prime minister under the DPJ from 2009 to 2012), and Yoshida Harumi (the only female candidate) competed in the four-person race. One of the significant issues in the 2024 election was the electoral coalition with other opposition parties, especially the JCP. This had remained an ongoing issue for the CDP since the 2021 general election.

4 THE CDP IN 2024: THE LEGACY OF THE ELECTORAL … 61

Of the four candidates, Edano and Noda attracted the most attention. Edano, who promoted an electoral coalition with the JCP in the 2021 general election, adopted a strategy of avoiding the JCP's leftist image in this contest. This was also a strategy designed to consider the needs of the JTUC and the conservative members of the CDP who opposed the electoral alliance with the JCP. Previously, Edano had referred to "zero nuclear power plants as soon as possible" in his policy manifesto, but in his campaign pledge, he used the phrase "aim for a society that does not depend on nuclear energy" to downplay the expression "zero nuclear power plants," as it might have given him a leftist image (*Jiji*, August 21, 2024). He also said that he would restructure his relationship with JCP. In a debate hosted by the Japan Press Club, he stated that "comprehensive cooperation is difficult" (*Sankei*, September 14, 2024).

Noda was cautious about electoral coalition with the JCP. His candidacy was supported by Ozawa Ichirō, who was reluctant to cooperate with the JCP (NHK, September 23, 2024). Noda said that he would seek to maximize the seats for opposition forces, arguing that he would work well with the DPP and go beyond it to capture even moderately conservative voters. He insisted that he would engage in dialogue with the JCP but would not share power (NHK, September 23, 2024). He frequently used the term "moderate conservatives" (*onkenna hoshu*) in his campaign (NHK, September 23, 2024).

The election was held on September 23. In the first round of voting, Noda received the most votes at 267, followed by Edano at 206, Izumi at 143, and Yoshida at 122. No candidate received a majority in the first round of voting, and a decisive vote was held between the top two candidates. Ultimately, Noda won the runoff, winning 232 votes against Edano's 180. After his victory, Noda said, "When the results are in, there is no side. I hope that everyone will unite their hearts and work toward overthrowing the LDP" (Nikkei, September 23, 2024).

CANDIDATE NOMINATION

The general election was announced on October 15, less than a month after Noda's victory. The CDP nominated a total of 237 candidates in both single-member districts (SMD) and the proportional representation (PR) tier. The number of candidates who ran in the SMDs and PR was 207 and 234, respectively. There was an overlap of 204 candidates between the SMD and PR tiers. As the House of Representatives has a majority of 233 members, this number allowed it to aim for a majority on its own. The main opposition parties, including the CDP and JCP, did not coordinate their candidates. In 239 constituencies, or approximately 80% of the 289 SMDs, the main opposition parties did not unify their candidates (*Asahi*, October 18, 2024). In addition, in 46 constituencies in which former candidates associated with the LDP's political finance fund controversy ran for office, only six constituencies united their candidates among the main opposition parties (*Asahi*, October 18, 2024). The JCP ran 216 candidates, competing with the CDP in more than 140 constituencies (*Nikkei*, October 10, 2024).

Table 4.1 summarizes the constituencies in which the CDP did not nominate any candidates in SMDs. Prefectures left blank indicate that the CDP nominated candidates in all constituencies. For example, Hokkaido is left blank, indicating that the CDP nominated candidates in all 12 constituencies. However, for example, Aomori is entered as 2, which means that the CDP did not nominate a candidate in the 2nd district.

Table 4.1 also illustrates the trends in the nomination of CDP candidates. First, in some prefectures where opposition parties have been strong since the DPJ days, they nominated more candidates. The most notable example is Hokkaido. Labor unions are prominent in Hokkaido, a prefecture known as the DPJ's Kingdom (*Minshu-tō Ōkoku*). Second, prefectures with key party members—that is, those with high name recognition and long tenure in the legislature—have candidates in all constituencies. For example, Iwate Prefecture is home to Ozawa Ichirō's constituency, and Ozawa is a key member of the CDP in Iwate. Mie has Okada Katsuya, and Nara has Mabuchi Sumio. Saga has Haraguchi Kazuhiro, and Fukushima has Genba Kōichirō. In these prefectures, candidates were nominated in all constituencies.

Trends can also be observed in prefectures with no CDP candidates. Even if they do not cooperate in the election, the CDP may have been wary of competing with other opposition parties. First, Ishin strongly influences the Kansai region, especially Osaka (Maeda 2022; Zenkyo 2025). In Osaka's 19 constituencies, only 4 (6, 10, 15, and 16 districts) fielded CDP candidates. It is difficult to say that the influence of Ishin was not considered in nominating candidates.

Another point is that there is a certain amount of candidate coordination between CDP and DPP. This is because both the CDP and DPP have their roots in the DPJ. Moreover, because of the fragmentation

Table 4.1 Districts where the CDP nominated no candidates

Prefecture (number of seats)	Districts with no CDP candidates	Prefecture (number of seats)	Districts with no CDP candidates
Hokkaido (12)		Shiga (3)	1, 3
Aomori (3)	2	Kyoto (6)	2, 4
Iwate (3)		Osaka (19)	1, 2, 3, 4, 5, 7, 8, 9, 11, 12, 13, 14, 17, 18, 19
Miyagi (5)	5	Hyogo (12)	3, 8, 11, 12
Akita (3)		Nara (3)	
Yamagata (3)	2	Wakayama (2)	
Fukushima (4)		Tottori (2)	
Ibaraki (7)	1, 2, 4, 5, 7	Shimane (2)	
Tochigi (5)	5	Okayama (4)	
Gunma (5)	2, 5	Hiroshima (6)	2, 4
Saitama (16)	4, 13, 14	Yamaguchi (3)	3
Chiba (14)	2, 7, 11	Tokushima (2)	2
Tokyo (30)	2, 4, 12, 13, 14, 17, 20, 25, 26	Kagawa (3)	2
Kanagawa (20)	11, 15	Ehime (3)	
Niigata (5)		Kochi (2)	2
Nagano (5)	4	Fukuoka (11)	4, 6, 8, 9, 11
Yamanashi (2)	2	Saga (2)	
Toyama (3)	3	Nagasaki (3)	1
Ishikawa (3)		Kumamoto (4)	2, 3
Fukui (2)		Oita (3)	1
Gifu (5)	1, 2, 3	Miyazaki (3)	2, 3
Shizuoka (8)	4	Kagoshima (4)	2, 4
Aichi (16)	2, 6, 7, 11	Okinawa (4)	1,2
Mie (4)			

of supporting parties within the JTUC, the CDP tends not to nominate candidates in prefectures where DPP-supporting allied labor unions are strong. For example, in Ibaraki, the party did not nominate candidates in five of the seven constituencies. Ibaraki is a prefecture in which Hitachi, a member of the alliance-affiliated Japanese Electrical Electronic and Information Union (*Denki Rengō*), has a company town. Hitachi City is located in the 5th District, and the CDP ran no candidates there. Aichi Prefecture is also where Toyota, a member of the Alliance-affiliated Confederation of Japan Automobile Workers' Unions (*Jidōsha Sōren*), has a company town. The 11th District, where the CDP had no candidates, includes Toyota City, where Toyota's headquarters is located.

Finally, I review the CDP's tactics in the 46 electoral districts associated with the LDP political fund scandal. The CDP nominated candidates in 37 constituencies and had no candidates in nine, including Aichi 7, Hyogo 3, Saitama 13, and Fukuoka 4, where the DPP nominated candidates. In Osaka 4, 13, and 19 districts, where Ishin had strong support, the CDP did not nominate candidates.

Electoral Campaign

One of the electoral strategies of the CDP is that high-profile members of the Diet, who hold key positions in political parties such as president and permanent advisor, visit constituencies to support candidates. Visits by party representatives tend to help the party's candidate receive more votes (McElwain 2009, 2015).

Figure 4.1 illustrates the number of times party executives visited prefectures during the election period. It also indicates the number of times the CDP's eight party executives, including Edano (party advisor, or *Seitō-Komon*), Okada Katsuya and Izumi (permanent advisors, or *Jōnin-Komon*), Noda (representative/president), Tsujimoto Kiyomi, Nagatsuma Akira, Ōgushi Hiroshi (acting representative/president) (*Daihyō-Daikō*), and Ogawa Junya (secretary general) (*Kanji-Chō*), visited constituencies.

Since the days of the former DPJ, the CDP has been an urban-focused party targeting independent voters (e.g., Lipscy 2016). In this

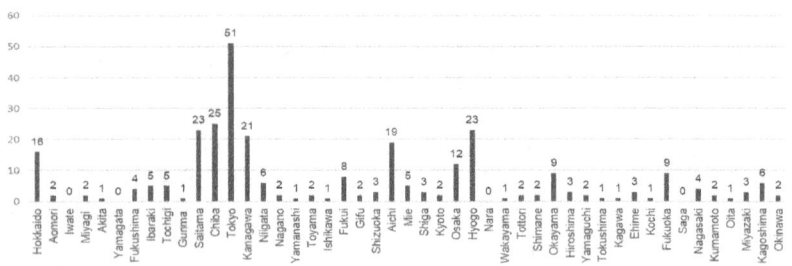

Fig. 4.1 Visits by prominent CDP party officials. *Source* CDP Website

election, the CDP adopted an election strategy centered on the Tokyo metropolitan area and other large metropolitan areas.

Tokyo was by far the most frequent destination, with 51 visits. Saitama, Chiba, and Kanagawa were next in the metropolitan area. In the West Japan metropolitan region (*Kansai*), party executives visited Hyogo, located next to Osaka, more than 20 times to support candidates. However, there were no visits to Iwate, Yamagata, Nara, or Saga. Prefectures with no visits can be divided into two types. The first category includes prefectures with strong leaders; for instance, Ozawa Ichirō in Iwate, Mabuchi Sumio in Nara, and Ōgushi Hiroshi and Haraguchi Kazuhiro in Saga. Because these leaders were famous figures with electoral strength and influence, support from the party was not necessary.

The CDP did not provide much electoral support to constituencies where the LDP was strong, and the CDP was weak due to factors such as the absence of incumbent Diet members. Hence, none of the party executives visited Yamagata. In Yamagata, the LDP took seats in all three districts in the 2021 general election and repeated that success in the 2024 general election. There were no CDP Diet members in the prefectures, and the prefectural branch (*kenren*) was headed by a prefectural assembly member. In Kochi, the representative of the prefectural branch was a former Diet member because there were no incumbent Diet members. Gunma is an LDP kingdom (*Jimintō Ōkoku*), and the LDP won every constituency in the 2021 election. Both prefectures were visited only once by party executives.

Table 4.2 details which party executives went to which constituencies and when to provide election support. The blank cells in Table 4.2 indicate they did not go to any constituency that day. There were differences in the number of visits by party executives. Noda, the party's representative, visited constituencies 62 times. However, other party executives were less active. For instance, Nagatsuma was absent on 7 of the 12 election campaign days, meaning he was less present than other key party members. Izumi visited constituencies 23 times and was absent five out of the 12 days. Edano visited constituencies 25 times but was absent for 3 days. Considering that Noda visited constituencies 62 times, Okada 45 times, and Ogawa 37 times, it can be said that Izumi and Edano were in support less often and had less presence as party officials.

Possible reasons why the two former representatives of the party appeared less frequently in the election campaign can be explained as

66 F. IKEDA

Table 4.2 Constituencies visited by major party officials

Date	Edano (Saikō Komon)	Okada (Jōnin Komon)	Noda (Daihyō)	Tsujimoto (Daihyō Daikō)	Ogawa (Kanjichō)	Izumi (Jōnin Komon)	Nagatsuma (Daihyō Daikō)	Ōgushi (Daihyō Daikō)
15-Oct	Hokkaido 1, 5, 3, 10, Saitama 3	Mie 1, 2, Saitama 1	Tokyo 24, Hyogo 9, Fukui 2	Osaka 10, Shiga 2	Hokkaido 5, Miyagi 3, Saitama 8, Tokyo 7, 11			
16-Oct		Saitama 3, Chiba 4, 13	Niigata 2, 3, 4, 5	Tokyo 21, 22, 23, 24	Saitama 10, 12, Ibaraki 3, 6, Tokyo 30			Hyogo 4, 10
17-Oct		Chiba 5, Tokyo 5, 10, 22, 29	Chiba 3, Tokyo 3, 15, Shimane 1, Tottori 2	Nagasaki 2, Fukuoka 5, Okinawa 4	Saitama 7, Fukushima 1, 4	Aichi 9, 10, 16, Gifu 5		Fukui 1, 2, Toyama 1
18-Oct	Aichi 16	Tokyo 7	Hyogo 2, 6, 7, Aichi 4, 8	Okinawa 3	Hiroshima 3, Yamaguchi 2, Okayama 1, 2	Gifu 4	Kagoshima 1, 3	Fukuoka 3, 7, Nagasaki 2
19-Oct	Aichi 5, Osaka 10, 16, Kyoto 5	Ibaraki 3, Chiba 8, Saitama 16, Tochigi 4	Aichi 1, 9, 16, Shizuoka 6, 8	Wakayama 1, 2, Osaka 6, 15, Tokushima 1	Chiba 3, 4, 5, 13			Nagasaki 3
20-Oct	Hokkaido 3, 4, 6, 11	Saitama 10, 12, Niigata 5	Tokyo 9, 10, 11, 18, 23, 29	Okayama 1, 2, Osaka 10	Kagawa 1, Ehime 2	Hyogo 2, 9, 10, Okayama 2		

Date	Edano (Saikō Komon)	Okada (Jōnin Komon)	Noda (Daihyō)	Tsujimoto (Daihyō Daikō)	Ogawa (Kanjichō)	Izumi (Jōnin Komon)	Nagatsuma (Daihyō Daikō)	Ōgushi (Daihyō Daikō)
21-Oct	Hyogo 2, 4, 6, 10, Okayama 4	Toyama 1, Fukui 2, Hyogo 6, 7, Osaka 16	Hokkaido 3, 4, 6, 10, Akita 1	Miyazaki 1	Aichi 1, 4, 8, 9	Kumamoto 1, 2, Kagoshima 1, 3		Kanagawa 1, 5, 6, 14, 18, 20
22-Oct	Tochigi 1, 3, Fukushima 1	Tokyo 15, Kanagawa 6, 13, 14, 18	Saitama 1, 7, 9, 16, Tochigi 4	Chiba 3, 4, 5, 6, 13	Nagano 5, Tokyo 24, 30		Tokyo 9, 10, 11, 15, 16, 29	Tokushima 1, Ehime 2
23-Oct	Fukuoka 1, Miyazaki 1	Kanagawa 1, 5, 7, 20	Yamaguchi 2, Fukuoka 2, 3, 10, Kagoshima 1, 3	Tokyo 7, 8, 10, 11, 15, 19, 24	Shimane 1, Tottori 2	Aichi 1, 3	Chiba 5, 6, 8, 10, 13, Ibaraki 3, Saitama 3	Hiroshima 1, 3, Okayama 1, 4
24-Oct	Saitama 3	Mie 2, Aichi 1, 4, 9, Okayama 2, 4	Ibaraki 6, Kanagawa 1, 5, 6, 7, 14, 20	Fukui 1, 2, Niigata 3, 4	Tokushima 1, Hyogo 2, 6, 7, 9, Osaka 16	Fukushima 4, Hokkaido 1, 3, 4, 5	Tokyo 3, 5, 6, 7, 22, 23	Aomori 1, 3
25-Oct	Oita 2	Fukuoka 2, Saitama 3, 16	Chiba 3, 4, 5, 6, 13, Kanagawa 18	Kochi 1, Ehime 2, 3, Osaka 3, 16	Fukui 2, Osaka 10, Shiga 2, Mie 2	Saitama 7, 9, Gunma 3, Kyoto 1, Shiga 2	Tokyo 18, 28, 30	Nagano 5, Yamanashi 1
26-Oct		Tokyo 18, 28, Shizuoka 6, Mie 2	Ishikawa 3, Tokyo 7, 9, 10, 11, 15	Hyogo 2, 4, 6, Osaka 10	Saitama 1, 7, 9, Kanagawa 18, Tokyo 5			Nagasaki 2, Fukuoka 3

Source CDP Website

follows. One reason is that they both carried an image of electoral cooperation with the JCP. The party's strategy was to keep the image of the JCP out of the election campaign as much as possible and to promote a centrist image (*Asahi*, November 19, 2024). While many of the eight members visited the Tokyo metropolitan area, including Tokyo and Kanagawa, where there are many independent voters, Edano and Izumi did not. Edano went to Saitama on October 24, but his constituency is also in Saitama's 5th District, and he was only there to support the prefecture in which his constituency is located. Among the 46 constituencies in which the LDP candidates were involved in political finance issues, nine were in Tokyo, Saitama, and Kanagawa. Neither Edano nor Izumi visited these constituencies.

Another trend is that many CDP executives visited constituencies where the DPP had a strong base due to its relationship with labor unions. For example, the data for Aichi and Ibaraki demonstrate that Edano, Okada, Noda, Izumi, and others repeatedly supported the DPP. Although they have not officially cooperated with the DPP in the election, it appears that they were making efforts to maintain a certain level of rapport with the DPP.

Electoral Results

The CDP won 148 seats, an increase of about 50 seats from before the announcement of the election. This is the first time an opposition party has won more than 100 seats in a general election since the DPJ won 113 seats in 2005, excluding the 2009 general election when the DPJ replaced the government. The CDP increased its seats since its founding in 2017 from 55 to 148, with 104 winners in the SMD tier and 44 winners in the PR tier.

Figure 4.2 illustrates the percentage of votes obtained by major parties in the PR tier in the 2017, 2021, and 2024 general elections. In the 2024 election, the CDP obtained 21.1% of the votes. The proportional district received approximately 1.156 million votes, an increase of approximately 70,000 (0.6%) from the 1.149 million votes received in the previous election in 2021, and won five more seats than the 39 it previously held (CDP, November 19, 2024). Despite this increase in the number of seats won, the CDP, in its summary of the elections, noted that support from independent and proportional votes generally remained flat and did not

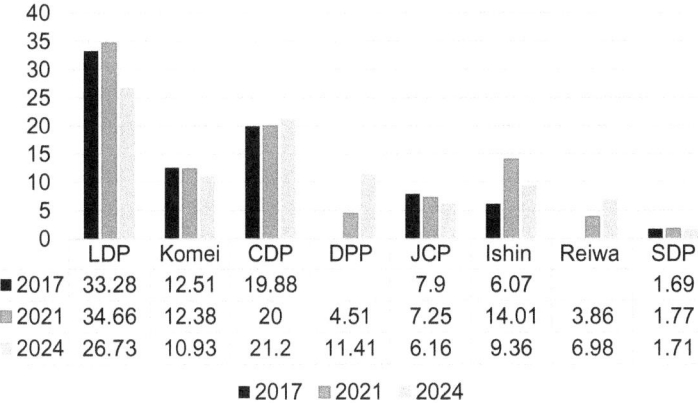

Fig. 4.2 The percentage of votes obtained by major parties in PR tier

lead to a large increase, which was positioned as a challenge for the future (CDP, November 19, 2024).

The DPP also made great strides in this election, increasing the number of seats from 11 before the announcement to 28. As Fig. 4.2 illustrates, the DPP's share of the proportional district vote in the 2024 general election increased dramatically from 4.51% in the 2021 general election to 11.41%. Compared to the last election, this is approximately 2.5 times higher. In contrast, the JCP fell from 10 seats before the announcement to 8, demonstrating a gradual decline from 2017 (e.g., Maeda 2018). The JCP's vote share has also been gradually declining in the PR tier: 7.9% in the 2017 general election, 7.25% in 2021, and 6.16% in 2024.

As Table 4.3 illustrates, the CDP won seats in 17 of the 47 prefectures' 1st Districts, which are generally considered urban areas. In metropolitan areas, such as Chiba, Tokyo, Kanagawa, and Hyogo, where many CDP executives visited to support candidates, the party won seats in the 1st Constituency. They also won seats in the 1st Districts of Iwate, Nara, and Saga, where there were core influential CDP members, even though none of the party executives visited. Looking exclusively at the Tokyo metropolitan area and urban prefectures, the CDP won 15 out of 30 seats in Tokyo and 11 out of 20 in Kanagawa. In Chiba, the party won 7 out of 14 seats, and in Saitama, it won 6 out of 16 seats. In Aichi, it won 8 out of 16 seats. Thus, it is fair to say that the CDP displayed a specific strength in the Greater Tokyo Area during this election. However, these

Table 4.3 The party that won in the 1st district

The party won in the 1st District	Prefecture	Total
LDP	Aomori, Akita, Yamagata, Tochigi, Gunma, Saitama, Toyama, Ishikawa, Fukui, Gifu, Shizuoka, Mie, Kyoto, Wakayama, Tottori, Okayama, Hiroshima, Yamaguchi, Tokushima, Ehime, Kochi, Fukuoka, Kumamoto	23
CDP	Hokkaido, Iwate, Miyagi, Fukushima, Chiba, Tokyo, Kanagawa, Niigata, Nagano, Yamanashi, Hyogo, Nara, Shimane, Kagawa, Saga, Miyazaki, Kagoshima	17
Other	Ibaraki, Aichi, Shiga, Osaka, Nagasaki, Oita, Okinawa	7

advances by the CDP were limited to East Japan (*Kantō*) and Middle Japan (*Chūbu*) regions, including Aichi Prefecture, with no change seen in the West Japan (*Kansai*) region, represented by Osaka. In Osaka, Ishin won seats in all the 19 electoral districts. In Hyogo, where party executives visited 23 times, the CDP won only 2 of the 12 seats.

Finally, I review the election results for the electoral districts where the LDP political finance scandal occurred. Table 4.4 summarizes the electoral districts where the CDP, LDP, or an independent or other party candidate won a seat. Of the 46 electoral districts, the LDP won in 14 electoral districts, while other parties won in 32. The CDP candidate won 21 of the 46 electoral districts. The DPP won seats in Saitama's 13th and Aichi's 7th Districts, where the DPP nominated candidates and the CDP did not. The CDP can be considered to have succeeded in capturing the critical votes of the LDP in these constituencies.

Table 4.4 Electoral outcomes of constituencies with political funding scandals

Winning party candidates	Districts
CDP candidates win (20 districts)	Hokkaido 5, Aomori 3, Iwate 3, Miyagi 3, Fukushima 1, Fukushima 3, Saitama 6, Saitama 9, Tokyo 1, Tokyo 7, Tokyo 11, Tokyo 21, Kanagawa 16, Niigata 2, Niigata 5, Fukui 2, Nagano 1, Shizuoka 3, Aichi 12, Ehime 2
LDP candidates win (14 districts)	Tochigi 3, Gunma 4, Saitama 8, Chiba 3, Toyama 1, Ishikawa 1, Ishikawa 2, Fukui 1, Nagano 5, Aichi 15, Mie 4, Hyogo 3, Fukuoka 4, Nagasaki 2
Independents or other parties win (12 districts)	Tokyo 17, Tokyo 24, Hyogo 9, Wakayama 2, Saitama 13, Aichi 7, Osaka 4, Osaka 10, Osaka 13, Osaka 19, Fukuoka 11, Oita 2

Conclusion

For the CDP, the 3-year period from the 2021 general election to the 2024 general election was a time to explore its relationship with opposition parties, especially the JCP. Izumi, who became the party's leader after Edano, avoided explicitly discussing the electoral coalition with the JCP but did not sever that relationship. For the CDP, the unification of candidates and JCP's community-based electoral base was attractive. In addition, the conclusion of whether to cooperate with JCP in the election was not easily reached, given that some incumbents had been elected through electoral cooperation with JCP in the House of Councillors election since 2016. Noda, who became leader in 2024, made it through the 2024 general election without an electoral alliance with the JCP.

In terms of electoral strategies in the 2024 general election, the CDP targeted urban areas. Party executives mainly visited urban and metropolitan areas, and did not run candidates in districts where they competed with the DPP. In addition, to dilute their association with the JCP in the eyes of the public, former representatives Izumi and Edano reduced the number of times they visited constituencies to demonstrate that the CDP was centrist. As a result of these election strategies, the CDP achieved a large increase in the number of seats compared to the previous election, winning seats in districts where there had been political funding problems and in urban and metropolitan areas. Thus, to a certain extent, the CDP succeeded in capturing votes critical of the LDP. However, challenges remain after the general election in 2024. The kind of relationship the CDP will seek with other opposition parties, especially the JCP, in the future is an ongoing issue. In addition, if the CDP aims to survive as a centrist party, as it claimed to do in this election, it will have to decide what type of policies it will pursue and how it will appeal to voters in the future.

REFERENCES

Carlson, Matthew M. 2025. "Scandals During the Kishida Administration." In *Japan Decides 2024: The Japanese General Election*, edited by Kenneth M. McElwain, Robert J. Pekkanen, and Daniel M. Smith, 217–233. Palgrave Macmillan.

CDP. November 30, 2021. "'Tagaiwo Mottomo Wakariaeteiruno ga Imano Kankyo de ha Naika' Daihyōsenshutsu wo Uke Kishakaiken de Izumi Kenta Shindaihyō". https://cdp-japan.jp/news/20211130_2646

CDP. October 15, 2024. "Shugiinsenkyo no Koji ni Atatte". https://cdp-japan.jp/news/20241014_8379

CDP. November 19, 2024. "Dai 50kai Shugiin Senkyo Sōkatsu". https://cdpjapan.jp/files/download/gLJ7/LgJ8/vULF/xkbC/gLJ7LgJ8vULFxkbCAu9E578p.pdf

CDP. "Dai 50kai Shugiin Senkyo Sōkatsu." November 19, 2024. https://cdpjapan.jp/files/download/gLJ7/LgJ8/vULF/xkbC/gLJ7LgJ8vULFxkbCAu9E578p.pdf.

Lipscy, Phillip Y. 2016. "DPJ Election Strategy: The Dilemma of landslide victory." In *The Democratic Party of Japan in Power: Challenges and Failures*, edited by Yoichi Funabashi and Koichi Nakano, 167–192. Routledge.

Maeda, Ko. 2018. "The JCP: A Perpetual Spoiler?" In *Japan Decides 2017: The Japanese General Election*, edited by Robert J. Pekkanen, Steven R. Reed, Ethan Scheiner, and Daniel M. Smith, 92–106. Palgrave Macmillan.

Maeda, Ko. 2022. "The 2021 Election Results: Continuity and Changes." In *Japan Decides 2021: The Japanese General Election*, edited by Robert J. Pekkanen, Steven R. Reed, and Daniel M. Smith, 137–152. Palgrave Macmillan.

McElwain, Kenneth M. 2009. "How Long Are Koizumi's Coattails? Party-Leader Visits in the 2005 Election." In *Political Change in Japan: Electoral Behavior, Party Realignment, and the Koizumi Reforms* Walter H, edited by Steven R. Reed, Kenneth Mori McElwain, and Kay Shimizu, 133–156. Shorenstein Asia-Pacific Research Center.

McElwain, Kenneth M. 2015. "Did Abe's Coattails Help the LDP Win?" In *Japan Decides 2014: The Japanese General Election*, edited by Robert J. Pekkanen, Steven R. Reed, and Ethan Scheiner, 129–141. Palgrave Macmillan.

McLaughlin, Levi. 2025. "Perennial Fears, Novel Responses: The Unification Church in Japan after the Abe Assassination." In *Japan Decides 2024: The Japanese General Election*, edited by Kenneth M. McElwain, Robert J. Pekkanen, and Daniel M. Smith, 235–253. New York: Palgrave Macmillan.

Nemoto, Kuniaki. 2025. "Reasons behind the LDP's Loss in the 2024 Election." In *Japan Decides 2024: The Japanese General Election*, edited by Kenneth M. McElwain, Robert J. Pekkanen, and Daniel M. Smith, 57–74. New York: Palgrave Macmillan.

Pekkanen, Robert J., and Steven R. Reed. 2022. "The Opposition in 2021: A Second Party and A Third Force". In *Japan Decides 2021: The Japanese General Election*, edited by Robert J. Pekkanen, Steven R. Reed, and Daniel M. Smith, 49–64. Palgrave Macmillan.

Zenkyo, Masahiro. 2025. "Why Did Public Support for the Japan Innovation Party Decline in the 2024 HR Election?" In *Japan Decides 2024: The Japanese General Election*, edited by Kenneth M. McElwain, Robert J. Pekkanen, and Daniel M. Smith, 91–105. Palgrave Macmillan.

News Sources

Asahi Shinbun. October 20, 2021. "Hatsu no Syugiinsen no Yatō Kyōtō 217 Senkyoku de Ipponka Tsuyosa Niha Notanka"
Asahi Shinbun. November 23, 2021. "Rikkenminsyutō Dihyōsen Tōronkai Osaka Seizi shi, Ogawa Junya shi, Izumi Kenta shi, Nishimura Chinami shi"
Asahi Shinbun. November 30, 2021. "Rengōkaichō 'Rikken,Kokumin Goryu wo' Kyosan tono Kyōto, Aratamete Hiteiteki"
Asahi Shinbun. December 1, 2021. "Rikken, Izumidaihyō, Shiren no Funade Yatō hearing wo Minaoshi 'Kyosankakugaikyoryoku' Reset"
Asahi Shinbun. January 26, 2022. "Rikken, Akueikyō wo Shiteki Kyosan tono Kyoryokugōi 'Gokai de Somerareta' Syugiinsennsokatsuan"
Asahi Shinbun. February 18, 2022. " 'Shienseitonashi' Ireino Hoshin Rengō Sangiin he Seishiki Kettei Rikken, Kokumin tono 'Renkei' tsuiki"
Asahi Shinbun. February 26, 2022. "Kyosan fukume Kōhoipponka Rengo,Rikken ga Kakunin Sangiinsen"
Asahi Shinbun. May 10, 2022. "Rikkenn, Kyosan Kyōtō ha Ichibuni Tōsyusyomei no 'Seisakugōi' Miokuri"
Asahi Shinbun. October 18, 2024. "Yatokyōgō Jimin ni Ri ? 289 Senkyokucyu 239 de Kyōgō 'Uragane' 46 Senkyoku, Ipponka ha 6 Shuginsen"

Asahi Shinbun. November 19, 2024. "Rikken ga Shugiinsensokatsu Chyudōsenryaku de 'Seika' mo SNS Katsuyō ha 'Kaizen no Yochi'"
Jiji Press. August 21, 2024. "Edanoshi Chudorosen Appeal 'Genpatsu Zero' Fuin Tai Kyosan mo Saikochiku Ritsumin". https://www.jiji.com/jc/article?k=202 4082100875&g=pol
Mainichi Shinbun. July 11, 2022. "Yatō 'Ichinin-Ku' 4 Shō 28 Ppai no Taihai 'Kyotō' Kuzure Seiken Hihan Hyo Bunsan". https://mainichi.jp/articles/20220711/k00/00m/010/024000c
NHK. July 9, 2024. "Rikken Tochijisen Renhōshi Sani de Yatōkan no Renkei Giron Kapptsu ni Narumitoshi". https://www3.nhk.or.jp/news/html/202 40709/k10014505621000.html
NHK. September 23, 2024. "Jimin ni Taiji suru Leader ha? Ritsumindaihyosen". https://www3.nhk.or.jp/news/html/20240923/k10014585081000.html
Nikkei Shinbun. September 23, 2024. "Rikkenminsyutō no Shindaihyō ni Noda Motoshushō Kessen Tohyō de Edanoshi Yaburu". https://www.nikkei.com/article/DGXZQOUA179580X10C24A9000000/
Nikkei Shinbun. October 10, 2024. "Kyōsan Shuinsen ni 216nin Rikken to 140cho de Kyōgō". https://www.nikkei.com/article/DGXZQOUA10C5 D0Q4A011C2000000/
Sankei Shinbun. September 14, 2024. "Torauma ni Nayamu Ritsumin no Kohosyatachi Yappari Kyōsan to Ketsubetsu Dekinai?" https://www.sankei.com/article/20240914-4ZPVIKUZ6BPLTBWVYJPSJ3SPOY/
Yomiuri Shinbun. 2 June, 2024 "Tochijisen de Yatō no Omowakukousa 'Yoyatō Taiketsu' Neraru Ritumin Kyosan, 'Saikyotō' ni Hanpatsu suru Kokuminminsyu to Rengō". https://www.yomiuri.co.jp/election/tochijisen/202 40601-OYT1T50216/

CHAPTER 5

A Costly Coalition: Kōmeitō's Enduring Partnership with the LDP

Axel Klein and Levi McLaughlin

INTRODUCTION: A BATTLE-WORN COALITION PERSISTS

The partnership between the conservative Liberal Democratic Party and the social welfare-oriented party Kōmeitō has lasted more than a quarter century. Japan has thus been governed for most of the past generation by one of the world's longest-lasting two-party coalitions.[1] Since they established their alliance in 1999, the LDP-Kōmeitō combine has sustained

---

A. Klein (✉)
Duisburg-Essen University, Duisburg, Germany
e-mail: axel.klein@uni-due.de

L. McLaughlin
North Carolina State University, Raleigh, NC, USA
e-mail: lmclaug2@ncsu.edu

---

[1] In Australia, the Liberal Party and the National Party have cooperated since 1946, remaining partners in government and in opposition. In Germany, the Christian Democratic Union and the Christian Social Union of Bavaria (CDU/CSU), an agreement known unofficially as the Union Parties, have shared a parliamentary group at the Bundestag since 1949. In Sweden, the Christian Democrats have cooperated with the Modern Party in a series of right-aligned minority governing coalitions since 1985. A comparative study of lasting party partnerships that emphasizes the importance of social

majorities and supermajorities in the Japanese Diet's Upper and Lower Houses and spent 3 years (2009–2012) relegated to the opposition. While the October 2024 general election saw dramatic losses, forcing the LDP and Kōmeitō to form a minority government for the first time since they joined forces, it also saw the perseverance of a long-lasting partnership that many predicted would collapse.

The past 25 years have seen the governing coalition's ideologically divergent partners grow closer in a symbiotic relationship that has proven resistant to division. Kōmeitō, sometimes glossed in English as the "Clean Government Party," was founded in November 1964 by Sōka Gakkai, a millions-strong lay Buddhist organization founded in the 1930s. The religion's adherents preserve the teachings and liturgies of the medieval reformer Nichiren (1222–1282) as they revere the Gakkai's Honorary President Ikeda Daisaku (1928–2023). Kōmeitō was founded on a platform of absolute pacifism and has long championed social welfare policies. It spent decades opposed to the LDP before the two parties forged an alliance that sees advantages for both sides. LDP candidates have benefited from Kōmeitō's unmatched vote-gathering power; Sōka Gakkai members have been cultivated for generations to treat electioneering for Kōmeitō and its allies as a core practice, providing between 10,000 and 20,000 votes per district where they campaign, and they have routinely directed their energies toward LDP Diet-level candidates. In exchange, Kōmeitō became part of the national government, guaranteeing that some of its policies would become law and that its controversial founding religion would be insulated from legal and political attacks (Nakano 2016; Klein and McLaughlin 2022a, b; Sohn 2024).

When Kōmeitō marked its 60th anniversary on 17 November 2024, however, there was little cause for celebration. All but four of the party's candidates in Lower House Single-Member Districts (SMDs), including its newly appointed party head, had just lost their races. Kōmeitō recorded its lowest-ever vote count in the proportional (PR) tier since partnering with the LDP. A combination of adverse factors worked against the party. Numbering among Kōmeitō's challenges were increasing difficulties mobilizing its aging Sōka Gakkai supporters and electioneering after the November 2023 death of Sōka Gakkai's charismatic leader Ikeda Daisaku; Ikeda's absence poses new challenges to a party and religion

conservatism and coalitions' capacity to mobilize religious communities would illuminate forces that have shaped postwar Japanese politics.

that have relied on adherents' affective links to Ikeda to motivate their activities. The LDP's slush-fund scandal (Carlson 2025) affected its junior coalition partner, dragging down voter confidence in a party linked to corrupt LDP officeholders. After Kishida Fumio became LDP president and Prime Minister in 2021, the relationship between the coalition partners suffered. Kishida's tenure as PM saw a decline in cordial coalition relations that were maintained by his predecessor, Suga Yoshihide. Worsening relations between Kōmeitō and the LDP affected electoral coordination. Additionally, as a party backed by a controversial "new religion," Kōmeitō endured collateral damage from the July 2022 assassination of former Prime Minister Abe Shinzō, whose murderer was driven by a grudge against the highly controversial new religious organization the Family Federation for World Peace and Unification, a group best known by its previous name, the Unification Church (UC) (McLaughlin 2023, 2025).[2]

This chapter provides a chronological overview of these factors and how they shaped Kōmeitō's electoral performances after Japan's 2021 general election. We conclude that, despite these challenges and a downward trend in its vote counts and election results, Kōmeitō remains a pivotal political force in Japan.

THE ASSASSINATION OF ABE SHINZŌ: A RELIGION-BACKED PARTY GROWS NERVOUS

Abe's murder and revelations about his assassin's motive exerted a negative impact on public perceptions of Kōmeitō and Sōka Gakkai. As was the case in March 1995, when the apocalyptic religion Aum Shinrikyō carried out sarin gas attacks on the Tokyo subways that triggered long-lasting moral panic about religion in Japan (Klein 2012; McLaughlin 2012), Kōmeitō and Sōka Gakkai suffered in 2022 as media outlets broadcast reports that raised popular suspicion of religious organizations in response to news about Abe's assassin being motivated by a grudge against the UC. The media blitz triggered by the assassination included coverage of Kōmeitō politicians who had taken part in UC-related events. According

---

[2] The label "new religion" generally refers to religious organizations founded after 1800. It is an academic category for groups that tend to be labeled as "cults" or by similarly stigmatized terms. For an overview of ways minoritized religions are categorized, see Stausberg, Van Der Haven, and Baffelli (2023).

to a survey by Kyodo News, 11 Kōmeitō politicians were recorded as having attended UC gatherings. Yoshida Shōko, for example, a Kōmeitō member of the Higashiōsaka city council, participated in an event for the Women's Federation for World Peace. She claimed to have been unaware that it was an organization affiliated with the UC (Klein 2023).

Kōmeitō was criticized in media coverage as impeding anti-cult legislation. The party clearly walked a tightrope between acting decisively as part of the ruling coalition and protecting religions from accusations of transgressing Article 20 of the 1947 Constitution, which affirms both that "freedom of religion is guaranteed to all" and that "no religious organization shall receive any privileges from the State, nor exercise any political authority" (Kantei 2025). The party's standard talking point on this matter was presented by then General Secretary Ishii Kei'ichi at a press conference on 19 August 2022, where he stated that the Unification Church was "a social problem, not an issue of 'religion and politics'" (*Kōmei Shinbun* 20 August 2022). In September 2022, then Kōmeitō leader Yamaguchi Natsuo warned about "the need to be extremely cautious" about implementing clauses in the Religious Juridical Persons Law to legally dissolve a religion based on its violations of civil law (*Asahi Shinbun* 26 September 2022). Yamaguchi asserted that the UC should not be primarily understood as a religion but as an "antisocial [group] committing illegal acts" (Klein 2023; McLaughlin 2025). By invoking the "anti-social" label, Yamaguchi equated the UC to organized crime, employing tactics adopted by the National Network for Lawyers Against Spiritual Sales and other UC opponents who have refined means of navigating past freedom of religion pitfalls to target the church's exploitative financial practices (Gaitanidis 2024). Following this logic, legislation passed by the LDP-Kōmeitō coalition from late 2022 that targeted the UC did not pertain to the law on religious juridical persons or to constitutional guarantees of religious freedom. Kōmeitō's draft bill stated that "prejudice and discrimination against religion in general must not be encouraged" (*Yomiuri Shinbun* 7 November 2022), and the bill passed by the Diet amended regulations for consumer protection.

The July 2022 Upper House Election: Kōmeitō's Declining Vote-Gathering Power

The most significant national-level contest between the 2021 and 2024 general elections was the 2022 Upper House election, held two days after Abe's murder. This election did not change the power balance in Japan's second chamber of the National Diet. Kōmeitō lost one PR seat and eventually contributed 27 to the ruling coalition's 146-seat majority. 6.2 million voters cast their ballot for the party, down 5.4% from 6.5 million in 2019 and in line with Kōmeitō's overall trend of falling PR support in national elections.

Kōmeitō's Leaders Delay Passing the Baton

One consequence of Abe's assassination was Kōmeitō's decision to postpone generational change in its leadership. Prior to Abe's murder, Ishii Kei'ichi had been chosen by the party to follow Yamaguchi Natsuo as Kōmeitō's leader, but on 16 September 2022 the 70-year-old Yamaguchi was reelected to an unprecedented eighth term. This was despite Yamaguchi having indicated earlier that he sought to pass the baton to a younger generation; he had served in the post from 2009. It is apparent that Kōmeitō's decision-makers were willing to overlook Yamaguchi's stewardship over a disappointing Upper House electoral return because they were concerned about changing leadership during the Unification Church crisis. Yamaguchi's proven capacity to mitigate criticism of Kōmeitō and his expertise in handling the relationship with the LDP seemingly proved indispensable at this crucial juncture.

Sustaining Yamaguchi's tenure as Kōmeitō leader may have smoothed over tensions that grew between the coalition partners. In the year leading up to the Abe assassination, relations between the LDP and Kōmeitō leaderships had taken a turn for the worse. Suga Yoshihide, Prime Minister between 2020 and 2021, had long maintained close ties with Kōmeitō and was regarded positively by the party. This was a relationship that dated back to the 1990s, when Suga cooperated with Kōmeitō as a municipal-level politician in Yokohama (Klein and McLaughlin 2022a). The LDP's former General Secretary Nikai Toshihiro, who retired in October 2021, had also fostered a long-term close association with Kōmeitō. When Kishida took over as LDP leader and Prime Minister, the changing of the guard added greater uncertainty for Kōmeitō during renewed public and political hostility to religion-affiliated political activism.

Yamaguchi ultimately stepped down to be replaced by Ishii on 28 September 2024. Ishii held the post for the shortest time of any leader in Kōmeitō's history. He lost his own seat in the October 2024 race in the SMD district Saitama 14. Prior to this, Ishii had served ten terms through Kōmeitō's proportional representation portion. Because Kōmeitō in October 2024 stuck with its party custom of not adding its SMD candidates to its proportional representation lists, he was out of office after the election. Ishii announced his resignation on 31 October, taking responsibility for his party's losses. Saitō Tetsuo, an engineering Ph.D. and long-term Lower House member, assumed Kōmeitō leadership on 8 November 2024.

The April 2023 Local Elections: Notable Kōmeitō Losses

A steady downward trajectory in Kōmeitō vote counts and seats won continued with the April 2023 unified local elections. In Tokyo, a record high 12 candidates failed to secure a seat in their local assemblies. Prior to this, Kōmeitō established a record of calculating its own voter turnout to very narrow margins of error, essentially ensuring that the candidates it ran won their seats (Smith 2014). However, in Tokyo's Nerima district, four Kōmeitō candidates ran unsuccessful campaigns. This sobering result was relevant because the eastern part of Nerima overlapped with the newly created Lower House SMD Tokyo 28 (see below), where Kōmeitō's policy affairs chief Okamoto Mitsunari was initially slated to run in October 2024. In Osaka's Miyakojima district, Kōmeitō's candidate Sasaki Kiyomi ran her campaign promising to become the first female delegate to be elected to the local assembly in twelve years. She came fourth out of four candidates.

Author discussions with Sōka Gakkai adherents indicate that these losses were greeted with dismay by local-level candidates and the Gakkai members who mobilized for them. One member pointed out to McLaughlin in April 2023 that, for another party, a 99.2% electoral success rate would be cause for celebration, but not so for Kōmeitō. Since 2007, all Kōmeitō candidates in local elections had been elected. And even though the number of unsuccessful candidates in 2023 pales in comparison to the 1,555 candidates Kōmeitō ran across Japan, the search for causes was on. Two assumptions stood out in media speculation: the aging of Sōka Gakkai's membership and outrage about the Unification Church and its political connections. The newspaper *Mainichi Shinbun* (11 April 2023), for example, quoted a Kōmeitō representative as saying that there was no effective medicine to stop the aging and decline of the party's strength, while the *Asahi Shinbun* (27 March 2023) cited an LDP campaign official who affirmed that those LDP supporters who previously had voted for Kōmeitō candidates had now abandoned the junior coalition party because of the Unification Church affair and instead chose Ishin candidates. Renewed public distrust of any relationship between religious organizations and political parties in the aftermath of the Abe assassination seemed to have cost Kōmeitō crucial support.

Perhaps the most painful loss in these local races was the defeat in Osaka. Miyakojima is historically a center of fervent dedication to Ikeda Daisaku, Sōka Gakkai's unequivocal authority in all matters. It is the neighborhood where Ikeda battled successfully against charges of violating elections law in 1957, an event Gakkai member refers to as the "Osaka Incident" that serves as a key episode in the apotheosizing of their leader. The religion selected Miyakojima as the site for a new Kansai Ikeda Great Memorial Lecture Hall, an impressive facility slated to open by late 2026, in advance of the seventieth anniversary of this event (*Seikyō Shinbun* 18 November 2022). Losing ground politically in an area sacralized through Ikeda's political sacrifice is a disturbing bellwether for members of Kōmeitō's founding religion.

The Death of Ikeda Daisaku: A New Era for Kōmeitō's Supporters

For decades, members of Sōka Gakkai in Japan have been cultivated to treat vote-gathering for Kōmeitō, the party founded by their mentor in 1964, and its political allies as *ongaeshi*, a "return of obligation" to Ikeda Daisaku. Maintaining an affective one-to-one mentor-disciple relationship with their living leader motivated Gakkai adherents to continue sacrificing time and resources to advance the coalition. These sacrifices persisted even after Ikeda disappeared from the public eye in May 2010. While to many adherents the news of Ikeda's passing in November 2023 did not come as a surprise, his death nonetheless tested Kōmeitō's ability to mobilize Gakkai members who no longer had a living mentor to whom they owe repayment of loyalty.

This challenge was exacerbated by difficulties an aging Gakkai constituency is facing in transferring enthusiasm for electioneering to a younger, and numerically smaller, generation that has not cultivated discipleship to Ikeda through connecting with him as a living presence. The dilemma of an aging voter base and the difficulty of motivating younger generations is an issue shared across Japan's political spectrum by legacy parties. However, Kōmeitō's generational gap is distinguished by the distinctive challenge of inspiring loyalty after the death of a central figure around whom electoral mobilization has been justified. Until 2023, Gakkai voters were inspired by the assurance that supporting the party Ikeda founded was what he wanted, no matter Kōmeitō's policy reversals. Now, they are liable to be assured by fellow campaigners that supporting Kōmeitō is what Ikeda *would have wanted*. This is an opinion expressed by fellow Gakkai adherents and is potentially one that can be contested, unlike the wishes of a living mentor. In the absence of a living charismatic leader, however affective his presence may have been, Kōmeitō has lost a key means of mobilizing its Sōka Gakkai base.

A 2023 Reapportionment Conflict in Tokyo

A contentious episode in 2023 illuminated ways mutual dependency of the LDP and Kōmeitō persists even as the coalition's conflict resolution capacities lose strength. Based on the results of Japan's 2020 national census, the Ministry of Internal Affairs recalculated the number of single-member districts to be distributed across the country. Five SMDs were added to Tokyo in late 2022. These new districts sparked contention between the partners. Each sought to preserve the coalition agreement of not running SMD candidates against one another while they maximized the number of seats for their parties. Kōmeitō demanded at least one of the new districts. The party initially aimed for Tokyo 28 but then settled for Tokyo 29. In January 2023, Kōmeitō announced its intention to run Diet member Okamoto Mitsunari, former vice Finance Minister under Kishida, but did so without first gaining the formal consent of the LDP (*Yomiuri Shinbun* 26 January 2023). Kōmeitō also announced that Saitō Tetsuo would run again in Hiroshima 3, an SMD the local LDP wanted back for its own candidate (Klein and McLaughlin 2022a).

What followed was an eight-month-long struggle during which Kōmeitō at one point threatened its coalition partner with withdrawing its party support for LDP candidates running in Tokyo in the next general election. This move, unprecedented during the coalition era, would have deprived LDP candidates in Tokyo of Sōka Gakkai vote-gatherer support for the first time in three decades, and it indicated increased willingness on the part of the junior coalition partner to remind the LDP of its reliance on Gakkai electioneering. By early September 2023, however, the electoral outlook for both parties had worsened to a degree that mending their strained relationship became a priority. Support rates for the cabinet were low (Yukio Maeda 2025), and Kōmeitō needed LDP partisan votes for its candidates running in Osaka against Ishin. Both party leaderships compromised: Kōmeitō kept Tokyo 29, promising to support Liberal Democrats running in other SMDs in Tokyo "while taking individual circumstances into account," and both parties agreed to aim for two successful Kōmeitō SMD candidates two elections from now in the Lower House (*Yomiuri Shinbun* 5 September 2023).

Kōmeitō's Election Manifesto and Policy Priorities

In October 2024, Kōmeitō ran on an unsurprising platform that featured its signature policy fields: controlling consumer prices and income tax, prioritizing support for education and child-raising stipends, and funding for healthcare and pensions, along with concern for disaster prevention and management, international peace, and progressive policies for women and young people (see Matsumoto 2025 for an overview of party manifestos). All these proposals were embedded in a narrative of crises which Kōmeitō promised to continue confronting to ensure a safe future for all. As then party leader Ishii's foreword concluded: "We will continue to pursue relatable politics and care for each and every individual, so that everyone can believe in a future of hope that can be realized." (Kōmeitō 2024: 1).

Acknowledging an issue at the forefront of its voters' concerns, the manifesto began with an announcement of "Political Reform for the Reiwa Period" (2024: 2). This was a reiteration of what has become Kōmeitō's standard response to ethical malfeasance on the part of its coalition partner. Kōmeitō's manifesto promise to "make clean politics happen," however, did not mention the LDP and stopped short of structurally transformative proposals, such as abolishing political donations by corporations or other significant means of addressing the funding scandals that afflicted the LDP from late 2023. Instead, Kōmeitō called for an independent third-party institution to annually assess political funds and to focus on "policy activities expenses" (*seisaku katsudō hi*). It also proposed that this institution take measures against "undignified" posters and campaign announcements, seemingly in response to concerns about electoral upheavals propelled by populist shifts (Umeda 2025).

The contentious issue of constitutional reform lost prominence with Abe's death, so much so that in 2024 Kōmeitō deleted discussion of this issue from the manifesto version the party used for street campaigning. Voters had to look to the 55-page-long version online and turn to the last two pages to find the party's reasoning for "adding to the constitution" (*kaken*) rather than changing existing constitutional language (Kōmeitō 2024). Even in this section, they would not find a clear statement on longstanding concerns about acknowledging the legality of Japan's Self-Defense Forces. Kōmeitō's proposals for constitutional additions were limited to provisions for emergency situations, adaptations to the risks of digital technology for democratic processes, and regulations for referenda. Notably, there was a proposal to add a constitutional obligation to conserve the global environment for future generations. In a party system in which campaigning for environmental protection is relegated to opposition parties on the left, Kōmeitō stands out for its proposals for this mostly untouched policy field.

Kōmeitō Voter Concerns with LDP Malfeasance

In October 2024, Kōmeitō faced the dilemma of convincing its supporters to get out the vote for a partner that had funneled millions of yen into untaxed slush funds. Kōmeitō faced heightened pressure in this regard, given that it relies on Sōka Gakkai's Women's Division, whose members have urged Kōmeitō to oust candidates who gained notoriety for improper behavior. For example, Kōmeitō up-and-comer Tōyama Kiyohiko lost Sōka Gakkai support after he was found to have visited night clubs with LDP colleagues in February 2021 at the height of COVID-era restrictions. He was forced to resign following tabloid attention and public outcry (Klein and McLaughlin 2022a). Given unwillingness on the part of Kōmeitō's base to tolerate unethical activities, it is unsurprising that the party's vote-gatherers were dismayed by the task of supporting LDP candidates caught up in the slush fund scandals. Our interviews with rank-and-file Gakkai members indicate that the LDP's money scandals have long put a strain on the relationship between Kōmeitō's voter base and its senior coalition partner. In 2024, Kōmeitō supporter anger about the LDP was palpable in its manifesto: "Kōmeitō is leading the debate on restoring trust in politics while confronting the anger and suspicion of the people head-on. Only Kōmeitō, with its spirit of standing with the masses, can correct Japanese politics" (Kōmeitō 2024: 2). It seems certain that the LDP's way of handling its financial misbehavior put downward pressure on Gakkai member willingness to support the coalition. Not for the first time, the LDP became a burden for Kōmeitō's electoral ambitions.

Election Results

Kōmeitō ran 11 candidates in SMDs and 39 on its party lists. Of those 50 politicians, 24 secured a seat, down from 31 in 2021. Four SMDs marked the second-lowest Kōmeitō SMD seat count since the start of the coalition in 1999 (see Fig. 5.1). The 2024 general election saw the number of SMD votes drop from 872,631 (2021) to 738,215 (2024), even though Kōmeitō ran two more SMD candidates than in 2021. The outcome of the PR tier confirmed a substantial loss of voter support for Kōmeitō. At 5.96 million votes, down 16% from 2021, this was the lowest number Kōmeitō had scored since the current electoral system was introduced in 1994. As Fig. 5.2 shows, the party has seen its total PR votes drop by one third over the last 20 years, from its highest of almost nine million in 2005 to just under six million in 2024.

The most prominent SMD loss was that of Ishii Kei'ichi. In previous elections, Ishii had won his seat in the North Kantō PR Bloc. In 2023, he moved to Saitama 14 as one outcome of the negotiations with the LDP regarding who would get to run in redesigned SMDs. Previously, Liberal Democrat Mitsubayashi Hiromi had held the Saitama 14 district, but because of his involvement in the LDP slush fund scandal, he was not formally endorsed by his party and moved to Saitama 13, where he lost his race to a DPP candidate. Even though forecasts based on previous election results seemed to give Ishii a substantial chance to win his SMD, more than half of the LDP voters in the district abandoned him in 2024, according to an *Asahi* exit poll (*Asahi Shinbun*, Saitama edition, 1 December 2024). As in Hiroshima 3, where LDP headquarters had given in to Kōmeitō's demand to endorse one of their candidates, local LDP chapters and supporters demanded instead that a new Liberal Democrat should be nominated. When this demand was not met, many LDP supporters did not follow their party's recommendation to vote for

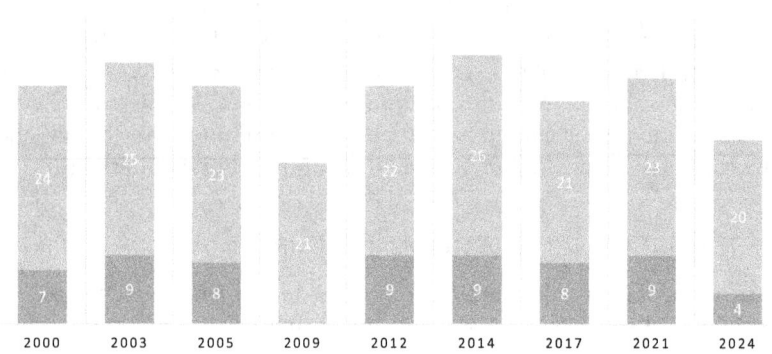

Fig. 5.1 Kōmeitō PR & SMD seats, 2000–2024

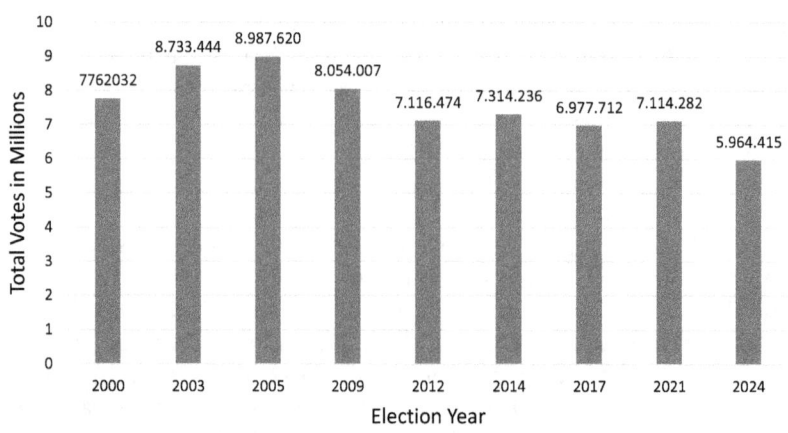

Fig. 5.2 Komeito PR votes in general elections, 2000–2024

the Kōmeitō SMD candidate. In Saitama 14, 25% of the LDP's supporters voted for Ishii's CDP competitor, who had previously served as a prefectural assembly member for the LDP (*Asahi Shinbun*, Saitama edition, 2 December 2024).

Another consequential outcome of the election was the result in Osaka. This area of western Japan is known within Sōka Gakkai as *jōshō Kansai*, "ever-victorious Kansai," and it was home to 1.15 million Kōmeitō PR voters in 2021. A primary cause of Kōmeitō's total defeat in four Osaka SMDs was Ishin. While Ishin lost seats overall in October 2024, it maintained its electoral strength in its Osaka home base. Had Kōmeitō secured anything close to its 2021 SMD results, it would have defeated all Ishin competitors in the region. The large number of LDP voters who abandoned Kōmeitō, however, denied the party any chance of success. While district-wide Kōmeitō support as measured in PR votes in Osaka fell by only 12%, the four Kōmeitō SMD candidates lost an average of 33.2% of their 2021 support (see Fig. 5.3), even though Kōmeitō lost fewer votes than Ishin lost nationally compared to 2021. In 2024, this number fell by 125,359, or a loss of 12%. At the same time, Ishin lost one-third of its 3.2 million PR votes from 2021 and ended up with 2.07 million votes in 2024. As was also confirmed by the Ishii defeat in Saitama, Kōmeitō's Osaka SMD results showed that, even in its stronghold, Kōmeitō candidates require LDP voter support to win in SMDs.

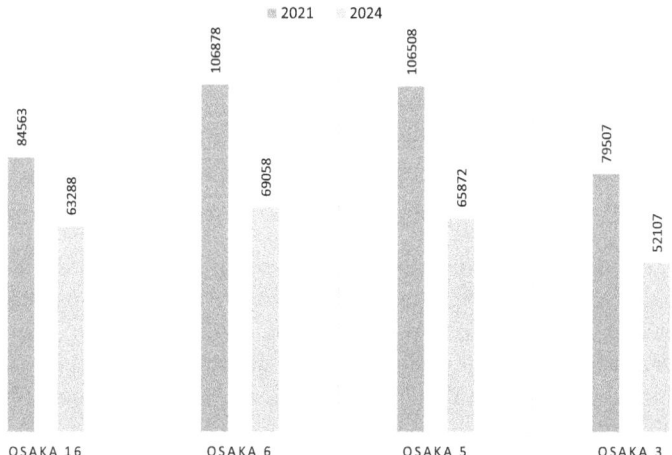

Fig. 5.3 SMD results for Kōmeitō in Osaka

Ishii's electoral failure served as proof of the danger of Kōmeitō's decision not to allow dual SMD and PR candidacies, a strategy that virtually guarantees party leaders a seat in parliament in other democracies with similar electoral systems. Minister of Land and Infrastructure Saitō Tetsuo was formally named party leader at an extraordinary party convention in early November 2024. He was 72 years old, older than Yamaguchi Natsuo was when he announced the need for a new generation to take the helm at Kōmeitō. Saitō's ascent reflected the fact that many of Kōmeitō's middle-tier hopefuls had lost their seats, deferring aspirations for generational change at the top of the party.

Conclusion: Kōmeitō's Enduring Strength

Despite the steep downward trend in its vote counts and election results, Kōmeitō, through its Sōka Gakkai base, remains capable of mobilizing millions of voters, and it remains Japan's most powerful organized voting bloc. Consequently, Kōmeitō is still a political force to be reckoned with. Despite its losses in the Lower House, the October 2024 electoral results may in fact have an upside for Kōmeitō. Having lost many more seats than its junior coalition partner and heading a minority government that requires multiparty agreement to pass budgets and new legislation, the LDP is potentially more dependent on Kōmeitō now than before. Negotiations with opposition parties from within the minority government provide Kōmeitō with new tactical options. Since some of its policy proposals are closer to those of opposition parties than those put forward by the LDP, Kōmeitō can form policy alliances with opposition parties and bring their parliamentary strength to the coalition table. Saitō himself commented on this situation after the election, saying that Kōmeitō was now more than just a brake on hawkish LDP policies (*Asahi Shinbun*, 19 November 2024).

It does appear as if Kōmeitō's leadership remains focused on transferring power to a new generation. After Saitō was selected as party leader, the party's homepage featured a picture of Taketani Toshiko, Kōmeitō's 55-year-old female deputy leader. This is perhaps an indication of how generational change may look in a party that depends on the commitment of women supporters.

REFERENCES

Carlson, Matthew M. 2025. "Scandals During the Kishida Administration." In *Japan Decides 2024: The Japanese General Election*, edited by Kenneth Mori McElwain, Robert J. Pekkanen, and Daniel M. Smith, 217–233. New York: Palgrave Macmillan.

Gaitanidis, Ioannis. 2024. "How Consumer Law in Japan Shapes Religion: 'Spiritual Sales' as a Legal Category. *Asia-Pacific Journal: Japan Focus* 22 (10): 3. https://apjjf.org/2024/10/gaitanidis

Kantei [Prime Minister of Japan and His Cabinet]. 2025. *The Constitution of Japan*. (https://japan.kantei.go.jp/constitution_and_government_of_japan/constitution_e.html).

Klein, Axel. 2012. "Twice Bitten, Once Shy. Religious Organizations and Politics after the Aum Attacks." *Japanese Journal of Religious Studies* 39 (1): 105–126.

Klein, Axel. 2023. "Kōmeitō and the Fallout of the Abe Assassination." criticalasianstudies.org Commentary Board, January 27, 2023; https://criticalasianstudies.org/commentary/2023/1/26/commentary-axel-klein-kmeit-and-the-fallout-of-the-abe-assassination?rq=Kōmeitō

Klein, Axel and Levi McLaughlin. 2022a. "Kōmeitō in 2021: Strategizing Between the LDP and Sōka Gakkai." In *Japan Decides 2021: The Japanese General Election*, edited by Robert J. Pekkanen, Steven R. Reed, and Daniel M. Smith, 71–85. New York: Palgrave Macmillan.

Klein, Axel and Levi McLaughlin. 2022b. "Kōmeitō: The Party and Its Place in Japanese Politics." In *The Oxford Handbook of Japanese Politics*, edited by Robert J. Pekkanen and Saadia M. Pekkanen, 201–222. Oxford: Oxford University Press.

Kōmeitō. 2024. *Kibō no mirai wa, jitsugen dekiru* [A desired future can be realized]. Party manifesto for the 2024 general election. (www.komei.or.jp/download/p372109/).

Maeda, Yukio. 2025. "Public Opinion and Scandals in Economic Hard Times." In *Japan Decides 2024: The Japanese General Election*, edited by Kenneth M. McElwain, Robert J. Pekkanen, and Daniel M. Smith, 163–179. New York: Palgrave Macmillan.

Matsumoto, Tomoko. 2025. "How Party Manifestos Framed Political Distrust in the 2024 Election." In *Japan Decides 2024: The Japanese General Election*, edited by Kenneth M. McElwain, Robert J. Pekkanen, and Daniel M. Smith, 143–161. New York: Palgrave Macmillan.

McLaughlin, Levi. 2012. "Did Aum Change Everything? What Sōka Gakkai Before, During, and After the Aum Shinrikyo Affair Tells Us About the Persistent "Otherness" of New Religions in Japan." *Japanese Journal of Religious Studies* 39 (1): 51–75.

McLaughlin, Levi. 2023. The Abe Assassination and Japan's Nexus of Religion and Politics. *Current History* 122 (845): 209–216.

McLaughlin, Levi. 2025. "Perennial Fears, Novel Responses: The Unification Church in Japan after the Abe Assassination." In *Japan Decides 2024: The Japanese General Election*, edited by Kenneth M. McElwain, Robert J. Pekkanen, and Daniel M. Smith, 235–253. New York: Palgrave Macmillan.

Nakano Jun. 2016. *Kōmeitō no kenkyū* [Kōmeitō research]. Tokyo, Iwanami Shoten.

Smith, Daniel M. 2014. "Party Ideals and Practical Constraints in Kōmeitō Candidate Nominations." In *Kōmeitō: Politics and Religion in Japan*, edited by George Ehrhardt, Axel Klein, Levi McLaughlin, and Steven R. Reed, 139–162. Berkeley, CA: Institute of East Asian Studies.

Sohn, Sukeui. 2024. "Between Appeasement and Accommodation: Kōmeitō's Policy Influence under Second Abe Administration." *Journal of East Asian Studies* 24: 197–220.

Stausberg, Michael, Alexander Van Der Haven, and Erica Baffelli. 2023. "Religious Minorities: Conceptual Perspectives." *Religious Minorities Online*, De Gruyter. https://www.degruyter.com/database/RMO/entry/rmo.2338 9320/html.

Umeda, Michio. 2025. "Electoral Campaigns in Japan's 2024 HR Election: Emerging Signs of Transformation." In *Japan Decides 2024: The Japanese General Election*, edited by Kenneth M. McElwain, Robert J. Pekkanen, and Daniel M. Smith, 109–124. New York: Palgrave Macmillan.

CHAPTER 6

Why Did Public Support for the Japan Innovation Party Decline in the 2024 HR Election?

Masahiro Zenkyo

The Japan Innovation Party (hereafter, Ishin) experienced a notable decline in proportional representation (PR) votes in the 2024 House of Representatives (HR) election despite obtaining a considerable number of PR votes in the 2021 HR election and the 2022 House of Councilors (HC) election. In the 2022 election, the Ishin achieved substantial voter support, with its proportional vote total surpassing that of the Constitutional Democratic Party of Japan (CDP)—the largest opposition party. Furthermore, in the unified local elections held in April 2023, numerous local assembly members endorsed by the Ishin secured seats. Although Ishin consistently expanded its political influence following the

Supplementary Information The online version contains supplementary material available at https://doi.org/10.1007/978-3-031-98797-7_6.

M. Zenkyo (✉)
Kwansei Gakuin University, Nishinomiya, Japan
e-mail: masahirozenkyo@kwansei.ac.jp

Table 6.1 Changes in Ishin's PR vote share in the 2021 and 2024 elections

PR block	2021 HR election			2024 HR election		
	N. of votes	Vote share (%)	Δ2021–2017 (in % points)	N. of votes	Vote share (%)	Δ2024–2021 (in % points)
Hokkaido	215,344	8.4	5.6	96,954	4.0	− 4.4
Tohoku	258,690	6.3	3.3	165,694	4.4	− 1.9
Kitakanto	617,531	10.0	6.6	391,136	6.7	− 3.3
Minamikanto	863,897	11.7	7.8	536,161	7.5	− 4.2
Tokyo	858,577	13.3	10.0	516,610	8.1	− 5.2
Hokuriku	361,476	10.3	5.7	228,617	7.0	− 3.3
Tokai	694,630	10.3	5.9	427,368	6.6	− 3.7
Kansai[Kinki]	3,180,219	33.9	15.6	2,069,796	23.3	− 10.6
Chugoku	286,302	9.2	4.5	187,517	6.4	− 2.8
Shikoku	173,826	10.2	5.3	103,237	6.7	− 3.5
Kyushu	540,338	8.6	4.3	382,034	6.5	− 2.1

2021 election, as summarized in Table 6.1, the party was unable to sustain this growth in the 2024 election. In contrast, the CDP—which maintained consistent criticism of financial scandals involving the Liberal Democratic Party (LDP)—and the Democratic Party for the People (DPP)—which prioritized policies advocating income growth for working people—increased their presence.

Why did many people who voted for Ishin in the 2021 and 2022 elections withdraw their support from the party in the 2024 election? In this election, the number of seats held by the LDP also declined compared to the 2021 election. This reduction stemmed from the LDP's repeated failure to address financial scandals and the "20 million yen" problem that emerged during the campaign (Carlson 2025; Nemoto 2025). In other words, many voters chose not to support the LDP because they viewed the issues related to "money and politics" as a pressing concern that required a resolution. In this context, Ishin's failure to gain voter support in the 2024 election raises a question. This is because Ishin has consistently maintained a strict stance on financial scandals, as symbolized by "Painful Reform (*Mi wo kiru kaikaku*)." Nevertheless, Ishin's vote count declined significantly in the 2024 election.

The decline in support for Ishin in the 2024 election cannot be attributed to a change in its policies or a liberal-conservative ideological stance. Iida (2023) provides empirical evidence to support the argument that the combination of (1) dissatisfaction with the LDP and (2) Ishin's conservative stance on constitutional revision contributed to its significant nationwide growth. However, Ishin's substantial loss of support cannot be explained by the change in its ideological stance because it maintained its pro-constitutional revision stance during the 2024 election (Taniguchi et al. 2025). In fact, Ishin's eight core policies (*Ishin-hassaku*) for the 2024 election explicitly declared its intention to "lead discussions on constitutional revision." Despite maintaining its ideological stance, Ishin experienced a significant decline in support.

This study focuses on evaluating party competence instead of the party's policy or ideological stance. Party competence reputation is an important determinant of voters' attitudes and behavior (Petitpas 2024; Petrocik 1996). Previous studies have demonstrated that the ownership strength of important issues (Dahlberg and Martinsson 2015; De Bruycker and Walgrave 2013), ideological positions (Johns and Kölln 2020; Stiers and Dassonneville 2024), the history of policy implementation (Bélanger and Meguid 2008; Petrocik 1996), and party size and status (Stiers and Dassonneville 2024) affect the evaluation of party competence. Additionally, this study assumes that inconsistent decision-making behavior also affects the evaluation of party competence. During the deliberations in the Japanese National Diet in 2024, Ishin exhibited inconsistent behavior because of the inadequate administrative competence of Baba Nobuyuki, the Ishin's party leader. This inconsistent behavior likely led to a decline in the evaluation of Ishin's competence as a political party, which in turn resulted in decreased support for the Ishin in the 2024 election.

In this chapter, I examine whether the evaluations of Ishin's leader or its party competence relate to support for the party or voting behavior in the 2024 election through two studies. The context for this was Ishin's inconsistent behavior during the amendment of the Political Funds Control Act (PFCA), which I explain in the next section. In the first study (Study 1), I analyze using an online survey of eligible voters who resided in the Osaka Prefecture before the 2024 election. I examine the relationship between evaluations of Baba and support for the Ishin, comparing it with the regional party that forms the basis of support for Ishin—Osaka Ishin no Kai (hereafter, Osaka Ishin). In the second study (Study 2), I examine the relationship between the evaluation of Ishin's competence and voting behavior in the 2024 election using a nationwide panel survey conducted before and after the 2024 election. Specifically, I analyze whether the evaluation of Ishin's party competence significantly affected continued voting for the party in the PR district in the 2024 election.

Inconsistent Decisions in Ishin: A Case of the 2024 Amendment to the Political Funds Control Act

The inadequate governing capability of Ishin has been highlighted by various problems, such as repeated scandals involving its members and the disarray surrounding its response to the scandal involving Saitō Motohiko, who serves as the Hyogo Prefectural Governor and was endorsed by Ishin in the 2021 Hyogo Prefectural election. The confusion within Ishin regarding the revision of the PFCA, which began around May 2024, was the most prominent example of the shortcomings of the Ishin's governability. During the PFCA revision process, Ishin exhibited contradictory behavior by supporting the bill in the HR while opposing it in the HC. Not only did the scandals, but also Ishin's decision to adopt such a contradictory stance, lead to a decline in its support.

In November 2023, it was revealed that a member of the LDP had received kickbacks from income generated through party ticket sales within the faction but failed to disclose this in the political funds report. This case was widely reported in the media as the "Illegal Funds Scandal," drawing widespread criticism. In response, the LDP and other political parties proposed amendments to the PFCA and submitted them to the National Diet. Three amendment proposals emerged: (a) the LDP's proposal, (b) a joint proposal by the CDP and the DPP, and (c) Ishin's proposal. On May 22, 2024, the House of Representatives' Special Committee on Political Reform formally initiated deliberations on the revisions.

The LDP encountered significant challenges regarding the amendment of the PFCA. While the LDP held a single-party majority in the HR, it lacked a majority in the HC. Thus, it was essential to secure the cooperation of Kōmeitō—its LDP coalition partner—to pass the bill. However, disagreements over several points—such as those related to disclosure standards for party-ticket purchasers—led to a deadlock with Kōmeitō. Consequently, the LDP sought support from Ishin to amend the PFCA. Ishin expressed its willingness to support the LDP's proposal on the condition that the LDP accepted the following terms: (a) imposing a cap on policy activity expenses, (b) ensuring the publication of receipts for such expenses after ten years, and (c) initiating discussions on the reform of "research, public relations, and accommodation allowances (*Chōsa-Kenkyu-Kōhō-Taizai-Hi*)." On May 31, 2024, the leaders of both the LDP and the JIP signed an agreement to formalize these terms. During a press conference following this agreement, Baba declared the party's commitment to supporting the LDP's amendment, while acknowledging the need for further discussions on specific details. Subsequently, on June 6, 2024, the HR passed the LDP's proposed amendments with support from the LDP, Ishin, and other parties.

However, Ishin took the unprecedented step of opposing the same amendment that it had agreed to in the HR when the House of Councilors' Special Committee on Political Reform convened on June 18, 2024. This reversal resulted from the LDP's decision to shelve passing legislation aimed at disclosing the use of research, public relations, and accommodation allowances during that Diet session. Ishin's leader, Baba, insisted that passing the legislation during that session had been an implicit condition of their agreement on the amendment of the PFCA. In response, the LDP maintained that the agreement did not specify explicit deadlines. Furthermore, it continued to provide vague answers concerning the establishment of an independent body to monitor such funds. Baba argued that the reversal decision regarding the amendment of the PFCA could be justified by these ambiguous responses from the LDP.[1]

Although Baba attempted to justify his contradictory decision, the inconsistent decision-making within Ishin likely raised doubts among voters regarding Ishin's competence as a political party. In fact, the support rate for Ishin declined after the party made an inconsistent decision regarding the amendment to the PFCA. As shown in Fig. 6.1, the results of the monthly public opinion polls conducted by Asahi, NHK, Nikkei, and Yomiuri from January to November 2024 revealed a decline in the average support rate for Ishin after June. This result implies that declining evaluations of Ishin's competence as a party—stemming from Baba's inconsistent decisions—contributed to the erosion of public support for Ishin and resulted in its major defeat in the 2024 election.

---

[1] *Asahi Shinbun*, June 8, 2024. "Otona no yakusoku, kodomo no kenka" https://digital.asahi.com/articles/ASS6Q4RPSS6QUTFK01WM.html (accessed January 15, 2025).

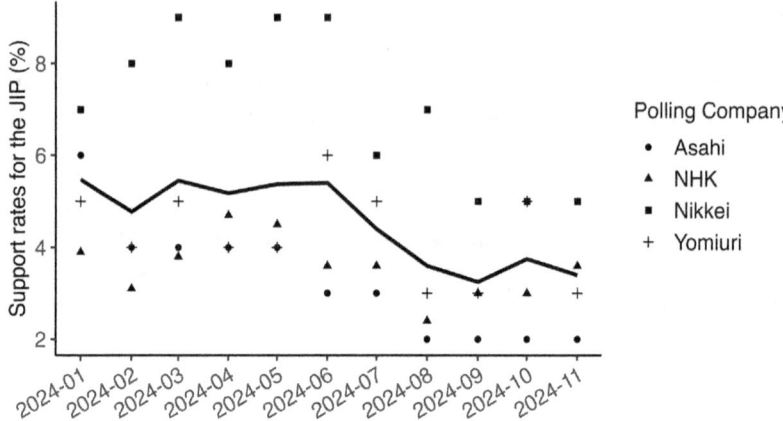

Fig. 6.1 The changes in support rates for Ishin in 2024

Study 1: Relationship Between Baba and Ishin Evaluations

Hypothesis

In this section, I examine the relationship between the evaluation of Baba and support for Ishin. The party leader is assumed to be responsible for decision-making, especially in a centralized party like Ishin. Thus, if the decline in support for Ishin in the 2024 election was caused by a deterioration in the party's reputation for competence, a significant correlation would be expected between the evaluation of Baba and support for Ishin. Conversely, if the correlation is insignificant, the decline in support for Ishin may be caused by other factors.

The strength of the correlation between evaluations of Baba and support for the Ishin is reinforced by comparing it to the association with support for Osaka Ishin. As shown in Table 6.1, the proportional share of votes for the Ishin in the Kansai region is exceptionally high, because Osaka Ishin enjoys strong support among a large number of voters in the Osaka Prefecture (Zenkyo 2018).[2] However, Osaka Ishin is not merely a subordinate branch of Ishin, but an independent political association with its own decision-making authority. In fact, the leader of Osaka Ishin is not

---

[2] Osaka Prefecture is one of the prefectures comprising the Kansai region.

Baba but Yoshimura Hirofumi, who has held the position of Governor of Osaka Prefecture since 2019. Even among voters in Osaka, evaluations of Ishin have been distinguished from those of Osaka Ishin (Zenkyo 2021). These facts suggest that the evaluation of Baba would have a stronger relationship with support for Ishin than with support for Osaka Ishin. The hypotheses examined in Study 1 are as follows:

H_1 The correlation between evaluations of Baba and Ishin would be positive and statistically significant, even when controlling for other covariates.

H_2 The correlation between evaluations of Baba and Ishin would be stronger than that between evaluations of Baba and Osaka Ishin.

Data and Method

To test the hypotheses, I used an online survey conducted between September 30 and October 4 on eligible voters who live in four electoral districts within the Osaka Prefecture (Electoral Districts 3, 5, 16, and 17) before the 2024 election.[3] Survey respondents for this survey were recruited from Rakuten Insight's online panel. The quota sampling method was used to match the marginal distribution of the sample by sex (male and female) and age categories (18–29, 30–39, 40–49, 50–59, and 60+) with that of the 2020 census. The total number of valid respondents, excluding survey satisficers,[4] was 1,557.

This survey included questions about attitudes toward major political parties (and Osaka Ishin) and their leaders using a feeling thermometer scale with options ranging from a minimum of 0 to a maximum of 100. Feelings toward Baba were operationalized as the evaluations of Baba, and feelings toward Ishin and Osaka Ishin were operationalized as support for these political entities. Furthermore, this survey measured covariate variables such as self-perceived position on liberal/conservative ideology, feelings toward Yoshimura, and the demographic characteristics of all

---

[3] The approval number of this survey by the Kwansei Gakuin University Institutional Review Board for Behavioral Research with Human Participants is 2024-40.

[4] This survey included a question instructing respondents to choose "Somewhat agree" for this item. Respondents who chose options other than "Somewhat agree" for this question were identified as survey satisficers and excluded from the analysis.

respondents. The descriptive statistics of these variables are summarized in Table A.1 in the Online Appendix.[5]

I estimated OLS regressions to examine the correlation between the evaluations of Baba and support for Ishin based on the following model:

$$Support_{ik} = \alpha_k + \beta_k Baba_i + \sum_{j=1}^{J} \gamma_{jk} Z_{ij} + \epsilon_{ik}, k \in \{Ishin, Osaka\},$$

where the subscript i denotes an observational unit, specifically an individual. The subscript j represents the covariate, and $k$identifies the target, either support for Ishin or Osaka Ishin. $Support_{ik}$ is the dependent variable, α_k is the intercept, β_k is the coefficient for the variable of interest—Baba's evaluation. Z_{ij} includes covariates such as the evaluation of Yoshimura, ideology, and demographic characteristics, and γ_{jk} denotes the coefficient corresponding to Z_{ij}. ϵ_{ik} is the error term. The dependent variables, intercepts, coefficients, and error terms depend on the target, k.

Results

Figure 6.2 shows the estimated correlations between the evaluations of Baba and support for both Ishin and Osaka Ishin. The left panel displays the estimation results when the dependent variable is $Support_{Ishin}$, whereas the right panel shows the results when the dependent variable is $Support_{Osaka}$. The circles in the figure represent the βIshin and $β_{Osaka}$ point estimates, and the horizontal lines indicate their 95% and 99% confidence intervals, respectively. Thinner outer lines represent the 99% confidence intervals, whereas thicker inner lines are the 95% confidence intervals. All the estimates were controlled for as the covariates. The details of the estimated results are summarized in Table B.1 in the Online Appendix.

The left panel in Fig. 6.2 demonstrates that the $β_{Ishin}$ is positive and statistically significant at the 1% level, even when controlling for the covariates. The expected value of $β_{Ishin}$ is 0.298 (SE = 0.028), and the horizontal bars do not overlap the dashed line at 0. These results support

---

[5] Online Appendix of this chapter can be accessed as supplementary material to this book and additionally via the URL on OSF (https://osf.io/k73eh).

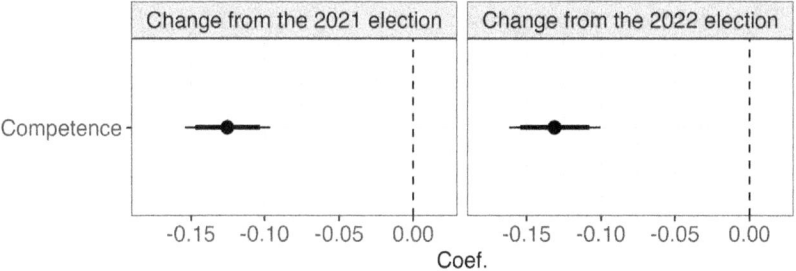

Fig. 6.2 Evaluations of Baba and support for both Ishin and Osaka Ishin

Hypothesis 1. Furthermore, in the model where support for Osaka Ishin is the dependent variable, the $β_{Osaka}$ is also positive and significant at the 1% level. While the difference in these coefficients for the evaluations of Baba is not statistically significant,[6] the point estimate for $β_{Ishin}$ is larger than that for $β_{Osaka}$. These findings are consistent with These findings are consistent with Hypothesis 2.

To examine the robustness of these findings, I conducted the following additional analyses.[7] First, $β_k$ were re-estimated using data with imputed missing values. As the feeling thermometers included many missing values, excluding respondents who did not report feelings toward parties or their leaders from the data may have introduced biased results. However, the estimated results using data sets with imputed missing values showed that $β_{Ishin}$ was estimated at 0.288 (SE = 0.029) and $β_{Osaka}$ at 0.252 (SE = 0.028). The results using imputed data sets further demonstrated that $β_{Ishin}$ was statistically significant and larger than $β_{Osaka}$.

Second, $β_{Ishin}$ was estimated based on a different model including support for Osaka Ishin as a covariate. If the results of $β_{Ishin} > 0$ were observed after controlling for a variable strongly correlated with support for Ishin, the correlation between evaluations of Baba and support for the

---

[6] The estimated difference between Ishin and Osaka by bootstrapping (the number of resamples is 2,000) was 0.040 (SE = 0.035). Although this result shows that there is not a statistically significant difference between these coefficients, this does not mean that Hypothesis 2 should be rejected.

[7] The details of the estimated results of the additional analyses in Study 1 are summarized in Tables B.2 and B.3 in the Online Appendix.

Ishin could be considered robust. The result of this additional analysis showed a significant relationship between these variables; the point estimate of β_{Ishin} was 0.138 (SE = 0.025). Although this estimated value was slightly smaller than that shown in Fig. 6.2, it remains statistically significant at the 1% level.

STUDY 2: PARTY COMPETENCE EVALUATION AND VOTING CHOICE IN THE 2024 ELECTION

Hypothesis

In this section, I examine the relationship between evaluations of Ishin's competence and changes in voting behavior from the 2021 and 2022 elections to the 2024 election. This chapter focuses on the reasons for the decline in Ishin's vote share in the 2024 election. It is assumed that this would be caused by a declining reputation for Ishin's competence due to its inconsistent decision-making and behavior. Thus, Study 2 investigates attitudinal or behavioral changes from past elections rather than the determinants of voting for Ishin in the 2024 election.

The hypothesis for Study 2 is:

H_3 Voters with negative evaluations of Ishin's competence are likely to switch their choice from Ishin to another party or abstain in the 2024 election.

Data and Method

To test this hypothesis, I used an online panel survey that was conducted before and after the 2024 election in Study 2.[8] The pre-election survey was conducted between October 9 and October 22, and the post-election survey was conducted between October 28 and November 1. Survey respondents for the pre-election survey were recruited from Rakuten Insights' online panel. The quota sampling method was used to match the marginal distribution of the sample by sex (male and female), age categories (18–29, 30–39, 40–49, 50–59, and 60+), and regional block (Hokkaido and Tohoku, Kanto, Hokuriku and Chubu, Kansai, Chugoku

---

[8] The approval number of this survey by the Institutional Review Board of Osaka School of International Public Policy at Osaka University is R61001-1.

and Shikoku, and Kyushu) with that of the 2020 census. Additionally, to ensure adequate representation across electoral districts, an upper limit of 120 respondents was set for each electoral district. Respondents for the post-election survey were recruited from the valid respondents of the pre-election survey, excluding those identified as survey satisficers, as well as the data used in Study 1. There were 28,949 valid respondents in the pre-election survey and 23,303 in the post-election survey. The response rate to the post-election survey was approximately 80.5%.

The panel survey included questions regarding voting choices in the 2024 and previous elections. Survey respondents were asked about voting choice in PR districts for both the 2021 and 2022 elections in the pre-election survey, and their choice in PR districts for the 2024 election in the post-election survey. I created two variables that measured the changes in voting choice from past elections by combining voting choice in the 2024 election with those in other national elections, namely $Choice_{2021HR}$ and $Choice_{2022UH}$. Both variables take the value of 1 if a respondent voted for Ishin in a past and the 2024 elections, and 0 if a respondent voted for Ishin in a past election but switched to another party or abstained from voting in the 2024 election. Thus, $Choice_{2021HR}$ indicates changes in voting choices from the 2021 election, and $Choice_{2022UH}$ indicates changes from the 2022 election. The descriptive statistics of these variables are summarized in Table A.2 in the Online Appendix. In the post-election survey, the questions designed to measure the governing competence (*Seiken tantō nōryoku*) of major political parties on a scale from "Low (1)" to "High (5)" were included. I used the evaluation of Ishin's governing competence as a proxy variable for the evaluation of Ishin's competence. Feelings toward the CDP and the DPP, self-perceived positions on liberal/conservative ideology, and demographic characteristics were also included in the estimation model as covariates.

I estimated OLS regressions to examine the correlation between evaluations of Ishin's competence and changes in voting choice in the 2024 election based on the following model:

$$Choice_{ik} = \alpha_k + \beta_k Competence_i + \sum_{j=1}^{J} \gamma_{jk} Z_{ij} + \epsilon_{ik}, k \in \{2021HR, 2022UH\},$$

where the subscript i denotes an observational unit, specifically an individual. The subscript j represents the covariate, and k identifies the target, either the change from the 2021 election or from the 2022 election.

$Choice_{ik}$ is the dependent variable, α_k is the intercept, and β_k is the coefficient for the variable of interest—the evaluations of Ishin's competence. Z_{ij} includes covariates such as feelings toward the CDP and the DPP, ideology, and demographic characteristics, and γ_{jk} denotes the coefficient associated with Z_{ij}. ϵ_{ik} is the error term. The dependent variables, intercepts, coefficients, and error terms depend on the target, k.

Results

Figure 6.3 shows the estimated correlations between the evaluations of Ishin's competence and change in voting choice from Ishin to another party or abstained from voting in the 2024 election. The left panel displays the estimation results when the dependent variable is $Choice_{2021HR}$, while the right panel shows the results when the dependent variable is $Choice_{2022UH}$. The circles in the figure represent the β_{2021HR} and β_{2022UH} point estimates, and the horizontal lines indicate their 95% and 99% confidence intervals. The thinner outer lines are the 99% confidence intervals, while the thicker inner lines are the 95% confidence intervals. All these estimates are controlled for covariates. The details of the estimated results are summarized in Table C.1 of the Online Appendix.

Both the estimated coefficients in Fig. 6.3 are negative and statistically significant at the 1% level; thus, these findings support Hypothesis 3. The point estimate of the coefficient associated with the evaluation of Ishin's competence for $Choice_{2021HR}$ was -0.0125 (SE $= 0.011$), and that for $Choice_{2022UH}$ was -0.131 (SE $= 0.012$). These results suggest

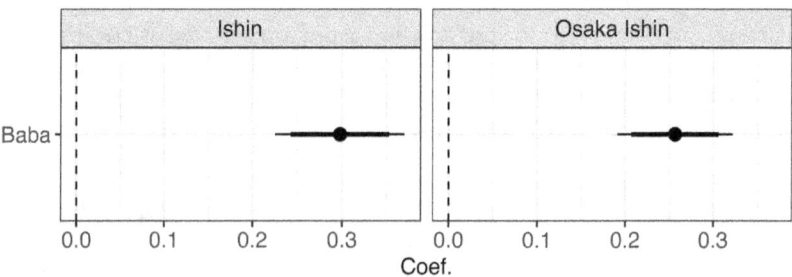

Fig. 6.3 Evaluations of Ishin's competence and voting shifts in the 2024 election

that those with a low evaluation of Ishin's competence were more likely to change their voting choices from Ishin to another party or abstain from voting in the 2024 election. Based on the estimation results, when the evaluation of governing competence decreases from the maximum value (=5) to the minimum value (=1), the probability of voters switching their votes from Ishin to another party, or abstaining, is estimated to increase by approximately 50%, regardless of whether the reference point was the voting choice in the 2021 or the 2022 elections. These findings suggest a strong relationship between evaluations of Ishin's competence and changes in voting behavior in the 2024 election.

I conducted two additional analyses to examine the robustness of the estimation results.[9] First, I examined whether the difference in evaluations of governing competence of Ishin between respondents who continued to vote for Ishin and those who did not was larger than those for other parties. For the evaluations of governing competence of major parties, excluding Kōmeitō, statistically significant differences were observed between consistent Ishin voters and others. However, the difference in the evaluations of Ishin's competence was the largest. Second, I conducted a further analysis, replacing the variable of interest from the evaluations of Ishin's competence with feelings toward Baba (0 to 10). As suggested by the results of Study 1, evaluations of the party leaders are assumed to be important determinants of party competence. Therefore, it is expected that evaluations of Baba would also strongly correlate with changes in voting behavior. The results of the additional re-analyses showed that β_{2021HR} was -0.077 (SE $= 0.006$) and β_{2022UH} was -0.082 (SE $= 0.006$). Both results indicate that lower evaluations of Baba are associated with a stronger tendency to switch votes from Ishin to another party, which is consistent with the findings shown in Fig. 6.3.

CONCLUSION

This chapter investigates the reason of Ishin's defeat in the 2024 election through empirical analyses based on two online surveys. Study 1 showed that evaluations of Baba were closely related to support for Ishin, even when controlling for its relationship with support for Osaka Ishin. Additionally, Study 2 demonstrated that evaluations of Ishin's competence and

---

[9] The details of the estimated results of the additional analyses in Study 2 are summarized in Tables C.2 and C.3 of the Online Appendix.

Baba were strongly associated with whether individuals who voted for Ishin in past national elections continued to do so in the 2024 election. The evaluations of Baba were relatively low, which led to lower evaluations of Ishin's competence reputation. The estimated results in this chapter do not rigorously demonstrate causal relationships; this chapter specifically focuses on the correlations between Ishin's competence reputation and voters' choices in the 2024 election. However, the findings from Studies 1 and 2 clearly suggest that the decline in evaluations of Ishin's party competence was likely the primary cause of its defeat in the 2024 election.

The findings of this chapter provide significant implications for the future of Ishin. Even if its leader is replaced, there is limited potential for an increase in support for Ishin unless its governing competence improves. Following Ishin's significant defeat in the 2024 election, Baba announced his intention to resign. Through Ishin's leadership election, Yoshimura was elected as the new leader of Ishin on December 1, 2024. However, support for Ishin is unlikely to recover unless the party's reputation for governing competence improves. Currently, Yoshimura has not implemented reforms substantial enough to enhance voters' evaluations of its competence. Unless Ishin enhances its competence, the level of voter support is likely to remain low.

This study has several limitations, and the determinants of support for Ishin should be further examined through more comprehensive and rigorous studies. One notable limitation is that this study assumes that inconsistent decision-making or behavior by Ishin leads to a decline in evaluations of its party competence. However, this assumption has not yet been empirically validated. Survey experiments to estimate the causal effects of inconsistent party decision-making on evaluations of Ishin's competence could strengthen the validity of these findings.

References

Bélanger, Éric., and Bonnie M. Meguid. 2008. "Issue Salience, Issue Ownership, and Issue-based Vote Choice." *Electoral Studies* 27 (3): 477–491. https://doi.org/10.1016/j.electstud.2008.01.001.

Carlson, Matthew M. 2025. "Scandals During the Kishida Administration." In *Japan Decides 2024: The Japanese General Election*, edited by Kenneth M. McElwain, Robert J. Pekkanen, and Daniel M. Smith, 217–233. Palgrave Macmillan.

Dahlberg, Stefan, and Johan Martinsson. 2015. "Changing Issue Ownership through Policy Communication." *West European Politics* 38 (4): 817–838. https://doi.org/10.1080/01402382.2015.1039377.
De Bruycker, Iskander, and Stefaan Walgrave. 2013. "How a New Issue Becomes an Owned Issue. Media Coverage and the Financial Crisis in Belgium (2008–2009)." *International Journal of Public Opinion Research* 26 (1): 86–97. https://doi.org/10.1093/ijpor/edt003.
Iida, Takeshi. 2023. "Kinpaku suru kokusai josei ka deno anzen hosho souten to tohyo kodo: 2022 nen Saninsen ni okeru Ishin no yakushin." *Japanese Journal of Electoral Studies* 39 (2): 74–90. https://doi.org/10.2307/1953324.
Johns, Robert, and Ann-Kristin. Kölln. 2020. Moderation and Competence: How a Party's Ideological Position Shapes Its Valence Reputation. *American Journal of Political Science* 64 (3): 649–663. https://doi.org/10.1111/ajps.12481.
Nemoto, Kuniaki. 2025. "Reasons Behind the LDP's Loss in the 2024 Election." In *Japan Decides 2024: The Japanese General Election*, edited by Kenneth M. McElwain, Robert J. Pekkanen, and Daniel M. Smith, 37–55. Palgrave Macmillan.
Petitpas, Adrien. 2024. "Media Coverage, Advertising, and Electoral Volatility: The Crucial Role of Party Competence." *Political Communication* 41 (6): 987–1008. https://doi.org/10.1080/10584609.2024.2329613.
Petrocik, John R. 1996. "Issue Ownership in Presidential Elections, with a 1980 Case Study." *American Journal of Political Science* 40 (3): 825–850.
Stiers, Dieter, and Ruth Dassonneville. 2024. "How Parties Can Shape Their Competence Reputations: Issue Attention, Position and Performance." *European Journal of Political Research*. https://doi.org/10.1111/1475-6765.12730.
Taniguchi, Masaki, Taka-aki Asano, Shōko Ōmori, and Shūsuke Takamiya. 2025. "Policy Positions of the Candidates." In *Japan Decides 2024: The Japanese General Election*, edited by Kenneth M. McElwain, Robert J. Pekkanen, and Daniel M. Smith, 125–142. Palgrave Macmillan.
Zenkyo, Masahiro. 2018. *Ishin shiji no bunseki: Popyurizumu ka yukensya no gorisei ka*. Yuhikaku.
Zenkyo, Masahiro. 2021. *Osaka no sentaku: Naze tookoso ha futatabi hiketsu sareta noka*. Yuhikaku.

PART III

The Campaign

CHAPTER 7

Electoral Campaigns in Japan's 2024 HR Election: Emerging Signs of Transformation

Michio Umeda

INTRODUCTION

The 50th General Election of the House of Representatives (HR) in Japan was held on October 27, 2024. On September 30, Ishiba Shigeru, the newly elected president of the Liberal Democratic Party (LDP) following a heated leadership race, officially announced his intention to call for a general election to be held on October 27, contingent upon his nomination as prime minister. The HR was subsequently dissolved on October 9, with the election formally announced on October 15. This sequence of events—where a newly elected prime minister (or the LDP president, who would be the prime minister soon) promptly calls for a general election—mirrors the actions of Kishida Fumio in 2021, who also called for an election shortly after winning the LDP presidential election.

After the official election announcement on October 15, campaign activities commenced, with the content of party leaders' speeches on the first day receiving significant media attention. These speeches offered

M. Umeda (✉)
Komazawa University, Setagaya, Tokyo, Japan
e-mail: umedam@komazawa-u.ac.jp

© The Author(s), under exclusive license to Springer Nature Switzerland AG 2025
K. M. McElwain et al. (eds.), *Japan Decides 2024*,
https://doi.org/10.1007/978-3-031-98797-7_7

insights into the parties' campaign priorities. Ishiba and Ishii Keiichi, the leader of the LDP's coalition partner, Kōmeitō (also known as the Clean Government Party), focused on emphasizing their policy achievements while in office. In contrast, opposition parties, particularly the Constitutional Democratic Party (CDP), Nippon Ishin no Kai (Ishin; also known as Japan Innovation Party), and the Japanese Communist Party (JCP), concentrated on criticizing the LDP over political money scandals. Meanwhile, newer parties such as the Democratic Party for the People (DPP), Reiwa Shinsengumi (Reiwa), and Sanseitō highlighted economic issues, despite their diverse ideological orientations.

This chapter begins by examining how structural factors in Japan—including institutional, electoral, and demographic dimensions—shape and constrain the electoral process while influencing outcomes. It first analyzes Japan's distinctive institutional framework, focusing on the prime minister's discretionary authority to dissolve the HR and the short campaign periods characteristic of Japanese elections. Furthermore, it explores key electoral and demographic dynamics, such as the impact of redistricting on the urban–rural balance, generational divides in voter behavior and their gradual evolution, and the expanding role of internet campaigning. These dynamics signal ongoing transformations in Japanese politics, which could significantly alter the political landscape in the near future, not only in terms of the party system but also in campaign strategies and tools.

The chapter then turns to key developments during the 2024 HR election campaign, focusing on Ishiba's tactical missteps, including his failure—or insufficient effort—to foster party unity, his outdated focus on rural constituencies, and his mishandling of political money scandals. By utilizing media reports on district-level campaigns, this chapter demonstrates how these tactical errors contributed to the rapid decline in the ruling coalition's electoral fortunes.

Structural Context of the Campaign

Institutional Factors

Some institutional features of Japan's HR are notably distinctive and significantly influence electoral dynamics by favoring governing parties. One key feature is the prime minister's authority to call early general elections. The prevailing convention has been to dissolve the HR and hold elections roughly three years after the previous one, with exceptions. Since the 1994 electoral reform, ten HR elections have occurred, with two held after two years (2005 and 2014), five after three years (1996, 2003, 2012, 2017, 2024), and three at the full four-year term's end (2000, 2009, 2021).

The discretionary dissolution of the HR under Article 7 of Japan's Constitution has long been a subject of scholarly and political debate. Critics argue that prime ministers frequently leverage this authority to secure strategic advantages for the governing parties. One such opportunity arises when newly elected prime ministers call snap elections to capitalize on the momentum generated by a fresh leadership mandate, especially when combined with Japan's short official campaign period, as discussed below. This tendency is particularly pronounced when the LDP presidential election includes participation by rank-and-file members, which often results in a temporary surge in public approval for the newly elected leader. The 2024 election exemplified this pattern: Ishiba assumed the LDP presidency following a competitive leadership race that garnered strong grassroots support. Yet, in a surprising development, his initial popularity deteriorated rapidly over the course of the general election campaign.

Dissolutions are also often timed to exploit opposition disunity, as seen during Abe's tenure, when opposition parties struggled to coordinate candidacies in single-member districts (SMDs). These strategic uses of HR dissolution underscore a broader structural asymmetry in Japan's electoral system, favoring governing parties over fragmented and less strategically positioned opposition forces. This practice contrasts with many democracies, where the executive's authority to call early elections is more constrained.

Another defining feature is Japan's short official campaign period. HR general elections allow only 12 campaign days, compared to 17 days for House of Councillors and gubernatorial elections. This brief period, coupled with strict campaign spending limits, is believed to benefit incumbents, particularly from the LDP (McElwain 2008).

The interval between election announcements and voting is also brief. Article 54 mandates elections within 40 days of HR dissolution, but recent elections have occurred within about three weeks—24 days in 2017, 17 in 2021, and 18 in 2024. This short timeframe reflects the ruling coalition's aim to optimize timing while limiting opposition preparation. In contrast, other democracies offer longer preparation periods.

For instance, Britain's 2024 general election allowed 36 days between Parliament's dissolution and voting, while Italy's 2022 election provided 62 days.

Japan also restricts campaign activities before official election announcements. During this pre-announcement phase, candidates can engage only in general political activities (*seiji katsudō*) and are prohibited from explicit electoral activities (*senkyo katsudō*), such as introducing themselves as district candidates. Instead, they identify as current members of parliament (MPs) or local party leaders.

However, not all pre-announcement campaigning is prohibited. Parties recruit candidates for open seats, coordinate with allies, deliver speeches (avoiding explicit candidacy references), and encourage constituents to join supporters' associations (*kōenkai*). These activities prepare the ground for official campaigns. Moreover, once elections are anticipated, candidates often escalate de facto campaigning, hiring staff and renting offices (Hayashi and Tsumura 2011), as seen in 2017 when the HR term neared its end.

Electoral Factors

This chapter next examines electoral factors distinctive to Japanese elections, including candidate-centered campaigns, weak partisan voting, and competitive district-level races. Scholars have studied the candidate-focused campaign style under the multi-member district/single non-transferable vote system (e.g., Curtis 1971). The electoral reform of 1994, which introduced SMDs and proportional representation (PR), eliminated intra-party competition among party candidates. Consequently, candidates shifted from particularistic appeals, such as securing local pork-barrel projects, to national policy platforms, including foreign and defense policies (e.g., Catalinac 2016). Electoral outcomes also became more influenced by national factors, such as party popularity, leadership, and policy agendas.

Despite this shift, weak grassroots party organizations compel most party candidates to invest heavily in personal visibility and in campaign networks such as kōenkai. To foster connections with constituents, candidates frequently engage in localized activities, including delivering morning speeches at train stations, attending community events, and advocating for local issues. The relatively large size of each district's constituency—around 346,000 voters on average, significantly higher than in most democratic countries' lower chambers (excluding the U.S. House of Representatives)—further intensifies the burden on individual candidates.

Another feature of Japanese elections is the instability of district-level outcomes. Weak partisan alignment and numerous competitive districts drive this volatility. Surveys indicate that independents—voters without strong party allegiance—comprise 25–30% of the electorate, similar to LDP supporters and exceeding any other single party's base. Independents' voting is often shaped by the political climate, leading to significant electoral shifts. Even among partisan voters, loyalty is inconsistent. In the 2024 *Yomiuri* exit poll, fewer than two-thirds of LDP supporters voted for LDP or Kōmeitō candidates in SMDs. Similar trends were observed among supporters of other parties, such as the CDP, revealing the challenges parties face in consolidating voter bases (*Yomiuri*, October 28, 2024, online edition).

District-level competitiveness is another defining feature of HR elections. In 2021, one-fifth of districts were decided by victory margins under 5%, and about one-third by under 10%, with urban districts particularly competitive. In contrast, only 9% and 17% of 2022 US House races were decided by similarly narrow margins. This competitiveness, combined with weak partisanship and many independent voters, intensifies pressure on candidates to secure support.

Finally, redistricting since the last election significantly increased the electoral weight of Tokyo and its surrounding metropolitan areas. Following a Supreme Court decision in 2011 requiring that inter-district (largely urban–rural) vote-value disparities be reduced to below two-to-one, the Adams rule was introduced as the new method of allocating seats among prefectures. Consequently, the previous system—which pre-allocated one seat per prefecture before applying the Hare largest remainder method—was abolished. This led to the redistribution of ten SMDs from rural to urban prefectures, mostly from LDP-dominated rural areas to competitive urban ones. Nine of these districts were reassigned to Tokyo, Kanagawa, Chiba, and Saitama, increasing their share from 71 to 80 out of 289, reflecting not only the rule change but also the rising population weight of these regions. Similarly, PR seats in the Tokyo and South Kantō Blocs rose from 39 to 42 out of 176.

Demographic Factors

The 2024 electoral campaign and its outcomes highlight a generational shift in Japan's electorate. Japan, one of the world's most aging societies, has a median electorate age of about 54 years. Voter turnout is highest among elderly citizens, underscoring their significant influence on election outcomes.

Generational cohorts in Japan exhibit distinct political preferences. The *dankai* generation, born between 1947 and 1949, has historically supported traditional leftist parties, including the Japan Socialist Party and its successors such as the Democratic Party of Japan, and more recently the CDP. This cohort has also been a key support base for the JCP. Additionally, a segment of the *dankai* generation has backed Kōmeitō, often due to their religious affiliation with *Sōka Gakkai* (see Klein and McLaughlin 2025). By 2024, this cohort, aged 75 to 77, continued to wield influence due to its size and political engagement. Electoral campaigns and public policy in Japan have traditionally targeted or heavily considered this cohort. However, as this generation ages into their 80s, their electoral influence is expected to decline due to natural attrition and reduced voter turnout.

This generational shift has already impacted political outcomes. Traditional parties that have historically relied on the *dankai* generation—such as the CDP, Kōmeitō, and JCP—experienced stagnation or losses in the 2024 HR election, particularly in the PR tier. Although the CDP gained seats in the majoritarian SMD tier, its growth in PR votes was marginal, increasing from 11.5 million (20.0%) in 2021 to 11.6 million (21.2%) in 2024 (see Ikeda 2025 for analysis of the CDP). Meanwhile, Kōmeitō's vote share fell from 12.4% (7.1 million votes) to 10.9% (6.0 million votes), and the JCP's share dropped from 7.3% (4.2 million votes) to 6.2% (3.4 million votes).

In contrast, newer parties appealing to younger generations, such as the DPP and Reiwa, saw substantial growth. The DPP's PR vote share increased from 4.5% (2.6 million votes) in 2021 to 11.3% (6.2 million votes) in 2024, while Reiwa rose from 3.9% (2.2 million votes) to 7.0% (3.8 million votes).

Exit poll data further illuminate this generational divide. As illustrated in Table 7.1, the LDP and CDP garnered 30% and 29% of the votes, respectively, from voters in their 70s, while among voters in their 20s, these figures fell to 20% and 15%. Conversely, the DPP and Reiwa secured

Table 7.1 The 2024 HR election PR vote preference by age group

	18–19 (%)	20s (%)	30s (%)	40s (%)	50s (%)	60s (%)	70s (%)	80s+ (%)
LDP	26	20	21	24	25	26	30	37
CGP	6	6	6	7	7	10	9	9
CDP	17	15	15	18	22	26	29	25
Ishin	8	10	12	12	10	8	7	6
JCP	5	5	5	4	5	6	8	8
DPP	19	26	21	14	10	7	5	3
Reiwa	9	10	11	12	10	6	3	1

Source Asahi (Oct 28, 2024). https://digital.asahi.com/articles/photo/AS20241028003415.html

only 5% and 3% of the vote among those in their 70s but achieved 26% and 10%, respectively, among voters in their 20s (*Asahi*, October 28, 2024, online edition).

Development of Internet Campaigning

The 2024 election signaled the onset of a new era in Japanese electoral campaigns, marked by the expanded utilization of internet platforms (see also Fahey 2025). A particularly notable development was the rapid rise of online campaigning, reflecting a strategic shift toward engaging younger generations, especially those in their 20s and 30s. This shift was evident not only in the 2024 HR general election but also in the gubernatorial elections held in Tokyo earlier in the year.

Although internet campaigning has been legally permitted in Japan since the 2013 House of Councillors (HC) election, its influence on electoral outcomes had previously been limited. In earlier elections, digital strategies often served to reinforce the dominance of the LDP, leveraging the party's superior financial resources and organizational capacity to maintain its electoral advantage.

In contrast, the 2024 election underscored the transformative potential of internet campaigning, particularly through the widespread use of YouTube videos. These platforms significantly contributed to the rise of smaller parties, most notably the DPP and, to a lesser extent, Reiwa. The effectiveness of digital campaigning was already evident earlier in the year during the Tokyo gubernatorial election in July. In that election, Ishimaru Shinji, a little-known mayor from a small city in Hiroshima Prefecture, utilized internet platforms to mobilize over 1.6 million votes. Although he ultimately lost to the popular incumbent governor Koike Yuriko, who secured 2.9 million votes with the backing of the LDP, Kōmeitō, and DPP, Ishimaru easily outperformed another prominent candidate, Renho, who received 1.3 million votes with support from the CDP and JCP. This outcome demonstrated the growing influence of digital campaigning, particularly for candidates with limited traditional political support.

During the 2024 election campaign, YouTube videos posted by the nine major political parties were viewed approximately 10 million times per day, a figure three times higher than during the 2022 HC election (*NHK*, November 9, 2024). Some of these videos were distributed as paid advertisements on platforms such as YouTube and X. Although paid advertising explicitly referring to candidacy or soliciting votes is prohibited under Japanese electoral law, parties employed such advertisements under the category of political activities. This allowed them to leverage the targeting capabilities of these platforms to reach specific regional or demographic subgroups effectively.

For example, a YouTube video posted by the DPP on October 9, featuring its leader Tamaki Yūichirō discussing policies to increase after-tax income, was viewed nearly 14 million times. Such messaging resonated particularly with younger voters dissatisfied with the heavy social insurance and tax burdens imposed under an aging population. These digital strategies clearly contributed to the DPP's strong performance in the election, underscoring the growing importance of internet campaigning in shaping electoral outcomes in Japan.

Key Campaign Developments

The 2024 electoral campaign resulted in substantial losses for Ishiba's LDP and its coalition partner, Kōmeitō. In contrast, emerging parties such as the DPP, Reiwa, and Sanseitō made significant gains, particularly in the PR tier. While external factors, such as the global inflation crisis and lingering public dissatisfaction with the LDP inherited from the previous administration, contributed to the governing coalition's setbacks (see Maeda 2025), these losses were exacerbated by tactical errors on Ishiba's part. Notably, his failure to foster unity within the LDP and his promotion of policy agendas that failed to resonate broadly with voters played critical roles. The following sections analyze these strategic missteps and the precipitous decline in the ruling coalition's electoral prospects over the course of the campaign.

Cabinet Formation and Rising Internal Division within the LDP

One of the key controversies arose with the composition of Ishiba's cabinet, formed on October 1, which was widely perceived as reward-oriented. Following a contentious presidential election featuring nine candidates, Ishiba narrowly secured victory in a runoff against Takaichi Sanae, a hawkish candidate with strong support from rank-and-file members in urban areas. Upon assuming office, Ishiba appointed many of his key backers to cabinet positions, including six of the nominators for his presidential candidacy.

In contrast, Takaichi and her supporters were not included in Ishiba's cabinet or in senior party executive roles, such as the LDP's three top officials. Members of the former Abe faction, longstanding rivals of Ishiba during the 2010s, were also notably absent from the cabinet. This approach differed significantly from the practices of previous LDP administrations, which had traditionally sought to incorporate competitors and their followers into cabinet or party leadership roles to maintain internal unity. For instance, following his defeat in the 2012 LDP presidential election, Ishiba himself was appointed as LDP Secretary-General under Prime Minister Abe Shinzō's leadership.

The lack of effort—or mutual willingness—to bridge internal divisions not only alienated key constituencies within the party but also weakened Ishiba's leadership credibility, contributing to the LDP's poor performance in the election.

Focus on the Traditional Rural Base

Next, Ishiba's policy focus on rural areas did not contribute positively to his performance in the election. Following the formation of his cabinet, Ishiba delivered the prime ministerial policy address to the Diet on October 4. Given its proximity to the promised dissolution of the HR, the speech drew significant public attention as a de facto campaign launch. While the speech included several policies consistent with those of previous LDP administrations, it notably emphasized efforts to revitalize rural areas under the initiative *Chihō Sōsei 2.0*, pledging to double subsidies for the project. This focus reflected Ishiba's background in agricultural policy, including his roles as Minister of Agriculture, Forestry and Fisheries (2008–2009) and Minister for Overcoming Population Decline and Vitalizing Local Economy (2014–2016). Ishiba's popularity among rank-and-file party members in rural areas—an influential group within the party, particularly in presidential elections due to their sheer numbers—played a key role in his rise to leadership.

However, Ishiba's emphasis on rural development was less appealing in urban areas, which encompassed many competitive districts. While the issue salience of rural development was relatively low, especially in comparison to the economy, social security, or child-rearing (see Maeda 2025; Tsuji 2025), his focus on rural policies gave the impression that he represented an outdated vision of the LDP, reminiscent of its past orientation, which recent LDP prime ministers had sought to move away from. This perception was particularly problematic in light of the increased electoral importance of urban areas following the redistricting implemented from this election.

Ishiba's focus on rural areas was also evident in his campaign stops. During the campaign period, he visited 67 districts, of which only 11 (16%) were in Tokyo and its neighboring prefectures. This figure contrasts with the campaign efforts of Kishida in 2021, who visited 82 districts, including 22 (27%) in the Tokyo area. This discrepancy is notable given that the number of districts in Tokyo and its surrounding areas increased following redistricting, as discussed earlier, creating additional open seats and battleground districts. In comparison, Noda Yoshihiko, the leader of the CDP, visited 62 districts during the campaign, a number comparable to Ishiba's. However, Noda devoted nearly half of his visits (30 districts, 48%) to Tokyo and its neighboring areas.

This divergence in focus could reflect not only the competitiveness of the districts but also the candidates' localized popularity. Ishiba may have strategically leveraged his established support in rural areas when selecting his campaign destinations, as suggested by previous studies (e.g., McElwain 2009). Nonetheless, the distribution of Ishiba's campaign visits underscores the rural-centric orientation of his electoral strategy.

(Mis-)handling of the LDP Political Money Scandal

In response to criticism over political money scandals, Ishiba implemented punitive measures within the LDP (See Nemoto 2025 and Carlson 2025 for more details). He decided not to nominate 12 candidates in SMDs and three candidates in the PR-only tier. Additionally, he nominated 34 candidates in the majoritarian SMD tier but barred them from being listed in the PR tier. Through these actions, Ishiba likely sought to distance himself from the scandal and demonstrate accountability.

These measures, however, failed to enhance Ishiba's public image and instead placed him in a precarious position. Within the party, the actions were widely perceived as excessive, particularly as they followed similar disciplinary measures enacted earlier in April 2024. This sequence of events created an impression of cumulative punishment imposed shortly before the election, disproportionately targeting members of the former Abe faction, Ishiba's longstanding rivals. Outside the party, however, the measures were criticized as insufficient. Ishiba's actions failed to successfully distance him from the scandal, as the electorate perceived the issue as a broader LDP scandal rather than one confined to the former Abe faction. Although Ishiba attempted to frame the controversy as unrelated to his leadership, this narrative did not resonate with voters.

Furthermore, Ishiba suggested that he might allow LDP candidates who were denied official nominations but succeeded in winning as independents to rejoin the party after the election, interpreting their victories as a mandate from their constituencies (*misogi*). This approach reflected practices from the multi-member district era, where similar accommodation was made, particularly in elections marred by scandals. However, this strategy appeared outdated to contemporary voters, who perceived it as an insufficient response to the scandal. Consequently, Ishiba's actions were criticized for being neither decisive enough to restore public trust nor conciliatory enough to unify the party. Additionally, his handling of the issue unintentionally amplified its visibility, aligning with the opposition's strategy to maintain public focus on the scandal.

The LDP's provision of campaign funds to candidates denied official nominations further reinforced perceptions of a lukewarm response. On October 23, just days before the election, *Akahata*, the JCP's official newspaper, reported that the LDP executive committee had allocated equal amounts of campaign funds—20 million JPY—to both officially nominated candidates and those excluded from nomination. This revelation was subsequently covered by other major media outlets (*Akahata*, October 23, 2024). LDP Secretary-General Moriyama Hiroshi explained that the funds were distributed to district-level party branches, for which the excluded candidates still served as branch managers and were intended to support party organizational activities rather than direct election campaigns. Nevertheless, this explanation failed to dispel public skepticism. Officially nominated candidates received 5 million JPY as a "nomination fee" (*kōninryō*), specifically designated as campaign funds, and 15 million JPY for "party organization expenses." In contrast, non-nominated candidates were given the entire 20 million JPY as "party organization expenses." The apparent inconsistencies in these financial arrangements further eroded confidence in Ishiba's handling of the scandal.

Sudden Shift of Electoral Prospects

As the campaign advanced, initial voter expectations shifted rapidly, with major media reporting a significant drop in the ruling coalition's projected seat share. This trend can be analyzed through media assessments of district-level campaigns. Japanese media conduct extensive polls during the official campaign, surveying hundreds of respondents in each SMD, generating a national sample of several hundred thousand. These polls require substantial investment, with some outlets conducting follow-up surveys to track trends, especially in competitive districts.

A unique feature of Japanese election reporting is the avoidance of publishing direct poll results, such as percentages favoring candidates. Instead, media offer qualitative assessments like "Candidate X is ahead" or "Candidates Y and Z are contesting closely," based on poll data and supplementary analysis, likely due to legal restrictions. Terms like "dominant," "stable," "leading," "catching up," "struggling," and "neck and neck" are used. Notably, in close races, the first-mentioned candidate is often seen as slightly ahead (Iida 2007).

For analysis, this chapter categorizes these descriptions into four groups: "Lean GC" (advantage for the governing coalition), "Toss-Up/Tilt GC" (slight GC advantage), "Toss-Up/Tilt Opposition" (slight opposition advantage), and "Lean Opposition" (opposition advantage). *Yomiuri*'s October 17 report categorized 108 districts as Lean GC and 52 as Lean Opposition, while *Nikkei*'s terms corresponded to 138 and 115, respectively, despite using the same data. Such discrepancies highlight differences in media assessments. Research suggests outlets like *Yomiuri* lean toward opposition parties, while *Asahi* favors the governing coalition

(Umeda 2023). These "house effects" likely result from varying methodologies or evaluative criteria, complicating comparisons of popularity shifts across different reports.

Therefore, initially this chapter focuses on reports from the same outlet for reliable comparisons. During the 2024 campaign, *Yomiuri* and *Nikkei* conducted surveys early (October 15–16) and later (October 22–24). In its second report, *Yomiuri* reassessed 133 competitive districts. Among the districts reassessed by *Yomiuri*, competitive districts favoring the governing coalition or classified as toss-ups but tilting toward them dropped from 14 and 61 to 5 and 58, respectively. Conversely, those favoring the opposition or tilting their way rose from 7 and 51 to 9 and 61 (*Yomiuri*, October 25, 2024).

Additionally, JX Press offered daily projections of party seat counts in SMDs throughout the 2024 campaign (JX Press 2024). These projections applied Umeda's item response theory-based methodology to aggregate four-level qualitative evaluations from various media outlets discussed earlier (Umeda 2023). As shown in Table 7.2, the JX projections highlighted a significant decline in the LDP's forecasted seats—from 157 on October 18 to 149 on October 22, and further to 138 by October 26, the day before the election. Ultimately, the LDP secured 132 seats in the final results. These trends indicate that the governing coalition lost approximately ten districts in the majoritarian SMD tier during the campaign's first week, another ten in the second week, and suffered similar losses in the PR tier.

Table 7.2 The 2024 HR election daily projections of party seat counts in majoritarian tier

	18 Oct	21 Oct	22 Oct	23 Oct	24 Oct	25 Oct	26 Oct	Shift b/w 18–26 Oct
LDP	157	155	149	149	146	141	138	-19
CGP	7	7	6	6	6	5	5	-2
CDP	89	91	97	97	99	103	104	15
Ishin	17	17	18	19	20	20	20	3
DPP	5	5	5	6	6	7	7	2
Others	14	14	14	12	12	13	15	1

Source JX Press (2024). https://prediction.election2024.newsdigest.jp

The campaign finance scandal described above had a particularly pronounced negative impact on LDP candidates who contested the election without an official party nomination. A regression analysis—modeling electoral outcomes as a function of nomination status and district-level campaign dynamics, using item response theory-based measures of competitiveness estimated a few days before the voting day and prior to media coverage of the scandal—reveals a significant disadvantage for these candidates.[1] Specifically, non-nominated LDP candidates received, on average, more than three percentage points fewer votes than their officially nominated counterparts, relative to expectations based on campaign-level conditions. This effect is statistically significant at the 5% level (one-sided test), underscoring the electoral costs associated with reputational damage arising from the funding controversy.

Conclusion

The 2024 Japanese HR election highlights both continuity and transformation in the nation's electoral landscape. Structural factors such as the prime minister's discretionary authority to determine election timing, the short, candidate-centered nature of campaigns, and the influence of an aging population continue to shape and constrain the behavior of political actors during electoral campaigns.

At the same time, the election underscores significant transformations in Japanese politics. A major shift is the gradual decline of the *dankai* generation, a once-dominant demographic with distinct partisan and political preferences. Urban areas, particularly Tokyo and its surrounding prefectures, have gained increasing electoral weight due to population

---

[1] The outcome variable in the regression analysis is the electoral outcome, defined as the relative vote-share advantage of the governing coalition candidate. Specifically, it is calculated as the difference between the vote share of the governing coalition candidate (v_g) and that of the strongest opposition party candidate (v_{o1}), divided by the sum of these two vote shares: Hence, it is ($v_g - v_{o1}$)/($v_g + v_{o1}$). Among the explanatory variables, the district-level campaign dynamics variable is measured using Umeda's item response theory-based methodology, as described above (Umeda 2023). Another key explanatory variable—nomination status—is operationalized as a dummy variable, coded as 1 for non-nominated and 0 for regularly nominated LDP candidates. Because the campaign dynamics variable reflects evaluations from media outlets prior to the emergence of the campaign finance scandal involving non-nominated LDP candidates, the nomination status variable is expected to exert a negative effect on the electoral outcome, conditional on pre-scandal campaign dynamics.

growth and electoral redistricting. Furthermore, the election marks the growing importance of digital campaigning, with internet platforms, especially YouTube, playing a pivotal role in engaging voters. This development signals a departure from traditional campaign methods focused on personal networks and localized activities.

These shifts have enabled newer parties like the DPP and Reiwa to rise, leveraging digital campaign tools such as YouTube videos to engage younger voters despite limited resources. Their campaigns emphasized economic issues rather than the traditional concerns of established opposition parties, such as political scandals. Conversely, traditional opposition parties like the CDP, JCP, and Ishin showed stagnation in the PR tier, despite the CDP's notable gains in the majoritarian tier.

The campaign also highlighted strategic missteps by Ishiba, which compounded the governing coalition's losses. His rural-centric focus, while appealing to traditional LDP bases, alienated younger and urban voters in competitive districts, particularly given generational shifts and the redistricting that amplified urban electoral weight. Ishiba's mishandling of political money scandals further damaged the coalition's image, creating perceptions of weak leadership and internal division. Media reports on district-level campaigns revealed a sharp decline in the coalition's projected seat share, with daily updates from sources like JX Press presaging significant losses, particularly in the campaign's final stages.

In conclusion, the 2024 HR election represents a turning point in Japanese politics, balancing entrenched structural constraints with emerging transformative forces. The setbacks faced by the ruling coalition, combined with the rise of newer parties and the digital transformation of campaigns, signal a shifting political landscape influenced by demographic change, urbanization, and technological innovation. These developments point to a gradual but inevitable evolution in Japanese democracy, with significant implications for party systems, voter behavior, and campaign strategies in the years ahead.

REFERENCES

Carlson, Matthew M. 2025. "Scandals During the Kishida Administration." In *Japan Decides 2024: The Japanese General Election*, edited by Kenneth. M. McElwain, Robert J. Pekkanen, and Daniel M. Smith, 217–233. New York: Palgrave MacMillan.

Catalinac, Amy. 2016. *Electoral Reform and National Security in Japan: From Pork to Foreign Policy*. Cambridge: Cambridge University Press.

Curtis, Gerald. 1971. *Election Campaigning, Japanese Style*. New York: Columbia University Press.

Fahey, Robert A. 2025. "Social Media in the 2024 General Election." In *Japan Decides 2024: The Japanese General Election*, edited by Kenneth M. McElwain, Robert J. Pekkanen, and Daniel M. Smith, 181–195. New York: Palgrave MacMillan.

Hayashi, Yoshimasa, and Keisuke Tsumura. 2011. *The Work of Members of Parliament: Politics as a Vocation (Kokkai Giin no Shigoto: Shokugyō toshite no Seiji)*. Chūōkōron-Shinsha.

Iida, Yoshiaki. 2007. "The analysis of the media electoral coverage—The 44th general election as a case (Shimbun no senkyo jyousei hodo no bunseki—dai 44 kai sousenkyo wo jirei to shite)." *Jissen Jyoshidai Ningensyakai Gakubu Kiyo* 3: 19–42.

Ikeda, Fumi. 2025. "The CDP in 2024: The Legacy of the Electoral Coalition with the JCP." In *Japan Decides 2024: The Japanese General Election*, edited by Kenneth M. McElwain, Robert J. Pekkanen, and Daniel M. Smith, 57–74. New York: Palgrave MacMillan.

JX Press. 2024. *2024 HR General Election Winning Probability Simulator.* https://prediction.election2024.newsdigest.jp. Accessed January 20, 2025.

Klein, Axel, and Levi McLaughlin. 2025. "A Costly Coalition: Kōmeitō's Enduring Partnership with the LDP." In *Japan Decides 2024: The Japanese General Election*, edited by Kenneth M. McElwain, Robert J. Pekkanen, and Daniel M. Smith, 75–90. New York: Palgrave MacMillan.

Maeda, Yukio. 2025. "Public Opinion and Scandals in Economic Hard Times." In *Japan Decides 2024: The Japanese General Election*, edited by Kenneth M. McElwain, Robert J. Pekkanen, and Daniel M. Smith, 163–179. New York: Palgrave MacMillan.

McElwain, Kenneth M. 2008. "Manipulating electoral rules to manufacture single-party dominance." *American Journal of Political Science* 52 (1): 32–47.

McElwain, Kenneth M. 2009. "How long are Koizumi's coattails? Party-leader visits in the 2005 election." In *Political Change in Japan: Electoral Behavior, Party Realignment, and the Koizumi Reforms*, edited by Steven R. Reed, Kenneth M. McElwain, and Kay Shimizu, 133–156. Walter H. Shorenstein Asia-Pacific Research Center.

Ministry of Internal Affairs and Communications. 2024. *An Easy Guide to Voter Turnout (Yoku Wakaru Tōhyōritsu)*. https://www.soumu.go.jp/main_content/000938531.pdf. Accessed January 20, 2025.

NHK. 2024. *Paid Online Advertisements by Political Parties: Why the Emphasis on Videos? (Seitō no yūryō netto kōkoku: Kokomade dōga jūshi no haikei wa?)*. Posted November 8, 2024. Accessed January 20, 2025.

Nemoto, Kuniaki. 2025. "Reasons Behind the LDP's Loss in the 2024 Election." In *Japan Decides 2024: The Japanese General Election*, edited by Kenneth M. McElwain, Robert J. Pekkanen, and Daniel M. Smith, 37-55. New York: Palgrave Macmillan.

Umeda, Michio. 2023. "Aggregating qualitative district-level campaign assessments to forecast election results: Evidence from Japan." *International Journal of Forecasting* 39 (2): 956–966.

CHAPTER 8

Policy Positions of the Candidates

Masaki Taniguchi, Taka-aki Asano, Shōko Ōmori, and Shūsuke Takamiya

INTRODUCTION

The UTokyo-Asahi Survey (UTAS) is a joint project between a research team led by Masaki Taniguchi of the University of Tokyo and the *Asahi Shimbun* newspaper. UTAS consists of surveys of voters and political leaders that have been conducted since 2003 during elections for the House of Representatives and the House of Councillors. By collaborating with *Asahi Shimbun*, one of Japan's largest newspapers, the response rate for the political leader surveys has always exceeded 90%, allowing us to obtain highly reliable elite survey data. This chapter summarizes the results of the 2024 UTAS Political Leader Survey.

M. Taniguchi (✉)
Graduate School of Public Policy and Graduate Schools for Law and Politics, The University of Tokyo, Tokyo, Japan
e-mail: taniguchi@j.u-tokyo.ac.jp

T. Asano
Faculty of Law, Kansai University, Osaka, Japan
e-mail: t-asano@kansai-u.ac.jp

CANDIDATE ISSUE ATTITUDES

Constitution, Diplomacy, Security

In this section, we compare the issue attitudes of the candidates by political party. Figures 8.1, 8.2, 8.3 and 8.4 shows the average responses of each party's candidates on these three issues. For questions asking whether they agree or disagree with a statement, 1 means they agree and 5 means they disagree. For questions that presented two opposing opinions and asked which one was closer to the respondent's own opinion, 1 indicates agreement with A and 5 indicates agreement with B. The English translations of the questions are provided in this chapter's Appendix.

In many developed countries, the left/right or liberal/conservative ideological divide is constructed around principles of economic policy. In Japan, however, the left/right ideological divide is primarily defined by views on the constitution, diplomacy, and security, including constitutional amendments, strengthening defense capabilities, and the Japan-U.S. security alliance. The right wing wants to revise the Constitution, including Article 9, and is in favor of strengthening Japan's defense capabilities and the Japan-U.S. Security Treaty. On the other hand, the left wing opposes these issues (Taniguchi 2020; Taniguchi and Mizushima 2021).

As shown in Fig. 8.1, there is a wide range of policy positions among the parties in 2024, from the LDP and CPJ, which take a right-leaning stance on these issues, to the JCP, SDP, and Reiwa, which take a far-left stance.

Regarding constitutional amendments, 57% of all candidates and 67% of successful candidates were in favor. Among those who favored constitutional amendments, the most frequently cited areas for change were maintaining the Self-Defense Forces (78%), extending the term of Diet

---

S. Ōmori
Faculty of Social Sciences, Hōsei University, Tokyo, Japan
e-mail: shoko_omori@hosei.ac.jp

S. Takamiya
Faculty of Political Science and Economics, Takushoku University, Tokyo, Japan
e-mail: stakamiy@takushoku-u.ac.jp

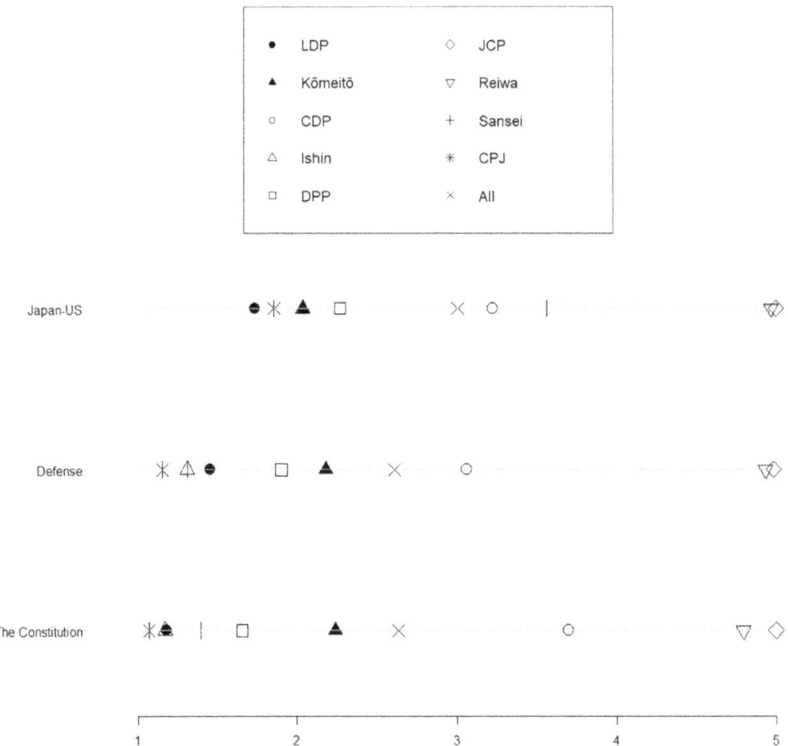

Fig. 8.1 Average values by political party for foreign policy and security issues

members in times of emergency (57%), and improving education (50%). The percentage of all Diet members in favor of retaining the Self-Defense Forces was just under half (49%), not enough to reach the two-thirds majority needed to propose constitutional amendments.

61% of the candidates are in favor of strengthening defense, and half of the candidates are in favor of strengthening the Japan-U.S. security alliance.

The positions of the CDP and the DPP on these issues are very different. Only 18% of CDP candidates are in favor of amending the Constitution, compared to 93% of DPP candidates. Only 35% of CDP candidates are in favor of strengthening Japan's defense capabilities, while 78% of DPP candidates are in favor. Regarding the Japan-U.S. Security

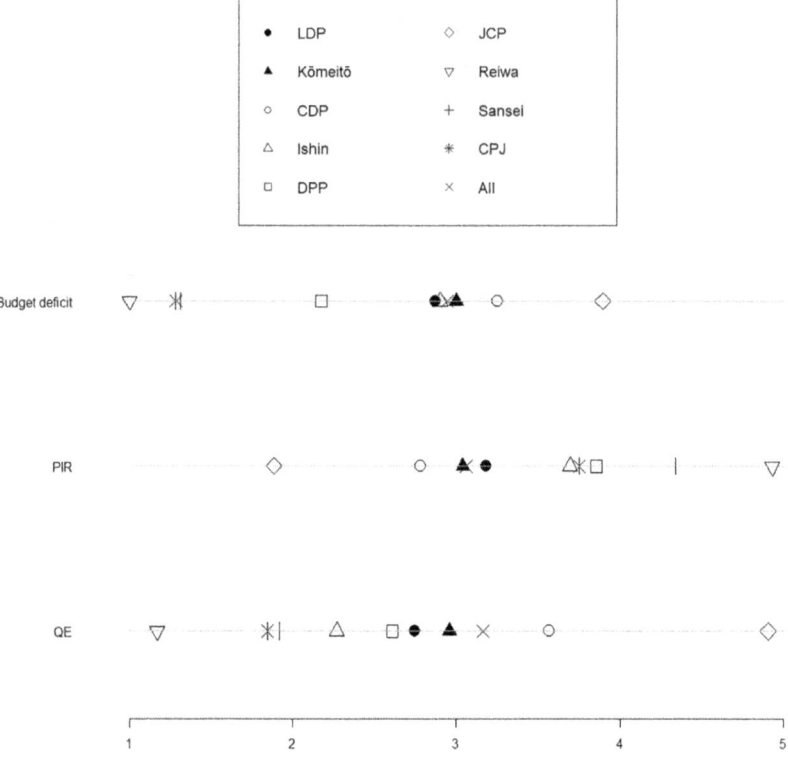

Fig. 8.2 Average values by political party for economic issues

Treaty, only 29% of CDP candidates believe it should be strengthened, while 71% of DPP candidates agree.

Economy

Japan's economic policies since 2000 have been characterized by wide fluctuations, including the neoliberal policies of the Koizumi Junichirō administration, the interventionist policies of the DPJ government that came to power after the global financial crisis, and the monetary easing policies of "Abenomics" since 2012. In addition, the political distance between the ruling party and the largest opposition party is not that great compared to constitutional and security policies. While maintaining

Fig. 8.3 Average values by political party for social issues

these characteristics, the 2024 general election showed signs of change (Fig. 8.2).

First, in terms of attitudes toward the idea that "the Bank of Japan will continue its policy of quantitative monetary easing, including purchases of Japanese Government Bonds" (QE), in 2021 40% of all candidates were in favor and 30% opposed, but in the 2024 survey the number of

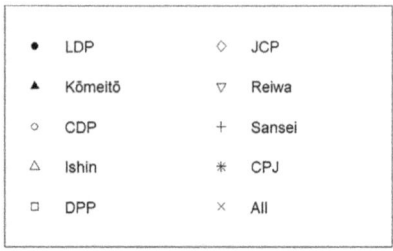

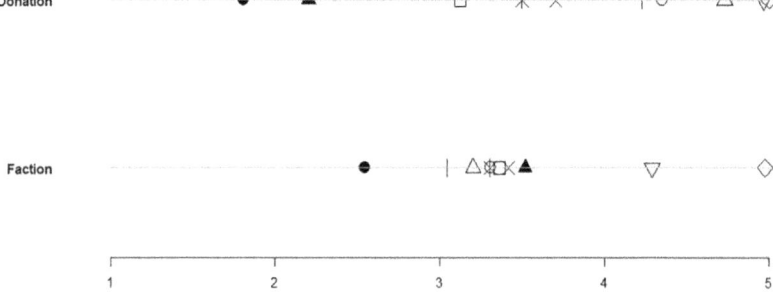

Fig. 8.4 Average values by political party for corporate and group donations and factions

candidates in favor decreased to 33%, while the number of candidates opposed increased to 38%. In particular, the LDP's support has dropped sharply from 61 to 34%, a clear sign of its departure from Abenomics. Among the opposition parties, 75% of Ishin candidates are in favor, while 57% of CDP candidates are opposed. About half of the DPP candidates are in favor.

Next, when asked whether they think "the Bank of Japan should raise its policy interest rate" (PIR), 27% of all candidates agree, 31% disagree, and 42% are undecided. The same trend was seen among LDP candidates (13% in favor, 61% neutral, 26% opposed). In contrast, the opposition parties were mostly opposed. 63% of DPP candidates, 69% of Ishin candidates, and all but one of Reiwa candidates said they were against raising interest rates.

Japan's outstanding debt is over 250% of GDP, which is much higher than in other countries. Regarding the budget deficit, the UTAS asked respondents whether they agreed more with the statement "There is no need to worry about the budget deficit as government bonds are being steadily purchased" (1 in Fig. 8.2) or the statement "The budget deficit is at a critical level, so the issuance of bonds should be controlled (5)." Overall, the candidates were evenly divided between those who said there was no need to worry (31%) and those who said it was at a critical level (33%). Among LDP candidates, many are not worried about the budget deficit (33% not worried, 23% at a critical level). Candidates from the DPP (71%), Reiwa (100%) and CPJ (93%) are also not worried about the budget deficit. On the other hand, many CDP candidates are aware that the budget deficit is at a critical level (44%).

With regard to economic policy, it is worth noting the emergence of Reiwa, Sanseitō, and the CPJ. As can be seen in Fig. 8.2, these new parties often take radical stances for or against the economic policies mentioned above. Moreover, while Reiwa takes a leftist stance on the constitution, diplomacy, and security, and Sanseitō and the CPJ take a rightist stance, they share the same stance on the economy, such as not worrying about the budget deficit and being in favor of QE. Although Reiwa, Sanseitō, and the CPJ are still small parties, if you consider that the DPP, which significantly increased its seats this time, is right next to them in terms of budget deficits and QE, it can be said that 2024 was the year that the seeds of populism were sown in Japan although it is impossible to predict at this point whether these seeds will sprout, take root, and grow.

Society

Figure 8.3 shows the parties' average issue positions on society. Regarding nuclear power plants, the overall proportion of candidates who support maintaining nuclear power plants increases from 30% in 2021 to 44% in 2024. The proportion of support within each party varies widely, with 86% of LDP candidates, 22% of Kōmeitō candidates, 6% of CDP candidates, 76% of Ishin candidates, and 90% of DPP candidates supporting nuclear power.

The number of politicians who support the introduction of a system of separate surnames for married couples and the legalization of same-sex marriage is increasing. About two-thirds of all candidates supported the system of separate surnames for married couples, the highest number ever. LDP candidates, however, were divided, with 30% in favor and 32% opposed. Regarding same-sex marriage, 57% of candidates were in favor, but only 14% of LDP candidates were in favor. In the case of Kōmeitō, the coalition partner, 98% and 90% of candidates are in favor of separate family names for married couples and same-sex marriage, respectively, in contrast to the LDP.

Similarly, while LDP candidates are reluctant, Kōmeitō and the main opposition parties (CDP, Ishin, JCP, DPP, and Reiwa) are in favor of introducing a quota system to allocate a certain percentage of seats and candidates in the Diet to women.

Political Reform

In the 2024 general election, political reform became a key issue due to the LDP's political funding scandal. According to the UTAS, "political and administrative reform" (17%) was the most important issue for candidates, ahead of "education and child-rearing" (15%) and "pensions, medical care and nursing care" (11%).

UTAS has asked similar questions since 2007, and this was the first time that most candidates named political and administrative reform as the most important issue. Among the political parties, Ishin and the CDP placed the most importance on "political and administrative reform" (62% and 25%, respectively), while the LDP placed the most importance on "industrial policy" (21%) and the Kōmeitō placed the most importance on "education and child-rearing" (34%).

Among the opposition parties, however, most DPP candidates chose "fiscal and monetary policy" (27%). In a single-issue election, the conflict between the ruling party and the largest opposition party was conspicuous, and there was a risk that smaller parties would not receive attention. In this election, the DPP significantly increased its number of seats by distinguishing itself from other opposition parties, which campaigned on the slogan of "increasing take-home pay" and the promise of tax cuts.

The assessment of the June 2024 revision of the Political Funds Control Law also differed by political party. While nearly half of the candidates from the LDP and Kōmeitō rated the revised law as "inadequate" and "appropriate," nearly all of the candidates from the opposition parties gave it a harsh "inadequate" rating.

One of the points of contention in the revision of the Political Funds Control Law was the issue of policy activity expenses paid by political parties to individual politicians. The revised law requires each politician to disclose the use of their policy activity expenses after ten years. In response, there were also opinions that individual politicians should be prohibited from receiving policy activity expenses.

This argument for abolishing policy activity expenses was supported by the majority of Kōmeitō candidates as well as the main opposition parties, but only 36% of LDP candidates supported it. Spending on policy activities was completely banned by a post-election revision of the Political Funds Control Law.

There are also some issues on which the opposition parties have different views. The political funds scandal this time was an incident in which the Abe faction and the Nikai faction of the LDP illegally concealed a large amount of income from political fundraising parties (see Carlson 2025). As a result, there were those who argued that political fundraising parties themselves should be banned. In response to these calls, the majority of CDP (62%) and Ishin (82%) candidates said they would not hold political fundraising parties, while half (55%) of DPP candidates said they would hold political fundraising parties if necessary, distancing themselves from the other parties. Most LDP (85%) and Kōmeitō (82%) candidates said they would continue to hold political fundraising parties as needed.

Opposition parties were also divided on corporate and group donations. The UTAS asked respondents to choose which of the following two statements they agreed with: "Corporations and groups have the freedom to engage in political activities (1)" or "Corporations and groups should be prohibited from making donations (5)."

As shown in Fig. 8.4, the LDP and Kōmeitō want to maintain corporate and group donations, while Ishin, CDP, and JCP call for a ban on corporate and group donations. However, the DPP is the only major opposition party that has not yet clarified its stance on corporate and group donations.

After the scandal broke, all factions of the LDP except the Asō Faction were dissolved, but many opposition parties are not necessarily negative about the existence of factions. When asked whether they agreed or disagreed with the statement "Factions or policy groups are necessary within the party for the study of policies and the development of human resources," candidates from the CDP, Ishin, and DPP gave more neutral responses (3) than those who disagreed (4 or 5).

LEFT/RIGHT IDEOLOGY

Comparison Between Political Parties

Next, we examine the differences in policy positions between political parties and candidates by systematizing individual issue attitudes as left–right ideology.

Based on previous candidate surveys, the LDP moved further to the right and away from the median voter throughout the 2010s, while the position of the largest opposition party (DPJ → DP → CDP) shifted to the left after the 2012 general election (Taniguchi 2020). In the 2021 general election, the LDP's position did not change significantly, but the CDP became more centrist on security issues (Asano 2023). What changes were seen in the ideological positions of candidates in the 2024 general election?

We estimated the ideological positions of candidates in the 2021 and 2024 elections based on UTAS. Specifically, we estimated the latent policy preferences of each candidate by analyzing their response patterns to about 30 questions on specific issue attitudes, such as security issues and economic policies, using the graded response model of item response theory (IRT). In addition, since eighteen questions were common to the 2021 and 2024 data, we equated the item parameters using the common-item method. As a result, it is possible to compare the positions of candidates and political parties on the same scale between 2021 and 2024. As mentioned in the first section, the estimated latent policy preference is highly correlated with attitudes toward constitutional reform and strengthening Japan's defense capabilities, and can be interpreted as the conventional left–right ideological axis in Japan.

Figure 8.5 summarizes the estimated ideological positions for each political party. The larger the estimate, the further to the right it is. The black dots are the median candidates within each political party. The gray dots are the positions of each candidate officially endorsed by that party. The dots representing the same candidate in the 2021 and 2024 elections are connected by a gray line.

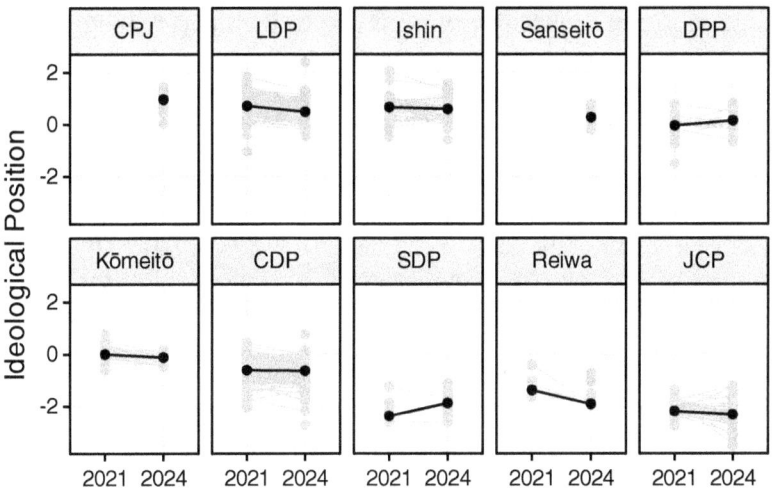

Fig. 8.5 The ideological positions of the candidates in the 2021 and 2024 elections

According to Fig. 8.5, we can summarize the ideological conflict between the parties in the 2024 general election as follows. First, the LDP became more centrist between 2021 and 2024. The median of LDP candidates was 0.72 in 2021, but it dropped to 0.49 in 2024. There was no significant change in the ideological cohesion within the LDP. The standard deviation of the ideological positions within the LDP was 0.35 in 2021 and 0.30 in 2024.

Second, the position of the CDP, the largest opposition party, did not change much (the median of candidates was -0.61 in 2021 and -0.63 in 2024). Similarly, the dispersion of ideological positions within the CDP also remained largely unchanged. The standard deviation within the CDP was 0.46 in 2021 and 0.44 in 2024.

Third, the new parties that gained seats in 2024 are at the extremes of the political spectrum. The Conservative Party of Japan (CPJ, Nippon Hoshutō), which won its first seats in the Diet in the 2024 election, is more to the right than the LDP. Sanseitō, which won its first seat in the House of Councillors in the 2022 election and also won a seat in the

House of Representatives this time, is also to the right. Among the left-wing opposition parties, we can see a shift to the left in the Reiwa Party, which increased its share of seats in this election.

In summary, the 2024 general election saw the political distance between the two major parties narrow, while new parties emerged on both the left and the right. The current Japanese party system can be described as moderate pluralism, with several smaller parties existing around the two major parties, the LDP and the CDP. Since nearly 40% of the members of the House of Representatives are elected by PR, the popular belief that the 1994 electoral reform was aimed at a two-party system is incorrect. However, there is no guarantee that the current electoral system will necessarily lead to moderate pluralism, and if Reiwa, CPJ, or Sanseitō were to expand their power in the future, there is a risk that it could turn into polarized pluralism similar to that in Germany or France, destabilizing democracy.

Comparison Between Candidates

Next, we examine the differences in ideological positions between candidates within the same political party. First, we focus on the gender gap. Previous elections have confirmed that male politicians are more right-wing than female politicians (Maeda 2019). We estimate a linear regression model with the ideological position of candidates in 2024 as the outcome variable and gender as the explanatory variable.[1] We found that female candidates were statistically significantly more left-leaning than male candidates in the LDP and CDP at the 5% level (see Table 8.1). The regression coefficient for the female dummy was − 0.16 for both the LDP and the CDP.

Next, we examined whether the differences in the electoral system affected ideological positions. Japan's general election is a mix of single-member districts (SMD) and proportional representation (PR), and candidates can run for both. However, just before the election, the LDP allowed only some of the members involved in a financial scandal to run in single-member districts and did not include them on the PR list. We

---

[1] The model also included the following as control variables: the candidate's age group (in 10-year age groups, with 70s and 80s in the same category), the number of times the candidate has been elected, whether the candidate ran only in SMD, and the candidate's ideological position in 2021.

Table 8.1 OLS estimations of ideological positions of the candidates in 2024

	LDP	CDP	Ishin
(Intercept)	0.28***	− 0.15*	0.32***
	(0.06)	(0.09)	(0.10)
Female	− 0.16***	− 0.16**	− 0.07
	(0.05)	(0.06)	(0.09)
Age	− 0.01	− 0.03	− 0.02
	(0.02)	(0.03)	(0.03)
# of Wins	− 0.01**	0.01	− 0.01
	(0.01)	(0.01)	(0.02)
Only SMD	− 0.02	− 0.15	0.04
	(0.04)	(0.21)	(0.08)
Ideological position (2021)	0.48***	0.65***	0.50***
	(0.05)	(0.06)	(0.07)
Observations	213	148	72
Adjusted R^2	0.37	0.53	0.44

Note Standard errors in the parentheses. Covariates are included but not shown
*$p < 0.1$, **$p < 0.05$, ***$p < 0.01$

estimated the average treatment effect of not being allowed to run in PR in the 2024 election for LDP candidates who ran in both SMD and PR in the 2021 election, using propensity score matching and inverse propensity weighting (IPW).[2] As Table 8.2 shows, there was no statistically significant difference in ideological position between candidates who ran only in SMD and dual candidates. In terms of ideological cohesion within the LDP, the electoral system appears to have had no effect.

However, it is possible that the electoral system affected the degree of importance given to ideological issues by LDP candidates. Table 8.2 also shows the results of estimating the degree of difference in the importance attached to foreign policy, security policy, and pork barrel policy by candidates who ran only in the SMD compared with those who ran in both the SMD and the PR. The importance of each policy area was measured on a four-point scale using questions about the most important, second most important, and third most important policies. Both the matching and IPW estimates show that LDP candidates who ran only for the SMD

---

[2] Candidates who were not allowed to run in the PR due to the LDP's internal "73-year-old retirement rule" were excluded from the analysis. As covariates, we also included each candidate's gender, age group, number of times elected, results in the previous election, and lagged outcome variable.

Table 8.2 Effects of running only in SMD on the electoral strategies of LDP candidates

	Ideological position		Emphasis of security policy		Emphasis of pork policy	
	Matching	IPW	Matching	IPW	Matching	IPW
(Intercept)	0.32*	0.19**	1.25	0.70**	0.20	0.66
	(0.18)	(0.08)	(0.76)	(0.34)	(1.10)	(0.49)
Only SMD	− 0.02	− 0.01	− 0.69**	− 0.62***	0.64*	0.52***
	(0.06)	(0.03)	(0.27)	(0.13)	(0.35)	(0.18)
Observations	56	173	56	173	56	173

Note Standard errors in the parentheses. Covariates are included but not shown
*p < 0.1, **p < 0.05, ***p < 0.01

placed less importance on foreign and security policy, which is an ideological issue. In addition, candidates who ran only for the SMD placed more importance than dual candidates on pork-barrel policies such as industrial policy, agriculture, forestry and fisheries, and infrastructure development, which lead to the distribution of benefits to the local area.

EMOTIONAL DISTANCE BETWEEN POLITICAL PARTIES

What does the narrowing of the policy gap between the LDP and the CDP, and the policies of the Ishin, DPP, and Kōmeitō in between, mean for the future of Japanese politics? In the past, the policy position of the Kōmeitō was closer to that of the DPJ than to that of the LDP, but the affinity between the DPJ and the Kōmeitō remained far apart. The 2017 DP split left an emotional gap between the CDP and the DPP, which should be close in terms of policy. Conversely, in 2021, the CDP and the JCP avoided competing candidates in many constituencies, and despite fundamental policy differences, the psychological distance between the two parties narrowed. This section highlights the emotional positioning of the major parties ahead of the 2024 election.

The UTAS asked candidates to rate the "affinity rating" of each party on a scale of 0 to 100 (Fig. 8.6). The Ishin candidates' rating of the CDP rose from 16 in 2021 to 43 in 2024. The evaluation of the DPP by the CDP candidates was 65, and vice versa, with a relatively high level of 52. The reason for the emotional closeness between the CDP, Ishin, and DPP is that Noda Yoshihiko, a right-wing member of the CDP, was elected as the party's leader in the September 2024 election. As a result of the CDP's shift to the center, the JCP's rating of the CDP plummeted from 77 in 2021 to 39 in 2024.

As a result of the general election, the LDP and Kōmeitō did not win a majority of seats, so Ishin and DPP, which are positioned between the LDP and CDP in terms of policy, also gained more bargaining power against the LDP. In the UTAS, 18%, 15%, 17%, and 33% of Ishin candidates said that they "should form a coalition" or "could form a coalition depending on the election results" with the LDP, Kōmeitō, CDP, and DPP. At the time of the survey, Ishin had no intention of forming a coalition with the LDP or Kōmeitō. In contrast, 56%, 66%, 79%, and 79% of DPP respondents said they could form a coalition with the LDP, Kōmeitō, CDP, and Ishin, respectively. A majority (57%) of LDP candidates also thought a coalition with the DPP was possible. For now, DPP leader Tamaki Yuichiro says his party aims to implement its policies while maintaining "equal distance" from both the LDP and the CDP. However, this is only a temporary lull, and by the summer of 2025, the psychological distance between the parties could change significantly again.

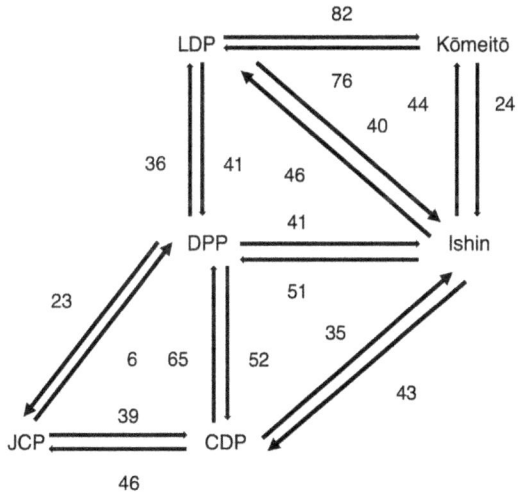

Fig. 8.6 Emotional temperature between political parties

Appendix: The 2024 UTAS Political Leader Survey

The 2024 UTAS Political Leader Survey was conducted from October 2 to October 27, 2024, targeting all 1344 candidates for the general election. The *Asahi Shimbun* distributed the survey forms, and the candidates responded by entering their answers online. The number of valid responses was 1255 (93.4%). The raw data and the codebook will be available at https://www.masaki.j.u-tokyo.ac.jp/utas/utasindex_en.html.

The questions used in this section are listed below. Other items used to assess ideology should be found in the codebook.

The Constitution: Do you think that the current Constitution needs to be amended or not? (1: It needs to be amended. 5: It does not need to be amended.)

(For those who answered "It needs to be amended" or "If anything, it needs to be amended") Which of the following items do you think need amendment?

Defense: The defense forces should be strengthened. (1 = Agree, 5 = Disagree)

Japan-U.S.:
A: The Japan-U.S. Security Treaty should be strengthened to ensure cooperation by the United States in times of crisis.
B: We should be cautious about strengthening the Japan-U.S. Security Treaty to avoid getting involved in wars that have nothing to do with Japan.
(1 = Close to A, 2 = Close to B)

QE: (Provided that this is long-term economic management) The Bank of Japan will continue its policy of quantitative monetary easing, including purchases of Japanese Government Bonds. (1 = Agree, 5 = Disagree)

PIR: The Bank of Japan should raise its policy interest rate. (1 = Agree, 5 = Disagree)

Budget Deficit:
A: There is no need to worry about the budget deficit as government bonds are being steadily purchased.
B: The budget deficit is at a critical level, so bond issuance should be controlled.
(1 = Close to A, 2 = Close to B)

Donation:

A: Corporations and groups have the freedom to engage in political activities.
B: Corporations and groups should be banned from making donations.
(1 = Close to A, 2 = Close to B)
Faction:
Factions or policy groups are necessary within the party for the study of policies and the development of human resources. (1 = Agree, 5 = Disagree)
Policies Emphasized: Which of the following policies is most important to you in this election? What is your second and third most important policy?
Feeling Thermometer: Do you have favorable or unfavorable feelings for or against the following parties and politicians? If you have neither favorable nor unfavorable feelings for a party or politician, please use the "Emotional Thermometer" below to set the temperature at 50 degrees. If you have favorable feelings, please answer with a number between 51 and 100 degrees, depending on the intensity of your feelings, and if you have unfavorable feelings, please answer with a number anywhere between 49 and 0 degrees. Please use an integer between 0 and 100, not a decimal point.
Coalition partners: Do you think that the political party to which you belong (or yourself, if you are not affiliated with any party) should participate in a coalition government after the election with the following parties?

1. We should form a coalition regardless of the election results.
2. Depending on the election results, we could form a coalition.
3. Regardless of the election results, we should not form a coalition.
4. The political party to which I belong.

REFERENCES

Asano, Taka-aki. 2023. *Supporters, Tolerators, and Fence-sitters: Responses to the LDP Government in the 2010s* [*Sandō, Kyoyō, Bōkan Sareta Jimintō Seiji*]. Yūhikaku.
Carlson, Matthew M. 2025. "Scandals During the Kishida Administration." In *Japan Decides 2024: The Japanese General Election*, edited by Kenneth M.

McElwain, Robert J. Pekkanen and Daniel M. Smith, 217–233. Palgrave Macmillan.

Maeda, Kentarō. 2019. *Democracy without Women* [*Josei no Inai Minshushugi*]. Iwanami Shoten.

Taniguchi, Masaki. 2020. *Representative Democracy in Japan: Voters and Politicians* [*Gendai Nihon no Daihyousei Minshu Seiji*]. University of Tokyo Press.

Taniguchi, Masaki, and Jirō Mizushima eds. 2021. *Economy, Society and Culture, and Globalization* [*Keizai, Shakai Bunka, Globalization*]. Nippon Institute of Research Advancement.

CHAPTER 9

How Party Manifestos Framed Political Distrust in the 2024 Election

Tomoko Matsumoto

Distrust in politics has been spreading across established democracies, garnering growing attention (see Citrin and Stoker 2018; Devine 2024 for a comprehensive review). Japan is no exception, with political distrust intensifying, particularly in response to the 2023 political funding scandals.

The 2024 House of Representatives election, overshadowed by political scandals, bears some resemblance to the pivotal 1993 election that marked the collapse of the 1955 system and the Liberal Democratic Party's (LDP) loss of power. While a detailed examination of political scandals and their effects is provided elsewhere (see Carlson 2025; Matsubayashi 2025; Nemoto 2025), it is noteworthy that Japan—where political trust has historically been low—experienced a pronounced surge in political distrust following revelations of illicit political contributions involving the LDP in December 2023. Public opinion survey data reflect this shift. According to a postal public opinion survey conducted by *Asahi*

T. Matsumoto (✉)
Tokyo University of Science, Tokyo, Japan
e-mail: tomoko.matsumoto@rs.tus.ac.jp

© The Author(s), under exclusive license to Springer Nature Switzerland AG 2025
K. M. McElwain et al. (eds.), *Japan Decides 2024*,
https://doi.org/10.1007/978-3-031-98797-7_9

Shimbun from late February to early April of each year, the percentage of respondents expressing significant or moderate trust in Japan's politics fluctuated around 44% in 2020, 47% in 2021, and 44% in 2023, before plummeting to 28% in 2024.[1] Similarly, the *Jiji* public opinion survey indicated that cabinet approval ratings remained below 20% from December 2023 to September 2024, rendering the government a lame-duck administration. Even after Kishida Fumio was replaced by Ishiba Shigeru as prime minister in October 2024, public opinion surveys indicated only a slight improvement, with disapproval ratings consistently surpassing approval as the election drew closer.[2] This evidence suggests that political distrust, including debates over political funding reform, undoubtedly influenced the 2024 House of Representatives election (see Maeda 2025 for a detailed discussion of public opinion trends).

This chapter employs qualitative and quantitative analyses to examine how political distrust was framed in party manifestos during the 2024 election. Although skepticism about politicians' fulfillment of campaign promises is widespread in Japan,[3] analyzing manifestos remains crucial for understanding how parties framed the political funding scandals and positioned themselves concerning political distrust. This chapter specifically addresses two key questions: first, how prominently were political funding issues featured in party manifestos; and second, how were these issues framed?

The remainder of the chapter is structured as follows. The next section develops hypotheses on the strategic incentives guiding ruling and opposition parties in their framing of political distrust. The following section outlines the data used in the analysis. Subsequent sections examine how political distrust was addressed in party manifestos and explore the influence of political distrust among young voters in Japan's aging society, before concluding with a summary.

---

[1] https://www.asahi.com/articles/ASS4C1RK5S4CUZPS008M.html, last accessed on January 9, 2025.

[2] https://www.jiji.co.jp/service/yoron/, last accessed on January 9, 2025.

[3] According to the 2016 International Social Survey Project, only 10.6% of Japanese respondents agreed or strongly agreed that "people we elect as MPs try to keep the promises they have made during the election" (ISSP Research Group 2018).

Framings of Political Distrust

Political distrust can be framed in two primary ways: distrust stemming solely from perception or distrust grounded in both perception and reality (i.e., actual corruption). When framed as a perception issue, political distrust is attributed to voters' lack of information. In such cases, proposed solutions typically focus on enhancing transparency and accountability to rebuild public trust.

Conversely, when distrust is framed as resulting from actual corruption, two subcategories emerge, as noted by Kishishita and Matsumoto (2024b): (i) the inefficient use of public funds and (ii) the prioritization of elite interests over ordinary citizens. The first subcategory focuses on wasteful government expenditures, even when the underlying projects may serve a public purpose. The second highlights collusion between politicians, business elites, and corporations, leading to policies that disproportionately benefit the wealthy. For instance, Gilens and Page (2014) document the limited influence of average citizens on U.S. policymaking compared to the substantial influence of economic elites and organized business groups.

Among them, the mildest criticism of the government attributes distrust to a mere lack of voter information. Therefore, the following hypothesis can be proposed: ruling parties are more likely to frame political distrust as a result of insufficient transparency and accountability, emphasizing informational remedies over allegations of misconduct.

On the other hand, opposition parties are more likely to frame political distrust as stemming from actual corruption, although their critique may vary in focus. Kishishita and Matsumoto (2024b) argue that concerns over government inefficiency make voters hesitant to accept tax increases, whereas concerns about plutocratic influence may prompt voters to support increasing taxes on the wealthy. Building on the argument, I hypothesize that the left-leaning opposition parties are more likely to frame political distrust as a result of plutocratic influence while the right-leaning opposition parties are more likely to frame it as a result of inefficient governance.

Additionally, in the context of political distrust in Japan, the distrust harbored by young voters toward the elderly warrants closer examination. Japan is the world's most rapidly aging society and holds the largest fiscal deficit among advanced economies. Since the mid-2010s, the term "silver democracy" has emerged, epitomizing the frustration among younger generations with a political system perceived to be dominated by older voters (Shimasawa 2017; Yashiro 2016).[4] They argue that politicians craft policies catering primarily to the elderly to secure electoral victories, as younger people not only constitute a smaller share of the population but also exhibit significantly lower voter turnout compared to the elderly.

Recently, this growing distrust among young people toward "silver democracy" has evolved into concerns over the sustainability of pensions and healthcare systems that have mainly benefited the elderly. Except for a minority of working people who express little concern about Japan's fiscal deficits, the majority do not support the burden increases, even when informed about the projected benefits they would receive upon reaching old age (Kishishita and Matsumoto 2024a).

Given Japan's demographic structure, where younger voters constitute a minority, it is not politically rational for major parties seeking a parliamentary majority to risk alienating older voters in exchange for garnering support from younger constituents. In contrast, for smaller parties that do not aim to secure a majority, at least in the short term, such as the Democratic Party for the People (DPP), it may be strategically viable to address the political distrust of young voters. This issue will be discussed in detail later.

PARTY MANIFESTOS IN JAPAN

This study utilizes party manifestos to analyze how political distrust was framed during the 2024 election for several reasons.[5]

First, party manifestos are strategic documents crafted by politically sophisticated elites (Laver and Garry 2000: 620). In contrast to media coverage, which is shaped by the media's editorial framing, party manifestos provide direct insight into how parties prioritize and frame key issues, such as political funding scandals.

---

[4] While Shimasawa et al. (2014) supports this skepticism, Takao (2022) demonstrates that older voters in Japan are less self-interested compared to their counterparts in other advanced economies.

[5] The use of standardized election bulletins (*senkyo kōhō*) has been a long-standing practice in Japan since 1934. However, the drafting of formal party manifestos by major political parties became a consistent tradition only after the 2003 House of Representatives general election. For discussions on the history of Japanese party manifestos and their international comparison, see Proksch et al. (2011) and Winkler and Hijino (2018).

Second, party manifestos provide sufficient textual data to analyze the framing of political funding issues chosen by each party. While election bulletins (*senkyo kōhō*) are another potential source of textual data,[6] their brevity limits their utility. Although these documents might indicate whether candidates address political funding issues, they do not provide enough textual content to analyze the nuances of how these issues are framed.

Finally, party manifestos more accurately reflect the official positions of political parties than candidate-specific materials such as candidates' pamphlets or social media posts, which may diverge from party strategies. As unified and strategic documents, party manifestos are therefore essential for understanding how parties framed political funding issues during the 2024 election.

For this study, party manifestos were collected from all political parties that secured at least one seat in the 2024 House of Representatives election. Party manifestos, as published on each party's official website in the lead-up to the election, were utilized as primary sources. Most parties' manifestos consist of two types of documents: (i) concise policy pamphlets and (ii) comprehensive policy compilations that detail all campaign promises. The concise policy pamphlets are instrumental in understanding which policies parties prioritize and highlight to appeal to voters. In contrast, the comprehensive policy compilations offer valuable insights into the full scope of a party's agenda and ideological stance. To capture the nuances of how parties framed political distrust and related issues, this study records and analyzes both types of documents as separate datasets. It should be noted that the Conservative Party of Japan (CPJ), Sanseitō, and the Social Democratic Party (SDP) did not provide a detailed policy compilation for the 2024 general election online, offering only a concise policy pamphlet. As a result, the comprehensive policy compilation from these parties is omitted from the dataset (see details in the Appendix.)

Additionally, to determine the left-right ideological positions of political parties, this study employs the "Expert Survey Results in Japan," conducted by Professor Junko Kato's Laboratory at the University of

---

[6] The advancement of quantitative text analysis methods since the 2000s has enabled numerous studies to analyze candidate election bulletins, both in Japan and internationally (Catalinac 2016, 2018; Hijino and Ishima 2021; Kajiwara 2014; Ono and Miwa 2023; Shinada 2011, 2018).

Tokyo during the 2021 House of Representatives election. The survey tasked experts with evaluating the ideological placement of each party on a 20-point scale, where 1 represents the most left-wing position and 20 the most right-wing.[7] The publicly disclosed average scores reveal that JCP scored 2.6, SDP 3.5, and Reiwa 3.5, designating these parties as the most left-leaning. The Constitutional Democratic Party of Japan (CDP) scored 7.1, reflecting a moderately left-leaning stance, while Kōmeitō and DPP scored 10.5 and 11.8, respectively, indicating centrist positions. In contrast, LDP scored 15.2, and Japan Ishin no Kai (Ishin) 16.3, signifying right-leaning tendencies. Although the newly established Sanseitō and CPJ were not included in this 2021 expert survey, Sanseitō leader Kamiya Sōhei remarked that their appeal resonated with "those holding conservative views."[8] Furthermore, the CPJ explicitly incorporates "conservative" into its party name. Based on these considerations, both parties are classified as right-leaning for the purposes of this analysis.

PARTIES DIFFERENTLY FRAMED POLITICAL FUNDING ISSUES

To assess how political parties prioritized and framed political funding issues during the 2024 House of Representatives election, Table 9.1 summarizes the election slogans and the prominence of these issues in party manifestos. While only two parties—Reiwa and JCP—explicitly mentioned political distrust in their slogans, a closer examination reveals that political funding issues were prominently featured in the manifestos of major parties. For example, the LDP, CDP, and Ishin listed political funding issues as their top priority. Although Kōmeitō did not formally list it as a pledge, it addressed the issue on the opening page of its manifesto, signaling its recognition of the topic's significance (see Klein and McLaughlin 2025). In contrast, smaller opposition parties displayed varying levels of engagement with political funding issues. Left-leaning parties such as the JCP and SDP placed these issues prominently at the forefront of their platforms. Meanwhile, DPP and Reiwa relegated political funding to the final items in their manifestos, reflecting

---

[7] An alternative approach to measuring ideology can be found in Taniguchi et al. (2025), which utilizes UTAS data for ideological classification.

[8] NHK https://www3.nhk.or.jp/news/html/20241027/k10014620871000.html, last accessed January 9, 2025.

a less emphatic prioritization. Notably, Sanseitō and CPJ entirely omitted political funding issues from their manifestos.

Additionally, Panel A of Fig. 9.1 visualizes the proportions of political funding-related keywords (e.g., "donations," "political funding," "policy activity expenses," "transportation costs," "correspondence expenses," "reserve funds," "lodging costs," and "money") in each party's manifesto.[9] Opposition parties such as the CDP, Ishin, DPP, and SDP referenced these issues more frequently than the LDP and Kōmeitō. This suggests that the ruling coalition, while acknowledging political funding issues, adopted a more reserved stance compared to opposition parties, which used the issue to criticize the government more aggressively.

Table 9.1 Campaign slogans and mentions of political funding in the 2024 election manifestos

Party	2024 election campaign slogan	Mention of political funding issues
LDP	Protect Japan. Harness Growth	1st out of 5 main pledges
Kōmeitō	A hopeful future is achievable	Mentioned at the start but not numbered as one of the six main pledges
CDP	Regime change is the greatest political reform	1st out of 7 main pledges
Ishin	Break the old politics	1st out of 8 main pledges
DPP	Increase take-home pay	4th out of 4 main pledges
Reiwa	Disappointed with the world? Then change it with Reiwa	6th out of 6 main pledges
JCP	Reform to correct the distortions of LDP politics through JCP's advance	1st out of 4 main pledges
Sanseitō	Don't underestimate Japan	No mention
CPJ	Make Japan prosperous and strong	No mention
SDP	Six plans to rebuild Japan	1st out of 6 main pledges

[9] The proportions were calculated as follows: First, the text was tokenized, removing punctuation, symbols, numbers, and URLs. Only tokens consisting of numerals, hiragana, katakana, and kanji were retained. Compound words, formed by co-occurring katakana and kanji sequences, were identified and merged. Stopwords and grammatical words were excluded. A document-feature matrix (DFM) was then generated, and document names were customized. Token frequencies were calculated per document, and the relative proportions of political funding-related keywords were determined by dividing their frequency by the total token count for each document. This method was also applied to calculate other ratios throughout this chapter.

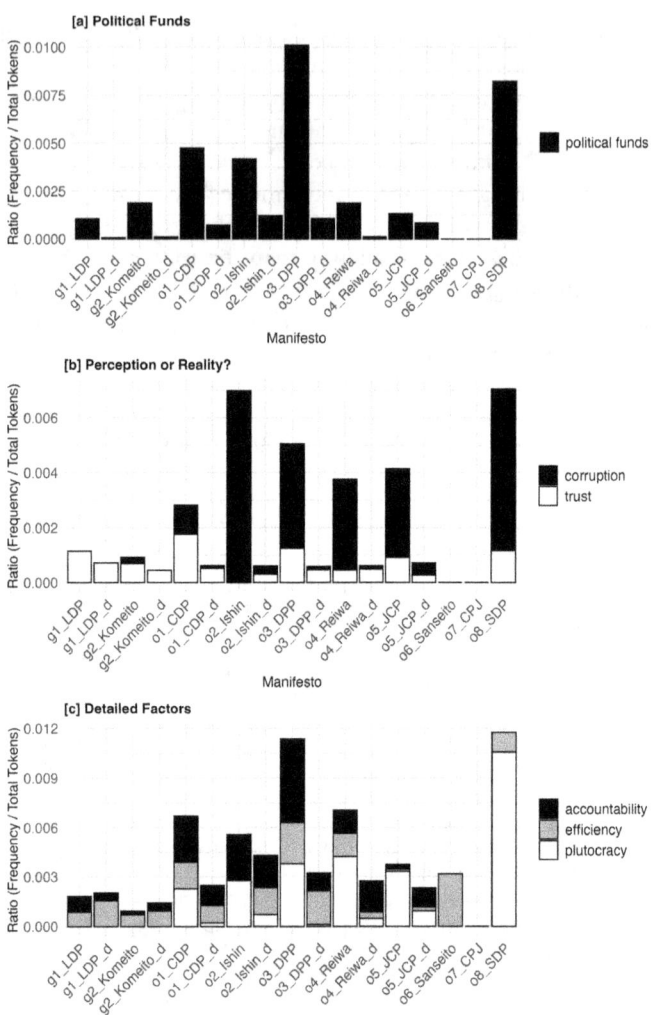

Fig. 9.1 How parties mentioned political distrust in their manifestos (*Note* "g" and "o" denote "government party" and "opposition party," respectively, with "g2" indicating the second largest ruling party. Sanseitō and CPJ each won three seats, but since Sanseitō received more proportional representation votes, it is listed first. Documents without "_d" are digest manifestos, while those with "_d" are comprehensive policy compilations.)

A particularly notable case is the DPP. Despite placing political funding issues last in its list of pledges, it devoted substantial manifesto content to the topic, indicating a strategic focus on detailed discussion without prioritizing it as a headline issue. Conversely, Reiwa and JCP, despite referencing political distrust in its slogan, exhibited a lower level of attention to political funding issues, the levels of which are similar to the one of Kōmeitō. Sanseitō and the CPJ, as previously noted, did not address the topic at all.

In summary, political funding issues played a significant role in the 2024 election, especially among major opposition parties, which leveraged these issues to differentiate themselves from the ruling coalition.

Next, I examine how each party framed political funding issues in the election. Panel B of Fig. 9.1 reports the proportions of corruption-related keywords (e.g., "dirty money," "graft," and "corruption") and trust-related keywords (e.g., "trust," "distrust," and "credibility") in party manifestos. Consistent with the hypothesis proposed previously, the LDP completely avoided explicit references to corruption, instead relying solely on trust-related terms. In the LDP's manifesto, the pledges concerning political funding issues emphasized "complying with the rules," asserting that the current controversy stemmed from failures to fulfill legal obligations for mandatory disclosures. The manifesto suggested that, had these disclosures been properly made, no issues would have arisen. This reflects the perspective that political distrust stems from a few Diet Members failing to comply with existing rules intended to ensure transparency for voters, even though the rules themselves do not allow corrupt practices.

Kōmeitō displayed a similar approach. The party indicates a strategic effort by the ruling coalition to frame political distrust as the result of isolated violations by certain individuals, rather than as evidence of systemic flaws in the regulations governing political funding.

In contrast, many opposition parties frequently invoked corruption-related language, framing political distrust as a direct consequence of systemic governance failures under LDP-led administrations. This approach allowed opposition parties to amplify their critique by connecting political distrust to tangible instances of corruption.

Panel C of Fig. 9.1 further analyzes manifesto content using three keyword categories: accountability (e.g., "accountability," "transparency," "disclosure," and "visualization"), government efficiency (e.g., "waste" and "[in-]efficiency"), and plutocracy ("slush fund," "donation," "money power," "collusion," "concession," and "bribe"). The right-leaning ruling party, LDP, emphasized accountability and government efficiency but avoided references to plutocratic influence, reflecting their focus on addressing political distrust through increased transparency and efficiency while sidestepping criticism of ties between wealth and politics. Kōmeitō took a similar approach in their manifesto.

In comparison, the CDP's manifesto addressed issues of accountability, inefficiency, and plutocracy in a balanced manner. It emphasized ensuring full transparency in political funding to prevent illicit activities and tax evasion. The manifesto proposed measures such as banning corporate and organizational donations, abolishing policy activity expenses, and amending the Political Funds Control Act to eradicate money-driven corruption in politics. Additionally, it advocated restricting the inheritance of political funding by Diet Members, diversifying political candidates, and ensuring that politics reflects the public's will. Furthermore, the manifesto underscored the importance of promoting transparency and efficiency in the use of taxpayers' money. While the CDP's detailed policy booklet places comparatively less emphasis on plutocracy-related corruption, it still addresses the interconnected issues of accountability, efficiency, and plutocracy. This balanced approach is similarly reflected in the DPP's manifesto.

Consistent with expectations discussed earlier, left-leaning opposition small parties such as Reiwa, JCP, and SDP prioritized critiques of plutocratic influence. By contrast, Sanseitō and the CPJ, right-leaning opposition small parties, entirely omitted references to plutocracy.

Contrary to expectations, Ishin—a right-leaning opposition party—emphasized accountability and plutocracy in its digest version but avoided addressing government efficiency. This omission may reflect an effort to deflect criticism over wasteful spending related to the Osaka World Expo 2025.

Youth Concerns Amid "Silver Democracy" and DPP's Strategies

In addition to examining general political distrust, this study highlights the specific distrust among young people, who believe that politicians primarily design policies to benefit the elderly rather than address the needs of younger generations. To investigate how political parties prioritize generational issues, Panel A of Fig. 9.2 presents the frequency of age-related keywords appearing in their manifestos. Keywords encompassed children (e.g., "child," "next generation," "school-age," "elementary school," "middle school," "high school," "kindergarten," "students"), youth (e.g., "student," "young," "young adults," "higher education," "university"), the working-age population (e.g., "parenting," "employment," "worker," "labor," "middle age"), and the elderly (e.g., "elderly," "retired," "senior," "end-of-life"). Additionally, I include keywords signifying inclusivity across generations (e.g., "Japanese," "people," "all generations") to capture non-explicit targeting of specific age groups (see Arami 2025 for a broader discussion of childcare and family policies).

Despite the prevalence of the "silver democracy" narrative, no evidence suggests that party manifestos exclusively target the elderly. On the contrary, younger generations often receive greater emphasis across party platforms. Even parties with higher mention rates for the elderly, such as Kōmeitō and Ishin, reference them less frequently than their demographic proportion would warrant. Interestingly, Kōmeitō and Ishin significantly reduced references to the elderly in their detailed policy booklets compared to the summary versions of their manifestos.

DPP emerged as a notable case, gaining substantial support from younger voters in the 2024 election (see also Fahey 2025). In the proportional representation vote, the DPP ranked second among 18- and 19-year-olds, capturing 19% of their votes compared to the LDP's 26%. Among voters in their 20s, the DPP surpassed the LDP, with 26% versus 20%, making it the most popular party in this age group. Additionally, the DPP tied with the LDP at 21% among voters in their 30s. In contrast, the CDP retained its position as the leading opposition party among voters aged 40 and above, further underscoring the DPP's strong appeal to younger demographics.

An analysis of the DPP's manifesto reveals minimal references to the elderly, with its primary focus directed toward the working-age population and younger generations. Simultaneously, the DPP emphasized inclusivity, appealing to "all generations" or "Japanese" more frequently than other major parties. This strategic focus on generational equity and inclusivity distinguishes the DPP in Japan's political landscape.

After the election, the DPP capitalized on its parliamentary leverage over the minority LDP, pressing demands such as raising the "income barrier." This term refers to a phenomenon in which surpassing a certain income threshold leads to disproportionate increases in taxes or social security contributions, effectively reducing take-home pay and discouraging additional earnings. The DPP's manifesto prominently advocated

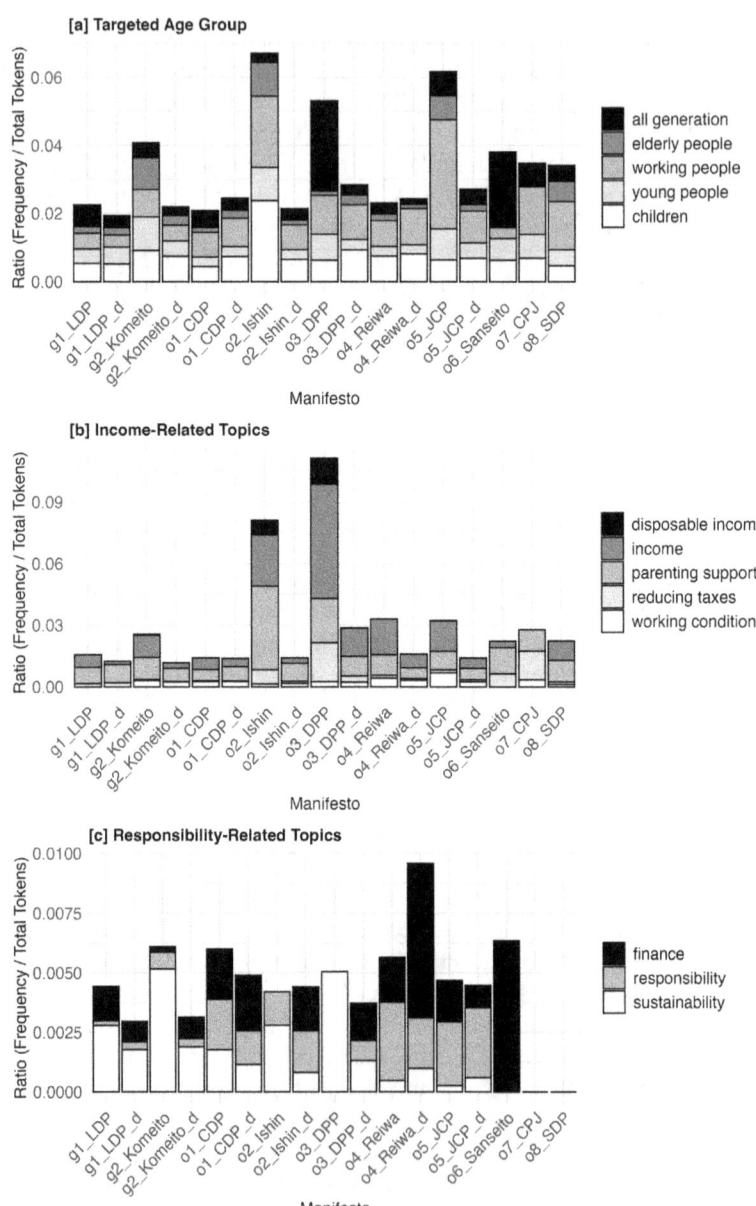

Fig. 9.2 Political distrust among younger voters
(*Note* Axis labels are the same as in Fig. 9.1)

for policies to "increase everyone's take-home income through tax reductions, reductions in social security contributions, and support for households and childcare." The issue of raising the income barrier emerged within broader discussions on tax cuts aimed at increasing the disposable income of the working-age population.

Panel B of Fig. 9.2 highlights the frequency of income-related keywords across party manifestos, including overall income (e.g., "income," "wages," "annual income," "salary," "household," and "wage increase"), disposable income (e.g., "take-home pay" and "disposable"), working conditions (e.g., "work," "overtime," "remote," "part-time," "employee," "full-time," "temporary," "reskilling," and "recurrent"), parenting support (e.g., "parenting," "education," and "scholarship"), and tax reductions (e.g., "tax cuts," "burden reduction," and "tax exemptions"). While Ishin also frequently mentioned income-related topics in its digest manifesto, the DPP outpaced all other parties. The DPP particularly prioritized increasing disposable income, prominently featuring this issue in its election slogan.

In contrast to the ruling LDP and Kōmeitō, as well as the CDP, which sought to position itself as an alternative ruling party and avoided discussing tax cuts due to fiscal discipline, the DPP took an active stance on reducing taxes and social security contributions. To provide further insight, Panel C of Fig. 9.2 examines keywords related to responsibility-focused topics, including "responsibility," "finance," and "sustainability." While the DPP addressed these issues in its detailed policy booklets, its condensed manifesto notably omitted any mention of responsibility or finance. This omission contrasts with the other major opposition parties, such as CDP and Ishin, which mentioned these themes in their manifestos, reflecting their governance ambitions.

The DPP's strategy is notable for its emphasis on short-term increases in disposable income while downplaying concerns about fiscal discipline and the long-term consequences of reducing social security contributions (Amano and Katada 2025). Worsening national finances could harm younger generations in the future, and diminished social security contributions may affect their retirement security. Nevertheless, the DPP's focused messaging on boosting immediate disposable income and supporting younger generations proved effective in capturing the attention and support of younger voters.

Conclusion

This chapter examined differences in how political parties addressed political distrust by analyzing their party manifestos. The findings reveal several key points. First, the ruling coalition led by the LDP viewed political distrust differently from opposition parties. While the LDP acknowledged political distrust and emphasized improving accountability and transparency, its manifesto refrained from discussing flaws in the current political funding system. This suggests that the LDP aimed to restore trust by demonstrating adherence to existing rules rather than questioning the system itself.

In contrast, major opposition parties not only acknowledged political distrust but argued that it stemmed from genuine instances of corruption. These parties highlighted two primary issues: misuse of public funds and collusion with business interests. Notably, left-leaning parties such as the JCP and SDP were particularly vocal in criticizing money politics, adopting a more assertive stance than centrist opposition parties.

The chapter also explored a form of political distrust specific to Japan: younger generations' skepticism that their interests are sidelined in favor of the elderly in a rapidly aging society. Contrary to this perception, an analysis of party manifestos revealed that most parties did not focus on the elderly much. Rather, they frequently mentioned younger generations, working-age populations, and children. Among these parties, the DPP, a non-mainstream opposition party, stood out for its targeted strategy to attract young voters. By minimizing references to the elderly and focusing instead on increasing disposable income for working generations—through tax reductions and social security contribution cuts—the DPP adopted a distinct approach compared to the major ruling and opposition parties. While questions remain about the long-term sustainability of prioritizing short-term benefits for younger generations, the DPP's focus on securing their votes marked a notable trend in the election.

Moving forward, two critical issues warrant attention: whether parties adhere to their manifestos and whether these manifestos demonstrate long-term consistency and sustainability. As mentioned earlier, the majority of Japanese citizens do not believe that politicians strive to fulfill their campaign promises. While parties like the DPP have taken steps to showcase their achievements in their manifestos, what is needed is not self-assessment but objective evaluations by third-party institutions. Efforts such as the Waseda University Manifesto Research Institute's initiative[10] to assess manifestos are a step in the right direction, but their visibility and evaluation criteria require further development. Establishing a robust framework for third-party evaluations of party manifestos could lay the foundation for addressing political distrust.

Appendix: Sources of Political Party Manifesto Data for the 2024 House of Representatives Election

The data for political party manifestos for the 2024 House of Representatives election were obtained as follows:

1. LDP: The LDP manifesto was accessed via the following link:

    - Digest manifesto: https://storage2.jimin.jp/pdf/pamphlet/202410_manifest.pdf
    - Comprehensive policy compilations: https://storage2.jimin.jp/pdf/pamphlet/20241015_j-file_pamphlet.pdf

2. Kōmeitō: The Kōmeitō manifesto was accessed via the following link: https://www.komei.or.jp/special/shuin50/manifesto/manifesto2024.pdf

    - Pages 1–22: Digest manifesto
    - Pages 23–106: Comprehensive policy compilations

3. CDP: The CDP manifesto was accessed via the following links:

    - Digest manifesto: https://cdp-japan.jp/election2024/downloads/2024_seisaku.pdf
    - Comprehensive policy compilations: https://cdp-japan.jp/assets/pdf/visions/2024/policies2024.pdf

4. Ishin: The Ishin manifesto was accessed via the following links:

    - Digest manifesto: https://o-ishin.jp/shuin2024/manifest/pdf/pamphlet.pdf

---

[10] https://www.waseda-manifesto.jp last accessed on January 10, 2025.

- Comprehensive policy compilations: https://o-ishin.jp/shuin2024/manifest/all.html

5. DPP: The DPP manifesto was accessed via the following link: https://new-kokumin.jp/file/DPFP-PolicyPamphlet_202206.pdf
   - Pages 1–16: Digest manifesto
   - Pages 17–26: Comprehensive policy compilations

6. Reiwa: The Reiwa manifesto was accessed via the following links:
   - Digest manifesto: https://shu50.reiwa-shinsengumi.com/wp-content/themes/shu50reiwa/assets/pdf/reiwa_2024_election_manifest.pdf
   - Comprehensive policy compilations: https://shu50.reiwa-shinsengumi.com/policy/

7. JCP: The JCP manifesto was accessed via the following links:
   - Digest manifesto: https://www.jcp.or.jp/web_download/2024/10/2024-senkyo-sei-p.pdf
   - Comprehensive policy compilations: Accessed from the links provided for each policy field at https://www.jcp.or.jp/web_policy/2024-sousenkyo.html

8. Sanseitō: The Sanseitō manifesto was accessed via the following link: https://sanseito.jp/2020/50th_hore_policy/#determination01

9. CPJ: The CPJ manifesto was accessed via the following link: https://hoshuto.jp/policy/

10. SDP: The SDP manifesto was accessed via the following link: https://sdp.or.jp/wp-content/uploads/2024/10/2024_Shuinelection_6plans_sdp.pdf

All data were downloaded on October 26, 2024, just before the House of Representatives election, and all links were last accessed on January 22, 2025.

References

Amano, Kenya, and Saori N. Katada. 2025. "Election Under Inflation: LDP's Choice of Macroeconomic Policy." In *Japan Decides 2024: The Japanese*

General Election, edited by Kenneth M. McElwain, Robert J. Pekkanen, and Daniel M. Smith, 317–331. New York: Palgrave Macmillan.

Arami, Reiko. 2025, "Childcare Policy in the 2024 Election: Who Resonated with the Public Amid an Unprecedented Birthrate Decline?" In *Japan Decides 2024: The Japanese General Election*, edited by Kenneth M. McElwain, Robert J. Pekkanen, and Daniel M. Smith, 293–315. New York: Palgrave Macmillan.

Carlson, Matthew M. 2025. "Scandals During the Kishida Administration." In *Japan Decides 2024: The Japanese General Election*, edited by Kenneth M. McElwain, Robert J. Pekkanen, and Daniel M. Smith, 217–233. New York: Palgrave Macmillan.

Catalinac, Amy. 2016. "From Pork to Policy: The Rise of Programmatic Campaigning in Japanese Elections." *The Journal of Politics* 78 (1): 1–18.

Catalinac, Amy. 2018. "Positioning Under Alternative Electoral Systems: Evidence from Japanese Candidate Election Manifestos." *American Political Science Review* 112 (1): 31–48.

Citrin, Jack, and Laura Stoker. 2018. "Political Trust in a Cynical Age." *Annual Review of Political Science* 21 (1): 49–70.

Devine, Daniel. 2024. "Does Political Trust Matter? A Meta-analysis on the Consequences of Trust." *Political Behavior* 46: 2241–62.

Fahey, Robert A. 2025. "Social Media in the 2024 General Election." In *Japan Decides 2024: The Japanese General Election*, edited by Kenneth M. McElwain, Robert J. Pekkanen, and Daniel M. Smith, 181–195. New York: Palgrave Macmillan.

Gilens, Martin, and Benjamin I. Page. 2014. "Testing Theories of American Politics: Elites, Interest Groups, and Average Citizens." *Perspectives on Politics* 12 (3): 564–81.

Hijino, Ken Victor Leonard, and Hideo Ishima. 2021. "Multi-level Muddling: Candidate Strategies to 'Nationalize' Local Elections." *Electoral Studies* 70: Article 102281.

ISSP Research Group. 2018. *International Social Survey Programme: Role of Government V—ISSP 2016*. GESIS Data Archive, Cologne. ZA6900 Data file Version 2.0.0, https://doi.org/10.4232/1.13052.

Kajiwara, Akira. 2014. "Who Supports Decentralization Reform in the Diet? Analyzing Candidates' Electoral Pledges in the Lower House General Elections in Japan." *Japan Election Studies* 30 (2): 91–104.

Kishishita, Daiki, and Tomoko Matsumoto. 2024a. "Self-benefits, Fiscal Risk, and Political Support for the Public Healthcare System." *European Journal of Political Economy* 85: 102597.

Kishishita, Daiki, and Tomoko Matsumoto. 2024b. "Political Trust and Preferences for Redistribution: Wasteful Spending and Plutocratic Influence." SSRN. https://doi.org/10.2139/ssrn.4976959.

Klein, Axel, and Levi McLaughlin. 2025. "A Costly Coalition: Kōmeitō's Enduring Partnership with the LDP." In *Japan Decides 2024: The Japanese General Election*, edited by Kenneth M. McElwain, Robert J. Pekkanen, and Daniel M. Smith, 75–90. New York: Palgrave Macmillan.

Laver, Michael, and John Garry. 2000. "Estimating Policy Positions from Political Texts." *American Journal of Political Science* 40 (3): 619–34.

Maeda, Yukio. 2025. "Public Opinion and Scandals in Economic Hard Times." In *Japan Decides 2024: The Japanese General Election*, edited by Kenneth M. McElwain, Robert J. Pekkanen, and Daniel M. Smith, 163–179. New York: Palgrave Macmillan.

Matsubayashi, Tetsuya. 2025. "Partisanship and Turnout in the 2024 General Election." In *Japan Decides 2024: The Japanese General Election*, edited by Kenneth M. McElwain, Robert J. Pekkanen, and Daniel M. Smith, 197–214. New York: Palgrave Macmillan.

Nemoto, Kuniaki. 2025. "Reasons Behind the LDP's Loss in the 2024 Election." In *Japan Decides 2024: The Japanese General Election*, edited by Kenneth M. McElwain, Robert J. Pekkanen, and Daniel M. Smith, 37–55. New York: Palgrave Macmillan.

Ono, Yoshikuni, and Hirofumi Miwa. 2023. "Gender Differences in Campaigning Under Alternative Voting Systems: Analysis of Election Manifestos." *Politics, Groups, and Identities* 11 (5): 1203–11.

Proksch, Sven-Oliver., Jonathan B. Slapin, and Michael F. Thies. 2011. "Party System Dynamics in Post-War Japan: A Quantitative Content Analysis of Electoral Pledges." *Electoral Studies* 30 (1): 114–24.

Shimasawa, Manabu. 2017. *Shirubā Minshushugi no Seiji Keizaigaku* [The Political Economy of Silver Democracy]. Tokyo: Nihon Keizai Shimbunsha.

Shimasawa, Manabu, Kazumasa Oguro, and Nao Toyoda. 2014. "Does Japan Have a Gray Democracy? An Empirical Analysis." *Hitotsubashi University Repository* 2014 (2): 1–18.

Shinada, Yutaka. 2011. "Policy Positions of the Japanese Parties in the 2009 General Election." *Japan Election Studies* 26 (2): 29–43.

Shinada, Yutaka. 2018. "The Transition of Japanese Campaign Manifestoes, 1990–2012." *Japan Election Studies* 34 (2): 5–17.

Takao, Yasuo. 2022. "Intergenerational Politics in an Aging Society: The Graying of Japanese Voters." *Asian Survey* 62 (4): 695–720.

Taniguchi, Masaki, Taka-aki Asano, Shōko Ōmori, and Shūsuke Takamiya. 2025. "Policy Positions of the Candidates." In *Japan Decides 2024: The Japanese General Election*, edited by Kenneth M. McElwain, Robert J. Pekkanen, and Daniel M. Smith, 125–142. New York: Palgrave Macmillan.

Winkler, Christian G., and Ken Victor Hijino. 2018. "Party Ideologies and Regional Inequality: An Analysis of Party Manifestos in Japan." *Asian Studies Review* 42 (4): 586–606.

Yashiro, Naohiro. 2016. *Shirubā Minshushugi: Kōreisha Yūgū o Dō Kokufuku Suru ka* [Silver Democracy: How to Overcome Favoritism Toward the Elderly]. Tokyo: Chūkō Shinsho.

CHAPTER 10

Public Opinion and Scandals in Economic Hard Times

Yukio Maeda

INTRODUCTION

The 2024 HR election marks the first general election following the assassination of Abe Shinzō, a strong leader who wielded considerable influence even after his premiership. In his second term, Abe served for more than 92 months and was immensely popular with the public. In the Jiji Opinion Poll, which has been tracking approval ratings of prime ministers since 1960, Abe's last approval rating of 46.3% is the highest among the preceding twenty-eight prime ministers (including Abe's first term). Succeeding a highly popular and long-serving prime minister is never easy, but in the wake of Abe's death, the Liberal Democratic Party (LDP) faced two major scandals: its ties to the Unification Church (UC) and the slush fund scandal, both of which can be traced back to Abe or his faction.

Furthermore, since early 2022, the Japanese economy has experienced a steady increase in consumer prices, which had remained stagnant since

Y. Maeda (✉)
University of Tokyo, Tokyo, Japan
e-mail: ymaeda@iss.u-tokyo.ac.jp

the latter half of the 1990s (Amano and Katada 2025). These changes in economic conditions have placed an additional burden on the government. While the rising consumer prices have generated discontent among the public, they have also compelled voters to significantly penalize the governing coalition in response to the slush fund scandals.

THE KISHIDA ADMINISTRATION, SCANDALS, AND THE ECONOMY

To understand how people reacted to public affairs between the 2021 and the 2024 HR elections, I rely on opinion polls conducted by media organizations that employ dual-frame Random Digit Dialing methodology. Figure 10.1 shows the approval and disapproval ratings of the Kishida Fumio cabinet from the Kyodo Opinion Poll.[1] The first approval rating for Kishida, just before the general election, was 55.7%.[2] Kishida easily won the 2021 HR election. By the summer of 2022, COVID-19 was no longer a political issue and the war in Ukraine, which started in February 2022, did not affect his approval ratings. Abe was assassinated on July 8, two days before the HC election. After the victory of the 2022 HC election, Kishida reached his highest approval rating of 63.2%. Though Abe's assassination was a shocking event, it had a negligible effect on the election results. 62.5% of respondents felt it had no effect on their voting decision (*Tokyo Shimbun*, July 13, 2023).

However, Kishida's approval rating began to decline shortly after the HC election for two reasons. First, Kishida held a state funeral for Abe, the first of its kind since Yoshida Shigeru's in 1967, but polling showed this did not receive widespread public support (*Yomiuri Shimbun*, September 5, 2022; *Asahi Shimbun*, September 13, 2022). The second and more significant reason was the revelations about Abe's connection with the UC, explained in more detail in other chapters of this volume, including McLaughlin (2025) and Nemoto (2025). The assassin, the son of a devout follower of the UC, apparently held a strong grudge against Abe due to his ties to the church. After the assassination, it was widely reported that Abe appeared in one of the videos prepared for the UC

---

[1] I consulted *Tokyo Shimbun* for the results of the Kyodo Opinion Poll.

[2] First approval ratings for Kishida reported by other news organizations are as follows: Asahi 45%, NHK 49%, Yomiuri 56%, and Nikkei 59%.

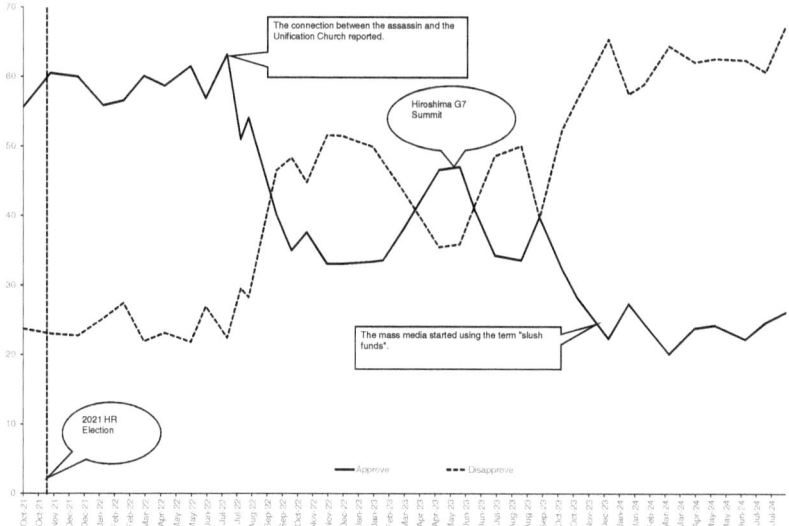

Fig. 10.1 Approval ratings of the Kishida cabinet, October 2021–August 2024 (*Source* Kyodo News Poll)

members. Indeed, the UC had a close connection with Abe's family since the days of his grandfather, Kishi Nobusuke (*Asahi Shimbun*, January 14, 2023).

As the UC was quite infamous, the revelation of its ties to Abe was a significant blow to Kishida. Furthermore, a subsequent series of news reports not only uncovered more on Abe's personal ties with the UC but also highlighted the broader, systematic relationship between it and the LDP. In polls conducted in July 11–12 and October 8–9, Kishida's approval rating dropped from 63.2% to 35.0%.

The UC scandal also led to the resignation of Economic Revitalization Minister Yamagiwa Daishirō in late October after he repeatedly failed to disclose his ties to the UC. Additionally, other scandals led to three more ministers resigning in quick succession from November to December. Justice Minister Hanashi Yasuhiro stepped down following insensitive comments regarding the death penalty, followed by the resignations of Internal Affairs and Communications Minister Terada Minoru over violations of political finance regulations, and Reconstruction Minister Akiba Kenya for issues related to political and campaign finance. Prime Minister

Kishida's approval ratings hovered around 33% from November 2022 to February 2023.

His approval rating experienced a brief surge from March to May 2023 because of his diplomatic efforts. Kishida's visit to Kyiv, Ukraine in March and bilateral meetings with South Korean President Yoon Suk-yeol in May contributed to an increase in his approval rating (*Yomiuri Shimbun*, April 18, 2023; *Nikkei Shimbun*, May 2, 2023). Additionally, his role in chairing the G7 summit in Hiroshima and successfully arranging visits by other G7 leaders to the Hiroshima Peace Memorial Museum in May left a positive impression on the public. Newspaper polls indicated that the G7 summit in Hiroshima boosted Kishida's approval rating (*Yomiuri Shimbun*, May 22, 2023; *Asahi Shimbun*, May 29, 2023). However, his approval rating soon began to decline again.

No single event or scandal clearly explains the decline in Kishida's approval ratings. His son tarnished his father's popularity by hosting a party at the official residence of the prime minister (*Nikkei Shimbun*, May 29, 2023). A series of troubles related to the My Number Card[3] and the presentation of his "extraordinary" policy to combat the declining birthrate were disappointing (*Asahi Shimbun*, June 19 and July 17, 2023; *Yomiuri Shimbun*, June 26 and July 24, 2023). Particularly, problems concerning the My Number Card and health insurance, which directly affect the daily lives of ordinary citizens, led people to question Kishida's leadership (*Asahi Shimbun*, August 21, 2023; *Yomiuri Shimbun*, August 28, 2023).

Kishida tried to revive his public support by reshuffling his cabinet in September 2023 but his approval rating improved only by a few percentage points: 6 in Kyodo News; 4 in *Asahi*; 3 in NHK; and no change in *Yomiuri*. His approval deteriorated through the successive scandal-related resignations of two state ministers and a parliamentary vice-minister. Furthermore, public discontent with the rise in consumer prices dating back to the start of the war in Ukraine was a continuous political issue. The government's ineffective economic policies fueled the

---

[3] My Number Card is linked to sensitive personal information registered in various government systems. The government has encouraged the public to apply for the My Number Card and has even offered monetary incentives. However, despite being advertised as highly secure, numerous errors have been reported, including the issuance of certificates for other individuals, the disclosure of medical information to unrelated parties, the incorrect association of a different person's bank account with one's card, and sending monetary rewards to unintended recipients (*Asahi Shimbun*, June 1, 2023).

public's anxiety and frustration (*Asahi Shimbun,* November 21, 2023; *Yomiuri Shimbun,* November 20, 2023). In late November, the mass media started reporting on the slush fund scandal in Abe's faction, which forced Kishida to expel four more ministers from his cabinet—Minister for Internal Affairs and Communications Suzuki Junji, Minister of Agriculture, Forestry and Fisheries Miyashita Ichirō, Minister of Economy, Trade and Industry Nishimura Yasutoshi, and Chief Cabinet Secretary Matsuno Hirokazu. This off-the-books slush fund scandal received massive media attention and further depressed Kishida's already low approval rating.

Underlying Economic Discontents

Reviewing the time series of approval ratings shows how people responded to the ongoing political affairs. In this section, utilizing the questions on the reasons why people approve or disapprove of the prime minister, I try to show what causes people's responses. The primary reason for using the Kyodo Opinion Poll in this chapter, among several other media opinion polls, is that its questions on the reasons for approval and disapproval include both economic policy and diplomacy, along with leadership, in its choice set.[4] Following chapters in previous volumes of *Japan Decides*, I calculated the percentage of respondents who approved or disapproved of Kishida for specific reasons within the entire sample.[5] Figure 10.2 shows how approval based on specific reasons changed over time.

Unlike his two predecessors, Kishida's approval was largely based on very passive reasons—his largest group of supporters chose "there is no one else suited to the job," and the second largest group chose "the Cabinet is a coalition between the LDP and Kōmeitō." When Abe took office, approval based on economic expectations was much larger than the support based on "there is no one else suited to the job." In the

---

[4] Asahi, Yomiuri, and NHK have similar questions, but none of them differentiate between diplomacy and economic policy when asking for the reasons respondents approve or disapprove of the cabinet.

[5] I calculate the percentage as follows: I multiplied the approval ratings by the percentage of respondents who selected each reason for approval and then divided by one hundred. For example, when an approval rating is 50% and 30% of those who approve of the prime minister select leadership as their reason, the approval based on leadership is 15%; 50 multiplied by 30 and then divided by 100 yields 15. The same procedure applies to the disapproval ratings for each reason.

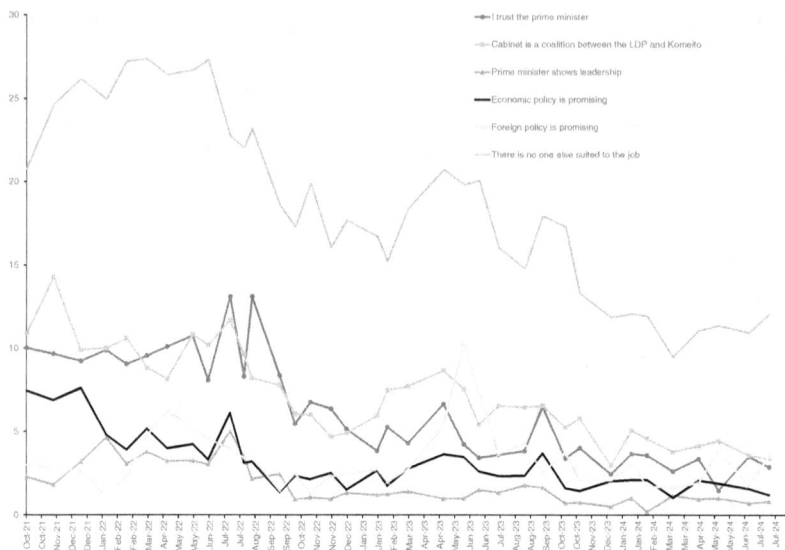

Fig. 10.2 Primary reason for cabinet approval, November 2021–August 2024 (*Source* Kyodo News Poll)

case of Suga Yoshihide, Kishida's immediate predecessor, the percentage of "I trust the prime minister" was equal to the percentage of "no one else." Kishida's approval was based on passive reasons from the beginning, and approval based on his leadership and economic policies remained low throughout his tenure.

Figure 10.3 shows trends in the primary reasons for disapproval. Initially, disapproval for each reason was low, but disapproval due to "economic policy is not promising" started to increase in the early spring of 2022 and accelerated over the summer. Disapproval based on leadership increased when Kishida suffered from the UC and the slush funds scandals, but its proportion is half that of disapproval based on the economy. Except for the scandal caused by his own son, who was an executive secretary for the prime minister, Kishida himself was not implicated in the high-profile scandals, which explains why disapproval based on distrust did not increase, but disapproval based on leadership did.

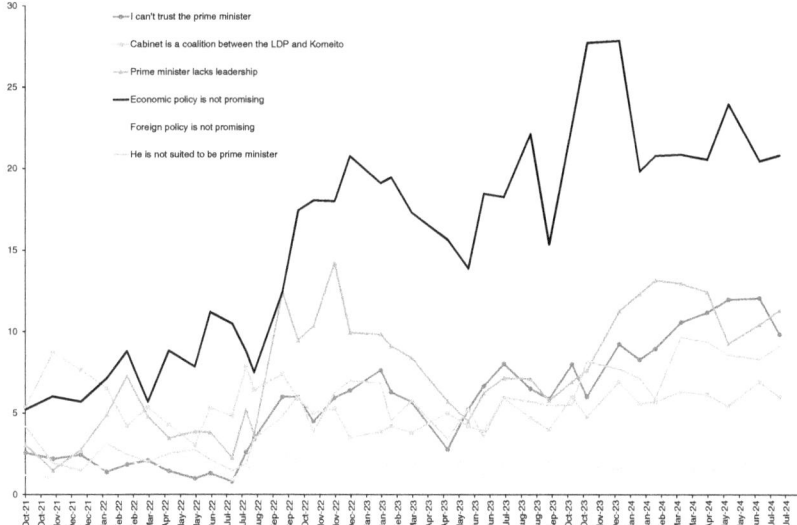

Fig. 10.3 Primary reason for disapproval, November 2021–August 2024 (*Source* Kyodo News Poll)

People's discontent with Kishida's handling of the economy can be more clearly seen in the Asahi Opinion Poll, which asked all respondents if they thought Kishida's economic policy was promising or not. The response to this question is shown in Fig. 10.4, along with disapproval and the Consumer Price Index. Unfortunately, Asahi asked this question only six times, ending in January 2023. Those who thought Kishida's economic policy was not promising increased at the same pace as the rise of the Consumer Price Index, along with Kishida's disapproval rating. Consumer prices kept soaring during his tenure, which hindered his chance to revive his approval.

THE RACE TOWARD THE NEXT PRIME MINISTER

The series of scandals was very unfortunate for Kishida, who apparently committed no wrongdoing himself, nor had anyone committed wrongdoing for him without his knowledge. He nevertheless paid a political price for misconduct by other LDP politicians. As people became more

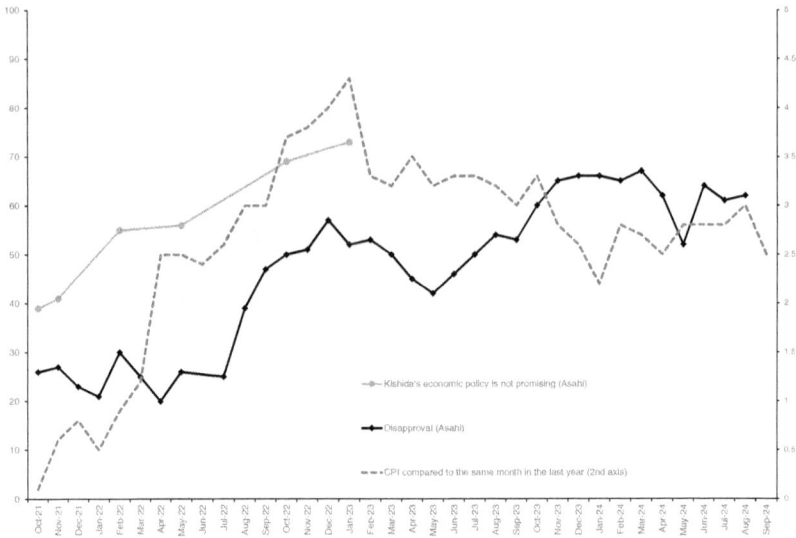

Fig. 10.4 Consumer price index and expectation for Kishida's economic policy (*Source* Cabinet Bureau and Asahi News Poll)

concerned about Kishida's management of the economy and his leadership in handling the scandals, media organizations began to focus on when he would step down and who would succeed him. Polls started asking how long respondents wanted Prime Minister Kishida to stay in power. Yomiuri asked the exact same question six times from May 2023 to June 2024: "How long would you like Prime Minister Kishida to remain in office?" The three options listed were "As long as possible," "Until his term as president of the LDP expires in September 2024," and "I want him to be replaced immediately." The second choice received very stable responses between 52% and 56% throughout, while the third choice of immediate replacement reached its peak of 36% in December 2023, after the revelation of the slush fund scandal (*Yomiuri Shimbun*, December 18, 2023). Looking across the results from other media opinion surveys confirms that very few people wanted Kishida to stay in power in the last half of 2023.

Then, the attention of media organizations turned to who would replace him. TV Asahi most frequently asked the question of who was best suited to be the next prime minister.[6] TV Asahi has asked this question in thirty-one polls since March 2018, fourteen of which were during the Kishida administration.[7]

Among the thirty-one TV Asahi polls, Ishiba Shigeru ranked first twenty-one times, followed by Kōno Tarō, who ranked first six times, and Koizumi Shinjirō, who ranked first four times. If we trace back to the LDP presidential election of September 2012, when the party was in opposition but expected to win the next HR election, Ishiba received 30% support compared to Abe's 21%. It is fair to say that Ishiba has been the public's most favored candidate for over a decade.

Figure 10.5 shows how the public's preferences for the next prime minister evolved during the latter half of Kishida's tenure.[8] When TV Asahi first posed this question, the leading candidate was Kōno Tarō, then the prominent Minister of Digital Transformation. However, his unapologetic communication style worked against him. Beginning in early summer 2023, news outlets reported numerous issues related to the incorporation of health insurance information into My Number Card, a hallmark policy of Kōno Tarō. Although he had been the most favored candidate at the end of 2022, his popularity declined due to these troubles.

After Kōno lost popularity, Ishiba and Koizumi obtained more favorable responses in TV Asahi polls. While they initially competed neck and neck, Ishiba pulled ahead in December 2023 and consistently maintained a lead of around 5 points. Surprisingly, Takaichi Sanae, winner of the first round of the LDP presidential election, averaged only 7% support from the public, in contrast to Ishiba's public support average of 22%. This discrepancy between the high number of first round votes Takaichi received and her weak public support suggests that the preferences of the public and those of the LDP members are quite different.

---

[6] The question wordings and frequencies of the TV Asahi (*Hōdō Station*) Public Opinion Poll since 2012 are available at https://www.tv-asahi.co.jp/hst/poll/.

[7] The wording of the questions changed in December 2022, when the question was first posed under the Kishida Administration. Prior to that, the question asked who was most suitable to be the president of the LDP. From December 2022, it asks who is most suitable to be the Prime Minister among the LDP lawmakers.

[8] The readers should be aware that the scale of the horizontal axis in Fig. 10.5 differs from that of the other figures in this chapter.

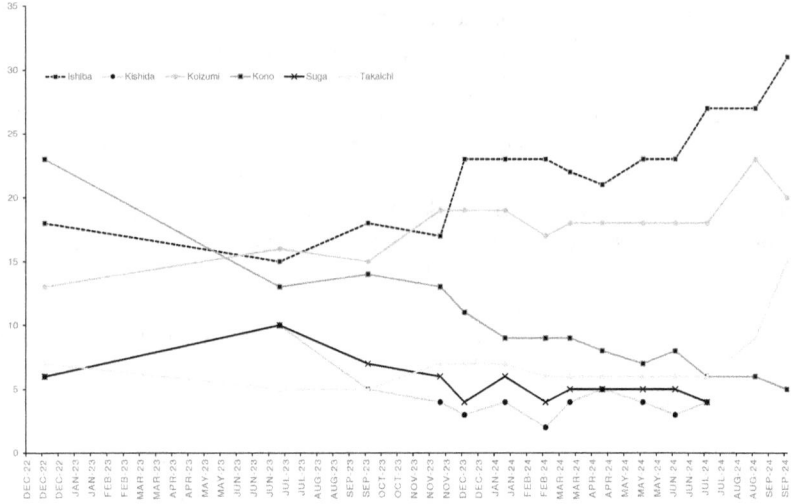

Fig. 10.5 Who is suited to be the next prime minister? (*Source* TV Asahi, *Hōdō Station*)

Most media organizations provide only frequencies of polling results in their publications, but *Asahi Shimbun* (not TV Asahi) provides cross-tabulation of opinion polls for subscribers of its electronic edition. The Asahi Opinion Poll in September 2024, taken ten days before the LDP presidential election, shows how each candidate mustered support across partisan groups. Table 10.1 shows the composition of partisan supporters for each candidate, who are listed according to their total share of support. Of the nine presidential candidates, only Ishiba, Koizumi, and Takaichi received double-digit support. Cell entries are percentages of the entire sample. For example, the number in Ishiba's row in the column of independents means 12% of the entire sample were independent voters who supported Ishiba.

These top three candidates have quite different profiles in terms of the partisan composition of their supporters. Takaichi had equal support from government supporters and independents. Koizumi had greater support from independents than from government supporters. The same was true for Ishiba, but he also received the most support from opposition supporters who are unlikely to vote for the LDP in a general election. If their favorite LDP lawmaker becomes the prime minister, independent

Table 10.1 The next prime minister by partisanship

	Government supporters	Opposition supporters	Independents	Total
Ishiba	9	5	12	26
Koizumi	8	1	12	21
Takaichi	5	1	5	11
Kamikawa	1	1	2	4
Kono	1	0	3	4
Kobayashi	1	0	2	3
Hayashi	1	1	1	3
Kato	0	0	1	1
Motegi	0	0	1	1
Can't find in the list	3	2	15	20
Other/NA	1	0	5	6
Total	30	12	59	100

Source Asahi Opinion Poll, September 14–15, 2024

voters may become more inclined to vote for the LDP in a general election. The same is not true for opposition supporters. The odds they would vote for the LDP if their preferred LDP candidate won a party election would remain slim to none.

These numbers indicate two things. First, because Ishiba attracted support from both governing and opposition party supporters, he may be able to bridge some partisan divides and lessen partisan animosities. Second, Ishiba attracted more supporters from the opposition and independents combined than from his own partisans. Thus, enacting policies that cater only to his own partisans is far more likely to backfire for him than it would be for Takaichi, whose primary supporters come from the LDP.

On August 14, Kishida announced he would not seek another term as prime minister. After his announcement, many potential contenders openly expressed their intention to run for the election because most factions, which played a crucial role in selecting candidates in the past, no longer officially existed within the LDP. These presidential hopefuls started their de facto campaigns early to secure the twenty endorsements from fellow LDP lawmakers needed to satisfy the condition of candidacy. Though the official election campaign period started September 12 and ended September 27, in practice, the LDP leadership campaign lasted more than a month (see Nemoto 2025 for details on the LDP presidential election).

The nine candidates discussed several issues, including the timing of the general election, during a joint appearance at the Japan National Press Club on September 14. Koizumi Shinjirō argued for holding the general election as early as possible, skipping all deliberation in the Diet. Most of the other candidates were skeptical of his idea. Ishiba made his position clear during the debate, stating, "It is the new prime minister's responsibility to provide the public with information to make their decision." He added, "A plenary session is basically a one-way street. The real exchange is in the Budget Committee" (*Asahi Shimbun*, September 16, 2024). It was widely expected that Ishiba would call a general election only after allowing enough time for debates in the Budget Committee in the Diet. However, a day before being officially selected as prime minister in both houses, he expressed his intention to dissolve the HR on October 9 and to have a general election on October 27 (*Asahi Shimbun*, October 1, 2024). Not only was it unusual to announce the general election schedule before assuming the premiership, but the announced schedule was also very tight, the second shortest in history after the 2021 HR election called by Kishida.

THE ELECTION CAMPAIGN AND ISSUES THAT MATTER

Media organizations ask respondents to pick their intended choice in the next general election when they foresee it on the political time horizon. The Kyodo Opinion Poll started asking this question in May 2024. While just 20.9% of respondents intended to vote for the LDP for the PR district at that time, that percentage gradually improved over time and reached 37.1% after Kishida announced he was stepping down. After Ishiba took office, 38.4% expressed intentions to vote for the LDP. However, just before the official announcement of the election on October 15, that number dropped to 26.4%.

Only Kyodo and NHK conducted opinion polls that cover the official campaign period and provide clues for this decline. There are two primary reasons for this sudden shift. The first reason is Ishiba's abrupt change of mind about the election timing. During the campaign for the LDP leadership selection, he repeatedly indicated an election would not be called before the Budget Committee had sufficient time for deliberations. Thus, his call for a quick election was considered a betrayal. The

NHK Opinion Poll asked the following question to respondents: "Prime Minister Ishiba dissolved the House of Representatives on October 9. What do you think about the timing of the dissolution?" 49.3% found it "not reasonable," while 36.7% found it "reasonable."[9] As Ishiba attracted support from independents and opposition supporters, his sudden change of strategy driven by partisan motives may have undermined his image.

Second, while Ishiba was considered a clear alternative to Abe and his legacy, he was unable to clean the slate of the faction's slush money scandals (cf. Carlson 2025; Nemoto 2025). Ishiba decided not to endorse the twelve representatives involved in the slush fund scandal as LDP candidates. He also removed another thirty-four representatives with much smaller political slush funds from the PR candidate lists to prohibit their dual candidacy. Nonetheless, the public still felt his response was not strict enough. A Kyodo Opinion Poll conducted on October 12 and 13 asked, "Do you think the LDP's response to the slush fund lawmakers was sufficient or insufficient?" Only 22.1% selected "sufficient," while 71.6% deemed it "insufficient."[10]

Not only did the tide of public opinion change immediately after Ishiba announced the election schedule, the voting intention for the LDP in the PR district also declined to 18.6% a few days before the election. For single-member constituencies, voting intention for the opposition parties rapidly increased from 22.9% to 41.6% in less than two weeks.

On October 23, four days before the voting date, it was revealed that the LDP headquarters provided twenty million Japanese yen for election campaigning not only to each of its officially endorsed candidates but also to candidates who were denied an official endorsement due to their involvement in the slush fund scandals (*Asahi Shimbun*, October 23, 2024). Giving the same amount of money to the scandal-tainted candidates ignited strong criticism from the opposition parties as well as from the mass media, which critically depressed voting intention for all the candidates from the governing coalition (for more details on this incident and its potential impact, see Nemoto 2025; Umeda 2025).

---

[9] This question was posed for the first wave of pre-election opinion polls fielded from October 12 to 14. Full results are available at https://www.nhk.or.jp/senkyo/.

[10] The frequencies from the three opinion polls conducted for the campaign period can be accessed at: https://www.47news.jp/politics/syuinsen/topic/results2?sjkd_page=cont_KA66f3b7de7a4f3_KA67224b54425fc.

The impact of the slush fund scandal on public opinion is evident in people's responses to questions regarding the key issues they considered when making their voting decisions. The Kyodo Opinion Poll asks respondents, "What is most important to you when voting in this election?" during the campaign period for each national election.

Though Kyodo adjusts the details of the policy areas each time, such as eliminating COVID-19 and adding disaster prevention for 2024, respondents can select up to two policy areas as important for them. As shown in Table 10.2, the largest decline occurred for Ishiba's trademark policy of "revitalizing localities" from 9.7% to 5.5%, while the largest increase occurred for "problem of money and politics" from 14.4% to 19.1%. A change of five points in policy considerations may not appear substantial enough to influence election outcomes. However, even minor changes can sometimes have a significant impact across districts, particularly when competition is exceptionally close. This last-minute revelation resulted in the governing coalition losing its majority status in the HR.

Table 10.2 What is most important for you in your voting decision for this election? Please select two from the ten listed

	October 12–13	October 12–19	October 25–26
Economy, employment, consumer price	57.0	60.8	57.9
Pension and social security	38.4	36.7	37.1
Child-rearing and low birth rate	20.5	23.8	20.5
Energy and nuclear power plant	3.5	6.7	6.2
Diplomacy and security	15.9	15.5	16.5
Constitutional reform	5.2	4.0	4.0
Administrative and fiscal reform	5.8	5.0	7.4
Disaster prevention	7.6	6.1	6.6
Revitalizing locality	9.7	6.2	5.5
Problem of money and politics	14.4	15.7	19.1
Other	0.7	0.3	0.5
DK/NA	2.6	2.0	1.3

Source Kyodo Opinion Poll, October 2024

Conclusion

The LDP-Kōmeitō coalition lost its HR majority in this election, the first time since 2009. No significant changes in the economy or foreign relations were observed between Ishiba's victory in the LDP leadership election and the 2024 HR election. The sudden shift is clearly driven by a series of short-term political events.

Before the 2024 HR election, it was expected that the LDP would lose seats. However, the predictions were divided regarding whether the governing parties would lose its HR majority in the early forecasts (*Yomiuri Shimbun*, October 17, 2024; *Tokyo Shimbun*, October 17, 2024). The second round of forecasts indicated a strong possibility that the government parties would lose control of the HR (*Tokyo Shimbun*, October 22, 2024; *Yomiuri Shimbun*, October 25, 2024). The last-minute revelation regarding funding for the election campaigns of non-endorsed candidates appears to have worsened an already difficult situation.

It is worthwhile to compare the short-term dynamics of public opinion regarding the 2021 and 2024 HR elections, using the question on which issues were most important to voters. Although the policy areas listed in the choice sets are not identical, the comparable choice of "economic policy" before the 2021 election campaign polls attracted only an average of 35.6%, which is more than twenty percentage points below that of 2024. In 2021, at the onset of the campaign, 19.4% of people chose "novel coronavirus countermeasures" as an important issue influencing their voting decisions, ranking second only to "economic policy." The election forecasts for the 2021 HR election were initially mixed. Some media organizations warned that the LDP-Kōmeitō coalition could lose control of the HR. However, Kishida benefited from the steep decline in COVID-19 infections, as the percentage of people who chose "novel coronavirus countermeasures" dropped to 13.7% within just two weeks. This decline appears to have contributed to an upward swing for the governing parties (Maeda 2022).

In contrast, the 2024 general election took place against a backdrop of rising consumer prices, which typically disadvantage the governing parties (Lewis-Beck 1988). As shown in Table 10.2, "Economy, employment, consumer price" attracted the most attention, with an average of 58.6%. The government might have secured a majority if nothing else had occurred. However, financial support for the scandal-tainted candidates was disclosed at the most inopportune moment, as economic discontent among the public intensified. When people are satisfied with the economy, government scandals have limited effects on people's evaluation of the government (Smyth and Taylor 2003). In economic hard times, people severely punish the government not only for its economic management but also for its scandals (Zechmeister and Zizumbo-Colunga 2013; Carline et al. 2015). The slush fund scandals may have acted as a catalyst; however, it is the economic conditions that compelled voters to severely punish the governing coalition in response to these scandals.

Acknowledgements I am grateful to Margaret Gibbons for proof-reading and editing this chapter. All the remaining errors are mine. This work was supported by JSPS KAKENHI Grant Number 22H00052.

References

Amano, Kenya, and Saori N. Katada. 2025. "Election Under Inflation: LDP's Choice of Macroeconomic Policy." In *Japan Decides 2024: The Japanese General Election*, edited by Kenneth M. McElwain, Robert J. Pekkanen, and Daniel M. Smith, 317–331. New York: Palgrave Macmillan.

Carlin, Ryan E., Gregory J. Love, and Cecilia Martínez-Gallardo. 2015. "Cushioning the Fall: Scandals, Economic Conditions, and Executive Approval." *Political Behavior* 37 (1): 109–130. https://doi.org/10.1007/s11109-014-9267-3.

Carlson, Matthew M. 2025 "Scandals During the Kishida Administration." In *Japan Decides 2024: The Japanese General Election*, edited by Kenneth M. McElwain, Robert J. Pekkanen, and Daniel M. Smith, 217–233. New York: Palgrave Macmillan.

Lewis-Beck, Michael S. 1988. *Economics and Elections: The Major Western Democracies*. Ann Arbor: University of Michigan Press.

Maeda, Yukio. 2022. "Public Opinion and COVID-19." In *Japan Decides 2021: The Japanese General Election*, edited by Robert J. Pekkanen, Steven R. Reed and Daniel M. Smith, 167–182. New York: Palgrave Macmillan.

McLaughlin, Levi. 2025 "Perennial Fears, Novel Responses: The Unification Church in Japan After the Abe Assassination." In *Japan Decides 2024: The Japanese General Election*, edited by Kenneth M. McElwain, Robert J. Pekkanen, and Daniel M. Smith, 235–253. New York: Palgrave Macmillan.

Nemoto, Kuniaki. 2025. "Reasons Behind the LDP's Loss in the 2024 Election." In *Japan Decides 2024: The Japanese General Election*, edited by Kenneth M.

McElwain, Robert J. Pekkanen, and Daniel M. Smith, 37–55. New York: Palgrave Macmillan.

Smyth, David J., and Susan W. Taylor. 2003. "Presidential Popularity: What Matters Most, Macroeconomics or Scandals?" *Applied Economics Letters* 10 (9): 585–588. https://doi.org/10.1080/1350485032000100189.

Umeda, Michio. 2025. "Electoral Campaigns in Japan's 2024 HR Election: Emerging Signs of Transformation." In *Japan Decides 2024: The Japanese General Election*, edited by Kenneth M. McElwain, Robert J. Pekkanen, and Daniel M. Smith, 109–124. New York: Palgrave Macmillan.

Zechmeister, Elizabeth J., and Daniel Zizumbo-Colunga. 2013. "The Varying Political Toll of Concerns About Corruption in Good Versus Bad Economic Times." *Comparative Political Studies* 46 (10): 1190–1218. https://doi.org/10.1177/0010414012472468.

CHAPTER 11

Social Media in the 2024 General Election

Robert A. Fahey

When Japan's Public Offices Election Law was revised in 2013 to allow candidates to communicate over the Internet during electoral campaigns, initial enthusiasm for the change—well summed up by a contemporaneous *Asahi Shimbun* editorial which declared that "Internet election campaigns can change Japan's politics" (*Asahi Shimbun* 2013)—rapidly faded as the transformative online grassroots campaigns some activists had hoped for failed to emerge. Eleven years later, the 2024 general election and several other electoral contests held within the same year suggest that Internet campaigning has finally become an important force in Japan's elections—but now the tone among media commentators discussing this change has become very cautious, even to the extent of having a note of being careful what you wish for about it (e.g., *Asahi Shimbun* 2024). This reflects a broad global trend in our understanding of the influence of social media on democratic society, which has changed significantly in the decade between Japan's adoption of online campaigning and its eventual rise to prominence. In 2013, perceptions of "Internet democracy" were largely utopian, with campaigns such as Barack Obama's 2008 presidential

R. A. Fahey (✉)
Waseda University, Tokyo, Japan
e-mail: robfahey@gmail.com

© The Author(s), under exclusive license to Springer Nature Switzerland AG 2025
K. M. McElwain et al. (eds.), *Japan Decides 2024*,
https://doi.org/10.1007/978-3-031-98797-7_11

run raising hopes that bringing politics online would engage and involve large swathes of voters, empower communities, and give voice to groups often ignored in traditional media coverage. In the following decade, however, this optimism has given way to deep concerns that online politics and social media have instead become a vector for misinformation, conspiracy theories, polarisation, and declining trust.

This chapter will explore how this changing social media landscape impacted the 2024 election, focusing on the use of polarising messaging and the exploitation of media fragmentation and declining trust by challenger parties such as the Democratic Party for the People (DPP), Conservative Party of Japan (Hoshutō; CPJ), and Sanseitō (the Party of DIY), and contrasting this with the arguably inadequate "business as usual" approach to online campaigning and social media seen from established parties. While significant barriers now exist to credible, in-depth analysis of social media content due to platforms' decisions to severely restrict researchers' access to the required data, we can still observe candidates' online campaigning activity and estimate their reach and popularity on these platforms. Later in the chapter, this data will be combined with insights into citizens' usage of different media types and information sources from electoral surveys to assess the risk of an emerging "information cleavage"—a socio-political divide between citizens who continue to trust traditional news sources and those who primarily rely on social media sources, with potentially major consequences for their political alignments and beliefs. In addition to discussing the 2024 general election, the chapter will also touch upon the clear influence of social media on a number of other key electoral contests during the same year, including the Tokyo and Hyogo gubernatorial contests (in July and November respectively) and the Tokyo-15 by-election in April. Taken together with the factors observed at the general election, a picture emerges of rapid changes to the information ecosystem and its relationship with political campaigning, to which mainstream political and media actors have yet to develop a clear response.

Japan is no exception to the global trend of rising concern over the negative impacts of social media on democratic society. Since the COVID-19 pandemic, there has been a significant rise in attention to the roles of misinformation and conspiracy theories in Japan, with the part played by social media in spreading and encouraging such beliefs being highlighted by many researchers (see for example Inoue et al. 2022; Demelius and Szczepanska 2024; Fahey 2023; Sato et al. 2024). In the years leading up to the 2024 election, several movements and parties emerged from an online social media ecosystem that is centered around platforms like YouTube and X/Twitter, and promotes nativist, nationalist, and conspiratorial views while purporting to offer an "uncensored" alternative to mainstream media narratives. These range from formally organized parties such as CPJ and Sanseitō, both of which contested and won seats in the 2024 election, to more fringe political groupings such as the Tsubasa Party (*Tsubasa no Tō*) and overt conspiracy theory groups such as YamatoQ (see Fahey and Marcantuoni 2025 for a discussion of the strategies of Sanseitō, and Demelius and Szczepanska 2024 for analysis of the evolution of YamatoQ). These groups and their supporters are very prominent in the online information environment, and while their electoral successes have been strictly limited, the narratives and ideas they promote can percolate widely across social media platforms.

The extent to which these ideas spread and take root among citizens on social media has, however, become very difficult to accurately measure. This is because the response of many social media platform operators to rising criticism related to issues of misinformation or extremism has been to shut out researchers' access to their data. Companies including X (formerly Twitter) and Meta (the operator of Facebook and Instagram) have disabled tools that allowed researchers to collect the large-scale data required to identify and analyze trends, study the spread of information across communities, or devise effective counterstrategies to misinformation (Blakey 2024). While some researchers have attempted to continue tracking audience engagement using keyword data aggregated by third parties (see Ito 2025 for an example of this approach to the 2024 election), in the absence of official tools provided by the platform, it is difficult if not impossible to verify the accuracy or representativeness of such data. Consequently, at this critical juncture in the intersection between social media and democracy, we have primarily been reduced to supply-side analyses of the ways in which politicians and other actors use social media to campaign, with little or no visibility of the demand-side, i.e., how regular social media users are responding to those strategies or engaging in political communication of their own.

It is often assumed that social media platforms provide an advantage to minor parties and candidates who would struggle to attract coverage in mass media outlets. While there is some truth to this assertion in general, in Japanese elections at least the most clear beneficiary of the spread of social media has historically been the Liberal Democratic Party (LDP), whose prominent politicians enjoy much larger followings on platforms such as X than those from minor parties do (see Fahey 2023 for following figures from the 2021 election, for example). This situation continued at the 2024 election, as can be seen in Table 11.1, which ranks the top candidates and party leaders in this election by their X follower count on polling day. Kōno Tarō is a clear outlier with more than 2.5 million followers; the only other Japanese politician to ever have a follower count in this range was the late Abe Shinzō. In total, there are five LDP politicians in the top ten, with only one apiece from other parties. In part, the LDP's lead in these figures simply reflects incumbency advantage—ordinary social media users who are not especially politically engaged often still choose to follow the Prime Minister's official account, for example, and three of the LDP politicians in the top ten (Kishida Fumio, Suga Yoshihide, and Ishiba Shigeru) are the three most recent prime ministers. However, setting aside the prime ministers, incumbency in senior offices does not appear to explain social media popularity particularly effectively. Both Kōno Tarō and Takaichi Sanae, in first and third place on this ranking respectively, have certainly occupied senior ministerial roles, with both also being serious challengers for the leadership of the LDP and thus for the Prime Minister's job; Sekō Hiroshige, just outside the top ten, has also held senior roles in government. However, the large majority of cabinet ministers and other senior figures in the LDP are not remotely as widely followed online. Excluding Prime Minister Ishiba, the mean follower count for members of his cabinet at the time of the election was only 27,000; many cabinet ministers had only a couple of thousand followers, which would arguably be a poor showing for even a backbench lawmaker.

An important factor in attracting a large social media following for many politicians appears to be not the holding of high office or legislative track record, but rather the courting of controversy. Right-wing LDP politician Sugita Mio is not included in this chart—she was denied inclusion in the LDP's proportional representation list due to her involvement in the party's financial scandals and chose not to put herself forward as an unendorsed candidate. With more than 410,000 followers at the time of the election, however, she would have broken into the top ten of candidates by following, despite never having held any particularly notable government or party positions. Instead, her online profile was boosted by hardline "culture war" rhetoric on social issues such as opposition to LGBT rights. The most-followed member of the CDP, the

Table 11.1 X (Twitter) follower counts for candidates and party leaders

	Name	Party	X screen name	Followers (000's)	Notes
1	Kōno Tarō	LDP	@konotarogomame	2524	
2	Kishida Fumio	LDP	@kishida230	863	Former Prime Minister
3	Takaichi Sanae	LDP	@takaichi_sanae	738	
4	Suga Yoshihide	LDP	@sugawitter	670	Former Prime Minister
5	Hyakuta Naoki	Hoshu/CPJ	@hyakutanaoki	660	Party Leader; did not run for election
6	Yamamoto Tarō	Reiwa	@yamamototaro0	571	Party Leader; member of Upper House
7	Ishiba Shigeru	LDP	@shigeruishiba	423	Prime Minister
8	Tamaki Yūichirō	DPP	@tamakiyuichiro	423	Party Leader
9	Haraguchi Kazuhiro	CDP	@kharaguchi	310	
10	Ozawa Ichirō	CDP	@ozawa_jimusho	277	
11	Sekō Hiroshige	LDP	@sekohiroshige	275	
12	Tachibana Takeshi	NHKP	@tachibanat	253	Party Leader; did not run for election
13	Fukushima Mizuho	SDP	@mizuhofukushima	253	Party Leader; member of Upper House
14	Koike Akira	JCP	@koike_akira	201	Party Secretary General; member of Upper House

Notes Follower data collected from X. Only party leaders and candidates in the House of Representatives election with over 200,000 followers are listed.

main opposition party in the Lower House,[1] meanwhile, is not any of the party's leadership, but rather Haraguchi Kazuhiro—a lawmaker who has frequently made controversial public statements including seeming to endorse conspiracy theories about COVID-19 vaccines and the invasion of Ukraine (*Mainichi Shimbun* 2024; *Asahi Shimbun* 2023). Among the smaller parties contesting the election, it is similarly controversy, rather than any track record of public service, that appears to determine a politician's following, and thus their potential reach and audience on social media. Hyakuta Naoki, leader of the nationalist/nativist CPJ, is the most followed politician outside the LDP; in second place is Yamamoto Tarō, leader of the left-wing populist and anti-establishment party Reiwa Shinsengumi. It is likely not a coincidence that both of these party leaders have prior careers in media and entertainment—Hyakuta as a novelist and TV commentator, and Yamamoto as a film and television actor—which may give them an advantage over most other politicians in appealing to groups of social media users who primarily see political discourses on these platforms as a kind of reality entertainment rather than being focused on issues of policy or governance. Tachibana Takeshi, whose leadership of the fringe NHK Party has been punctuated with attention-grabbing public stunts (such as his use of a party political broadcast time allocated to the party to gleefully repeat allegations that an NHK executive had engaged in "adulterous car-sex"; see Guerrera-Sapone 2021), similarly has a larger social media following than most politicians, including leadership figures in much more well-established parties.

The online campaigning style of political figures from small challenger parties like Hyakuta, Yamamoto, and Tachibana, along with those of more "fringe" figures among mainstream parties such as the LDP's Sugita or CDP's Haraguchi, tends to be aggressive, combative, and accusatory, including making claims that they are speaking truths to their followers that are deliberately censored or suppressed by mainstream politicians and media. Such claims are built upon declining trust in establishment media on the part of some citizens, while at the same time spreading and advancing that same narrative of untrustworthiness. This rhetorical style aligns closely with many aspects of populist speech—suggesting to their

---

[1] Focusing on candidates for the House of Representatives and their party leaders means that Table 1 excludes CDP lawmaker Renho, who has over 580,000 followers but sits in the House of Councillors. Similarly, LDP members of the House of Councillors such as Satō Masahisa, who has over 520,000 followers, are excluded.

followers that they are locked in struggle with a conspiring group of elites who must be defeated to restore the sovereignty of the good, ordinary people of Japan; or to put it more simply, engaging in the "politics of making enemies" (Toru 2011, 56). This contrasts sharply with the rather bland approach to social media campaigning that has consistently been employed by many mainstream politicians over the past decade. Far from picking fights or throwing metaphorical punches online, the majority of politicians from mainstream parties have treated social media simply as a channel for promoting their existing campaign activities, with most posts either being announcements of upcoming campaign events, photographs of prior events, or links to coverage of the candidate in traditional media outlets. To the extent that policy positions or achievements are promoted over social media, they tend to be in the form of direct statements that are not followed up by discussion, with very few politicians engaging in actual dialogue with users on these platforms (beyond occasionally re-posting supportive messages and thanking the users who sent them). Interaction and discussion among political opponents, meanwhile, though a relatively common feature of social media discourse in some other countries, is almost unheard of among candidates from mainstream parties in Japan.

This established, "traditional" approach to social media campaigning saw few changes at the 2024 election. If anything, although the unavailability of comprehensive data makes direct comparison impossible, the heavy focus on the LDP's financial scandals during the 2024 campaign (cf. Carlson 2025; Nemoto 2025; Umeda 2025) appears to have led to further reduced attention to policy issues in online campaigning for this election than in 2021, when there was at least a significant degree of engagement with questions such as the LDP's record on vaccination (Fahey 2023, 191). A reasonably representative case to consider is Shimomura Hakubun, a senior LDP figure who faced an extremely close race in the Tokyo-11 constituency after losing the party's official endorsement due to his role in the financial scandals. One might reasonably expect a candidate in such a close race to use every tool available to him for his campaign, but his social media campaign consisted almost entirely of posting pictures from rallies and speech events on X and occasionally posting videos of them on YouTube. He posted to X only 59 times during the campaign, with less than a dozen of those posts mentioning a policy position of any description; did not repost from any account other than his own (with the exception of a single post from Takaichi Sanae about her schedule for campaigning on his behalf); and did not reply to a single question or comment from other users on the platform. Shimomura's low focus on his social media campaign meant that he had only 6300 followers by election day despite being in one of the most closely watched constituency races in the country. As with the large proportion of mainstream candidates with similar approaches to social media, Shimomura barely uses these platforms at all outside of election campaigns; prior to the start of the general election campaign in early October he had not posted on X since July, and after a thank-you message to supporters on the day after the election, he did not post again until late February. However, even candidates who use social media more regularly tended not to stray from this low-engagement approach to online campaigning. Sekō Hiroshige, for example, was running for re-election in the Wakayama-2 district having also lost the party endorsement over financial scandals. He is a regular poster on X outside of campaign periods and has more than 270,000 followers, but while his online campaign did feature more professionally produced video content than Shimomura's, the frequency of posting was much the same—as was the complete lack of any interaction with other social media users.

Such anodyne usage of social media by establishment candidates has unsurprisingly left a significant gap to be exploited by other political actors, especially as the relative importance of social media as an information source has increased over the years. Fringe figures from extremist parties have certainly benefited, as seen in the outsized social media reach of politicians like Tachibana or Yamamoto. In the 2024 general election, however, it was the Democratic Party for the People (DPP) and its leader Tamaki Yūichirō who most effectively took advantage of the mainstream parties' blind spot for social media campaigning. The DPP's overall campaign message struck a chord with many groups of voters to an extent that apparently took the party itself by surprise to some degree, with its increase in seats (from 11 to 28) being limited by its failure to run enough candidates to capitalize on its elevated vote share. While the DPP campaigned in all the traditional ways expected of a Japanese party—with speech events, rallies, sound trucks, and so on—the party also focused a significant amount of its efforts on online campaigning. At least from the perspective of growing its audience and reach on social media, this campaigning was extremely effective. Tamaki grew his follower count on X from 378k at the outset of the campaign to 423k by its end, a growth rate far outpacing that of any other political leader. The second highest follower growth rate among individual politicians was that of DPP

Secretary-General Shinba Kazuya, followed by Reiwa leader Yamamoto and Sanseitō leader Kamiya Sōhei. The DPP's official party account also grew its reach far faster than its rivals, with its followers increasing at four times the pace of the LDP's official account, and more than twice as fast as the Reiwa and Sanseitō accounts (Okazaki 2024).

The contrast between Tamaki's approach to social media and that of establishment politicians like Shimomura and Sekō is quite stark. During the campaign, Tamaki posted to X dozens of times each day—often posting more in a single day than many establishment candidates did during the entire campaign period. Notably, he was also a prolific poster before the campaign, and maintained a similar pace after its end, suggesting that he and his party view social media as a primary channel for communicating with the electorate at all times, not just a campaign tool. Tamaki frequently engaged with other users on social media, reposting their comments, thanking supporters, and even directly criticizing or denying posts he felt misrepresented or misunderstood the DPP's positions. The "voice" of the account gives the impression that Tamaki is posting himself (whether that is actually the case or not), and alongside posts about policies, campaign videos, and photographs and updates from rallies and events, Tamaki frequently gave personal updates and anecdotes from the campaign trail.

In terms of content, much has been made of the DPP's use of "meme culture" to promote its policy ideas—one example being a widely circulated TikTok video in which various clips of cats were edited together to music to provide a simplified explanation of the DPP's policy around the "¥1.03m wall" in the taxation system. The majority of that content, however, was actually created by DPP supporters online rather than being commissioned by the party itself, although DPP politicians did re-share some of this content through their official accounts. The party's own social media content instead featured graphics with simple, punchy sound-bites about policy ideas, or well-designed infographics that explained the party's ideas and their potential impact on voters, with both of these types of content being widely shared by social media users. While political rivals criticized much of the DPP's messaging on these issues for being over-simplified or incorrect, they tended to do so in the mainstream media, rather than engaging with this content on social media where it originated—thus leaving it largely unchallenged on those platforms.

This capacity for the DPP to spread messages across social media with relatively minimal pushback helps to explain a stark messaging gap that grew between the party and its mainstream rivals during this election. Based on keyword analysis on X, Ito Masaaki has charged that Tamaki effectively opened and capitalized upon an inter-generational cleavage that found its strongest expression on social media platforms, where the user demographics skew towards younger generations (Ito 2025). His findings suggest that there was a wellspring of resentment among young and middle-aged social media users over various perceived iniquities and imbalances between Japan's generation cohorts, with keywords such as "silver democracy" and "working generation" seeing far higher uplift in frequency over the course of the campaign than keywords related to conventional policy issues such as "constitutional amendment", "separate surnames", or "nuclear power". Even as these issues became central to electoral discussions on social media, however, they were absent or relatively under-emphasized in mainstream media coverage—creating a gap between mainstream media agendas and social media agendas which no doubt fuelled some social media users' perceptions that mainstream media was suppressing or covering up the "real issues". In this sense, while Tamaki and the DPP have a much more moderate set of policies and priorities than radical fringe parties like Sanseitō or the CPJ, their online communication strategies are very similar—employing somewhat populist, aggressive rhetoric, and exploiting a belief held by some citizens that Japan's mass media is putting its thumb on the scale on behalf of the conspiring, undemocratic elites.

The argument that the DPP's communication strategy resembles the radical parties' approaches, even if its policies are dissimilar in many regards, is supported further by evidence regarding the different sources of information preferred by supporters of each party. Figure 11.1 shows a heatmap of this distribution based on data from an electoral survey conducted by Waseda University researchers, with darker shading indicating that a larger proportion of voters for that party (in columns) indicated a preference for receiving political information from that medium (in rows). The most notable contrast in this chart is that voters for the LDP, CDP, Kōmeitō, Ishin, and the JCP were all significantly more likely to say that they got their political information from newspapers or TV news (with NHK in particular being a major information source for both LDP and CDP voters), while voters for the DPP, Reiwa, Sanseitō, and CPJ all had a strong tendency to prefer receiving political information from online news or social media. Voters for the far-right parties in particular—Sanseitō and CPJ—tend to eschew traditional mass media

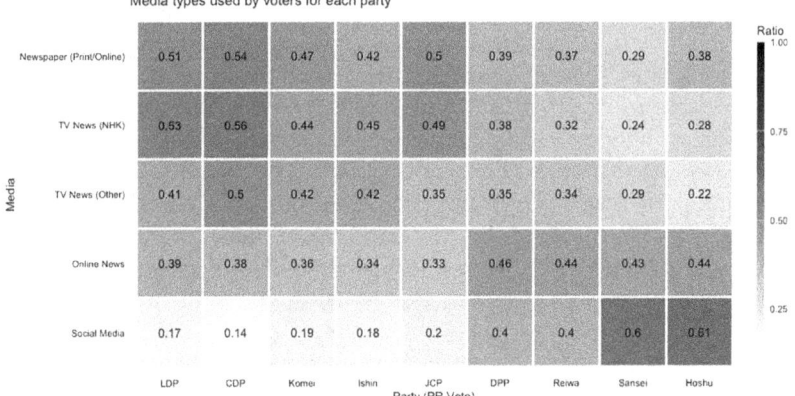

Fig. 11.1 Types of media used for political information, by party supported (*Notes* Data from an online electoral survey of 4588 voters conducted by the author along with Airo Hino [Waseda University] and Ling Liu [Waseda Institute for Advanced Study])

sources and strongly prefer receiving their information from social media. A further breakdown of these figures reveals that YouTube is the most popular information source among voters for these parties, followed by X. By contrast, looking across all respondents in the survey, NHK is by far the most popular information source, selected by 47%, followed by Yahoo! News (32%) and TV Asahi (31%). YouTube was indicated as a preferred information source by only 14% of respondents in total, and X by just 10%.[2] This sharp divergence in media preferences according to party alignment can be seen as an indication of a growing divide in Japanese politics (cf. Matsumoto 2025; Umeda 2025)—not just an intergenerational divide, though this is certainly part of the underlying reason, but a growing cleavage between voters who continue to trust the mainstream media, and those who are increasingly seeking their information elsewhere.

Any discussion of the role of social media in the 2024 general election is incomplete without touching at least briefly on its even more pronounced role in other elections over the course of the year. In

---

[2] Respondents could indicate multiple preferred sources in this question, so the totals add up to over 100%.

the Tokyo-15 by-election in April, many fringe parties put forward candidates, with particular controversy being stirred by the right-wing, conspiracy theorist Tsubasa Party, whose members obstructed the campaign events of other candidates by interrupting their speeches with loudspeakers and car horns, and even engaging in dangerous vehicular pursuits of other parties' campaign trucks. Three members of the party, including party leader Kurokawa Atsuhiko, were later arrested for these actions; what is notable in the context of social media is that the party's candidate and leadership had been streaming video of all of these events online on a social video platform. This arguably represents the very unwelcome arrival of so-called "nuisance streaming" (an online subculture in which viewers give financial donations to encourage live-streaming broadcasters to carry out increasingly extreme nuisance activities in public) in Japanese political campaigning, although the strong response of the Tokyo Metropolitan Police after the election may help to discourage further such activity. A few months later in the Tokyo gubernatorial election, the main opposition candidate Renho was unexpectedly pushed into third place by Ishimaru Shinji, an independent candidate with no party backing whose only prior experience of governance was as mayor of Akitakata City (which has a population of under 30,000 people) in Hiroshima Prefecture. Ishimaru does, however, have a major online following, and employs very similar social media strategies to those of figures like Tamaki Yūichirō—which he was able to leverage into 1.7 million votes in the Tokyo election, compared to only 1.3 million for the establishment opposition candidate.

Finally, in Hyogo Prefecture's gubernatorial election in November, the former governor Saitō Motohiko—who had been removed by a unanimous vote of the Prefectural Assembly following allegations of harassment of an employee leading to their suicide—won re-election by a large margin on significantly higher turnout than the previous election. Saitō's re-election campaign was largely based on claims that he was a reformer who had been targeted by corrupt elites in the political establishment and the media, a claim that was widely taken up and amplified across social media. His supporters framed the election in part as a referendum on what they saw as media corruption; after his victory, comments on the social media pages of mass media outlets demanded that the media must now apologize for reporting on the harassment allegations in the first place. While social media played a significant role in all of the elections throughout the year, the specific targeting of the media in this campaign—with its echoes of the Trump campaign in the United States—seemed to provoke the most concern among commentators, leading to editorials highlighting the potential risks to democracy from the Internet, such as the one mentioned at the beginning of this chapter (*Asahi Shimbun* 2024).

The immediate aftermath of the general election and the Hyogo gubernatorial race saw some political figures openly musing about the possibility of tighter regulation of social media—for example, LDP Secretary General Fukuda Tatsuo told a press briefing that a calm discussion of social media regulation was required (NHK News 2024). However, any such discussions quickly seemed to disappear off the administration's list of priorities, perhaps in part because the LDP-led minority government needed the cooperation of parties such as the DPP to pass legislation. Nonetheless, some will does appear to exist for a more robust effort to combat online misinformation—but not only does the current administration lack the political capital for new regulations in this sphere, doing so in a way that does not simply ignite further mistrust and claims of censorship or suppression is something that has largely eluded governments around the world thus far. Perhaps a more straightforward response from establishment political forces would simply be to increase and improve their own engagement on social media platforms, rather than allowing the messaging of challenger parties and fringe groups to run largely unchecked in these spaces. If the elections of 2024 tell us anything, it is that the fragmentation of the information ecosystem seen in other parts of the world is rapidly catching up to Japan as well, and the era in which mainstream political actors could largely ignore the social media platforms without consequence is firmly behind us.

References

Asahi Shimbun. 2013. "EDITORIAL: Internet Election Campaigns Can Change Japan's Politics." *The Asahi Shimbun*, December 4.

Asahi Shimbun. 2023. "Riken Okuta-shi 'Futekisetsu' to Haraguchi Kazuhiro-shi wo Chūi 'Neo-Nachisu Seiken' hatsugen de [CDP's Okuta Warns Haraguchi Kazuhiro of 'Inappropriateness' Over 'Neo-Nazi Administration' Comments]." *The Asahi Shimbun*, September 14. https://www.asahi.com/articles/ASR9G5VTDR9GUTFK00S.html?iref=ogimage_rek.

Asahi Shimbun. 2024. "After 11 Years, Internet Begins to Dominate Japan's Elections." *The Asahi Shimbun*, December 17. https://www.asahi.com/ajw/articles/15553411.

Blakey, Elizabeth. 2024. "The Day Data Transparency Died: How Twitter/X Cut Off Access for Social Research." *Contexts* 23 (2): 30–35. https://doi.org/10.1177/15365042241252125.

Carlson, Matthew M. 2025. "Scandals During the Kishida Administration." In *Japan Decides 2024: The Japanese General Election*, edited by Kenneth M. McElwain, Robert J. Pekkanen, and Daniel M. Smith, 217–233. New York: Palgrave Macmillan.

Demelius, Yoko, and Kamila Szczepanska. 2024. "Conspiracy Theories and the COVID-19 Pandemic in Japan: The Rise, Radicalization, and Fall (?) of YamatoQ-Kai." *Social Science Japan Journal* 27 (2): 149–168. https://doi.org/10.1093/ssjj/jyae003.

Fahey, Robert A. 2023. "Yoron Chōsa Ni Miru Nihonjin No Inbōron Shiji [Support for Conspiracy Theories Among Japanese Citizens as Seen in Public Opinion Surveys]." *Chuo Koron* 127 (12): 62–69.

Fahey, Robert A., and Romeo Marcantuoni. 2025. "From Conspiracy Theory Movement to Challenger Party: The Case of Japan's Sanseitō." WIAS Discussion Paper 2024-001, January. https://www.waseda.jp/inst/wias/assets/uploads/2025/01/dp2024001.pdf.

Guerrera-Sapone, Max. 2021. "YouTube and Japan's New Political Underground: The Rise and Decline of the Party to Protect the People from NHK." *Asia-Pacific Journal: Japan Focus* 19 (2). https://apjjf.org/2021/2/gurrera-sapone.

Inoue, Mami, Kanako Shimoura, Momoko Nagai-Tanima, and Tomoki Aoyama. 2022. "The Relationship Between Information Sources, Health Literacy, and COVID-19 Knowledge in the COVID-19 Infodemic: Cross-Sectional Online Study in Japan." *Journal of Medical Internet Research* 24 (7): e38332. https://doi.org/10.2196/38332.

Ito, Masaaki. 2025. "'Ōrudo na mono' he no tekii: Sau tairitsu no shōshitsu to arata na senten [Hostility to 'Old Things': The Vanishing of Left-Right Competition, and New Lines of Conflict]." *Sekai* 990 (February): 72–81.

Mainichi Shimbun. 2024. "Japan Pharma Mulls Suing Lawmaker Who Likened New COVID Vaccine to 'Biological Weapon'." *The Mainichi Shimbun*, November 2. https://mainichi.jp/english/articles/20241102/p2a/00m/0na/003000c.

Matsumoto, Tomoko. 2025. "How Party Manifestos Framed Political Distrust in the 2024 Election." In *Japan Decides 2024: The Japanese General Election*, edited by Kenneth M. McElwain, Robert J. Pekkanen, and Daniel M. Smith, 143-161. New York: Palgrave Macmillan.

Nemoto, Kuniaki. 2025. "Reasons Behind the LDP's Loss in the 2024 Election." In *Japan Decides 2024: The Japanese General Election*, edited by Kenneth M. McElwain, Robert J. Pekkanen, and Daniel M. Smith, 37–55. New York: Palgrave Macmillan.

NHK News. 2024. "Komei Saito Daihyō Nagoya-shichōsen 'Masashiku kanpai' SNS eikyō mo bunseki he [Komeito's Representative Saito: Nagoya Mayoral Election 'Certain Total Defeat'; Influence of Social Media to Be Analysed]." *NHK News*, November 25. https://www3.nhk.or.jp/news/html/20241125/k10014648851000.html.

Okazaki, Yuuji. 2024. "Sōsenkyo kōshi kikan no X forowā no nobi, Kokuminminshu ga Reiwa, Sansei no bai, Jimin no go bai yo [X Follower Growth During General Election Campaign, DPP Is Double Reiwa, Sansei; Five Times LDP]." *Atta*, November 28. https://www.atta-sophia-journalism.com/post/sns-and-2024-general-election.

Sato, Yukihiro, Ichiro Kawachi, Yasuaki Saijo, Eiji Yoshioka, Ken Osaka, and Takahiro Tabuchi. 2024. "Correlates of COVID-19 Conspiracy Theory Beliefs in Japan: A Cross-Sectional Study of 28,175 Residents." *PLoS ONE* 19 (12): e0310673. https://doi.org/10.1371/journal.pone.0310673.

Yoshida, Toru. 2011. *Popyurizumu wo kangaeru Minshushugi he no sainyūmon* [Thinking About Populism: A Reintroduction to Democracy]. NHK Shuppan.

Umeda, Michio. 2025. "Electoral Campaigns in Japan's 2024 HR Election: Emerging Signs of Transformation." In *Japan Decides 2024: The Japanese General Election*, edited by Kenneth M. McElwain, Robert J. Pekkanen, and Daniel M. Smith, 109–124. New York: Palgrave Macmillan.

CHAPTER 12

Partisanship and Turnout in the 2024 General Election

Tetsuya Matsubayashi

INTRODUCTION

Voter turnout in the 2024 general election was 53.85%, which was 2.08 percentage points lower than the 2021 general election. Given that the number of eligible citizens is approximately 100 million in the recent national elections in Japan, the drop in turnout might occur because approximately 2 million people who voted in 2021 decided not to vote in 2024, while all other people made the same decision in 2021 and 2024. Alternatively, the drop might occur because there were more people who voted in 2021 but abstained in 2024 than those who abstained in 2021 but voted in 2024, while all others made the same decision in the two elections. Since voter turnout fluctuates across elections, it is essential to understand the factors that drive the change in people's decisions from turnout to abstention or vice versa.

This chapter explores who was more likely or less likely to vote in the 2024 general election. My explanation is simple: the electoral context, in

T. Matsubayashi (✉)
University of Osaka, Osaka, Japan
e-mail: matsubayashi.osipp@osaka-u.ac.jp

particular the electoral choices presented to voters, affected who voted in 2024 (Zipp 1985; Rogowski 2014; Hobolt and Hoerner 2020). I focus on the role of partisanship. Using large-scale web survey data collected before and after the 2024 general election, I first show that Liberal Democratic Party (LDP) supporters were less likely to vote while DPP supporters were more likely to vote, compared to Constitutional Democratic Party (CDP) supporters as a baseline (and supporters of other major parties). This pattern was much weaker in the 2021 election.

Building on literature that highlights the importance of alienation from parties as a determinant of voter abstention (Davis et al. 1970; Plane and Gershtenson 2004; Adams et al. 2006), I argue that LDP supporters were dissatisfied with the Kishida Fumio cabinet and the handling of the major scandal involving the misuse and misreporting of campaign funds by members of the LDP. As a result, LDP supporters felt alienated from their party, which demobilized them from voting. In contrast, Democratic Party for the People (DPP) supporters were strongly attracted to their own party's leader and ideological/policy positions, which led especially young people to perceive the DPP as an appealing choice to justify the cost of voting. Hence, DPP supporters were mobilized to vote.

My additional analyses help to verify these interpretations. First, LDP supporters who were dissatisfied with the Kishida cabinet were much less likely to vote than those who were satisfied with the cabinet. This pattern is most evident among LDP supporters. Second, the support for DPP was strongly associated with turnout among the young and the middle-aged, typically with a lower propensity to vote. This pattern did not exist among the seniors and the supporters of other parties. Third, DPP supporters evaluated their own party's leader more positively and perceived less ideological distance between their position and the party's position compared to the supporters of other parties. LDP supporters were less positive about the leader and perceived a larger ideological distance. Taken together, these results suggest that the alienation from the party among LDP supporters and attachment to the party among DPP supporters explain their decision to vote in 2024.

Finally, I analyze municipality-level data in the 2021 and 2024 elections to evaluate whether the overall turnout change was associated with the vote shares of the LDP and DPP. The results demonstrate that a larger drop in turnout was associated with a larger drop in the LDP's absolute vote share in 2024, while a larger increase in turnout was associated with a larger increase in the DPP's absolute vote share in 2024, compared to 2021.

Partisanship and Turnout in the 2024 General Election

In the 2024 general election, the LDP experienced a significant loss of votes, from 34.66% in 2021 to 26.73% in 2024 in the PR tier. In contrast, the DPP increased its vote share from 4.51% to 11.31. These results might reflect the change in the turnout decision among LDP and DPP supporters. In other words, the LDP's loss is partly attributable to the fact that LDP supporters were demobilized to vote for the party, while the DPP's gain is partly attributable to the fact that DPP supporters were mobilized to do so.

To examine the role of partisanship in shaping the turnout decision in the 2024 general election, I compare the probability of self-reported turnout among survey respondents who showed support for the major parties. The data were obtained from a large-scale panel survey collected before and after the election. The pre-election survey was fielded from October 9 to 22, while the post-election survey was fielded from October 28 to November 1. The sample was drawn by one of the major survey research companies in Japan—Rakuten Insight Inc. Respondents were randomly selected from this survey company's subject pool after adjusting their demographics to be matched with the 2020 Population Census on age and sex. The total number of respondents was 28,949 in the pre-election survey and 19,294 in the post-election survey, after those who failed to pass attention checks were excluded.

The pre-election survey asked the respondents about their party support. The respondents are categorized into one of the following ten categories: a supporter of the LDP, the DPP, the CDP, Ishin, Kōmeitō, the Japanese Communist Party (JCP), Reiwa, other parties, those who did not feel close to any of the parties, and those who reported "don't know" (DK). In the following analyses, I use the indicator variables for each party and set CDP supporters as the baseline category. This is because the CDP was the largest opposition party and received the second-highest share in PR in 2021 and 2024 (see Ikeda 2025). In addition, the election returns in 2024 indicate that the vote share of the CDP in the PR tier stayed quite similar between the two elections, suggesting that most CDP supporters did not alter their turnout and vote choice between the 2021 and 2024 general elections.

The post-election survey asked the respondents whether they voted in the 2024 general election. I code one if the respondent reported that they voted and zero otherwise. In addition, I use the same coding for the recall of turnout in the 2022 Upper House election, which is the most recent national election. The latter is used to check if a similar relationship between partisanship and turnout existed in 2022.

Figure 12.1 reports the relationship estimated by a linear probability model where turnout in the 2024 election is regressed on the nine indicator variables for party support and five demographic indicator variables. The demographic variables for controls are coded one for female, college graduate, married, and those aged 18–39, 40–59, and 60 and older (baseline). The same analysis was repeated for the 2022 election. Figure 12.1 displays the estimated coefficients and 95% confidence intervals based on robust standard errors. The results for the demographic variables are omitted from the figure. The coefficients for the 2024 election are displayed as a circle, while those for 2022 are displayed as a triangle.

The results show that LDP supporters were less likely to vote in 2024 compared to CDP supporters. The estimated coefficient for the LDP supporter is 7.1. This means that LDP supporters were less likely to vote by 7.1 percentage points than CDP supporters. In contrast, DPP supporters were more likely to vote by 4.5 percentage points than CDP supporters. The estimated coefficients for Ishin and Reiwa in 2024 are also negative, indicating they were less likely to vote than the CDP supporters. Those without party support (None and DK) were least likely to vote, as expected.

Importantly, the estimated coefficients for LDP and DPP supporters are much smaller in 2022 than in 2024. In the 2022 Upper House election, compared to CDP supporters, LDP supporters were less likely to vote by 1.9 percentage points, while DPP supporters were more likely to vote by 0.2 percentage points, which is not statistically significant. Note that the turnout in 2022 was measured by recall, which might be driven by the actual turnout in 2024 and other factors. Yet, the difference in the estimated coefficients between the 2022 and 2024 elections provides suggestive evidence that election-specific factors demobilized LDP supporters and mobilized DPP supporters more strongly in 2024 than in 2022.

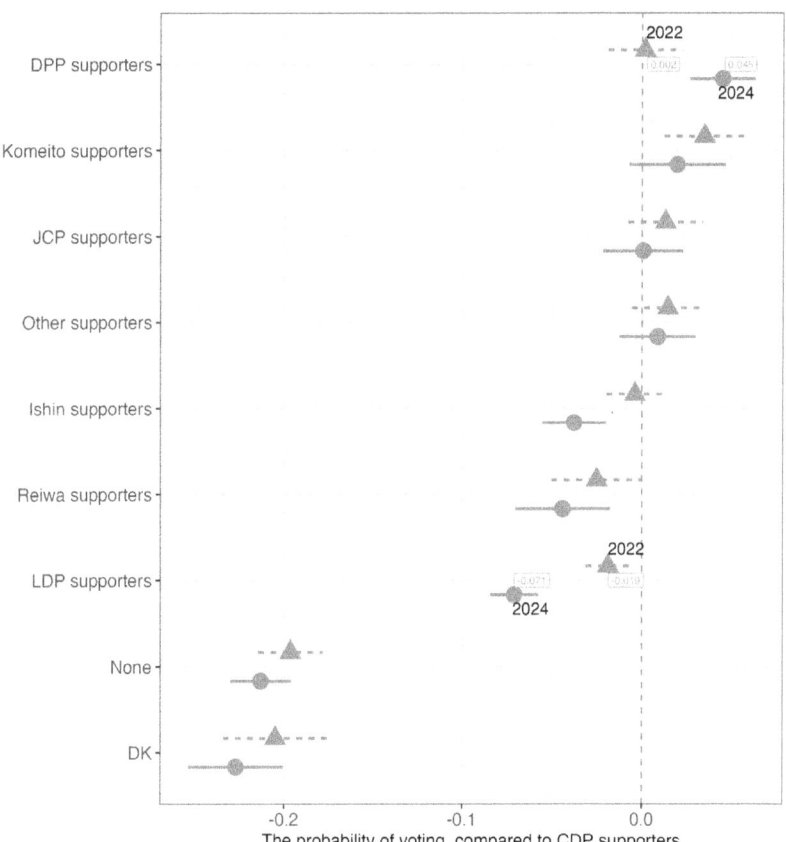

Fig. 12.1 The probability of voting in 2022 and 2024 by party support

Indifference, Alienation, and Turnout

What accounts for the revealed relationship between partisanship and turnout in 2024? My explanation relies on the unified model of turnout and vote choice by Adams et al. (2006). This model is based on the spatial model of voting and turnout by Downs (1957) and Davis et al. (1970). In his classic model, Downs (1957) argues that the party differential, defined as the difference in the utility between voting for one of the parties in a two-party system, affects people's decision to vote. If the party differential is sufficiently large relative to the cost of voting, they will vote. If the party differential is trivial, they abstain because they are indifferent between the two parties, and the indifference does not justify the cost of voting. In Japan, the cost of voting includes the time to travel to a polling place and gather information about candidates and parties.

Davis et al. (1970) argue that the greater party differential does not always lead to a greater probability of voting. They highlight the importance of alienation, suggesting that abstention is more likely when the utility people associate with their preferred party decreases. This means that the party differential is non-zero because people prefer one party over the other, but the utility of voting for their preferred party is not sufficiently large, and thus, they feel alienated, which leads to abstention.

The roles of indifference and alienation as determinants of turnout have been empirically verified primarily by operationalizing the party differential as a distance among the policy or ideological positions of parties and voters (Lefkofridi et al. 2014; Leighley and Nagler 2014; Rogowski 2014; Sakaiya 2015). This approach becomes more salient in the era of greater party polarization in many parts of the world. Scholars have sought to understand whether people are more or less likely to vote when they perceive a greater ideological distance between themselves and the parties as well as between the parties (Béjar et al. 2020; Ellger 2024; Hobolt and Hoerner 2020; Muñoz and Meguid 2021).

Importantly, the unified model of turnout and vote choice indicates that the party differentials are not exclusively determined by policy and ideological distances. The utility of voting for a particular party could be a function of non-policy factors, such as partisanship and valence evaluations of the parties. For example, people might perceive the greater utility of choosing one of the parties because they have an attachment to this party and view the party leader as appealing and the party's competence satisfactory, regardless of the party's policy or ideological position. In their unified model, Adams et al. (2006) argue that people vote if the party differentials as a function of policy and non-policy factors exceed their threshold of indifference, and the utility associated with their preferred party exceeds their threshold of alienation.

I argue that the unified model is useful to explain the larger probability of abstention by LDP supporters and of turnout by DPP supporters in 2024, compared to that among the supporters of the CDP and other parties. The explanation for LDP supporters also applies to Ishin supporters who voted less in 2024 (see Zenkyo 2025). Party support is arguably the most powerful among the determinants of the utility of voting for a particular party. Among those attached to one party, it is natural to predict that the utility of voting for this party is larger than those associated with all other parties. Thus, the party (or utility) differentials are likely to outweigh the indifference threshold among those with party support. In other words, LDP and DPP supporters (and supporters of all other parties) are not indifferent among the parties and find a reason to vote for their party. In contrast, those without party attachment find smaller party differentials, and their indifference leads to abstention.

The above argument does not mean that the other factors are irrelevant. Given the historically low support for the Kishida cabinet during the months preceding the 2024 election, many LDP supporters might be strongly discontent with the policies pursued by the Kishida cabinet (see Nemoto 2025; Maeda 2025). This dissatisfaction could be further exacerbated by the major scandal involving the misuse and misreporting of campaign funds by members of the LDP. Importantly, Kuriwaki et al. (2025) argue that non-policy, valence considerations, such as trust in the party, motivate LDP supporters and others to vote for the party. This implies that lower trust in the party and the leader might play a particularly important role in the decision to vote among LDP supporters in 2024. If the larger policy distance and dissatisfaction with the performance of the party decreased the utility of voting for the LDP but had little influence on the utilities associated with other parties, the utility of voting for the LDP becomes trivial and falls below the alienation threshold. Accordingly, LDP supporters are less likely to vote compared to the supporters of other parties who were not particularly unhappy with their party.

In contrast, the DPP was increasingly popular in the months leading up to the election, especially among the young. Many people viewed the DPP's leader, Tamaki Yūichirō, known for his personality and communication skills, as attractive and appealing. The DPP's policy proposal, "Increase take-home pay (*tedori wo fuyasu*)," received considerable public attention, potentially because it was a simple and easy economic policy to understand even among the politically uninformed, such as the young. These positive features of the party induced some people to perceive the DPP as a viable option and support it. Independent of this, the utility of voting for the DPP may have increased due to the smaller distance between the party's and supporter's positions and the more positive evaluation of the party and its leader. Thus, DPP supporters were more likely to vote compared to the supporters of other parties who were not particularly attracted to their party.

Taken together, the above argument leads to several expectations. First, the probability of voting was notably lower among the LDP supporters who were discontent with the Kishida cabinet. Second, the probability of voting was particularly higher among young DPP supporters. Third, the perceived ideological distance between supporters' position and their preferred party's position was smaller among DPP supporters and larger among LDP supporters compared to supporters of the other parties. Fourth, the favorability of the own party's leader was higher among DPP supporters and lower among LDP supporters compared to supporters of the other parties.

The Mechanisms for Lower Turnout Among LDP Supporters and Higher Turnout Among DPP Supporters

I test the first expectation associated with LDP supporters by splitting the entire sample based on the respondent's evaluation of the overall performance of the Kishida cabinet and then estimating the same regression model as in Fig. 12.1. The subsample of the respondents who reported "very good" and "good" about the performance is defined as those who were "happy" with the Kishida cabinet. In contrast, the subsample of the respondents who reported "poor" and "very poor" is defined as those who were "unhappy" with the Kishida cabinet. The latter includes approximately 77% of the entire sample ($N = 19{,}294$ in the post-election survey), consistent with the low support for the cabinet in the months preceding the election.

Figure 12.2 shows the results. The coefficients for the respondents who were happy with the Kishida cabinet are displayed as a circle, while those for the respondents unhappy with the cabinet are displayed as a triangle. The probability of voting was lower by approximately 9% points among the LDP supporters unhappy with the Kishida cabinet and by 4% points among the LDP supporters happy with the Kishida cabinet, compared to the CDP supporters. No similar pattern is found among the supporters of the other parties, except for those without party support (i.e., "None" and "DK"). These results suggest that discontent with the Kishida cabinet was one of the factors that demobilized many LDP supporters from voting in 2024.

For the second expectation associated with DPP supporters, I split the entire sample based on the respondent's age. Those 59 years old and younger are defined as "Below 59" (60% of the respondents in the post-election survey), while those 60 years old and older are defined as "Above 60". Fig. 12.3 shows that the probability of voting was higher by approximately 4% points among the young to middle-aged DPP supporters

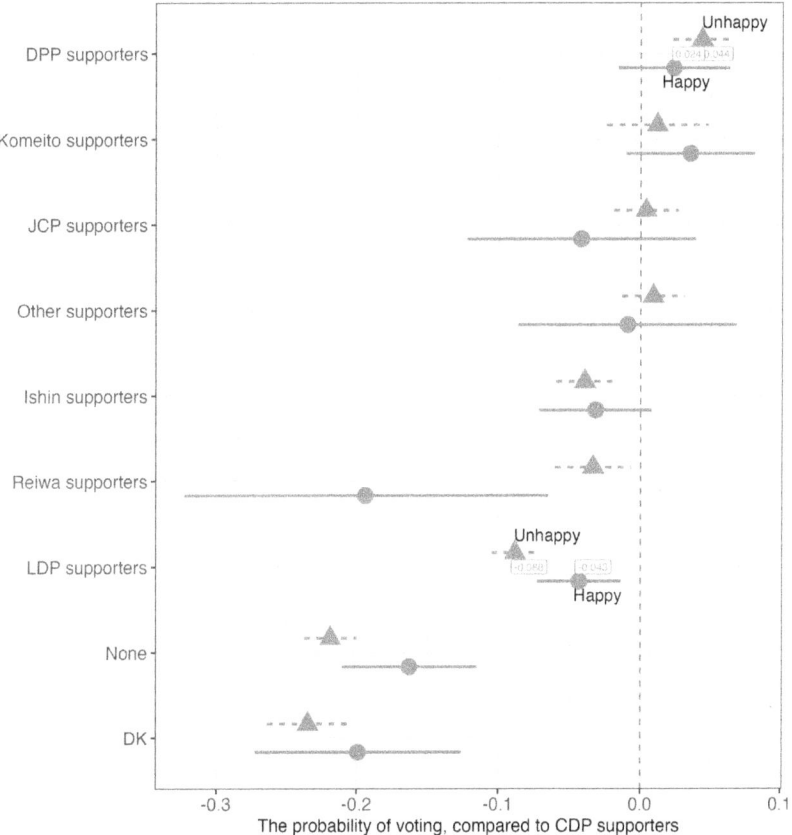

Fig. 12.2 Voter turnout in 2024 by party support and Kishida cabinet support

compared to the CDP supporters of the same age. The probability of voting is not different between the older DPP supporters and the older CDP supporters. Among the supporters of Ishin, Reiwa, and LDP, the probability of voting is lower among younger supporters than older supporters, which is typically found in the relationship between age and turnout. Taken together, it appears that the younger DPP supporters were strongly attracted to the party, which mobilized their turnout in 2024.

The last two expectations are tested by using questions about the perceived ideological distance and the favorability of party leaders. The

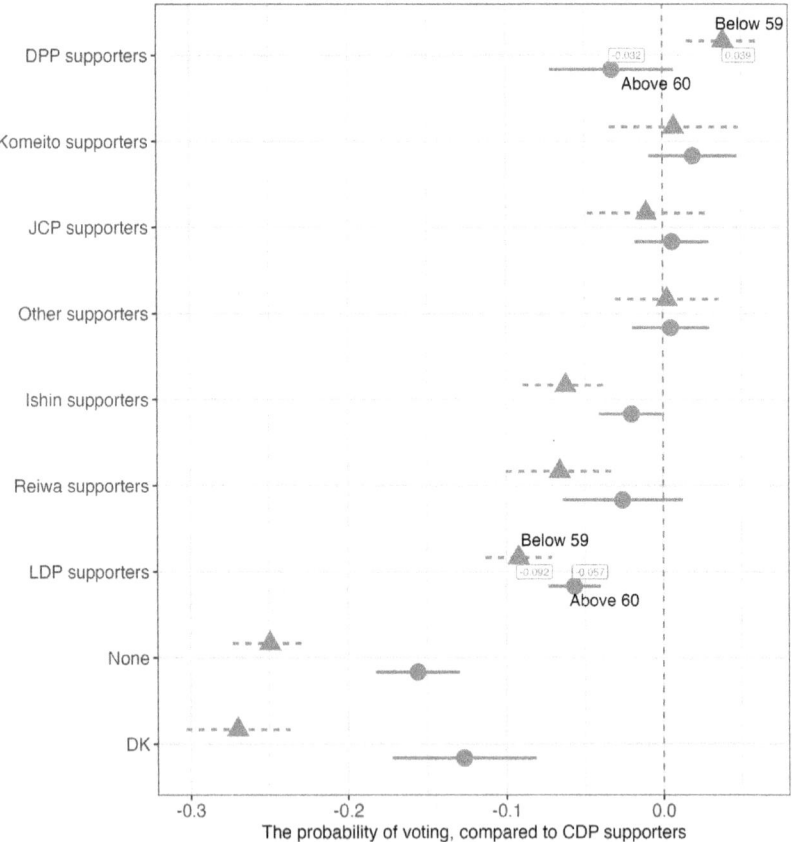

Fig. 12.3 Voter turnout in 2024 by party support and age

perceived ideological distance is measured by the squared difference between the ideological position of the respondent and the party they support on an eleven-point left–right scale from 0 to 10. The larger the value, the larger the distance between the respondent's position and the party's position. The favorability of the party leaders is measured on an eleven-point scale from 0 to 10, where zero means "strongly dislike" and 10 means "strongly like". I focus on the favorability toward the leader of the party the respondent supports. This part of the analysis focuses on the major parties, including the LDP, the DPP, the CDP, Ishin, Kōmeitō, the JCP, and Reiwa, while excluding the supporters of smaller parties and the respondents without party support.

Figure 12.4 reports the results using the perceived ideological distance. The perceived ideological distance is regressed on the indicator variables of party support, controlling for the demographic variables. Compared to CDP supporters, DPP supporters showed a smaller ideological distance of 0.5 points between the position of the party they support and their own. In contrast, LDP supporters, along with the JCP, Ishin, and Reiwa supporters, showed a larger ideological distance. Figure 12.5 reports the estimation results using the favorability of the party leaders. Compared to CDP supporters, DPP supporters evaluated their party's leader much more positively, whereas LDP and Ishin supporters evaluated their party leaders much more negatively (see Zenkyo 2025 for a discussion of perceptions of Ishin's leadership).

In short, these results indicate that both policy/ideology factors and non-policy valence factors shaped the decisions to vote among LDP and DPP supporters more strongly than among the supporters of other parties. LDP supporters were demobilized from voting because their utility of voting was decreased by the lack of policy-and valence-related appeals, while the DPP supporters were mobilized because their utility of voting was increased by the policy-and valence-related appeals.

Turnout and Party Vote Shares in the 2024 General Election

If LDP supporters were discouraged and DPP supporters were encouraged to vote in the 2024 election, their (in)actions might have a substantial influence on the party vote shares at the municipality level. In particular, I anticipate that a larger drop in turnout from 2021 to 2024 is associated with a larger drop in the LDP's absolute vote share,

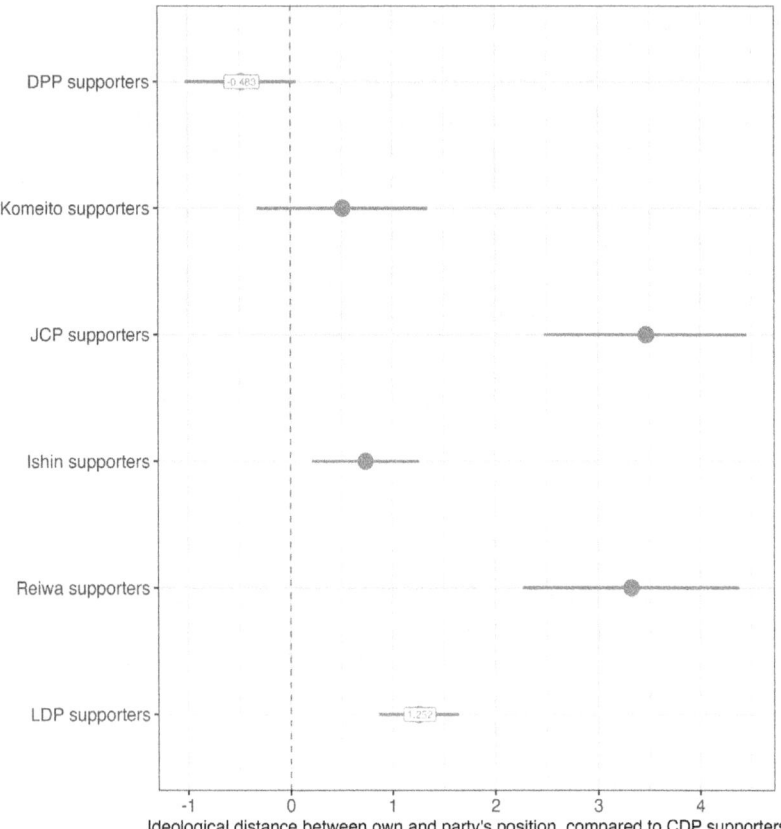

Fig. 12.4 Ideological difference between own position and party position by party support

while a larger increase in turnout is associated with a larger increase in the DPP's absolute vote share. I use the absolute vote share, defined as the percentage of the votes each party received among all eligible citizens in each municipality because it directly captures the relationship between the number of people who cast a ballot and the number of people who voted for the LDP or DPP, after considering the number of eligible citizens as a denominator.

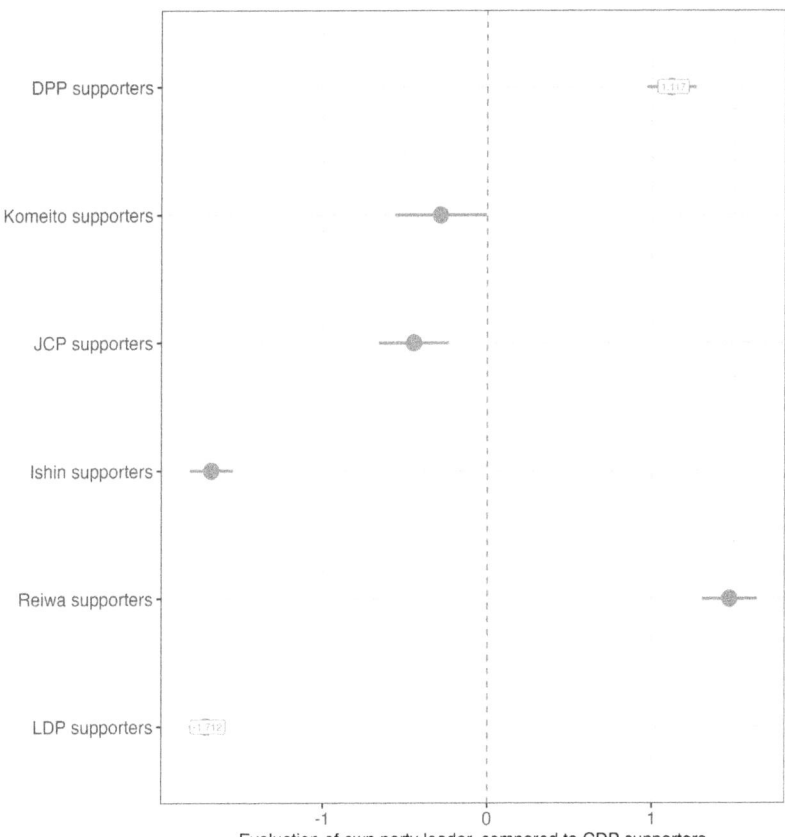

Fig. 12.5 Evaluation of own party leader by party support

I examine these relationships by using the municipality-level data obtained from each of the 47 Prefectural Election Commissions. The data include the number of eligible citizens, the number of citizens who cast a ballot, and the number of valid votes received by each party in the PR tier in the 2021 and 2024 general elections. Turnout is defined as the percentage of citizens who cast a ballot among eligible citizens in the municipality. The number of observations is 1890, which covers almost all the municipalities and wards in Japan. I treat 175 wards in 20 major cities as separate units.

Figure 12.6 shows the scatter plots of the change in turnout on the horizontal axis and the change in the absolute vote share on the vertical axis for each party. Each panel represents the share by the LDP at the top-left, the DPP at the top-right, the CDP at the middle-left, Ishin at the middle-right, Kōmeitō at the bottom-left, and the JCP at the bottom-right. The size of the point represents the population of the municipality. The bold line represents the linear regression line (estimated with the population weight), while the horizontal dashed line represents no change in the vote share between 2021 and 2024.

Most panels in Fig. 12.6 present a clear positive relationship between the change in turnout and the change in the absolute vote share, suggesting that higher (or lower) turnout was generally associated with a larger (or smaller) vote share for each party. The top-left panel shows that this relationship is strongest for the LDP vote share. The intercept is estimated to be −4.1, indicating that the LDP's vote share decreased by 4% points on average nationwide from 2021 to 2024. The LDP lost additional votes in the municipalities where turnout decreased from 2021 to 2024. The estimated slope of the regression line is 0.3 and highly significant, indicating that the LDP's absolute vote decreases by 0.3% points as turnout decreases by 1% point. The LDP lost a more significant number of votes in the municipalities where turnout decreased, implying that those who abstained in 2024 were LDP voters in 2021.

The top-right panel of Fig. 12.5 also shows a clear positive relationship between the changes in turnout and the DPP's absolute vote share. The intercept is estimated to be 3.8, indicating that the DPP's vote share increased by 3.8% points on average nationwide from 2021 to 2024. Additionally, in the municipalities where turnout increased from 2021 to 2024, the DPP vote share also increased proportionally. The estimated slope of the regression line is 0.2 and highly significant, indicating that the DPP's absolute vote rose by 0.2% points as turnout increased by 1% point. This implies that those who abstained in 2021 turned out to vote for the DPP in 2024, increasing the DPP's vote share.

The other four parties show a weaker positive relationship between the changes in turnout and their absolute vote shares, except for the CDP. Like the DPP, the CDP's absolute vote increases by 0.2% points as turnout increases by 1% point.

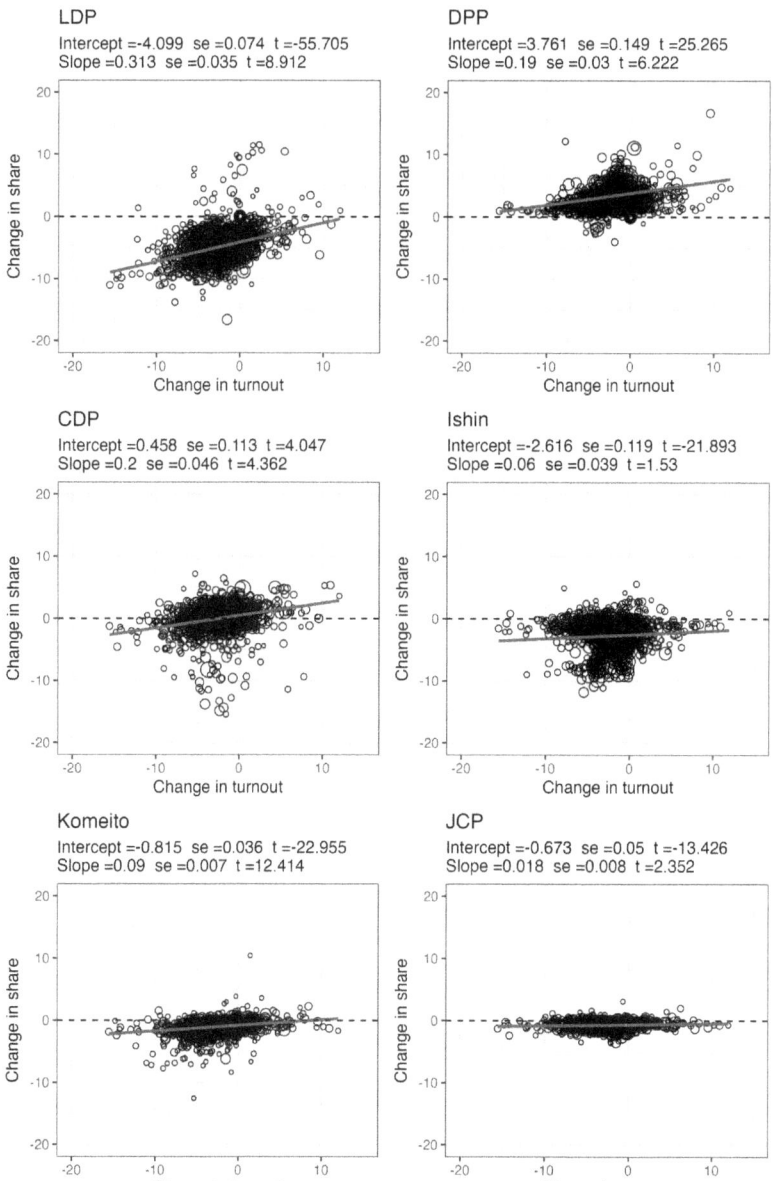

Fig. 12.6 Turnout and absolute party vote share

Conclusion

This chapter highlights the importance of partisanship in shaping people's decision to vote in the 2024 general election. Building on the unified model of turnout and vote choice, I argue and show that LDP supporters were less likely to vote because they felt alienated from their party. In contrast, DPP supporters were more likely to vote because they were attracted to their party's policy and valence appeals. These patterns ultimately led to a large loss in the LDP's vote share and a large gain in the DPP's vote share from the 2021 to 2024 elections.

The findings of this chapter have important implications for the study of voter turnout and electoral behavior in Japan. Even in the era of declining turnout, politics and electoral choices remain key factors in shaping people's decision to vote. When the electoral choices presented to voters change and look more or less appealing, many people change their actions from turnout to abstention or vice versa accordingly. Declining turnout is often attributed to the lack of interest in and attention to politics among (especially young) voters. Yet, the findings of this chapter suggest people decide to vote or abstain in accordance with the political parties and their policy and valence appeals. Recent scholarship on voter turnout tends to pay closer attention to the influences of electoral reforms and institutional characteristics on turnout. While these factors are undoubtedly important as determinants of the cost in the calculus of voting, this chapter underscores the importance of the benefits of voting in the same calculus.

Acknowledgements This study received financial support from JSPS grant number 23H00040. I thank the participants of JPOSS for their helpful comments on an earlier version of this chapter. The author declares that the collection of the survey data used in this article was reviewed and approved by the Institutional Review Board of Osaka School of International Public Policy, University of Osaka (No R61025-1).

References

Adams, James, Jay Dow, and I. I. I. Samuel Merrill. 2006. "The Political Consequences of Alienation-Based and Indifference-Based Voter Abstention: Applications to Presidential Elections." *Political Behavior* 28 (1): 65–86.

Béjar, Sergio, Juan A. Moraes, and Santiago López-Cariboni. 2020. "Elite Polarization and Voting Turnout in Latin America, 1993–2010." *Journal of Elections, Public Opinion and Parties* 30 (1): 1–21.
Davis, Otto A., Melvin J. Hinich, and Peter C. Ordeshook. 1970. "An Expository Development of a Mathematical Model of the Electoral Process." *American Political Science Review* 64 (2): 426–48.
Downs, Anthony. 1957. *An Economic Theory of Democracy*. Harper.
Ellger, Fabio. 2024. "The Mobilizing Effect of Party System Polarization. Evidence from Europe." *Comparative Political Studies*. 57 (8): 1310–38.
Kuriwaki, Shiro, Yusaku Horiuchi, and Daniel M. Smith. 2025. "Winning Elections with Unpopular Policies: Valence Advantage and Single-Party Dominance in Japan." *Quarterly Journal of Political Science*, 20 (4): 439–476.
Hobolt, Sara B., and Julian M. Hoerner. 2020. "The Mobilising Effect of Political Choice." *European Journal of Political Research* 59 (2): 229–47.
Ikeda, Fumi. 2025. "The CDP in 2024: The Legacy of the Electoral Coalition with the JCP." In *Japan Decides 2024: The Japanese General Election*, edited by Kenneth M. McElwain, Robert J. Pekkanen, and Daniel M. Smith, 57–74. Palgrave Macmillan.
Lefkofridi, Zoe, Nathalie Giger, and Aina Gallego. 2014. "Electoral Participation in Pursuit of Policy Representation: Ideological Congruence and Voter Turnout." *Journal of Election. Public Opinion, and Parties* 24 (3): 291–311.
Leighley, Jan E., and Jonathan Nagler. 2014. *Who Votes Now? Demographics, Issues, Inequality and Turnout in the United States*. Princeton University Press.
Maeda, Yukio. 2025. "Public Opinion and Scandals in Economic Hard Times." In *Japan Decides 2024: The Japanese General Election*, edited by Kenneth M. McElwain, Robert J. Pekkanen, and Daniel M. Smith, 163–179. Palgrave Macmillan.
Muñoz, Maria Murias, and Bonnie M. Meguid. 2021. "Does Party Polarization Mobilize or De-Mobilize Voters? The Answer Depends on Where Voters Stand." *Electoral Studies* 70: 102279.
Nemoto, Kuniaki. 2025. "Reasons Behind the LDP's Loss in the 2024 Election." In *Japan Decides 2024: The Japanese General Election*, edited by Kenneth M. McElwain, Robert J. Pekkanen, and Daniel M. Smith, 37–55. Palgrave Macmillan.
Plane, Dennis L., and Joseph Gershtenson. 2004. "Candidates' Ideological Locations, Abstention, and Turnout in U.S. Midterm Senate Elections." *Political Behavior* 26 (1): 69–93.
Rogowski, Jon C. 2014. "Electoral Choice, Ideological Conflict, and Political Participation: Electoral Choice, Ideological Conflict, and Political Participation." *American Journal of Political Science* 58 (2): 479–94.
Sakaiya, Shiro. 2015. "Parties' Ideological Positions and Voters' Electoral Participation in Postwar Japan". *Leviathan* 57 (Fall): 47–71.

Zenkyo, Masahiro. 2025. "Why Did Public Support for the Japan Innovation Party Decline in the 2024 HR Election?" In *Japan Decides 2024: The Japanese General Election*, edited by Kenneth M. McElwain, Robert J. Pekkanen, and Daniel M. Smith, 91–105. Palgrave Macmillan.

Zipp, John F. 1985. "Perceived Representativeness and Voting: An Assessment of the Impact of 'Choices' vs. 'Echoes'." *American Political Science Review* 79 (1): 50–61.

PART IV

Issues

CHAPTER 13

Scandals During the Kishida Administration

Matthew M. Carlson

INTRODUCTION

Scandals are common in all democracies and Japan is no exception. In the last three years, Japanese politics has experienced a slush fund scandal, bureaucratic policy failure scandals, financial scandals linked to politicians, as well as scandals and controversies linked to religion. The assassination of former Prime Minister Abe Shinzō, who led the Liberal Democratic Party (LDP) from 2012 to 2020, generated a strong societal reaction toward the South Korean-based Family Federation for World Peace and Unification, known more commonly by its former name, the Unification Church. This helped generate a new scandal ingredient in 2022 and 2023: lawmakers' ties to the church. The discovery of faction slush funds in 2022 also became a major scandal in 2023. This chapter focuses on the causes and consequences of the church controversy and the slush fund scandal for the 2024 lower house election and Japanese politics and society more broadly.

The scandals considered in this chapter provide important context for thinking about the underlying developmental symptoms of corruption

M. M. Carlson (✉)
University of Vermont, Burlington, VT, USA
e-mail: Matthew.Carlson@uvm.edu

© The Author(s), under exclusive license to Springer Nature Switzerland AG 2025
K. M. McElwain et al. (eds.), *Japan Decides 2024*,
https://Doi.org/10.1007/978-3-031-98797-7_13

that exist in each society. One study classifies Japan as an "influence market" society (Johnston 2005). Its corruption syndrome, *influence market corruption*, works mostly within the confines of established institutions and focuses on winning offices and influencing those who hold them.[1] In influence market societies such as Japan, it is common for politicians to rely on organized groups (including religious organizations) to mobilize support and win elections. The LDP system of factions also served as a mechanism for selecting party leaders, dividing important posts in the party and government, and nominating and supporting individual members in elections. The scandals and controversies discussed in this chapter offer critical insights into how Japan's influence market operates and provide context for why the LDP failed to maintain its lower house majority in the 2024 election.

One useful definition of scandals is "actions or events involving certain kinds of transgressions which become known to others and are sufficiently serious to elicit a public response" (Thompson 2000: 13). Among their characteristics, scandals involve the transgression of values, norms, or moral codes. Scandals also require the involvement of non-participants, who express their disapproval to others after a transgression shocks or offends them. In the publication of a scandal, the news media plays a dominant role in getting information out to the public (Lull and Hinerman 1997). Another concept related to scandal is moral panic, which occurs when "a condition, episode, person or group of persons emerges to become defined as a threat to societal values or interests" (Cohen 1980: 9). Moral panics arise when the mass media exaggerates this threat in a way that creates fear and reinforces stereotypes. These concepts will be used to first discuss the controversy surrounding the Unification Church and its ties to lawmakers followed by an examination of the LDP faction slush fund scandal.

---

[1] Johnston uses country-level statistical indictors and cluster analysis to derive four ideal types intended to highlight patterns. Besides influence market corruption, elite cartel corruption is linked to networks of elites that use corrupt exchanges and is a common syndrome in consolidating democracies and reforming markets (i.e., Italy or South Korea). The two final types (oligarch and clan and official mogul corruption) are most relevant for transitional and undemocratic regimes.

Abe's Assassination and the Unification Church

In 1954, Sun Myung Moon founded the Unification Church (UC) in South Korea. Missionaries came to Japan after and established the UC of Japan as an official religious corporation in 1964. Moon, who was an ardent anti-communist, later created a political group in Japan called the International Federation for Victory over Communism in 1968. In Japan, one of the major controversies surrounding Moon and the UC is the so-called practice of "spiritual sales." Members of affiliated groups sold expensive pots, seals, and other items to believers claiming that such items were necessary to ward off misfortune and bad karma. Criticism of this practice led to the formation of the National Network of Lawyers Against Spiritual Sales (hereafter the National Network) in 1987.

The LDP formed in 1955 and traditionally has relied upon a wide array of organizations and interests within society to stay in power. The LDP and the UC shared a similar conservative ideology and dislike of communism. LDP members have relied upon UC followers to help them mobilize to win votes and seats. They signed policy pledges drafted by the church, attended events of the church or its affiliated groups, and participated in interviews with UC-affiliated magazines and other publications. The UC's ties to the LDP likewise helped further the economic and political goals of the Moon organization through its global network of affiliated groups, businesses, and nonprofit corporations (Nippon.com 2023).

Some scholars have mentioned the concept of moral panic in trying to explain the intense public reactions to the UC after the assassination of former Prime Minister Abe on July 8, 2022 (McLaughlin 2023, 2025; Kingston 2023). Yamagami Tetsuya, who admitted to the killing, told investigators that he held a grudge against the UC because his mother was a member and had donated large sums of money to the church that led her to declare bankruptcy in 2002. Yamagami searched the internet for information about the UC and believed that Abe and his grandfather had helped spread the UC's influence in Japan. He also corresponded with journalists and online bloggers who had taken a critical stance against the UC. While this chapter will focus only on some aspects of media coverage, it is important to mention that social media, television stations, and investigative journalists played important roles in shaping public reactions (see McLaughlin 2023, Poppe 2022, Prusa 2024, and Saitō 2024).

The immediate sympathy expressed for Yamagami as a victim was possible because journalists and lawyers who were critical of the UC defended him and used the killing to repeat criticisms of the UC as well as the Japanese government. Days after the killing, the National Network held a press conference and released a statement that described Yamagami's actions as despicable but also claimed that his resentment against the Church is understandable. As lawyers, they viewed the Church as being responsible for widespread suffering by current and former members and blamed the government and politicians of the ruling party for doing nothing about the activities of the UC that had been destroying families for more than 30 years (National Network, July 12, 2022).

The UC held an earlier press conference where it expressed condolences for Abe's killing and expressed pity for the tragedy that struck Yamagami's family. It released a statement on the ensuing media frenzy, where it strongly protested the "biased reporting, which has been carried out by lawyers belonging to the association as commentators, severely damaging the reputation of our organization and its members, violating their human rights, and potentially inciting hate crimes" (WPUFF, July 17, 2022). In the weeks that followed, the UC and National Network waged a public relations battle over who was responsible. Introvigne (2022) argues that powerful opponents of the UC convinced the media that the Church bore partial responsibility for Abe's death. This led to hate incidents and discrimination and the creation of scandals focusing on politicians' connections to the church.

The negative media campaign levied against the UC negatively impacted public opinion and created a new political problem for the Kishida Fumio administration and for politicians with ties to the UC (cf. Yukio Maeda 2025; McLaughlin 2025). In the first public opinion surveys on cabinet approval after Abe's killing, the *Asahi* showed that the approval rating of Kishida's cabinet fell from 57% in July to 47% in August (*Asahi Shinbun*, August 29, 2022). When the poll asked respondents about Kishida's response to problems surrounding the church, 21% expressed approval while 65% said they did not approve. When asked whether the politicians should sever their ties with the UC, 82% said they should while 12% said there was no need.

Media Efforts to Shame Politicians

One important characteristic of the moral panic was the frantic search to identify the politicians who had ties to the UC. In the weeks following Abe's death, the press sent out questionnaires, interviewed politicians and scrutinized social media postings to identify any public official associated with the UC. One of the first revelations of a politician who was involved was Education Minister Suematsu Shinsuke, who acknowledged that church members had bought tickets to his fundraising parties in 2020 and 2021 (*Yomiuri Shinbun*, July 24, 2022). Defense Minister Kishi Nobuo also admitted that UC followers had helped him in past election campaigns, but in the capacity of volunteers rather than as representatives of the church (*Jiji*, July 26, 2022). Even leaders from various opposition parties, such as Izumi Kenta of the Constitutional Democratic Party (CDP), acknowledged ties, and pledged to investigate the details.

Senior leaders of the LDP tried to rebuff the intensive media onslaught by refusing to investigate individual members and the sorts of political activities that have been a normal matter of course (cf. Nemoto 2025). Secretary-General Motegi Toshimitsu explained that the LDP headquarters has never had a formal relationship with the UC. Prime Minister Kishida also denied having personal connections to the UC. Kishida's government relied heavily on members of the Abe faction. After Abe's killing, Kishida wanted to show his respect for Abe, which included organizing a state funeral. This generated significant controversy since taxpayers would have to shoulder the costs. There were also members of the public who knew about Abe's involvement and support of the UC because of the media coverage, which generated opposition to Kishida's plans for a state funeral.

With the LDP refusing to investigate itself, major media organizations tried to obtain information about the connections between the UC and politicians through their own efforts. One of the first major efforts in this regard was a *Kyodo* survey sent to 712 lawmakers (*Kyodo News*, August 31, 2022). Out of the 583 responses obtained, more than 106 members acknowledged ties to the UC. The majority of those (82) heralded from the LDP. *Kyodo* published the names online, which journalists used to target their reporting and to identify politicians not on the list or suspected of hiding their ties.

The search for names and the publishing of name lists reached the pinnacle with the *Asahi* newspaper. *Asahi* journalists wanted to show that the Church's influence had spread to local politics, which is why it sent its questionnaire to 3333 politicians not only at the national level, but also to prefectural assembly members and governors (*Asahi Shinbun*, September 4, 2022). Of the 447 respondents who acknowledged ties to the UC, 290 were local assembly members, 150 were from the Diet, and seven were governors. Among the prefectural assembly and Diet members, those from the LDP made up 80% or more of the respondents. *Asahi* correspondents used the survey to emphasize how the influence of the Church had spread to local areas across Japan and urged the LDP to investigate its ties.

Under relentless media pressure, the LDP decided to send its own questionnaire to 379 of its members (*Asahi Shinbun*, September 30, 2022). Like the polls before, the LDP focused not only on identifying which members have ties, but also on the basic contours of such ties. The LDP survey listed a total of eleven connections, ranging from sending telegrams to accepting election support. Sending a congratulatory telegram to an organization is a common courtesy when politicians are unable to attend an event. The LDP survey confirmed that half of its membership had ties to the UC or its affiliated organizations. LDP leaders initially hesitated on whether to release partial or full results for the survey. They decided to disclose the names of 125 members, keeping the names of fifty-five members secret. The undisclosed names are from three categories: sending telegrams, cases where a secretary attended a meeting, and interviews with church-related publications. These are the categories where politicians resisted disclosure because they could point to the heavy involvement of their secretaries.

Table 13.1 shows the responses linked to the 180 members who indicated that they have one or more connections across the eleven categories. The most common connections are greetings given by the Diet member while attending the event of a related organization to the Unification Church, sending a congratulatory telegram, and having a secretary attend an event in person. Under the intense glare of the media, opposition parties, and anti-UC groups in society, these ties became an important scandal ingredient and added fuel to the moral panic over religion. The LDP's attempt to investigate itself generated considerable backlash. The survey failed to investigate former lower house speaker Hosoda Hiroyuki, despite a viral photograph showing him at an event sponsored by a UC-affiliated group (*TBS News*, July 26, 2022).

Table 13.1 Results of the LDP survey on contacts with Unification Church

Connection to UC or related organization	Number of responses
Greeting given at a meeting of a related religious organization	102
Sent congratulatory telegram to event	97
Secretary attended meeting	76
Participated in interview with publication	24
Membership fees paid to related organization	24
Speech given at a meeting of a related religious organization	20
Volunteer election support received	17
Attended meeting directly hosted by Unification Church	13
Donations or other income received from related organization	4
Election support requests accepted	2

Sources *Yomiuri* and *Tokyo Shinbun* (September 8, 2022) as well as the LDP's additional release of names (*Asahi Shinbun*, September 30, 2022)

KISHIDA'S CABINET PURGE AND CABINET RESIGNATION SCANDALS

One of the most urgent and visible political problems for Prime Minister Kishida was what to do about the ministers in his second cabinet that the media had exposed as having UC ties. After Abe's killing, the media had identified a total of eight ministers, with seven linked to one of the major factions. Their connections to the church reflected the typical things revealed in the media and LDP surveys. None of these ministers had broken any laws although critics called on them to resign. Kishida decided to reshuffle his second cabinet, hoping that he could reappoint new members without associations to the UC. In the first reshuffle of his second cabinet in August, Kishida replaced the scandal-tainted ministers. However, Kishida's reshuffled cabinet failed to solve Kishida's urgent and visible problem.

Immediately before and after the appointment, the media identified eight new ministers with known ties to the UC. One explanation for Kishida's misfire is that he reshuffled too quickly and did not implement a stringent vetting process. As suggested above, Kishida and the LDP were reluctant to directly investigate their individual members and their political activities and connections to other organizations. LDP members often defended their activities and ties by stressing that the Constitution guarantees the freedom of religion, but the media campaign to expose these ties and cast the UC as an anti-social group was intense. In this environment, it is not surprising that the media managed to find and expose LDP members that concealed their ties, including high-profile cabinet ministers. This led to public distrust that Kishida or the LDP would be able to sever ties with the UC.

The failure of the LDP and Kishida to thoroughly investigate and vet cabinet ministers also contributed to the creation of significant cabinet resignation scandals, such as the case of Yamagiwa Daishirō. Kishida appointed Yamagiwa as Economic Revitalization Minister and Minister for Novel Coronavirus Response in his first cabinet and kept him in this position through his reshuffled second cabinet. None of the various searches uncovered any significant and direct ties between Yamagiwa and the UC. When Yamagiwa or his office filled out the LDP survey, he indicated that he had attended a meeting with a UC-affiliated organization. Later, it became apparent that he had downplayed his association or did not tell the truth: the event in question was an actual UC meeting led by the new leader and widow of Sun Myung Moon.

While the opposition parties publicly called on Yamagiwa to resign, Kishida took a cautious approach and asked him to give a sincere and thorough explanation to the public. Yamagiwa tried to shift blame on his office staff for not reporting the meeting on the LDP questionnaire. What doomed him was that whoever had reported his attendance to the media had convincing evidence. A viral photo circulated that showed Yamagiwa in a group photo standing next to the widow of the group's founder. Yamagiwa admitted that he had posed for the photo. When it was clear that the scandal was not going away, Kishida reversed his cautious stance and forced Yamagiwa to resign (*Kyodo News*, October 24, 2022).

Besides the case of Yamagiwa, Kishida dismissed three additional ministers during the last two months of 2022.[2] While the Unification Church had become an important scandal ingredient in Yamagiwa's case, the additional cabinet minister scandal resignations included other ingredients such as inappropriate statements or problems related to money. The Kishida administration also had to deal with the fallout from numerous errors related to the "My Number" national identification system, controversies linked to the discharge of treated water from the

---

[2] Kishida dismissed Hanashi Yasuhiro over a gaffe. He then removed Terada Minoru and Akiba Kenya after various financial scandals.

Fukushima nuclear power plant, as well as the arrest of LDP member Akimoto Masatoshi in 2023 for bribery.

The intense media campaign and moral panic led the ruling and opposition parties to work on efforts to pass legislation to help victims of the UC. The first legal enactment in December 2022 focused on preventing the inappropriate solicitation of donations, whereas a second enactment in 2023 focused on monitoring the assets of religious groups and helping citizens get legal assistance. In March 2025, the Tokyo District Court ordered the UC to be dissolved of its corporate status as a religious group, although the UC has filed an appeal (*Kyodo News*, March 25, 2025).

LDP Faction Slush Fund and Kickback Scandal

The origins of this scandal began in 2022 when journalists from communist newspaper *Akahata* published a story alleging that LDP factions were breaking the law by not disclosing the names of all large purchasers of party fundraising tickets (*Akahata*, November 6, 2022). The law requires factions to disclose the name of anyone who purchases more than 200,000 yen of tickets. *Akahata* reporters investigated to what extent LDP factions were following this rule. They collected disclosure reports for factional groups along with reports from donor organizations that purchased tickets. Because studying all reports is too time consuming, they limited their investigation to a three-year period in the Tokyo and Osaka area. When a political group disclosed that it purchased tickets exceeding 200,000 yen, they checked whether the faction disclosed details about the donor in its own report. Overall, they uncovered fifty-nine cases of non-reporting involving an amount of 24.2 million yen. The issue of non-reporting was systematic and involved all LDP factions.

The *Akahata* article also included commentary from Kamiwaki Hiroshi, a professor of constitutional law at Kobe Gakuin University, who argued that extensive non-reporting was likely part of a deliberate and widespread scheme linked to the creation of LDP factional "slush funds" (*uragane*). Professor Kamiwaki filed a complaint with the Tokyo District Public Prosecutors Office and launched his own investigation using the income and expenditure reports of LDP factions. In October 2023, he submitted another complaint after completing his investigation. He told prosecutors that LDP factions had understated their party fundraising income by a total of forty-one million yen over a four-year period, an amount double of what *Akahata* had reported at the end of 2022.

The tipping point that generated a massive scandal was when the Special Investigation Department of the Tokyo Prosecutors Office decided to launch their own probe, beginning with the voluntary questioning of factional officials (*Jiji*, November 19, 2023). In parliament, members of the opposition began to question Kishida and other leaders or former leaders of various factions (*Asahi Shinbun*, November 21, 2023). The Ministry of Internal Affairs and Communications released campaign finance disclosure reports for the 2022 cycle in November, which provided new material for journalists and prosecutors to pore over. The picture that emerged was that LDP factions returned the slush funds to individual faction members in a kickback scheme. They potentially ignored or violated campaign finance rules when either the sending or receiving side did not properly disclose the amount in their disclosure report.

LDP factions assigned quotas for ticket sales by individual members based on the number of times they have won elections and their position (*Asahi Shinbun*, December 3, 2023). It is not clear when the slush funds and kickback scheme started, but one possibility is that the practice goes back to the period when former Prime Minister Mori Yoshirō led the faction from 1998 to 2006 (*Mainichi Shinbun*, April 22, 2024). Factions allowed members who sold more than their quota to keep the income above the quota. The media focused the most on the use of slush funds and kickbacks linked to the Abe faction.

Prime Minister Abe led the faction until his assassination in 2022. It became the largest in the LDP with approximately one hundred members, which is more than a quarter of the party's membership. The faction allegedly reimbursed members with ticket revenue totaling around five hundred million yen over a five-year period until 2022 (*Kyodo News*, December 8, 2023). At least ten Diet members from this faction accepted kickbacks of ten million yen or more. In the fundraising events for upper house members running for re-election, the faction kicked back all collected funds, which neither the faction nor the upper house members disclosed. To distance himself from factional politics, Kishida resigned as the leader of his faction. He also decided to purge key members of the Abe faction from his cabinet and party, leading him to dismiss four cabinet ministers along with five senior vice ministers on the same day (*Asahi Shinbun*, December 14, 2023).

Investigators from the special investigation unit of the Tokyo District Public Prosecutors Office started with the voluntary questioning of LDP members and then searched the offices of the Abe and Nikai factions on suspicion of violating campaign finance laws (*Asahi Shinbun*, December 19, 2023). They also searched the homes and offices of two LDP Abe faction members: Ōno Yasutada and Ikeda Yoshitaka (*Asahi Shinbun*, December 29, 2023). Prosecutors believe that Ōno accepted more than fifty million yen in undisclosed kickbacks. They indicted him and his secretary without arrest. Prosecutors also indicted Ikeda for receiving kickbacks worth around forty-eight million yen over five years (*Asahi Shinbun*, December 27, 2023). Unlike Ōno, prosecutors arrested Ikeda after the discovery of damaged data storage drives and other telltale signs that Ikeda and his secretary were attempting to destroy evidence (*Asahi Shinbun*, January 8, 2024).

Prosecutors also issued indictments against current or former accountants linked to the Abe, Nikai, and Kishida factions and to another Abe faction member, Tanigawa Yaichi, for not disclosing forty million yen in kickbacks (*Asahi Shinbun*, January 11, 2024). Due to a lack of evidence, prosecutors made the decision not to charge any of the senior LDP politicians that had served as top executives in the Abe faction (*Yomiuri Shinbun*, January 16, 2024). Kishida had already purged them from important leadership posts, but the slush fund scandal showed no signs of abating. In one *Asahi* (January 23, 2024) poll taken around this time, Kishida's approval rating stood at 23%, the lowest since the LDP returned to power in 2012. When the poll asked respondents how Kishida has responded to the slush fund problem thus far, 75% were against and 17% approved.

The failure to charge the most influential players linked to the Abe faction and the resulting public backlash stirred Kishida to respond. Kishida pushed his faction group Kōchikai to dissolve its legal standing allowing it to raise and spend funds (*Mainichi Shinbun*, January 20, 2024). The Abe and Nikai factions followed suit. Other factions such as the Asō and Motegi factions, however, did not dissolve their faction headquarters and expressed their intention to continue operating as a "policy group." In the past, LDP factions have disbanded only to resume their activities later. Kishida also urged the LDP to establish what was known as the Political Reform Headquarters, which adopted new internal party rules.[3]

---

[3] The new LDP rules prohibit the creation of factions that wield influence in raising and dispensing money and personnel issues. Policy groups are allowed to form but cannot hold

With the legal investigation concluding, the opposition parties urged Kishida and the LDP to investigate and provide a list of every faction member who did not report kickbacks and threatened to boycott parliamentary sessions if the government failed to meet their demands. Following the same playbook when it investigated UC ties, the LDP sent a questionnaire to its members about undisclosed kickbacks (*Asahi Shinbun*, February 2, 2024). When the LDP finished the survey, it made public the list of 82 LDP members, the majority from the Abe faction, who failed to report kickbacks. The opposition parties wanted the list to publicly shame these politicians and criticize Kishida and the LDP's response.

Opposition parties urged the LDP to hold meetings in the lower house's Deliberative Council on Political Ethics. They wanted to use this committee to question senior members of the Abe and Nikai factions about their involvement in the scandal. After Abe faction members demanded that the committee hold the sessions behind closed doors, the committee quickly became bogged down in conflict. Kishida, however, helped break the impasse by attending the first session. The other members then attended sessions open to the press (*Mainichi Shinbun*, March 1, 2024).

As part of the LDP's political reform efforts, the party initiated disciplinary measures to punish key LDP members who were involved. The LDP targeted thirty-nine members. It asked two members to leave the party (Sekō Hiroshige and Shionoya Ryū), suspended three from party membership (Shimomura Hakubun, Nishimura Yasutoshi, and Takagi Tsuyoshi), suspended seventeen from holding party positions, and gave another seventeen a warning (*Kyodo News*, March 23, 2024). The LDP published the names of all thirty-nine members on its webpage.[4]

The slush fund scandal led to significant changes to existing campaign finance laws in June 2024. The changes lower the minimum threshold for disclosing the names of those who buy fundraising tickets from 200,000

fundraising parties. The party also added new disciplinary measures intended to punish Diet members whose accountants are arrested or indicted, such as suspension or expulsion from the party (*Asahi Shinbun*, March 8, 2024).

[4] Faction leader Nikai Toshihiro was not on this list because he had struck a secret deal with Kishida to announce his political retirement instead (*Yomiuri Shinbun*, May 4, 2024).

to 50,000 yen. The new rules require lawmakers to confirm a document that they have checked over the contents of their campaign finance report. The revisions also highlighted a gradual move toward disclosing policy activity funds that the party headquarters gives to individual Diet members. Although political leaders left the specific details on implementation to a later date, the basic idea is to have lawmakers disclose policy activity expenses (*Asahi Shinbun*, June 19, 2024).[5]

SCANDALS AND THE 2024 ELECTION

The slush fund scandal contributed to the LDP's poor showing in the April 2024 lower house by-elections for seats in Tokyo, Nagasaki, and Shimane. LDP member Kakizawa Mito vacated his seat from the Tokyo 15th district due to his arrest and conviction of vote-buying in a Tokyo ward mayoral election. The LDP failed to field a candidate, which helped pave the way for the opposition to win. Tanigawa Yaichi represented the Nagasaki 3rd district until his resignation after prosecutors indicted him for not disclosing forty million yen in Abe faction kickbacks. The LDP did not field a candidate, paving the way for the CDP candidate to win the seat. Finally, Shimane 1st district was vacant due to the death of former LDP lower house speaker Hosoda Hiroyuki. The media had linked Hosoda to multiple scandals. The LDP-backed candidate lost to the CDP candidate by more than 17% of the vote.

The slush fund scandal was one of the significant challenges faced by Kishida that played a vital role in his decision to not run for a second term as LDP president, paving the way for the 2024 LDP presidential election that featured a record number of nine candidates (cf. Nemoto 2025). Ishiba Shigeru won this contest in the second round after coming in third in the first round. Part of his victory may be because Kishida encouraged junior members to support Ishiba over Takaichi Sanae, a close ally of former Prime Minister Abe.

---

[5] Some of the first legal cases initiated by prosecutors have now concluded. The Tokyo District sentenced a former accountant of the Nikai faction to a two-year jail sentence, which he will not have to serve if he stays out of trouble as it was suspended for five years (*Mainichi Shinbun*, 10 September 2024). A former accountant of the Abe faction received a three-year sentence, which was also suspended for five years (*Mainichi Shinbun*, September 30, 2024). Prosecutors also reached a decision to not indict sixteen current or former Diet members due to insufficient evidence (*Asahi Shinbun*, July 9, 2024).

Prime Minister Ishiba called for a snap election and the official campaign period for the lower house began on October 15. Journalists from the Communist Party-linked newspaper *Akahata* noticed an important detail that shook up the election. Throughout the year, the LDP allocates funds from the taxpayer-funded political party subsidy to its local party branches, typically managed by the endorsed LDP candidate in the single-member constituencies. Journalists from *Akahata* saw that the LDP had transferred twenty million yen to its branches, including to those managed by former LDP members denied the party endorsement due to their involvement in the slush fund scandal (*Akahata*, October 23, 2024). This scoop generated major headlines and provoked the question: why was the LDP distributing a large amount of funds to candidates they refused to endorse? Opposition parties used this controversy to criticize the LDP in the home stretch of the campaign while the non-endorsed candidates tried to distance themselves from the uproar by returning the funds.

In preparation for the election, the LDP and the Kōmeitō made important decisions on which LDP candidates to endorse or support. Once the official campaign began, the media quickly focused coverage on what they labeled the "slush fund" politicians: a group that had now grown to forty-four members linked to undisclosed faction kickbacks. In the 2024 election, the LDP endorsed thirty-four of them, but banned them from being dual candidates in the PR tier. There were also ten non-endorsed candidates forced to run as independents. The LDP had previously disciplined nine of them with either a warning or a suspension from holding party leadership positions. Kōmeitō supported thirty-five of them because these members could help the party get more votes under PR.

The media focused intensely on the "slush fund" candidates and the prevailing story line after the election was that 61% of them (27 of 44) failed to win a lower house seat. Of the thirty-four endorsed candidates, twenty lost their seat while seven of the ten non-endorsed candidates lost. Using a regression analysis, Nemoto (2025) shows that politicians involved in either the church controversy or slush fund scandal had significantly lower vote shares. Another factor that negatively affected the vote shares of independent candidates was the LDP's punishment of denying some candidates the party nomination. The LDP had banned some of the losing candidates from competing in the PR tier, making it more difficult for them to win particularly if they faced a strong challenger in the 2024 election.

In the 2024 general election, the media primarily focused on politicians with undisclosed slush fund kickbacks, although sometimes there was mention of the church controversy. The media focused on unendorsed candidates such as Hagiuda Kōichi in Tokyo's 24th District. Hagiuda not only maintained close ties to the UC, but also the LDP had suspended him from party posts over undisclosed faction kickbacks. Without the Kōmeitō's support, he won partly by relying on ties with members of his old faction (Abe) and benefited from the fractured opposition (*Asahi Shinbun*, October 20, 2024). Besides Hagiuda's case, an additional twenty-one members "participated" in both the slush fund scandal and the church controversy. Of this group, fourteen lost their seats. Most struggled to raise funds and attract votes, while others competed with more resources and connections, such as Hagiuda.

In the wake of Abe's killing, the media focused on blaming the UC and shaming politicians by revealing details about their connections. The various lists of names published by the media complicated the efforts of the Kishida government to appoint "untainted" LDP members in the party or government. Anti-UC groups and opposition parties used the controversy to push for legal remedies. Unlike the faction scandal, the church controversy and moral panic over religion lost steam before the 2024 election. The initial efforts to name politicians implicated more than half of the LDP, but attention later shifted to enacting new legislation. The slush fund scandal that emerged was subject to a criminal investigation, which made for interesting and more dramatic coverage. The media thus focused intensely on the fate of forty-four "slush fund" politicians in the 2024 election rather than the UC controversy.

The major scandals in 2022 and 2023 revealed underlying features of Japan's influence market society where the dominant focus is on winning offices and influencing those that hold them. Forging connections with religious organizations and other groups to help generate funds and votes is commonplace in Japan and in other influence market societies. The LDP leaders were reluctant to investigate the activities of its members in relation to the Unification Church. The moral panic over religion and the various scandals related to the church created major political problems for the Kishida administration in such areas as ministerial appointments, party endorsements of election candidates, and led to loss of public support and low cabinet approval ratings.

The emergence of the slush fund scandal added to Kishida's problems with significant consequences for Japan's political system and the

2024 election. This major scandal helped reveal Japan's problems with its factional and campaign finance system. The scandal also exposed the battle between factions and its campaign finance system. The former Abe faction struggled after Abe's death, and its exposure in the slush fund scandal weakened its position after the 2024 election. The LDP's failure to maintain its majority in the 2024 election marks an end to the period of dominance that began with former prime minister Abe in 2012.

References

Cohen, Stanley. 1980. *Folk Devils and Moral Panics: The Creation of the Mods and Rockers*. New York: St. Martin's Press.

Introvigne, Massimo. 2022. "The Assassination of Shinzo Abe and the Unification Church." *The Journal of CESNUR* 6 (6): 74–96.

Johnston, Michael. 2005. *Syndromes of Corruption: Wealth, Power, and Democracy*. Cambridge: Cambridge University Press.

Kingston, Jeff. 2023. "Bad Karma? Abe's Assassination and The Moonies." *Asia-Pacific Journal* 21 (12): 5. https://apjjf.org/2023/12/kingston.

Lull, James, and Stephen Hinerman. 1997. "The Search for Scandal." In *Media Scandals: Morality and Desire in the Popular Culture Marketplace*, edited by James Lull and Stephen Hinerman. New York: Columbia University Press.

Maeda, Yukio. 2025. "Public Opinion and Scandals in Economic Hard Times." In *Japan Decides 2024: The Japanese General Election*, edited by Kenneth M. McElwain, Robert J. Pekkanen, and Daniel M. Smith, 163–179. Palgrave Macmillan.

McLaughlin, Levi. 2023. "The Abe Assassination and Japan's Nexus of Religion and Politics." *Current History* 122 (845): 209–216.

McLaughlin, Levi. 2025. "Perennial Fears, Novel Responses: The Unification Church in Japan after the Abe Assassination." In *Japan Decides 2024: The Japanese General Election*, edited by Kenneth M. McElwain, Robert J. Pekkanen, and Daniel M. Smith, 235–253. Palgrave Macmillan.

National Network of Lawyers Against Spiritual Sales. "Statement on Fatal Shooting of Former Prime Minister Shinzo Abe." July 12, 2022. https://www.stopreikan.com/english/index-e.htm.

Nemoto, Kuniaki. 2025. "Reasons Behind the LDP's Loss in the 2024 Election." In *Japan Decides 2024: The Japanese General Election*, edited by Kenneth M. McElwain, Robert J. Pekkanen, and Daniel M. Smith, 37–55. Palgrave Macmillan.

Nippon.com. 2023. "An Unholy Alliance: How the Unification Church Penetrated Japan's Ruling Liberal Democratic Party." https://www.nippon.com/en/japan-topics/c12101/.

Poppe, Stevie. 2022. "'From Y': A Mixed-Method Analysis of the Twitter Account of Abe Shinzō's Killer." https://www.digital-japan.org/2022/08/19/analysis-of-the-twitter-account-of-abe-shinzos-killer/.

Prusa, Igor. 2024. "The Unification Church Scandal: Assassination of Abe Shinzô and Religio-Political Collusion in Japan", *Ejcjs* 24 (3). https://www.japanesestudies.org.uk/ejcjs/vol24/iss3/prusa.html

Saitō, Masami. 2024. "The Abe Assassination, the Unification Church, and Local Media: A Case Study of Journalism in Toyama Prefecture." *The Asia-Pacific Journal: Japan Focus* 22: 1–22.

Thompson, John B. 2000. *Political Scandal: Power and Visibility in the Media Age*. Cambridge: Polity Press.

Perennial Fears, Novel Responses: The Unification Church in Japan after the Abe Assassination

Levi McLaughlin

Shortly before noon on July 8, 2022, on the streets of Nara in western Japan, Japan's political world transformed. Abe Shinzō, Japan's longest-serving prime minister and still the most powerful politician in the country after he stepped down as Prime Minister in 2020, was campaigning there on behalf of Satō Kei, a candidate in Abe's Liberal Democratic Party (LDP) seeking reelection in the July 10 House of Councillors race. Abe was shot and killed by Yamagami Tetsuya, a lone gunman who had manufactured a projectile weapon following instructions downloaded from the internet. Media reports in the hours immediately following Abe's shocking murder reported that Yamagami was motivated by hatred of "a specific religious organization." Most outlets dropped references to religion until the results of the July 10 Upper House race were confirmed, reportedly out of fear of losing access

L. McLaughlin (✉)
North Carolina State University, Raleigh, NC, USA
e-mail: lmclaug2@ncsu.edu

to politicians who were sensitive about their links to religious groups. Rumormongering nonetheless erupted online and in print journalism, most notably in the pages of tabloid magazines and newspapers. The tabloid *Nikkan Gendai* confirmed the assassin's motive on July 9, and by the time Prime Minister Kishida Fumio held a press conference on July 14 to announce plans to hold a state funeral for Abe in September 2022, Japan's media was awash with reports about Yamagami's motive: resentment of the former prime minister because of his and his family's generations-long ties to the South Korea-based Family Federation for World Peace and Unification (FFWPU), a highly controversial religious organization better known by its former name, the Unification Church (UC) (Kingston 2023; McGill 2022).

This chapter provides an overview of legal and political developments that have unfolded in Japan following the Abe assassination; the murder for which Yamagami will stand trial should indeed be categorized as an assassination, given that his motive was to target a powerful political figure who supported a religion against which he held a grudge. Here, I consider responses to public outrage by the Japanese government following revelations about longstanding ties between conservative politicians and the UC, beginning with the immediate aftermath of the assassination and ending with the Tokyo District Court decision in March 2025 to proceed with stripping the FFWPU of its legal juridical persons status, marking the first time since the end of the Occupation Era (1945–1952) that a religious corporation in Japan has lost juridical personhood based solely on violations of civil law.

It is important to place these events within a broader modern Japanese historical and political context. While the Abe murder inspired unprecedented legal responses, reactions to it can also be characterized as the latest in a long line of high-profile panic-induced episodes in which a religion stigmatized in Japan receives media scrutiny, usually following a tumultuous event, sparking condemnation from the public and dramatic reactions by governmental officials. Condemnation of the Unification Church consumed Japanese media and political discourse from July 2022 until the end of 2023, when news of the LDP's slush fund scandal diverted public interest (Carlson 2025; Nemoto 2025). Attention directed at the Unification Church after the Abe murder marks a reprise of moral panic about "new religions," organizations founded from the nineteenth century onward that are frequently labeled as heterodox sects or cults. Approximately once a generation, widespread anxiety about a new religion exerts a significant impact on Japanese politics, inspiring public scrutiny of an enduring close relationship between elected officials and controversial religious organizations (McLaughlin 2025). In this way, responses to the Unification Church following the Abe murder join a tradition of outraged reaction to stigmatized religions that operate in the public sphere.

Since it began its activities in Japan in 1959, the Unification Church has attracted a dedicated community of Japanese devotees for whom adherence to the religion's teachings and leadership is a non-negotiable aspect of their personal identities and community belonging. The group has also gained a reputation for exploitative practices that have specifically targeted Japan to extract monetary and human capital. These practices include "spiritual sales" (*reikan shōhō*), which have involved sophisticated marketing strategies organized within an elaborate combination of non-profit and for-profit entities aimed at eliciting large sums in exchange for promised spiritual benefits (Gaitanidis 2024). Spiritual sales and related strategies have encouraged dedicants to make ruinously large donations to the religion: Yamagami's mother, who reportedly converted to the church in 1991, donated millions of yen, forcing her family into bankruptcy in 2002, and the family's resulting poverty stoked Tetsuya's ire for the church (McLaughlin 2023). Converts have also been cultivated to take part in the religion's famed mass weddings, resulting in a decades-long flow of devotees, mostly women, from Japan to Korea, inspiring advocacy against the church by their families and other anti-cult activists (Sakurai 2010).

The Unification Church's controversial practices had proceeded steadily for decades only to be thrown into sharp relief by press attention to the Abe murder. The church's most active parishioners, and the majority of members and non-members involved in the church's financial schemes, have been women, but it took the murder of Japan's most powerful man by a male assassin to spark widespread public outrage against the UC. Legal and political responses to Abe's murder have arguably made this homicide the most successful political assassination in living memory, in terms of producing an outcome that suits the assailant's intentions. The Family Federation for World Peace and Unification did not murder Abe Shinzō. The religion is, however, effectively being punished for this crime by having its religious juridical persons status, along with its vital tax exemptions, removed by Japan's courts. In the meantime, media coverage of the murder, along with scholarly and political attention to the church, has continued to largely ignore those who will bear the burden of the religion's legal dissolution, namely its majority female grassroots-level membership, who remain dedicated to their religion and committed to its leadership.

DIMINISHED PUBLIC SYMPATHY FOR ABE, RISING SYMPATHY FOR HIS MURDERER

Twitter exploded in the days following Abe's assassination. According to data gathered by Matthew Brummer, a political scientist at the National Graduate Institute for Policy Studies (GRIPS) in Tokyo, the Abe murder sparked Japan's largest-ever social media event, inspiring a conservative estimate of at least ~350 million tweets, making this one of the largest online events recorded to date (SAAD 2025). This surge in online interest both inspired and promoted a steady stream of broadcast and print media exposés of politicians who had maintained ties to the Unification Church (Carlson 2025). Such was the high pitch of media reaction that news of a single photo of a politician at an event convened years previously by the church or one of its affiliate organizations was likely to receive hundreds of retweets and thousands of views. As Matthew Carlson details in this volume, Prime Minister Kishida attempted damage control with a cabinet reshuffle and forced resignations of cabinet ministers in efforts to oust LDP Diet members who had been revealed as connected with the church. On August 10, 2022, Kishida dismissed seven ministers from his cabinet in a reshuffle after they disclosed ties to the church, including Abe's brother Kishi Nobuo, who was then Minister of Defense. The newspaper *Asahi Shinbun* conducted a survey between August 18 and September 2, 2022, in which it found that 447 lawmakers, including 150 Diet members, 290 prefectural assembly members, and seven governors affirmed links to the UC (*Asahi Shinbun* September 4, 2022). These connections ran the gamut from congratulatory messages sent on the occasion of a church-related gathering to more involved engagements, such as lawmakers receiving clerical and electoral assistance from the religion's adherents. On September 12, LDP Secretary General Motegi Toshimitsu announced at a press conference that 179 of his party's Diet members (of 379) admitted to ties to the church. Reporters immediately leapt on this report to flag others, notably Economic Revitalization Minister Yamagiwa Daishirō, who at first attempted to downplay ties to the UC, including his appearance at an event attended by the UC's leader

Hak Ja Han Moon, before ultimately resigning in October 2022 (*Kyodo News* October 24, 2022).

Kishida fought a losing battle with plummeting public confidence in his government as plans proceeded to hold a state funeral for Abe Shinzō in late September. This would have been a controversial decision irrespective of circumstances surrounding Abe's death, given that the only prime minister to receive a state funeral after World War II had been Yoshida Shigeru, whose death in 1967 came after he was credited with laying the groundwork for Japan's postwar economic revival. The Japanese public reacted negatively to Kishida's state funeral plan. Even conservative news outlets, such as the newspaper *Sankei Shinbun*, reported that a majority of those polled opposed the event (*Sankei Shinbun* September 19, 2022). Reasons given on conservative media platforms tended to emphasize objections to the cost of the funeral, which was estimated at ~1.65 billion yen. However, the public was being swayed by media saturated with scoops about close ties between the church and the Abe family, extending back to his father Shintarō and grandfather Kishi Nobusuke, who has served as Prime Minister of Japan from 1957 to 1960 and as a wartime minister of commerce and industry under Tōjō Hideki. Approval ratings for Kishida's cabinet dropped from a high of 64% prior to the Abe murder to as low as 29% in the weeks before the September 27, 2022 state funeral. The event, convened at the Nippon Budōkan sports arena in central Tokyo, hosted 4,183 attendees, far short of a reported 7,000 invited, and no G7 leaders attended (McLaughlin 2023).

During the funeral, an estimated 25,000 members of the public lined the Tokyo streets to pay respects at a shrine erected a short distance from the Budōkan, a number large enough to undermine easy reliance on a narrative of broad-based rejection of sadness at Abe's death (*Nikkei Shinbun* September 28, 2022). Meanwhile, outside the National Diet, as many as 15,000 protestors bearing placards from opposition parties such as Reiwa Shinsengumi and other opponents of the LDP and the Unification Church gathered to voice their objection to the event (*Tokyo Shinbun* September 27, 2022). Photos of several protestors dressed up as Yamagami Tetsuya, sporting the clothes and facemask he wore when he perpetrated the murder, circulated online. These pictures fed into a largely social media-driven Yamagami fandom, amplifying sympathy and even enthusiasm for his actions. The Osaka Detention Center, where Yamagami was held after his arrest, reportedly ran out of space for gifts sent to him by well-wishers, including over one million yen in cash, and a change.org petition calling for a reduced or commuted sentence, mostly in consideration of his mother's experience in the church, garnered close to 14,000 signatures.

On January 13, 2023, Yamagami was indicted by prosecutors for the murder of Abe Shinzō and violations of Japan's firearms and swords law. He had been declared fit to stand trial following six months of psychiatric evaluations. The *Asahi Shinbun* reported on March 27, 2025 that "a religion scholar" had visited Yamagami multiple times in the Osaka Detention Center, eliciting testimonial from him to aid defense lawyers in making a case that experience growing up affected by the Unification Church should be factored into his sentencing. It is clear that negative sentiments for the church will play a significant role in deliberations about Yamagami's punishment and hostility to the religion will certainly shape public reactions to the trial.

The Unification Church in Japan and the "Second Generation Religious": Controversial Doctrinal Commitments and Religion Framed as Abuse

Yamagami is the most prominent representative of a constituency labeled the *shūkyō nisei*, or "second generation religious." This is a term that coalesced prior to the Abe assassination but has since become common parlance in Japan, functioning as the working equivalent of "cult survivor." People growing up with one or more parents strongly committed to organizations that bear the label "cult," such as the Unification Church, Jehovah's Witnesses, Happy Science (Kōfuku no Kagaku), Sōka Gakkai, and other new religions that have gained a negative reputation, now have access to the *shūkyō nisei* identity to articulate their experiences using a framework that elicits sympathy from the general public and possesses the capacity to mobilize lawmakers. "Second generation religious" is a narrative taken up by media outlets, governmental agencies, lawyers, some academics, anti-cult activists, and other advocates. They characterize proselytizing, highly demanding religious teachings and practices, and intensive sacrifice of resources to faith-based causes, along with parental demands that children take part in these challenging and frequently stigmatized undertakings, as forms of child abuse (Ogiue 2022; Tsukada et al. 2023; Yokomichi 2023).

Testimonials from the Unification Church's "second generation religious" following the Abe assassination greatly amplified public awareness about the Korea-based religion's Japan-specific doctrines and practices. Japan has been central to the Unification Church's institutional growth, revenue-generating activities, and theological exegeses since early in its global expansion. After the Abe murder, global attention returned to the church founder Sun Myung Moon (1920–2012), his teachings regarding Japan, and his views on what was owed as repayment for Japan's brutal dominance of the Korean peninsula up to 1945. Academic and media treatments brought attention to a December 19, 1990, speech Moon delivered to the Unification Church National Conference at the religion's World Mission Center, where the religion's leader made this pronouncement:

> Korea is the Adam nation, Japan is the Eve nation, and the three archangels are the United States, the Soviet Union and Red China. In Japan, the Eve nation, the women are controlling the money. A women's purse there is always full…Japan must realize that it is not Japan's money; it is Eve's money to be used for the sake of Adam, for Rev. Moon and Korea's unification. Japanese wealth has to be contributed for the unification of Asia and the unification of the world. (Moon 2025)

This speech develops themes expounded in the *Divine Principle*, an edition of Moon's teachings published in 1966 that serves the religion as scripture. This text interprets Jewish and Christian doctrines to assert that Eve entered into a sexual relationship with Satan, thereby establishing a fallen world in which all people were born Satan's children. Order will be restored through the church, which will create the "Kingdom of Heaven on Earth." An attempt to establish this kingdom was made by God when he sent Jesus with the intent that he establish the perfect family, only to see Jesus not fulfill this mission because he was crucified. We live now in the Last Days, the era of the second coming of Christ, when God has sent the "True Parents of humanity" in the form of Sun Myung Moon and his spouse Hak Ja Han Moon (1943–), who is the church's "True Mother" and current head of the organization (Sakurai and Nakanishi 2010).

Investigations of the Unification Church by academics and journalists reveal that approximately 80% of the church's global revenue was produced by Japanese members and the non-profit and for-profit ventures they run in Japan during the height of the UC's Japanese mission (Sakurai

2010). An estimated 90% of donor names listed at the entrance to Cheongjeong Palace, the religion's world headquarters in South Korea's Gyeonggi province, are Japanese, attesting to the crucial importance of Japanese donors to the UC's global operations (*Hankyoreh* 12 July 2022). At the height of the bubble economy years in the 1980s, the Unification Church in Japan was sending as much as 10 billion yen per month to the Korean headquarters. Today, donations are considerably lower than this. Before the Abe assassination, the church claimed 600,000 adherents in Japan, while scholars estimated that its active membership was likely between 50,000 and 70,000. Judging by ethnographic observations since July 2022, adherent numbers have dropped below this more modest pre-assassination estimate and will continue to shrink as the church fights legal dissolution.

Children born into Unification Church families are raised to seek union through "holy marriage blessing ceremonies." These are the famed mass weddings convened at arenas and church facilities at which, on some occasions, thousands of couples, many of whom having never met previously in person, are paired up under the authority of the religion's True Parents. For believers, it is only children of heterosexual couples married at the church's blessing ceremonies who are born without original sin, and it is the children born of these unions who will bring about the Kingdom of God. This doctrinal stance is a principal motivation for the Unification Church's advocacy in Japan against legislation aimed at gender equality and securing rights for LGBTQ+ people. For decades, Japan has been a primary source of brides for the church's blessing ceremonies. Critics of the religion charge that the group created the working equivalent of human trafficking by convincing Japanese women adherents to enter arranged marriages with Korean men, or men of other ethnic origins, in ceremonies held in South Korea (Sakurai and Nakanishi 2010; Higuma 2022). Families of some of these brides contend that their daughters were effectively disappeared by the church, having cut contact with their natal families, and some "second generation religious" testimonials are given by women who escaped these unions or were pressured by their UC adherent relatives to seek matrimony through the church's mass weddings (Kaburagi 2022; Ogawa 2023).

A Religion/Politics Quid Pro Quo

Given the Unification Church's doctrinal dictates that Japan must provide Korea indemnity, it may seem odd that the religion's leaders and grassroots-level followers forged ties with conservative Japanese figures, including some of Japan's most strident nationalists. Critics of the church aver that the organization has evaded legal scrutiny and managed to bridge ideological divides thanks to a cordial relationship between Sun Myung Moon and Prime Minister Kishi Nobusuke that sanctioned a norm for LDP politicians to maintain UC links. Shared conservative commitments between the church and at all levels of the LDP solidified bonds across nationalist divides and facilitated a quid pro quo that saw the church offer electoral and other practical support in exchange for the LDP's imprimatur.

Moon oversaw the construction of the Unification Church's Japan headquarters in 1964 next to the Kishi family compound in Shibuya, central Tokyo. This was the same year in which the church received religious juridical persons status from Japan's Agency for Cultural Affairs. Moon and Kishi bonded over their mutual animosity toward communism. In January 1968, Moon founded the International Federation for Victory over Communism, basing this group in South Korea and Japan. The Federation enjoyed patronage from Kishi and other prominent conservatives, including business leader Sasakawa Ryōichi and other influential figures who mobilized against communism in the postwar decades (Saitō 2024). The Moon-Kishi connection served as a template for generational transmission of UC-LDP links. Abe Shinzō's father Shintarō received support from the church during his tenure in office, which included stints as the LDP Secretary General and Minister of Foreign Affairs. Abe Shinzō perpetuated his family's connections by supporting the Unification Church leadership and receiving electoral aid from the religion's adherents. In a speech broadcast for the twentieth anniversary of 9/11 for the Universal Peace Federation, a UC affiliate NGO, Abe praised Hak Ja Han Moon; it was reportedly this speech that inspired Yamagami to plan his assassination. During his tenure as Prime Minister and thereafter, church members mobilized to support Abe and those in his circle. Inoue Yoshiyuki, who had served as Abe's secretary, received campaign support in his successful bid for an Upper House seat in the July 2021 race (*Asahi Shinbun* August 7, 2022). Inoue spoke out in a campaign speech against same-sex marriage, mirroring language and policies promoted by the church. Adherent supporters, who announced that "Inoue is fighting the Satan force," declared that the politician had become a "member" of the church at a rally where he greeted his UC vote-gatherers. Inoue received approximately 165,000 votes in the 2022 race, up from ~88,000 in his unsuccessful 2019 electoral attempt, demonstrating that the church possessed the capacity to ensure election for favored candidates (Saitō 2024).

After the first Abe government passed a revision of the Basic Act on Education in 2006, which paved the way toward promoting "family education" in Japan, the Unification Church in Japan elevated its proactive opposition to policies on gender equality and LGBTQ+ rights. Anthropologist Yamaguchi Tomomi, one of few researchers who has carried out a sustained investigation of the Unification Church since before the Abe murder, notes that as its anti-communism agenda lost salience with the end of the Cold War, "family values" became the religion's core concern and the basis for its political engagements, particularly below the national level (Yamaguchi 2022). The church took its cue from Nippon Kaigi and other conservative activist groups that were instrumental in powering anti-feminist policy promotions (Yamaguchi and Saitō 2023). The Unification Church has made a practice of opposing municipal-level same-sex partnership ordinances, most notably the 2015 Shibuya Ward ordinance, which was enacted in the municipality where the religion maintains its Japan headquarters. Though the church's efforts to forestall these ordinances have not been successful, getting LDP politicians and other conservative lawmakers to sign onto socially conservative "policy pacts" in exchange for electoral support became conventional means for the UC to tighten bonds with local-level and national-level candidates (*Asahi Shinbun* October 20, 2022). News of these policy pledges powered media-driven investigations into UC-LDP ties in the wake of the Abe murder. (See Kawasaka 2025 for a broader discussion of LGBTQ+ issues in the 2024 election.)

THE ABE MURDER REIGNITES PERENNIAL FEARS ABOUT RELIGION IN THE PUBLIC SPHERE

In surveys conducted by newspapers and polling organizations, Japan routinely ranks as one of the world's least religious countries, with as few as one in ten respondents replying in the affirmative to variations of the question "do you have religious faith?" This aversion prevails even though there are more than 180,000 religious juridical persons in Japan, and religious practices and organizations from Buddhist, Christian, Shintō, and other origins remain regular features of Japanese life. Popular nervousness about identifying as religious is a product of Japan's modern political development. *Shūkyō*, the Japanese word for "religion," is a translation of the English term and its European language variants. As Japan began transforming into a modern imperialist nation-state in the mid-nineteenth century after its forced opening by the United States, *shūkyō* coalesced as an umbrella category that designated legal boundaries of sects that were required after this time to register as corporations subject to governmental regulation. This exercise of designating "real" religions was heavily influenced by predominantly Protestant associations with the category "religion," which include the centrality of interiorized faith, emphasizing the study of scripture, regular worship attendance, and the presumption that a person belongs to *a* religion. "Religion" presumptions have consistently been an awkward fit in Japan, where the average person will be "born Shintō, die Buddhist," will most likely not study sacred texts, and may not regard participation in a ritual calendar as a felt obligation (McLaughlin 2025).

As religion developed as a concern for the modernizing Japanese state, the category's putative opposites came into focus. From the late nineteenth century onward, chronologically new faith-based organizations, folk traditions, and other worship communities that did not enjoy high social status or governmental sanction were liable to be smeared with epithets in the popular press and in political discourse. Religion scholar Janine Sawada describes how new religions served as "whipping boys in [ideologues'] discursive circumscription of the modern Japanese ideal" (Sawada 2004). Organizations such as Ōmoto-kyō, Renmonkyō, and others that arose from the late nineteenth century onward were routinely vilified by government officials and other powerholders as *inchiki shūkyō* (fake religion), *meishin jakyō* (superstitious false teachings), and other precursors to the contemporary use of the term "cult."

The "cult" category is complicated by a history of a small minority of organizations given this label that have perpetrated harm and tarnished the broader category of "religion." One landmark episode in the living memory of most people in Japan cements "religion" as a negative designation and equivalent to "cult." On March 20, 1995, members of the apocalyptic religion Aum Shinrikyō boarded subways in Tokyo that passed through Kasumigaseki station, near Japan's National Diet. They released sarin gas in five trains, killing fourteen, injuring thousands, and destroying positive connotations with the term "religion" for a generation (Baffelli and Reader 2012). The so-called "Aum laws" enacted in 1996 were ostensibly aimed at policing Aum Shinrikyō, but were in practice attempts on the part of LDP members and other political opponents of Kōmeitō to target this party and its founding religion Sōka Gakkai, relying on popular anger at "cults" to achieve their political aims (McLaughlin 2012). An ironic result of the political targeting of Sōka Gakkai after the Aum attack was a 1999 coalition agreement between Kōmeitō and the LDP, which has persisted into the present. Thus, in the 1990s, as in the 2020s, moral panic about new religions as a threat to Japanese state and society produced spillover effects that reshaped Japanese politics.

The Unification Church Sends the Government into New Legal Territory

While he was fighting a losing battle with declining poll numbers and a persistent onslaught of media exposés about links between the Unification Church and politicians in his party, Prime Minister Kishida on October 17, 2022 announced a government-led probe that aimed at stripping the church of its religious juridical persons status (*Mainichi Shinbun* October 18, 2022). A government hotline for victims of the UC received 1,002 calls in the first five days after it launched on September 5, 2022, with many callers identifying financial abuse by the church (*Asahi Shinbun* September 13, 2022). On October 18, the two parties in the LDP-Kōmeitō governing coalition joined a bid launched by the opposition parties Ishin no Kai and the Constitutional Democratic Party (CDP) to push for new legislation aiding those who had suffered financially from the UC's manipulative contractual demands.

The following day, Kishida announced during a House of Councillors Budget Committee meeting that removing religious juridical persons status from the Unification Church could be justified based on violations of civil law (*Mainichi Shinbun* October 19, 2022). This declaration moved the Japanese government into new legal territory. Only three religious juridical persons have been stripped by the Japanese courts of their legal status since the Religious Juridical Persons law was enacted in 1951. These are (1) Aum Shinrikyō, the organization that committed mass murder, which was dissolved in 1996, (2) Myōkakuji Group, a temple-based Buddhist organization that was convicted on felony fraud charges, dissolved in 2002, and (3) Dainichizan Hokekyōji, a Nichiren Buddhism-based entity that was dissolved in 2009 after it was embroiled in a complex fraud case in which the temple was seized by the Resolution and Collection Corporation of Japan, a semi-governmental agency responsible for purchasing non-performing loans (Gaitanidis 2024). To justify court orders for these legal dissolutions, criminal court proceedings were used in lieu of following Article 78-2 of the Religious Juridical Persons Law, which allows the Agency for Cultural Affairs to investigate religions suspected of violating their terms of incorporation.

News that civil law violations were sufficient to press forward with an order to remove religious juridical persons status from the Unification Church was greeted with enthusiasm by Japan's National Network for Lawyers Against Spiritual Sales. This is a collective of attorneys who have brought cases against the UC and its affiliate organizations since 1987. On July 12, 2022, four days after the Abe murder, the National Network held a press conference at which it produced documents for 34,537 consultations between 1987 and 2021 amounting to 123.7 billion yen lost by their claimants to the Unification Church (Gaitanidis 2024; Kitō 2022). From July 2022 onward, lawyers for this organization coordinated with the Japanese Communist Party (a long-term UC opponent), several prominent academics, sympathetic journalists, and other activists to hold dramatic press conferences and advise participants in government hearings at which "second generation religious" and other victims delivered searing testimonials about malfeasance by the church. These testimonials and related efforts by the Network and their allies informed advisory committees who voted on the results of investigations undertaken by government agencies. The Religious Juridical Persons Inquiry Board advised investigators from the Agency for Cultural Affairs, the government body under the Ministry of Education, Culture, Sports, Science, and Technology (MEXT) that oversees Japan's religious corporations, and the Investigative Commission for Policies on Malicious Sales Practices, Including Spiritual Sales informed investigators for the Consumer Affairs Division.

The Agency for Cultural Affairs began its first of seven formal questioning sessions of the Family Federation for World Peace and Unification on November 22, 2022. In the meantime, the coalition government moved to address claimant needs, shrewdly avoiding concerns about violating constitutional guarantees of religious freedom by focusing on consumer affairs. The Diet approved laws on December 10, 2022, that aimed at restricting malicious solicitations for donations and offer repayment to victims. Critics noted that the new laws lacked sufficient donation limits and did not promise adequate redress for "second generation religious," while defenders of the church claimed that this new legislation formed part of a continued assault on religious freedom (*Kyodo News* December 10, 2022). On October 12, 2023, the Religious Juridical Persons Inquiry Board reported that its members voted unanimously in favor of recommending that a court order proceed to remove corporate status from the FFWPU (*Yomiuri Shinbun* October 12, 2023). The committee noted that church officials failed to satisfactorily answer approximately one hundred of five hundred questions asked by Agency investigators. This recommendation was made in keeping with Article 81 of the Religious Juridical Persons Law, which allows the government to dissolve a religion "clearly found to have harmed public welfare."

The following day, Prime Minister Kishida filed a request with the Tokyo District Court for an order to remove corporate status from the Family Federation. Church leaders responded on November 8, 2023, by announcing plans to allocate up to 10 billion yen in compensation to victims of its forced donations practices. The church made this announcement as part of an attempt to forestall worries that it would unload its assets and send them out of Japan before having to compensate claimants (*Asahi Shinbun* November 8, 2023). On November 15, lawmakers from the LDP and Kōmeitō submitted proposed amendments to the Religious Juridical Persons Law that would require religions facing dissolution to notify the government before disposing of their assets. This new measure responded to warnings from "second generation religious" advocates and opposition parties that the church would seek to sell its real estate and other holdings and transfer funds overseas. At the same time, FFWPU leaders and lawyers for the church issued protests about the nature of the Agency for Cultural Affairs investigation, pledging to fight dissolution in the courts. It is worth pointing out that the Agency's deliberation process was held behind closed doors, rendering the nature of the questions and responses opaque, and that dissolving a religion justified solely by perceptions of harm to public welfare may set a worrying precedent for other religious entities that may fall afoul of popular or political fury.

After months of closed-door deliberations, on March 24, 2024, Judge Suzuki Kenya of the Tokyo District Court ruled that "violation of laws and regulations" justifying dissolution of a religious juridical person "includes civil law torts," thereby laying the groundwork for the court to proceed with an order to strip the FFWPU of its legal status (*Asahi Shinbun* March 24, 2024). Violations were determined by twenty-two civil court rulings on donations exceeding 1.5 billion yen solicited by the Unification Church. As a result, the church's Japan president Tanaka Tomihiro was ordered to pay a 100,000 yen fine for not responding appropriately to investigators' questions.

Almost exactly one year later, on March 25, 2025, the Tokyo District Court issued a ruling to remove religious juridical persons status from the Family Federation for World Peace and Unification (*Kyodo News* March 25, 2025). The court decision stipulated that the church's problems were "extensive and continuous," that it had caused "unprecedented damage" to Japanese society, and that a dissolution order was necessary because it was unlikely that the FFWPU "could voluntarily reform." Lawyers for the church appealed this decision to the Tokyo High Court on April 7, 2025.

Conclusion: Who Will Bear the Cost of the Church Dissolution?

By the time Kishida Fumio ceded his premiership to Ishiba Shigeru on October 1, 2024, news about Unification Church ties to LDP politicians had taken a back seat to a stream of reports about the party's slush fund scandal (Yukio Maeda 2025; Umeda 2025). However, Kishida is likely to be remembered first and foremost as the prime minister in office during the Abe assassination and the Unification Church affair. The specter of the church has clung to the Liberal Democratic Party, which did not regain a positive approval rating under Kishida after the Abe murder and only briefly reached parity between approval and disapproval under Ishiba (NHK 2025). It is apparent that spillover distaste for religion in politics reignited by furor over the UC affected electoral results after 2022 (Ko Maeda, 2025). While candidates for local elections in April 2023 who were known for prior ties to the church mostly avoided dire consequences for these connections, Kōmeitō suffered conspicuous losses in Tokyo and Osaka, perhaps partly because of popular aversion to religion-linked voter mobilization (Klein and McLaughlin 2025). In other cases, the lingering specter of UC ties has obviously taken a toll. For example, Negita Masanobu, mayor of Hekinan, a small city in Aichi Prefecture, failed in his April 21, 2024, reelection bid when he was defeated by a candidate who publicized Negita's longstanding adherence to the church (*Asahi Shinbun* April 21, 2024). And it is certain that continued public outrage about the church sparked voter anger that drove the LDP into minority party status on October 27, 2024. Critics of Ishiba's government have routinely listed the slush fund and Unification Church scandals together as collective reasons why voter confidence dropped.

To conclude, I will briefly consider the ramifications of the Family Federation for World Peace and Unification's legal dissolution. Article 20 of Japan's 1947 Constitution stipulates that "freedom of religion is guaranteed to all." This ensures that adherents of the Unification Church may continue their faith-based practices. However, by losing religious juridical persons status, the church loses tax exemption on revenue generated by faith activities and tax relief on property. The Tokyo District Court also ordered the religion to liquidate its assets to provide compensation to claimants who lost money to its financial schemes. Church representatives with whom I have spoken anticipate a rise of 40–50% on their operation costs. This unmanageable price hike, in combination with the practical difficulties they will face finding landowners who will rent or sell property to their highly stigmatized organization, convince members I spoke with that the religion will be forced into bankruptcy in Japan.

Critics of the Unification Church will declare the dissolution a triumph, a righteous victory that has been too long delayed. It is worth emphasizing, however, that it is not the church's top leaders who are likely to suffer the dissolution's effects. It is the religion's most devoted local-level adherents who will shoulder responsibility to maintain the organization. At regional FFWPU churches, adherents arrive as early as 5:00 a.m. to take part in their complex ritual calendar, and many will stay at the church for the entire day, preparing meals and caring for one another. The majority of these devotees are women, and many are elderly. They are largely educationally, financially, and socially disenfranchised. And they are rendered invisible in most academic, legal, political, and media treatments.

A member I will refer to as Mrs. B, who was thirty-eight years old when I spoke with her in the autumn of 2022, lives in a small city in western Japan. She was raised in the Unification Church as a second-generation adoptee. Her birth mother, a convert to the church, had bestowed her on another adherent family, following a custom of Unification Church family adoptions (mostly of girls) that has attracted intense critique. Mrs. B characterized her upbringing in mostly positive terms, however, and is raising her own family in the church. She is the mother of three young children (nine, six, and two years old when we spoke), and she was married at twenty years old in a mass wedding ceremony to a pastor whose primary responsibility is to the *shukufuku nisei*, the "blessed second generation" who are the future of the organization. Mrs. B is an intelligent and forthright person who spoke in strikingly critical terms about her religion. She expressed frank critiques of the church's administration and resentment about its excessive financial demands, particularly those she endured when she was young. However, she emphasized repeatedly to me that, in stark contrast to characterizations that dominate Japan's media, "I am *not* a victim." Instead, she is terrified of governmental measures taken against her religion and what they portend for her family. She avoids most mainstream media, finding its portrayals of the church inaccurate and personally hurtful. And she hides her church identity from most neighbors and only divulges it to the most trusted teachers in her children's schools. In short, she is a sophisticated, self-determined woman who maintains her faith simultaneously as a critic and supporter of the church, devising the best ways to protect her family as she navigates the post-Abe era.

It is women such as Mrs. B who will voluntarily take on the daunting task of maintaining the church. To fully comprehend the scope of fallout from the Abe assassination, it is incumbent on those who study politics and religion to attend to women such as Mrs. B as incipient fears of stigmatized religion continue to unfold.

References

Baffelli, Erica, and Ian Reader. 2012. "Editors' Introduction: Impact and Ramifications: The Aftermath of the Aum Affair in the Japanese Religious Context." *Japanese Journal of Religious Studies* 39 (1): 1–28.

Carlson, Matthew M. 2025. "Scandals During the Kishida Administration." In *Japan Decides 2024: The Japanese General Election*, edited by Kenneth M. McElwain, Robert J. Pekkanen, and Daniel M. Smith, 217–233. New York: Palgrave Macmillan.

Gaitanidis, Ioannis. 2024. "How Consumer Law in Japan Shapes Religion: 'Spiritual Sales' as a Legal Category." *Asia-Pacific Journal: Japan Focus* 22 (10): 3. https://apjjf.org/2024/10/gaitanidis.

Higuma, Takenori. 2022. *Tōitsu kyōkai=Shōkyō rengō to wa nani ka* [*The Unification Church: What is the International Federation for Victory over Communism?*]. Tokyo: Shin Nippon Shuppansha.

Kaburagi, Keiko. 2022. *Karuto hanayome* [*Cult Bride*]. Tokyo: Gōdō Shuppan.

Kawasaka, Kazuyoshi. 2025. "LGBTQ+ Rights Issues and the 2024 Japanese Election." In *Japan Decides 2024: The Japanese General Election*, edited by

Kenneth M. McElwain, Robert J. Pekkanen, and Daniel M. Smith, 273–291. New York: Palgrave Macmillan.

Kingston, Jeffrey. 2023. "Bad Karma? Abe's Assassination and The Moonies." *Asia-Pacific Journal: Japan Focus* 21 (12): 5 (December 22). https://apjjf.org/2023/12/kingston.

Kitō, Masaki. 2022. *Karuto shūkyō* [*Cult Religions*]. Tokyo: Ascom.

Klein, Axel, and Levi McLaughlin. 2025. "A Costly Coalition: Kōmeitō's Enduring Partnership with the LDP." In *Japan Decides 2024: The Japanese General Election*, edited by Kenneth M. McElwain, Robert J. Pekkanen, and Daniel M. Smith, 75–90. New York: Palgrave Macmillan.

Maeda, Ko. 2025. "The 2024 Election Results: A Political Earthquake." In *Japan Decides 2024: The Japanese General Election*, edited by Kenneth M. McElwain, Robert J. Pekkanen, and Daniel M. Smith, 17–34. New York: Palgrave Macmillan.

Maeda, Yukio. 2025. "Public Opinion and Scandals in Economic Hard Times." In *Japan Decides 2024: The Japanese General Election*, edited by Kenneth M. McElwain, Robert J. Pekkanen, and Daniel M. Smith, 163–179. New York: Palgrave Macmillan.

McGill, Peter. 2022. "The Dark Shadow Cast by Moon Sun Myung's Unification Church and Abe Shinzo." *Asia-Pacific Journal: Japan Focus* 20 (17): 10 (October 15). https://apjjf.org/2022/17/McGill.

McLaughlin, Levi. 2012. "Did Aum Change Everything? What Sōka Gakkai Before, During, and After the Aum Shinrikyo Affair Tells Us About the Persistent "Otherness" of New Religions in Japan." *Japanese Journal of Religious Studies* 39 (1): 51–75.

McLaughlin, Levi. 2023. "The Abe Assassination and Japan's Nexus of Religion and Politics." *Current History* 122 (845): 209–16.

McLaughlin, Levi. 2025. "Politics and Governance." In *The New Nanzan Guide to Japanese Religion*, edited by Matthew McMullen and Jolyon B. Thomas, 351–65. Honolulu: University of Hawai'i Press.

Moon, Reverend Sun Myung. 2025. *Speech to the Unification Church National Conference*. December 19, 1990. https://www.tparents.org/Moon-Talks/sunmyungmoon90/901219.htm.

Nemoto, Kuniaki. 2025. "Reasons Behind the LDP's Loss in the 2024 Election." In *Japan Decides 2024: The Japanese General Election*, edited by Kenneth M. McElwain, Robert J. Pekkanen, and Daniel M. Smith, 37–55. New York: Palgrave Macmillan.

NHK. 2025. *Naikaku shijiritsu* [*Cabinet Approval Ratings*]. https://www.nhk.or.jp/senkyo/shijiritsu/.

Ogawa, Sayuri. 2023. *Ogawa Sayuri, shūkyō nisei* [*Ogawa Sayuri, Second Generation Religious*]. Tokyo: Shōgakkan.

Ogiue, Chiki, ed. 2022. *Shūkyō nisei: "Kamisama" yori mo "tasuke" o kudasai* [*Second-Generation Religious: Offer Us Aid Rather Than God*]. Tokyo: Ōta.
SAAD (Shinzo Abe Assassination Database). 2025. https://www.saadataset.org/about.
Saitō, Masami. 2024. "The Abe Assassination, The Unification Church, and Local Media: A Case Study of Journalism in Toyama Prefecture." *Asia-Pacific Journal: Japan Focus* 22 (10): 3. https://apjjf.org/2024/10/saito.
Sakurai, Yoshihide. 2010. "Geopolitical Mission Strategy: The Case of the Unification Church in Japan and Korea." *Japanese Journal of Religious Studies* 37 (2): 317–34.
Sakurai, Yoshihide, and Hiroko Nakanishi. 2010. *Tōitsu kyōkai: Nihon senkyō no senryaku to kannichi shukufuku* [*The Unification Church: Its Mission Strategy in Japan and Blessed Korea–Japan Relations*]. Sapporo: Hokkaido Daigaku Shuppankai.
Sawada, Janine Tasca. 2004. *Practical Pursuits: Religion, Politics, and Personal Cultivation in Nineteenth-Century Japan*. Honolulu: University of Hawai'i Press.
Tsukada, Hotaka et al. eds. 2023. *Dakara shitte hoshii: "shūkyō nisei" mondai* [*That's Why I Want You to Know: The "Second-Generation Religious" Problem*]. Tokyo: Chikuma Shobō.
Umeda, Michio. 2025. "Electoral Campaigns in Japan's 2024 HR Election: Emerging Signs of Transformation." In *Japan Decides 2024: The Japanese General Election*, edited by Kenneth M. McElwain, Robert J. Pekkanen, and Daniel M. Smith, 109–124. New York: Palgrave Macmillan.
Yamaguchi, Tomomi. 2022. "Abe and the Unification Church: Opposing Gender Equality and LGBTQ+ Rights." In *The Abe Legacy: A Compendium*, edited by David McNeill. *Asia-Pacific Journal: Japan Focus* 20 (16) (November 11). https://apjjf.org/2022/16/mcneil.
Yamaguchi, Tomomi, and Saitō, Masami. 2023. *Shūkyō uha to feminizumu* [*The Religious Right-wing and Feminism*]. Tokyo: Seikyūsha.
Yokomichi, Makoto. 2023. *Minna no shūkyō nisei mondai* [*Everyone's Second-Generation Religious Problem*]. Tokyo: Shōbunsha.

CHAPTER 15

Increase in Women's Representation and Candidates' Positions on Gender Equality Issues

Yuki Tsuji

INTRODUCTION

The 2024 general election broke records for women's representation in the House of Representatives (HR). After leveling off at approximately 10% in six general elections since 2005, the number of women elected increased from 45 in 2021 to 73 in 2024, or an increase in the percentage of women elected from 9.7% to 15.7% out of 465 seats, although this rate remains much lower than the global average of 27.0% (Inter-Parliamentary Union 2024). Thirty-two of the women were newcomers, meaning they were neither incumbents nor former members of the HR. Women also account for 23.4% of all candidates compared with 17.7% in 2021. How did this change occur and what are its potential effects? This chapter aims to identify the profiles of female candidates and winners and

Y. Tsuji (✉)
Tokai University, Hiratsuka, Japan
e-mail: ytsuji@tokai.ac.jp

to examine the positions of political parties and candidates on gender equality issues.

After reviewing the context regarding gender issues up until the 2024 general election, I will examine the results of the election by gender, party, and constituency of candidates and classify the previous careers of female newcomer candidates and winners in the following sections. I will then examine the positions of candidates on the issue of the legislation on dual surnames, paying particular attention to the changes among Liberal Democratic Party (LDP) members.

Changing Social Norms on Gender and the 2024 Election

The issues of gender equality and women's political representation were less salient in the 2024 election, as attention was focused more on the slush fund money scandal of the LDP (see Carlson 2025; Nemoto 2025). However, the average perception of the Japanese electorate on gender equality has seemingly changed. The annual release of the Global Gender Gap Index by the World Economic Forum reported that the gender gaps in the political and economic spheres in Japan are large. People now share a basic understanding that eliminating gender disparity in all areas of society is necessary for addressing many challenges arising from a shrinking population. A stronger attitude also exists that sexual violence, sexual assault, and harassment should not be tolerated in the media and entertainment industries, as well as in workplaces and schools.

Social pressure on political parties is also increasing. The Act on Promotion of Gender Equality in the Political Field, which was first established in 2018, was amended in 2021 with additional text that further encourages political parties to take initiatives to ensure an equal number of male and female candidates for public office as much as possible (Miura 2021). Specifically, in addition to setting numerical targets for female candidates, the 2021 amendment suggests measures such as an improvement in candidate selection methods, development of political human capital, and prevention of sexual and maternity harassment to be implemented by political parties. Six years after the enactment of the Act and three years after the amendment, the excuse that there is not enough time to recruit female candidates is no longer acceptable.

Among contentious issues regarding gender, one of the prolonged agendas is legislation on dual surnames for married couples, which would enable spouses to retain their respective surnames if they wish. Opinion polls demonstrate an increasing number of people in favor of legislation on dual surnames, although differences exist depending on the method of questioning (*Asahi Shinbun* Globe+ 2024). For example, an opinion poll by the Japan Broadcasting Corporation (NHK) reports that 62% of respondents are in favor of this legislation (NHK 2024). In June 2024, the Japan Federation of Economic Organization (Keidanren) officially recommended that the government proceed with dual surname legislation. It stated that the current Civil Law that enforces the same surname for married couples could hinder women's advancement in the business field, and that the increased use of maiden names as common names in workplaces, a choice made by more and more married women as a stopgap measure, could be a business risk abroad (Keidanren 2024).

Even the LDP, which had been the biggest barrier to the legislation, has shown signs of change in recent years. One factor may be the revelation of a close relationship between LDP politicians and the former Unification Church (see McLaughlin 2025). After the murder of former Prime Minister Abe Shinzō in 2022, it became well known that the former Unification Church and other religious right-wing forces have been supporting the election of members of parliament (MPs), especially those of the LDP, and that these religious right-wing forces have firmly opposed the legislation on dual surnames (Yamaguchi and Saitō 2023). This issue did not even appear on the policy agenda within the LDP under the Abe administration, whose core supporters included solid conservative or right-wing organizations (Tsuji 2024). After 2022, however, when the LDP declared that it would sever ties with organizations affiliated with the former Unification Church, some LDP members began to speak positively about the issue. In the LDP presidential election held in October 2024, Koizumi Shinjirō and Kōno Tarō supported the legislation on dual surnames, while Ishiba Shigeru expressed his intention to proceed with discussions within the party. Alternatively, Takaichi Sanae and Kobayashi Takayuki, known for their right-wing positions, opposed it by expressing their concerns about possible disadvantages to children.

Regarding LGBT+ issues, the Act on Promoting Public Understanding of Diversity in Sexual Orientation and Gender Identity was passed in 2023 after consultation between ruling and opposition parties. Although the legalization of same-sex marriage has not been realized, an increasing number of local governments have enacted partnership certification systems between same-sex spouses (see Kawasaka 2025).

Expansion of Women's Representation

Table 15.1 presents the number and percentage of female candidates and those elected, by political party. The total number of candidates (both genders) in this election was 1,344, which increased from 1,051 in 2021. A total of 314 women ran in 2024, compared with 186 women in 2021. The percentage of women among all candidates in 2024 was 23.4%, up from 17.7% in 2021. Compared with the 2021 general election, the number of female candidates in all major parties increased except for the Social Democratic Party (SDP), as the LDP increased from 33 to 55 candidates, Kōmeitō from four to eight, Ishin from fourteen to 29, the Constitutional Democratic Party of Japan (CDP) from 44 to 53, the Japanese Communist Party (JCP) from 46 to 88, the Democratic Party for the People (DPP) from eight to nine, and Reiwa Shinsengumi (Reiwa) from five to twelve. However, only three parties, namely, JCP, Reiwa, and Sanseitō, fielded female candidates above the benchmark of 30%.

Table 15.1 Number and percentage of female candidates and winners by party

	Candidates			Winners		
	Total	Women	%	Total	Women	%
LDP	342	55	16.1	191	19	9.9
Kōmeitō	50	8	16.0	24	4	16.7
Ishin	164	29	17.7	38	4	10.5
CDP	237	53	22.4	148	30	20.3
DPP	42	9	21.4	28	6	21.4
SDP	17	5	29.4	1	0	0.0
JCP	236	88	37.3	8	3	37.5
Reiwa	35	12	34.3	9	4	44.4
Sanseitō	95	36	37.9	3	2	66.7
CPJ	30	6	20.0	3	1	33.3
Other parties	15	2	13.3	0	0	–
Independents	81	11	13.6	12	0	0.0
Total	1,344	314	23.4	465	73	15.7

Source Ministry of Internal Affairs and Communications (2024). Given that the Conservative Party of Japan (CPJ) fulfilled the legal party requirements after the election, the numbers of female members were counted according to their party affiliation after the election (the same applies to the following tables)

Not only were the parties' efforts to recruit more women successful to a certain extent, but the weak electoral cooperation among opposition parties also resulted in the increase of candidates in total. In the 2021 election, the opposition parties attempted to coordinate candidates to defeat the ruling party, but they were reluctant to do so this time and fielded their own candidates more aggressively (*Nikkei Shinbun*, October 11, 2024; cf. Ikeda 2025). For example, while the JCP limited the number of candidates to 130 in 2021, it fielded 236 candidates this time. Reiwa also increased the number of candidates from 21 to 35. Ishin increased the number of candidates from 96 to 164, although it was not involved in the electoral cooperation in 2021. Notably, the newly established Conservative Party of Japan (CPJ) and Sanseitō also fielded more than a few female candidates despite their socially conservative ideologies.

What initiatives have political parties taken to recruit more women? One notable initiative is the *women-only open recruitment* conducted by the LDP and CDP, in which only women could apply for nomination (Cabinet Office, Gender Equality Bureau, 2024). In March 2023, the LDP Tokyo federation conducted this women-only open recruitment for the 18th district in Tokyo despite protests from municipal branches. The CDP employs a separate application process for female candidates in addition to the general open application process. Most of the major parties have set numerical targets for female representation, including the LDP, CDP, DPP, SDP, and JCP (Cabinet Office, Gender Equality Bureau, 2024). The LDP and SDP are also running *schools of politics (seiji juku)* that target women and provide training programs to identify and support female aspirants (Oki 2018). In addition, the LDP, Ishin, CDP, DPP, and SDP provide financial assistance to female candidates and/or candidates raising children. Most of the major political parties also established an anti-harassment committee and/or a consultation service for members.

In terms of the number of women being elected, the largest number was 30 for the CDP, followed by nineteen for the LDP. Compared with 2021, the number increased by seventeen for the CDP, five for the DPP, and three for Reiwa, and decreased by one for the LDP, with no change for the other parties (Fig. 15.1). The LDP, Kōmeitō, and Ishin increased the number of female candidates, but doing so did not lead to more women being elected. In summary, the increase in the number of women elected is mainly due to the better performance of opposition parties in gaining votes and seats, especially the CDP and DPP, which fielded a moderate degree of female candidates (21%–22%).

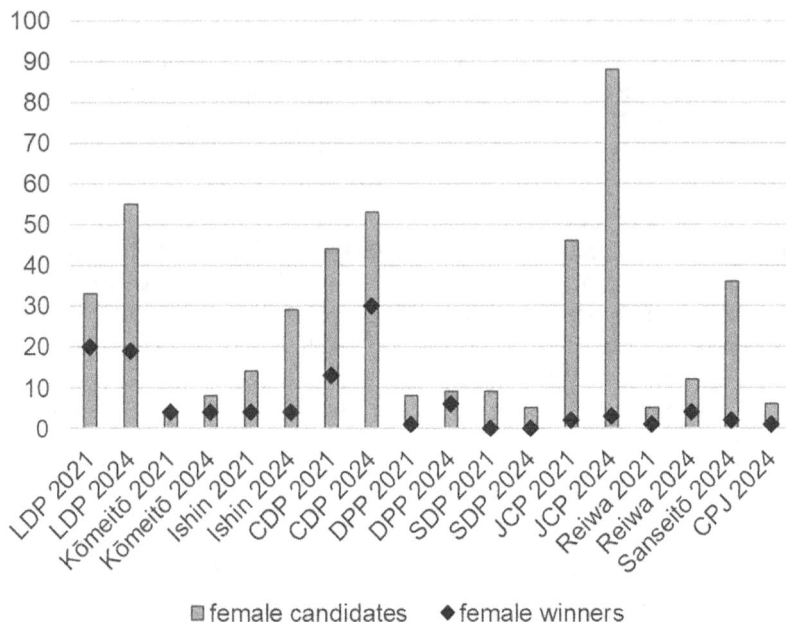

Fig. 15.1 Number of female candidates and winners by party in 2021 and 2024 (*Source* Ministry of Internal Affairs and Communications (2021, 2024))

Table 15.2 depicts the percentage of women and men elected among candidates of the respective gender groups (Table 15.2). Out of the five parties that fielded 20 or more female candidates, the winning rates of male candidates exceeded that of female candidates for the LDP, Ishin, and CDP. For these major parties, the increase in the number of female candidates did not directly lead to an increase in the number of women elected. By contrast, women in Kōmeitō, Reiwa, Sanseitō, and the CPJ had a better chance of winning than did their male counterparts.

Did the newcomers win in the single-member districts (SMDs) or in the proportional representation (PR) tier? In this election, newcomers occupied 99 out of 465 seats, including 67 men and 32 women. PR candidates are divided into two groups, namely, dual-listed candidates who run both in the SMD and in the PR and won the PR seat according to the *best-loser* principle, and PR-only candidates who run only in the PR tier. Among 99 newcomers, 34 won in the SMDs, 52 won by dual

Table 15.2 Winning rates among candidates by party and gender

	Men (%)	Women (%)
LDP	59.9	34.5
Kōmeitō	47.6	50.0
Ishin	25.2	13.8
CDP	64.1	56.6
DPP	66.7	66.7
SDP	8.3	0.0
JCP	3.4	3.4
Reiwa	21.7	33.3
Sanseitō	1.7	5.6
CPJ	8.3	16.7
Other parties	0.0	0.0
Independents	17.1	0.0
Total	38.1	23.2

Source Ministry of Internal Affairs and Communications (2024)

candidacy, and thirteen secured seats as PR-only candidates. Comparing winning rates between genders, Table 15.3 indicates that the winning rates of male newcomers are higher than those of female ones in the SMDs, but women exhibited a greater chance to be elected in the PR tier.

Notably, women in the DPP were more successful than men in the SMDs. Two out of seven female newcomers (28.6%) won in the SMDs, while only two out of 22 male challengers (9.1%) gained seats in the SMDs. These two elected newcomer women in the DPP seemingly ran in *winnable districts*, with only two rivals running from the LDP and JCP in their respective districts (Aichi 7th and 11th), and the LDP candidate of Aichi 7th was involved in the slush fund money scandal.

If political parties are serious about increasing the number of female MPs, they should position women at the top of the list in PR alone (Gaunder and Wiliarty 2020). In particular, candidates running from small parties are unlikely to win seats in the SMDs, such that their chance of winning is dependent on their placement on the PR list.

In fact, the LDP fielded 28 out of 34 newcomer women in the PR-only list, but these women were placed in ranks lower than those of dual-listed candidates. As a result, most of these newcomer women could not gain a seat, except for Morishita Chisato (a former TV personality), who was

Table 15.3 Winning rates of newcomer candidates by party, gender, and constituency

	SMD		PR (dual-listed)		PR (list only)	
	Men (%)	Women (%)	Men (%)	Women (%)	Men (%)	Women (%)
LDP	16.2	16.7	13.9	20.0	0.0	3.6
Kōmeitō	0.0	0.0	–	–	11.8	50.0
Ishin	6.9	0.0	1.2	8.3	0.0	–
CDP	16.7	14.3	27.1	32.1	0.0	0.0
DPP	9.1	28.6	50.0	42.9	100.0	–
SDP	0.0	0.0	0.0	0.0	0.0	0.0
JCP	0.0	0.0	0.0	16.7	33.3	11.1
Reiwa	0.0	0.0	20.0	20.0	7.7	33.3
Sanseitō	0.0	0.0	0.0	33.3	0.0	50.0
CPJ	0.0	0.0	–	–	4.8	20.0
Other parties	0.0	0.0	–	0.0	0.0	–
Independents	6.5	0.0	–	–	–	–
Total	5.9	3.5	15.4	21.7	5.0	12.1

Source Ministry of Internal Affairs and Communications (2024). The author corrected an error in the number of DPP newcomers in the original data

placed in the second rank on the LDP's PR list for the Tohoku bloc—higher than that of dual-list candidates—and won. By contrast, the CDP positioned most of its dual-listed candidates in the same rank (i.e., the first on the PR list), so the *best-losers* could get elected. As an exception, two women (a former MP and a newcomer) were positioned in the first rank of the CDP's PR list for Hokkaido bloc, while all other dual-listed candidates were placed in the third rank. Out of these two women, the former MP won in the SMD, while the newcomer woman was elected from the PR list. Similarly, Ishin, the DPP, and Reiwa gave an equal chance to dual-listed candidates in most cases when determining the orders of the PR rosters.

In contrast, Kōmeitō did not use the dual-list method and placed two of the four new female candidates in second place on the PR list with a high chance of winning. For example, in the South Kantō bloc, an incumbent male candidate was placed in first place, a female newcomer in second, and two male newcomers in third and fourth place, out of whom the top two were elected. The same is true for the Tokyo bloc.

In summary, even though female newcomer candidates could not win as many seats as their male counterparts, many of them fought well in the SMDs, which, combined with an increase in PR votes for the opposition parties, led to an increase in the number of newly elected female members.[1]

Previous Careers of Newcomer Women

What kind of experiences do newcomer women have? Table 15.4 presents the classification of the current or previous titles or jobs of the female newcomer candidates from the five parties that fielded 20 or more such candidates. Information on the titles and jobs of the candidates was obtained from the NHK's website. NHK lists up to two titles per candidate instead of one on other websites. Using the NHK data allows us to obtain more accurate background profiles, because candidates for general elections are typically expected to have pursued political and nonpolitical careers prior to running.

Parties seemingly recruited female candidates from different pools. First, the LDP recruited only a small number from local politics, such as former governors, mayors, and local assembly members. At the same time, the LDP recruited more women from among former members of the House of Councillors, the party's branch chiefs, staffers, and secretaries of politicians. Given that the top three previous jobs of LDP candidates for the Diet have been local assembly members, secretaries, and bureaucrats (Hamamoto 2022: 22), resources for women candidates may be partially different from those of conventional aspirant groups. One explanation for the small number of candidates who were local politicians may be the small number of vacant constituencies in the SMDs where the newcomers could run. As mentioned earlier, most of the LDP newcomer women were placed in lower ranks on the PR list as PR-only candidates, having little chance of winning. Local politicians with proven records would not agree to run under such unfavorable conditions. Instead, the LDP recruited more women with diverse backgrounds, including directors and staffers of civic organizations, corporate executives, and company employees.

Second, many of the new female candidates in Ishin, the CDP, and JCP appear to have climbed up the political pipeline, running for national office after gaining political experience as local politicians, party officers or staffers, or secretaries. In addition, many women had careers in medical,

---

[1] Female incumbents were slightly more likely to be elected than male incumbents (83.0% female and 78.8% male).

Table 15.4 Classification of careers of female newcomer candidates in the five parties

	LDP	Ishin	CDP	JCP	Sanseitō
Number of female newcomer candidates	34	24	34	83	36
Members of the House of Councillors	4	0	1	0	0
Governors, mayors, local assembly members	3	11	15	38	0
Branch chiefs or staff members of political parties, secretaries of politicians	11	4	10	72	4
Bureaucrats (national or local)	4	3	1	1	0
Medical, nursing, welfare, care professionals	5	2	8	14	6
Directors or staff members of civic organizations (NPOs, labor unions, associations)	9	2	3	7	1
Company executives, self-employed	7	6	3	0	13
Company employees	6	4	5	5	10
TV personalities, celebrities, athletes	3	4	0	0	0
Consultants, think-tank members	2	0	4	0	1
Teachers, lawyers, accountants, other legal professionals	1	2	6	9	3
Others	2	5	2	6	15

Source Classified and compiled by the author based on data from the NHK's website. The NHK website lists up to two titles per candidate, such that the sum of titles does not match the total number of female newcomer candidates

nursing, welfare, and care-related occupations or were former teachers and legal professionals. The CDP also fielded several candidates with consulting or think-tank careers.

Third, Sanseitō seemingly adopted a very distinctive recruitment policy. Since its formation in 2020, Sanseitō has gained seats in local assemblies. However, none of the candidates in this election were recruited from among local assembly members. Instead, its candidates present diverse backgrounds, including corporate executives, company employees, a cartoon artist, and a housewife. The party may have searched for women who are not steeped in political color.

Among the 32 newcomer women elected, nine were former local assembly members, and nine held former/current positions as party officers. Six have built careers in medical, nursing, welfare or care services, and six have worked for private companies. An expanded female representation through these newcomer women may bring more diverse perspectives in policy deliberations in the HR on issues such as the elimination of gender disparities in the labor market.

Another issue I would like to mention at the end of this section is the problem of the *zero-women district*. In recent national and supplementary elections, electoral cooperation has been observed between opposition parties in terms of fielding candidates. While it was justified for the purpose of taking seats away from ruling parties, it has also reduced the number of candidates in the SMDs. There were fewer open districts where newcomers could run due to party coordination. Given that incumbents with a high likelihood of winning tend to be prioritized when parties select one *unified candidate*, electoral cooperation results in the sluggish growth of female candidates, unless parties are seriously committed to fielding women (Miura 2017). In the 2021 election, 179 out of 289 (61.9%) SMDs did not have a single female candidate. In these districts, even if voters value the information of a candidate's gender and wish to vote for a female candidate, they would have no place to vote.

In contrast, the number of female candidates increased in 2024 because the opposition parties did not actively cooperate. Nevertheless, many constituencies remained without female candidates, accounting for 116 out of 289 (40.1%) SMDs. Although this problem has not been widely pointed out, electoral cooperation among opposition parties entails the problem of curtailing candidate diversity.

Candidate's Issue Positions on Dual Surnames

Most voters do not highly prioritize gender equality policy when casting votes in general elections. However, expanding media coverage of the stance of political parties on gender issues is putting pressure on the parties. Items on one's position on gender equality issues, especially the item on the approval or disapproval of dual surnames, are frequently included in party/candidate questionnaires sent prior to the election by news media, researchers, and civic organizations. Online voting advice apps and websites, typically known as a *vote match* in Japan, are based on the responses to these questionnaires, such that the positions of political parties and candidates on this issue become more visible than ever.

The current issue positions of the political parties are divided into three groups. The LDP's pledges indicate a cautious position in legislating dual surnames, while other major opposition parties are generally in favor of the idea, except for Ishin, who proposed an original measure to decrease the disadvantage and inconvenience caused by changing surnames. New right-wing parties, namely Sanseitō and the CPJ, clearly oppose the dual surname legislation.

Overall, gender gaps of issue positions among candidates exist, but they are smaller than partisan differences, which have been also observed in the past elections (Miura 2017). According to the UTokyo-Asahi Survey (UTAS) in 2024, 72.6% of female candidates agreed or somewhat agreed with the dual surname legislation, compared with 57.2% of male candidates.[2] The introduction of a gender quota system was also favored by 68.2% of female candidates, compared with 43.7% of male candidates. With regard to party affiliations, while most of the candidates in Kōmeitō, Reiwa, the CDP, DPP, SDP, and JCP are in favor of the legislation on dual surnames, all candidates from Sanseitō and the CPJ opposed and candidates in Ishin were divided (Taniguchi et al. 2025; see also Nippon Television Network Corporation & JX PRESS 2024).

The positions of LDP members on the dual surnames were divided widely with approximately 30% in favor, 38% undecided, and 31% not in favor (*Asahi Shinbun*, October 19, 2024). However, the average position of LDP members has shifted toward greater favorability (Taniguchi et al. 2025). To determine if the position change differed by gender, I examined the positions of male and female LDP candidates in UTAS between 2021 and 2024. As Fig. 15.2 demonstrates, a gender difference already existed in 2021, but this difference further widened in 2024. In fact, no significant change occurred in the proportion of male candidates for or against the issue. Instead, the "cannot say either way" response decreased by six points, and the number of respondents who chose either side slightly increased. The recent vitalization of the debate on this issue within the LDP, on such an occasion as the party's presidential election, may have encouraged some male candidates to clarify their positions. In contrast, among female candidates, 36.4% agreed or somewhat agreed in 2021, but this percentage increased by eighteen points in 2024. The percentage of those who responded "cannot say either way" also increased by ten points. Conversely, the percentage of women who answered either disagree or somewhat disagree decreased by 20 points, while the percentage of women who did not answer decreased by seven points. In summary, many female LDP candidates shifted toward approval. A possible explanation is that changes in social norms since

---

[2] The calculation is conducted by the author based on the UTAS data posted on the *Asahi* digital 2024 election page.

2021 have made expressing a more women-friendly attitude easier for women in the LDP. As for the introduction of the gender quota, once again, a large difference exists between male and female candidates in the LDP. According to UTAS 2024, 56.4% of LDP female candidates opted for agree or somewhat agree, while only 20.6% of male candidates did so.

Finally, I examined whether the LDP members who had connections with the former Unification Church changed their attitudes on this issue after breaking off the relationship. I selected 81 LDP candidates running for the 2024 election, who were reported to have had certain forms of connection with the former Unification Church, including donations or sending congratulatory telegrams to affiliate organizations (see Carlson 2025; McLaughlin 2025).[3] Examining whether their positions changed on the issue of dual surnames in the UTAS between 2021 and 2024, I found no clear trend. Among these 81 members, eighteen and seventeen

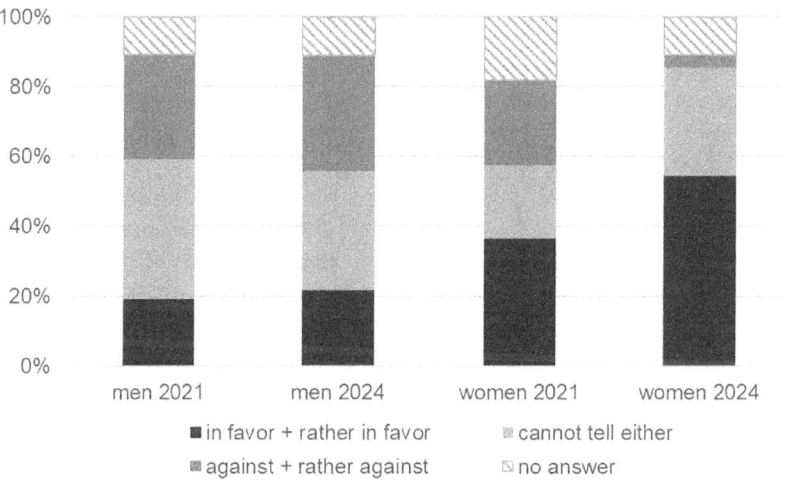

Fig. 15.2 Shifts in issue positions of the LDP candidates on the dual surname legislation between 2021 and 2024 by gender (*Sources* UTokyo-Asahi Survey (2021, 2024))

---

[3] Identification of the LDP members with the former Unification Church connection is based on media reports between July and December 2022, the survey by *Asahi Shinbun* (2022), and the survey conducted by the LDP headquarters (*Asahi Shinbun*, September 8, 2022, online edition).

shifted in the direction of approval and disapproval, respectively, while 38 made no change, and eight did not respond. Among five women, two shifted their positions from "cannot say either way" to "somewhat agree," one from "somewhat disagree" to "cannot say either way," and two women remained in the same position (one "cannot say either way" and one "somewhat agree").

Conclusion

To summarize the 2024 general election from the gender perspective, each political party exerted efforts to increase the number of female candidates, but the extent to which women were prioritized in the placement on the PR list varied among parties. Most of the LDP newcomer women were placed in a low rank with little chance of winning. The increase in the number of women elected was due to an increase in voters' support for opposition parties, combined with the fact that female candidates fought well in the SMDs. As a result of the election, the HR welcomed many female newcomers with rich political experience in local politics and political parties, but also a few women with previous careers in various professions. It could lead to the representation of more gender-balanced and diversified views in the HR.

Based on previous experiences, there are various hurdles to translating increased women's descriptive representation into policy outputs (Gaunder 2012; Gaunder and Wiliarty 2020). In particular, women's substantive involvement in decision-making within each party as well as in the Diet is essential for policy change. For the LDP, we should closely monitor if and to what extent the widened differences in attitudes toward gender issues between female and male MPs will lead to changes in intra-party cultures as well as policies.

Acknowledgements This work was supported by JSPS KAKENHI Grant Number JP24K04728. The author would like to thank Enago (www.enago.jp) for the English language review.

References

Asahi Shinbun. 2022. "Kyū Touitsu Kyōkai tono Kankeiwa, Kokkaigiin Chiji Ankēto [Survey on Connection with the Former Unification Church to

MPs and Governors]." https://digital.asahi.com/special/unificationchurch-survey/. Accessed on January 10, 2025.
Asahi Shinbun Globe+. 2024. "Same-Sex Marriage, Dual Surname: What Kind of Questionnaire Design Moves Japanese Opinions? Standard University Survey." https://globe.asahi.com/article/15421790. Accessed on January 10, 2025.
Cabinet Office, Gender Equality Bureau. 2024. "Kakuseitō niokeru Danjo Kyōdō Sankaku no Torikumijōkyō to Kadai, Reiwa 5 nendo [Gender Equality Initiatives and Challenges in Each Political Party]." https://www.gender.go.jp/policy/seijibunya/seijibunya_yousei.html. Accessed on January 10, 2025.
Carlson, Matthew M. 2025. "Scandals During the Kishida Administration." In *Japan Decides 2024: The Japanese General Election*, edited by Kenneth M. McElwain, Robert J. Pekkanen, and Daniel M. Smith, 217–233. New York: Palgrave Macmillan.
Gaunder, Alisa. 2012. "The DPJ and Women: The Limited Impact of the 2009 Alternation of Power on Policy and Governance." *Journal of East Asian Studies* 12: 441–466.
Gaunder, Alisa, and Sarah Wiliarty. 2020. "Conservative Women in Germany and Japan: Chancellors versus Madonnas." *Politics & Gender* 16: 99–122.
Hamamoto, Shinsuke. 2022. *Nippon no Kokkai Giin: Seiji Kaikakugono Genkai to Kanōsei [Diet Members in Japan: Limitations and Possibilities after the Political Reforms]*. Tokyo: Chūōkōron Shinsha.
Ikeda, Fumi. 2025. "The CDP in 2024: The Legacy of the Electoral Coalition with the JCP." In *Japan Decides 2024: The Japanese General Election*, edited by Kenneth M. McElwain, Robert J. Pekkanen, and Daniel M. Smith, 57–74. New York: Palgrave Macmillan.
Inter-Parliamentary Union. 2024. "Global and Regional Averages of Women in National Parliaments, Average as of 1st November 2024." https://data.ipu.org/women-averages/. Accessed on January 10, 2025.
Kawasaka, Kazuyoshi. 2025. "LGBTQ+ Rights Issues and the 2024 Japanese Election." In *Japan Decides 2024: The Japanese General Election*, edited by Kenneth M. McElwain, Robert J. Pekkanen, and Daniel M. Smith, 273–291. New York: Palgrave Macmillan.
Keidanren. 2024. "Sentakushi noaru Shakai no Jitsugen wo Mezashite: Josei Katsuyaku nitaisuru Seido no Kabe wo Norikoeru [Aiming to Realize a Society with Choices: Overcoming Systemic Barriers to Women's Advancement]." https://www.keidanren.or.jp/policy/2024/044_honbun.html#s4. Accessed on January 10, 2025.
McLaughlin, Levi. 2025. "Perennial Fears, Novel Responses: The Unification Church in Japan after the Abe Assassination." In *Japan Decides 2024*, edited by Kenneth M. McElwain, Robert J. Pekkanen, and Daniel M. Smith, 235–253. New York: Palgrave Macmillan.

Ministry of Internal Affairs and Communications. 2021. "Reiwa 3 nen 10 gatsu 31 nichi Shikkō, Shūgiinsōsenkyo, Saikōsaibansho Saibankan Kokuminshihsa Sokuhōkekka [Preliminary Results of the General Election for the House of Representatives and the National Examination of Supreme Court Judges]."

Ministry of Internal Affairs and Communications. 2024. "Reiwa 6 nen 10 gatsu 27 nichi Shikkō, Shūgiinsōsenkyo, Saikōsaibansho Saibankan Kokuminshihsa Sokuhōkekka [Preliminary Results of the General Election for the House of Representatives and the National Examination of Supreme Court Judges]."

Miura, Mari. 2017. "Persistence of Women's Under-Representation." In *Japan Decides 2017: The Japanese General Election*, edited by Robert J. Pekkanen, Steven R. Reed, Ethan Scheiner, and Daniel M. Smith, 185–202. London: Palgrave Macmillan.

Miura, Mari. 2021. "Seiji Bunya niokeru Danjo Kyōdō Sankaku Suishinhō no Kaisei omeguru Giron to Igi [Discussion and Significance of the Amendment to the Act on Promotion of Gender Equality in the Political Field]." *Josei Tenbō = Women's Perspective* 712: 19–21.

Nemoto, Kuniaki. 2025. "Reasons Behind the LDP's Loss in the 2024 Election." In *Japan Decides 2024: The Japanese General Election*, edited by Kenneth M. McElwain, Robert J. Pekkanen, and Daniel M. Smith, 37–55. New York: Palgrave Macmillan.

NHK. 2024. "Sentakuteki Fūfu Bessei, Sansei ga 62%, Hantai wa 27% ni, NHK Yoron Chōsa [NHK Poll: 62% in Favor of Dual Surname, 27% Opposed]." https://www3.nhk.or.jp/news/html/20240501/k10014437371000.html. Accessed on January 10, 2025.

Nippon Television Network Corporation & JX PRESS. 2024. "ZERO 2024 General Election Candidates Survey." https://www.ntv.co.jp/election2024/research/party/. Accessed on January 10, 2025.

Ōki, Naoko. 2018. "'Seijijuku' to Josei no Seijisanka: Rikurūtomento no Kanten kara ['School of Politics' and Women's Political Participation in Terms of Recruitment]" *Joseigaku (Women's Studies)* 25: 44–62.

Taniguchi, Masaki, Taka-aki Asano, Shōko Ōmori, and Shūsuke Takamiya. 2025. "Policy Positions of the Candidates." In *Japan Decides 2024: The Japanese General Election*, edited by Kenneth M. McElwain, Robert J. Pekkanen, and Daniel M. Smith, 125–142. New York: Palgrave Macmillan.

Tsuji, Yuki. 2024. "Skillful Agenda-Setting for Women's Policy." In *Critical Review of the Abe Administration: Politics of Conservatism and Realsim*, edited by Yoichi Funabashi and Koji Nakakita, 187–211. Abington, OX and New York: Routledge.

UTokyo-Asahi Survey (UTAS). 2021. Political Leader Survey, 2021 HoR Election. https://www.masaki.j.u-tokyo.ac.jp/utas/utasindex_en.html. Accessed on January 10, 2025.

UTokyo-Asahi Survey (UTAS). 2024. Political Leader Survey, 2024 HoR Election. Asahi Digital, 2024 Election Page. https://digital.asahi.com/senkyo/shuinsen/2024/asahitodai/. Accessed on January 10, 2025.

Yamaguchi, Tomomi and Masami Saitō with Politas TV, eds. 2023. *Shūkyō Uha to Feminizumu* [*Religious-Right and Feminism*]. Tokyo: Seikyūsha.

CHAPTER 16

LGBTQ+ Rights Issues and the 2024 Japanese Election

Kazuyoshi Kawasaka

INTRODUCTION

Japan has a long history of LGBTQ+ (Lesbian, Gay, Bi, Trans, Queer or Questioning, and more) activism that has tried to influence public office elections. In 1971, Tōgō Ken became the first openly gay candidate for public office, standing for the House of Councillors election. The LGBTQ+ civil rights group *Akueriasu* (Aquarius), established in 1999, started to conduct questionnaires on LGBTQ+ issues among candidates of elections since the 2000s, although initially it only received responses from a handful of candidates. Now it has become the norm for major political parties to propose their own LGBTQ+ rights policies in their manifestos. Their wording and policies reflect each party's ideological position on family and human rights issues, one of the few topics on which parties and candidates in Japan present diverse positions.

This chapter analyzes the major Japanese parties' political positions on LGBTQ+ rights issues through a study of their manifestos. It begins

K. Kawasaka (✉)
University of Tokyo, Bunkyo City, Japan
e-mail: kawasaka@g.ecc.u-tokyo.ac.jp

with a summary of the LGBTQ+ rights issues currently being faced in Japan and their historical context, followed by a discussion of the first LGBTQ+-related law since the 2004 GID Act and the major LGBTQ+ rights judicial cases during the 2021–2024 Diet term. It then discusses the weaponization of LGBTQ+ rights by the Japanese religious right. Finally, the chapter proceeds to an analysis of Japanese ruling and opposition parties' LGBTQ+ policies in the 2024 general election, exploring the kinds of LGBTQ+ issues that became politically divisive—and why—and their influence on the 2024 election.

LGBTQ+ Rights in Japan

The Japanese LGBTQ+ situation has often been described as unique by scholars compared to countries in the Global North (Frühstück 2022; Kawasaka and Würrer 2024; McLelland 2005). Japan has historically had a rich queer culture, as it never criminalized cross-dressing and same-sex sexual conduct, except during a short period at the beginning of the Meiji era in the nineteenth century. Although modern medical discourses have stigmatized non-normative genders and sexualities, there has been no moral authority like the Christian Church over sexual conduct. Japanese law has a "loophole" for same-sex couples to form a family—a parent–child relationship—via a special system of adult adoption (Maree 2004). In this sense, Japan could be described as a tolerant society for LGBTQ+ people compared to other countries that have sodomy laws (McLelland 2005, 71–72; Liberal Democratic Party of Japan 2016).

Nevertheless, Japan has failed to keep up as LGBTQ+ rights have become an international human rights issue and related institutions have been introduced transnationally. So far, Japan does not have any LGBTQ+ rights protection laws, such as anti-discrimination, anti-hate speech, or hate crime protection laws; a human rights or equality act; or a same-sex marriage or civil union law. Many Japanese local authorities have started to introduce a same-sex partnership certificate system after the first one was established by Tokyo's Shibuya ward in 2015, but this is only a symbolic gesture and barely offers any legal rights, as the national government retains authority over family law. Japanese LGBTQ+ rights organizations such as Japan Alliance for LGBT Legislation (J-ALL 2016) express concern regarding potential discrimination in the workplace or against those renting accommodation, due to the lack of an anti-discrimination law that includes LGBTQ+ people, but there are no official statistics for how common such discrimination is. With regard to transgender rights, the so-called Gender Identity Disorder (GID) Act, enacted in 2004, sets one of the most stringent conditions for trans people to legally change their gender marker in the Global North (Human Rights Watch 2021). The law demands that trans people be sterilized, have a sex-reassignment operation, and be single without any minor children. Owing to its slow adoption of LGBTQ+ human rights reforms, Japan is now one of the lowest-ranked countries in the Organization for Economic Co-operation and Development (OECD 2020) in terms of its protection of LGBTQ+ legal rights.

While the contemporary governments led by the Liberal Democratic Party (LDP) and the Kōmeitō in recent years have been reluctant to introduce any LGBTQ+ rights-related legal reforms, Japanese public opinion began leaning toward being more LGBTQ+ friendly from the 2010s. According to an international poll by Pew Research Center in 2023, 68% of respondents support same-sex marriage (strongly/somewhat favor), which is the second highest percentage of support in Asia–Pacific countries, following Australia, and higher than in the United States (Gubbala et al. 2023). However, the majority of those in favor indicated "somewhat favor," and in terms of the percentage of those who responded "strongly favor" (11%), Japan ranks among the lowest countries in the survey. A similar trend can also be found in Ipsos's (2024) international poll, which found that opposition to same-sex marriage in Japan was the lowest (6%) among 23 countries, but support for same-sex marriage (42%) or an antidiscrimination law (42%) was also among the lowest. In this sense, the Japanese public does not seem to have steadfast personal opinions on LGBTQ+ issues: they do not strongly oppose or support LGBTQ+ rights, in contrast to other countries such as the United States, where LGBTQ+ equality is treated as a partisan issue.

LGBTQ+ Issues in the 2021–2024 Diet Term

LGBTQ+ rights are not sufficiently protected by law in Japan compared to other OECD countries, being one of the lowest alongside Turkey and South Korea (OECD 2020). This lack of LGBTQ+ legal protection was seriously challenged in the 2021–2024 Diet term. In June 2023, under international pressure, the LDP passed the first law pertaining to LGBTQ+ rights since the 2004 GID Act. In addition, the lack of

LGBTQ+ rights protection began to be regarded as unconstitutional by the Japanese justice system.

Japan's first LGBTQ+ law in response to international pressure

2023 was a symbolic year for Japanese LGBTQ+ activism, as the first LGBTQ+-related law was passed in the LDP-majority Diet since the GID Act was enacted in 2004: the Act on Promoting Public Understanding of Diversity in Sexual Orientation and Gender Identity, or the so-called LGBT *Rikai Zōshin Hō* (hereafter, "Act on Promoting LGBT Public Understanding"). While the law was intended to improve Japanese public awareness about LGBTQ+ issues, it does not legally improve LGBTQ+ rights or prohibit discrimination based on sexual orientation and gender identity (SOGI).

The original plan for introducing the law was announced by the LDP in 2016 as part of the preparations for the Tokyo 2020 Olympics and Paralympics (Kawasaka 2024; Maree 2020). The IOC Charter was revised to ban discrimination based on sexual orientation in 2014, as the Sochi Winter Olympics suffered turmoil and boycotts due to Russia's "anti-gay propaganda" law. In announcing the party's principal position on LGBTQ+ rights, the LDP (2016) explained why it considered promoting public awareness and understanding of LGBTQ+ issues to be a better policy than banning discrimination. First, social discrimination against LGBTQ+ people in Japan is caused by people's ignorance rather than intentional hostility. Japan's traditional tolerance of the diversity of gender expression and sexuality was changed by Westernization/modernization. Second, if the government were to introduce an anti-discrimination law, the LDP claimed, it could result in people being prosecuted for unintentional offences because the Japanese public, especially older generations, still lack awareness of LGBTQ+ issues. Nikaidō Yuki (2017), a journalist specializing in LGBTQ issues, points out that ultraconservative groups within the party strongly opposed introducing an anti-discrimination or same-sex marriage law. Promoting LGBTQ+ public understanding was a pragmatic compromise between ultraconservative groups and preparations for the Tokyo Olympics.

The Act on Promoting LGBT Public Understanding was a proposed legislation promised in the LDP's 2017 and 2019 manifestos. However, in May 2021, just before the delayed Tokyo 2020 Olympics, ultraconservative groups started opposing the bill, claiming it had become a de facto anti-discrimination law because of the inclusion of the passage "discrimination based on gender identity shall not be allowed" (Furugaki and Nakamura 2021),[1] although the bill did not penalize discrimination of LGBTQ+ people. Due to the failure to reach consensus within the party, the LDP decided to scrap the bill without sending it to be read in the Diet.

After the Tokyo Olympics, the hosting of another international event—the G7 summit in 2023—politicized LGBTQ+ rights in Japan again. As a member of the G7, Japan's international official position is to support LGBTQ+ rights, as stated in the G7 Leaders' Communiqué: "We seek to ensure full, equal and meaningful participation of women and girls in all their diversity as well as LGBTIQ+ persons in politics, economics, education and all other spheres of society" (G7 2022, 24). The LDP's resistance to LGBTQ+ rights created a contradiction between Japan's domestic policy and its international stance as a G7 member.

In April 2023, Rahm Emanuel, the US ambassador to Japan (2022–2025), sent a clear message to the Kishida administration at a media conference that he expected the Diet to "take the steps necessary to be a clear, unambiguous voice not only for tolerance but against discrimination" toward LGBTQ+ people (*The Japan Times*, February 16, 2023). In addition, Emanuel took the initiative to release a video message with the ambassadors of thirteen other countries, expressing their support for LGBTQ+ rights as universal human rights and their opposition to discrimination against LGBTQ+ people. This exerted political pressure on Japan before the summit to pass a bill on the Act on Promoting LGBT Public Understanding (Kawasaka 2025).

Although the Kishida administration moved to pass this bill, which the LDP had long promised in previous elections under political pressure from Japan's allies, ultraconservative opposition to it was also persistent. In response to requests by Ishin and the Democratic Party for the People (DPP), the bill was revised with the phrase "discrimination on the basis of sexual orientation or gender identity shall not be acceptable" to "there should be no unfair discrimination," which implies and legitimizes the potential for "fair" discrimination. It was further revised with a condition that consideration should be paid to "all citizens being able to lead their lives without concern," which implies that the existence of LGBTQ+

---

[1] All translations from Japanese sources are my own, unless otherwise indicated.

people can cause concern for people. LGBTQ+ activists were concerned about the potential for this condition to be utilized to oppose education and policies in schools and local governments in relation to LGBTQ+ issues (J-ALL 2023). Due to these problems, the Constitutional Democratic Party of Japan (CDP), the Japanese Communist Party (JCP), Social Democratic Party (SDP), and Reiwa voted against the bill, but it was passed when the LDP, Kōmeitō, DPP, and Ishin voted in favor of it.

The Act on Promoting LGBT Public Understanding obligates the government to formulate a basic plan for implementing policies on LGBTQ+ public awareness and understanding, which the Kishida administration failed to do by the 2024 general election. The newly enacted law and the LDP's failure to formulate a basic plan became one of the issues in the 2024 general election.

Legal decisions on LGBTQ+ rights

As the Supreme Court of Japan has traditionally been extremely cautious in deciding whether an existing law is unconstitutional or not, it has been "widely and justifiably considered the most conservative constitutional court in the world" (Law 2009, 1545). However, the Japanese justice system has begun to recognize and advance LGBTQ+ rights since the 2021 election, in stark contrast to the political resistance to such progress.

In 2023, the Supreme Court unanimously decided that the sterilization requirement under the GID Act for changing one's legal gender was unconstitutional, ruling that it violated a person's bodily autonomy protected by the Constitution, forcing them into the harsh dilemma of either undergoing sterilization or abandoning the option of legally changing their gender on their family registry (Saikō Saibansho Hanketsu 2023, 9). When deliberating such cases earlier in 2019, the Supreme Court had decided that the requirement was constitutional, in contrast to other international courts such as the European Court of Human Rights, which decided that such a requirement was a violation of human rights in 2017 (A. P. and Others v. France). However, in 2023, the Supreme Court set a new precedent, finding the law unconstitutional in what was only the twelfth Supreme Court decision that an existing law was unconstitutional in postwar Japan.

The lack of a same-sex marriage law has recently been challenged in Japanese courts as well. In February 2019, lawsuits were filed in four district courts—Sapporo, Tokyo, Nagoya, and Osaka—followed by the Fukuoka district court in September, to challenge and clarify the constitutionality of the Japanese legal family system, which does not allow same-sex couples to marry. These lawsuits are collectively called the "Freedom to Marry for All" litigation, characterized as policymaking lawsuits within the LGBTQ+ movement (Taniguchi 2024, 63). Although a Supreme Court decision has not yet been made as of January 2025, the lawsuits have been successful. As of January 2025, seven out of eight decisions concluded that the current ban of same-sex marriage was unconstitutional (*iken*) or a state of unconstitutionality (*iken jōtai*). In particular, the Sapporo High Court and the Tokyo High Court made decisions in 2024 that the Constitution of Japan equally guarantees the freedom to marry for both same-sex couples and opposite-sex couples and that banning same-sex marriage was discriminatory based on sexual orientation.

Thus, Japanese courts have started to render decisions of unconstitutionality on the lack of same-sex marriage, based on the equality and pursuit of happiness clauses in the Constitution. These judicial decisions led to debates over the revision of unconstitutional parts of the GID Act and the legalization of same-sex marriage in the lead-up to the 2024 election.

LGBTQ+ Issues and Conservative Politics in the 2024 Election

LGBTQ+ issues are one of the essential political interests of the religious right such as the Unification Church and Japan Conference (Nippon Kaigi), which have supported the LDP for decades (McLaughlin 2025). In the early 2000s, anti-gender movements grew in response to the Gender Equality Act (1999). The movements targeted sex education and the term "gender-free," which was extensively used in gender-awareness education. In such anti-gender movements, homosexuality and transgender expression were often symbolically featured as the result of "extreme sex education" and "gender-free" feminist movements, and presented as a departure from and destruction of the Japanese "traditional" family system (Kawasaka 2023). The movements were incited by religious groups such as the Unification Church and the Association of Shinto Shrines (*Jinja Honchō*) and supported by powerful conservative politicians, including Abe Shinzō even before he was elected as prime minister (Yamaguchi 2014; Yamaguchi and Saitō 2023). Many ultraconservative politicians, including Yamatani Eriko, who became famous and built a close relationship with Abe through the anti-gender movements in the 2000s, are still influential in the LDP and serve as the main political force against any reforms of the Japanese family system, such as allowing married couples to have separate family names (*fūfu bessei*) and the recent resistance to the Act on Promoting LGBT Public Understanding (see Matsumoto 2025; Taniguchi et al. 2025).

When LGBTQ+ rights institutions, including same-sex marriage, were transnationally expanded and started to influence Japanese society, anti-LGBTQ+ policies became a priority of the Japanese religious right, especially since the late 2010s. The political branch of the Unification Church in Japan, which is called the International Federation for Victory over Communism (IFVOC), set four annual doctrines in 2021, one of which was to "stop the legalization of same-sex marriage and extreme 'LGBT' human rights movements and promote accurate views of marriage and family" (IFVOC 2022), in addition to organizing Constitution-revision movements. The influence of the Association of Shintō Shrines was also strong due to its connection to LDP lawmakers. In 2022, the Shinto Association of Spiritual Leadership distributed a pamphlet to lawmakers, mostly from the LDP, at a meeting for affiliated members of the Diet, including a transcript of a lecture recommending conversion therapy for homosexuality, which it described as "an acquired mental disorder, an addiction" (Rich and Hida 2023). As these activities suggest, LGBTQ+ issues are prioritized by the Japanese religious right and ultraconservatives (see also McLaughlin 2025).

However, following the assassination of former prime minister Abe Shinzō in 2022, the role and political influence of religious right groups over Japanese LGBTQ+ rights were widely recognized, especially in terms of their connection with the LDP. *Mainichi Shinbun* reported in April 2023 that the Unification Church's anti-LGBTQ+ activities have visibly expanded in Japan since the Japanese translation of its founder Sun Myung Moon's book of quotations was published in 2002, which included 74 anti-homosexuality remarks (Sakaguchi et al. 2023). These activities, which were fueling anti-gender movements, were widely discussed among feminist and LGBTQ+ scholars and activists in Japan (Yamaguchi and Saitō 2023). But such mainstream news attention contributed to the public understanding of how deeply the religious right groups influence the LDP-led governments over gender equality and LGBTQ+ rights in Japan.

The relationship between the LDP and religious right groups became complicated after the slush fund scandal among LDP lawmakers and the enactment of the Act on Promoting LGBT Public Understanding in 2023. Religious right groups traditionally had a close relationship with lawmakers of the Abe faction, but the slush fund scandal hit the largest LDP faction, removing its power within the party after Kishida Fumio ordered the dissolution of the party factions (see Carlson 2025; Nemoto 2025). At the same time, by passing the Act, the LDP also lost trust from the religious right as a party resisting LGBTQ+ rights. As a result, the Conservative Party of Japan (CPJ) was established by Hyakuta Naoki, a novelist who had originally been Abe's close ally. He established this new anti-LGBTQ+ party in 2023 in response to the LDP passing the LGBTQ+ law, which he claimed "would destroy Japan, ignoring Japanese culture and tradition" (*Abema Times*, September 29, 2023). Anti-LGBTQ+ policies and anti-immigration policies were the CPJ's key policies for the 2024 election and attracted voters (Fukatsu 2024). Sanseitō, arguably the most far-right and anti-vaccination party, stands against LGBTQ+ rights, including the new LGBTQ + law and proposals for same-sex marriage, claiming the party supports the protection of a Japanese national identity and avoiding social confusion.[2]

While the CPJ cultivated its supporters with its anti-LGBTQ+ policies, the LDP's stance on LGBTQ+ rights has become increasingly confusing. Ishiba Shigeru (2024a, 118) expressed support for institutionalizing same-sex marriage in his book published just before the LDP leadership campaign: "On same-sex marriage, discussions should not rely on personal favor or dislike nor political right or left ideologies. We should think about it only based on the viewpoint of respect for fundamental human rights guaranteed by the Constitution, which postwar Japan has treated as the most important foundation of the nation." However, after being elected prime minister in 2024, he backtracked, noting in an address to the Diet: "[Same-sex marriage] is closely related to each citizen's perspective on family. It is essential to closely monitor public opinions, parliamentary discussions, and the status of legal proceedings" (Ishiba 2024b). His statement follows previous government positions

---

[2] For the relationship between Japanese national identity and queer gender and sexuality in Japanese modernity, see Kawasaka (2018).

that implied same-sex marriage would negatively affect the traditional family unit and should not be introduced to Japanese society. The close relationship between the LDP and religious right groups has long functioned to prevent any legal reforms for advancing LGBTQ+ rights in Japan (Yamaguchi and Saitō 2023). As a result, Japan faces international pressure from its allies. However, such an openly anti-LGBTQ+ position became difficult for the LDP in the 2021–2024 Diet term, as the LDP's close relationship with religious right groups, especially the Unification Church, fueled political scandals.

The Ruling Parties' Positions on LGBTQ+ Rights Issues in the 2024 Election

The Liberal Democratic Party (LDP)

As a ruling party, the LDP promised to respect the existing Act on Promoting LGBT Public Understanding and the Supreme Court's decision of unconstitutionality on the requirement of forced sterility by the GID Act for changing one's legal gender. At the same time, however, the LDP did not promise or even mention further policies on LGBTQ+ issues. The LDP's (2024, 34) manifesto states:

> To alleviate the societal challenges faced by sexual minorities, efforts will be made to promote better understanding in various social contexts, including local communities, schools, and workplaces. Furthermore, in regards to the 2023 Supreme Court ruling on gender dysphoria, necessary legal revisions will be undertaken, emphasizing the protection of human dignity.

What is notable is that the LDP was reluctant to include SOGI issues in the school curriculum, although it proposed to "promote better understanding in schools." To questionnaires for the 2024 general election conducted by J-ALL (2024), the LDP responded that "addressing the diversity of sexual minorities as part of the school curriculum should be carefully considered, taking into account factors such as the developmental stages of individual students, the understanding of parents and the broader public, and the assurance of appropriate guidance by educators." Although the LDP promised to promote better public understanding of LGBTQ+ issues as its essential policy on LGBTQ+ human rights, the party expressed a cautious approach to the inclusion of SOGI issues in the school curriculum, citing issues of "the understanding of parents and the broader public."

The Kōmeitō

The Kōmeitō's LGBTQ+ policy is very similar to the LDP's as a ruling coalition party. The Kōmeitō promised to work for a better public understanding of LGBTQ+ issues and revise the GID Act following the Supreme Court's decision. In addition to these issues, it proposed an expansion of the same-sex partnership certificate system by local governments, which is not legally binding unlike the civil union introduced by other countries, as well as improving the support system for sexual minorities.

THE OPPOSITION PARTIES' POSITIONS ON LGBTQ+ RIGHTS ISSUES IN THE 2024 ELECTION

Radical Right Parties

The most prominent anti-LGBTQ+ radical right parties in Japan are the CPJ and Sanseitō. Due to their opposition to LGBTQ+ rights policies, they did not respond to questionnaires about LGBTQ+ related policies by J-ALL for the 2024 general election.

- The **Conservative Party of Japan (CPJ)** proposed to revise the Act on Promoting LGBT Public Understanding, especially the part pertaining to the education of minors. What is notable in its policy is the contextualization of LGBTQ+ issues under the category of "protecting Japanese national essence [*kokutai*] and traditional culture" (Conservative Party of Japan 2024), not the education category, implying that the party regards LGBTQ+ issues as threats to the Japanese national essence.
- The **Sanseitō** expressed in its 2024 manifesto its opposition to the Act on Promoting LGBT Public Understanding and same-sex marriage because of the "lack of sufficient discussion" (Sanseitō 2024). Similar to the CPJ, the party also put LGBTQ+ rights issues under the category of "protecting Japanese national culture and national interests/constructing national identity" (Sanseitō 2024).

Left-Leaning Parties

Left-leaning opposition parties in Japan have promised more comprehensive LGBTQ+ rights policies, including an anti-discrimination law and the legalization of same-sex marriage, rather than mainly symbolic policies like the Act on Promoting LGBT Public Understanding.

- The **Constitutional Democratic Party of Japan (CDP)** seeks to promote social issues such as gender equality and LGBTQ+ issues to differentiate itself from the current ruling LDP. The largest opposition party, it devoted 12 pages to gender equality policies and one whole page to SOGI issues. The CDP promised LGBTQ+ rights policies, including an anti-discrimination law banning discrimination in governmental agencies, workplaces, and education; the legalization of same-sex marriage; a revision of the GID Act following the Supreme Court's decision; and the inclusion of SOGI issues in the school curriculum (CDP 2024). What is notable in the CDP manifesto is that it sets out an agenda on human rights and business, including SOGI issues in this category. In this sense, the CDP promised a comprehensive reform of the current human rights policy in Japan.
- The **Social Democratic Party (SDP)**, which is declining and may lose its political party status for failing to meet minimum requirements in the foreseeable future, has been regarded as "feminist" since the party was established in 1996, promoting policies for gender equality. In the 2024 general election, the party announced six key policies, the fifth of which was on gender equality and diversity, calling for same-sex marriage and anti-discrimination laws (SDP 2024).
- The **Japanese Communist Party (JCP)** proposed comprehensive policies for LGBTQ+ rights on its website, including the legalization of same-sex marriage, a revision of the GID Act, an anti-discrimination law, and the expansion of human rights education (JCP 2024b). Its manifesto for the 2024 general election, however, lacks such details and only mentions the party's support for same-sex marriage. It does not mention LGBTQ+ rights issues despite devoting an entire page to human rights issues, including disabled people, foreigners, refugees, and the Ainu (JCP 2024a, 19). What is characteristic of the JCP approach to LGBTQ+ rights issues is that

the JCP did not consider sexual minorities in worker's issues in either its manifesto or website, unlike the CDP, although the JCP's 2024 campaign focused on working people's issues.

- **Reiwa Shinsengumi (Reiwa)** proposed the legalization of same-sex marriage and the LGBTQ+ Equality Act, as well as gender sensitive education as part of compulsory education which "reduces gender stereotypes and enforced traditional gender roles" (Reiwa 2024, 21). Reiwa, like the CDP, is one of the few parties which mentioned educational policy for gender equality and sexuality education including LGBTQ+ issues.

Parties that Changed Their LGBTQ+ Positions Since the 2021 General Election

A noticeable change for LGBTQ+ issues in the 2024 general election was that the DPP and Ishin subtly changed their tone in their manifestos between 2021 and 2024, after these parties intervened to revise the bill and voted for the revised LGBTQ+ Act in 2023. Due to their revisions, the bill became more conservative than the LDP's original bill. For example, the bill modified the section on education, demanding parental and community agreements for LGBTQ+ related education, saying "to deepen understanding of the diversity of sexual orientation and gender identity, educational or awareness-raising initiatives shall be undertaken with the cooperation of families, local residents, and other relevant stakeholders." This opened up the potential for the religious right and conservatives to intervene in gender and sex education in schools. Moreover, they added the phrase "all citizens being able to lead their lives without concern," suggesting LGBTQ+ people and education about them can cause concern to other citizens. These additional terms and legislative developments were well reflected in anti-LGBTQ+ campaigns, causing concern among many LGBTQ+ activists about Japanese politicians' understanding of LGBTQ+ human rights issues in general (Marriage for All 2023).

- **The Democratic Party for the People (DPP)** called for an anti-discrimination law for LGBTQ + equality as well as inclusive education in its 2021 manifesto, although there was no mention of same-sex marriage or partnership (DPP 2021, 10). In its 2024 manifesto, however, the DPP (2024, 31) dropped its policies of inclusive education and anti-discrimination law and promised an anti-hate speech law for social discrimination issues, although the proposed anti-hate speech law only covers "race, ethnicity, and place of origin," which carefully avoided issues of hate speech against LGBTQ+ people and discrimination based on SOGI, which are covered by hate speech laws in many other Global North countries. For LGBTQ+ issues, the DPP (2024, 31) followed the wording of the Act on Promoting LGBT Public Understanding, saying "the party aims for creating a society in which all people are naturally accepted regardless of sexual orientation and gender identity."

- **Ishin** also changed its tone on LGBTQ+ issues between its 2021 and 2024 manifestos, although it had not been pro-LGBTQ+ rights, unlike left-leaning parties in 2021. Ishin called for expanding same-sex partnership certificates by local governments, which also includes heterosexual couples, rather than the institutionalization of same-sex marriage. Whereas Ishin (2021) did not call for same-sex marriage, it still supported an anti-discrimination law as part of LGBTQ+ rights issues in 2021. In 2024, however, Ishin (2024) dropped its support for an anti-discrimination law including LGBTQ+ people but instead started supporting same-sex marriage.

Conclusion

The 2021–2024 Diet term was a groundbreaking period for Japanese LGBTQ+ rights progress. The first LGBTQ+-related law since the GID Act was enacted in Japan in 2023. The number of local governments introducing a same-sex partnership certificate system—which was symbolically important for same-sex couples despite being legally very limited—continued to increase. Numerous important legal decisions were made for expanding LGBTQ+ rights, including the Supreme Court decisions on trans rights and lower court rulings of unconstitutionality on banning same-sex marriage in Japan. Furthermore, the G7 leaders communiqué started to advocate for LGBTQ+ equality worldwide.

However, the Japanese political parties' manifestos in the 2024 general election indicate that LGBTQ+ policies and narratives in general are moving in a more conservative and less LGBTQ+-friendly direction. The ruling parties, the LDP and Kōmeitō, did not propose further LGBTQ+

policies other than what they promised in the previous election, reducing issues into "public understandings" without reforming the educational curriculum. The radical right CPJ, which was established as part of the backlash against the Act on Promoting LGBT Public Understanding, stood for Japanese national identity and tradition against LGBTQ+ rights, attracting new supporters from other conservative parties, especially the LDP. The analysis showed that each party has its own distinctive ideological position on LGBTQ+ issues. As LGBTQ+ issues are a sensitive subject for some parties, especially when they have a connection to religious and moral conservative groups, the policies are carefully worded in each party's manifesto and distinguished from other parties or their own past position. The Act on Promoting LGBT Public Understanding made the DPP and Ishin more conservative on LGBTQ+ rights issues, dropping some important policies such as the anti-discrimination law. In addition, the legislative process of the Act highlighted the potential for the political weaponization of anti-LGBTQ+ rights positions, prompting these two parties to start changing their stance on these issues.

The pro-LGBTQ+ left-leaning parties also showed distinctive approaches to LGBTQ+ issues. The JCP treated them as human rights issues but did not make them a major policy for its political campaign. Conversely, the CDP proposed the most comprehensive set of policies for gender and LGBTQ+ issues among Japanese political parties in the 2024 general election, very similar to European center-left parties' positions on LGBTQ+ issues. In 2024, the CDP gained 50 more seats than it had in the previous election, consolidating its position as the largest opposition party, threatening the LDP's majority. In this sense, despite an increase in conservative-leaning and more radical anti-LGBTQ+ parties, the 2024 general election showed some positive signs for the future of Japanese LGBTQ+ rights.

References

Abema Times. 2023. "Hyakuta Naoki ga hikiru Nihon Hoshu-tō Ga mezasu 'kyokutan janai hoshu' to wa?" [What is the "Non-Radical Conservatism" Aimed for by Naoki Hyakuta's Japan Conservative Party?]. September 29. https://times.abema.tv/articles/-/10097319?page=1.

Carlson, Matthew M. 2025. "Scandals During the Kishida Administration." In *Japan Decides 2024: The Japanese General Election*, edited by Kenneth M.

McElwain, Robert J. Pekkanen, and Daniel M. Smith, 217–233. Palgrave Macmillan.
Conservative Party of Japan. 2024. *Nihon Hoshu-tō no jūten seisaku kōmoku* [Key Policy Agenda of the CPJ]. https://hoshuto.jp/policy/#h01.
Constitutional Democratic Party of Japan. 2024. *Rikken minshutō seisakushū 2024* [Policies of the CDP]. https://cdp-japan.jp/assets/pdf/visions/2024/policies2024.pdf.
Democratic Party for the People. 2021. *Kokumin minshutō seisaku panfuretto* [The DPP Manifesto]. https://new-kokumin.jp/file/DPFP-PolicyPamphlet_202110.pdf.
Democratic Party for the People. 2024. *Kokumin minshutō seisaku panfuretto* [The DPP Manifesto]. https://new-kokumin.jp/file/DPFP-PolicyCollection2024.pdf.
Frühstück, Sabine. 2022. *Gender and Sexuality in Modern Japan. New Approaches to Asian History*. Cambridge University Press.
Fukatsu, Makoto. 2024. "Nihon Hoshu-tō wa 'Jimintō o bukkowasu' no ka: LGBT hō hanpatsu de ugoita ganban [Will the JCP "Destroy the LDP"? The Base Mobilized by Opposition to the LGBT Law]." *Mainichi Shinbun*, October 28. https://mainichi.jp/articles/20241027/k00/00m/010/038000c.
Furugaki, Hiroto, and Daisuke Nakamura. 2021. "'Sabetsu wa yurusarenai' wa dame? LGBT hōan ni yureta Jimintō [Is "Discrimination is Unacceptable" Not Allowed? The LDP Shaken by the LGBT Bill]." *NHK*, June 16. https://www.nhk.or.jp/politics/articles/feature/62170.html.
G7. 2022. "G7 Leaders' Communiqué." https://www.g7germany.de/resource/blob/974430/2062292/fbdb2c7e996205aee402386aae057c5e/2022-07-14-leaders-communique-data.pdf.
Gubbala, Sneha, Jacob Poushter, and Christine Huang. 2023. *How People Around the World View Same-Sex Marriage*. Pew Research Center. https://www.pewresearch.org/short-reads/2023/11/27/how-people-around-the-world-view-same-sex-marriage/.
Human Rights Watch. 2021. "The Law Undermines Dignity." May 25. https://www.hrw.org/report/2021/05/25/law-undermines-dignity/momentum-revise-japans-legal-gender-recognition-process.
Ipsos. 2024. *LGBT+ PRIDE 2024: A 26-Country Ipsos Global Advisor Survey*. https://www.ipsos.com/sites/default/files/ct/news/documents/2024-05/Pride%20Report%20FINAL_0.pdf.
Ishiba, Shigeru. 2024a. *Hoshu seijika saga seisaku, saga tenmei* [Conservative Oolitician: My Policies, My Destiny]. Kōdansha.
Ishiba, Shigeru. 2024b. "Tōbenshō" [Response to a Question], Naikaku Sanshitsu 214 Dai 13-gō. https://www.sangiin.go.jp/japanese/joho1/kousei/syuisyo/214/touh/t214013.htm.

Ishin. 2021. *Nihon Ishin no Kai seisaku teigen* [Ishin Manifesto]. https://o-ishin.jp/policy/8saku2021.html.
Ishin. 2024. *Nihon Ishin no Kai seisaku teigen* [Ishin Manifesto]. https://o-ishin.jp/shuin2024/manifest/all.html.
Japan Alliance for LGBT Legislation. 2016. *LGBT sabetsu kinshi hō ga areba* [If There Were an LGBT Discrimination Prohibition Law]. https://lgbtetc.jp/wp/wp-content/uploads/2016/03/ポンチ絵付き私案.pdf.
Japan Alliance for LGBT Legislation. 2023. *Seiteki shikō oyobi jendā aidentiti no tayōsei ni kansuru kokumin no rikai no zōshin ni kansuru hōritsuan no seiritsu ni tsuite no seimei* [Statement on the Enactment of the Bill to Promote Public Understanding of Diversity in Sexual Orientation and Gender Identity]. June 19. https://lgbtetc.jp/news/2878/.
Japan Alliance for LGBT Legislation. 2024. "LGBT (SOGI) o meguru kadai ni kansuru Rakutō no seisaku to kangaekata ni tsuite no chōsa kekka hōkoku" [Report on Survey Results Regarding Party Policies and Perspectives on Issues Surrounding LGBT (SOGI)]. *LGBT Hō Rengō Kai* (blog). October 16. https://lgbtetc.jp/news/3139/.
The Japan Times. 2023. "U.S. Envoy to Japan Hopes for 'Clear, Unambiguous' LGBTQ Legislation." February 16. https://www.japantimes.co.jp/news/2023/02/16/national/us-japan-hopes-lgbtq-legislation.
The Japanese Communist Party. 2024a. *Nihon Kyōsantō sōsenkyo seisaku* [The JCP Manifesto]. https://www.jcp.or.jp/web_download/2024/10/2024-senkyo-sei-p.pdf.
The Japanese Communist Party. 2024b. "Seiteki mainoritī, LGBT/SOGI" [Sexual Minority, LGBT/SOGI]. https://www.jcp.or.jp/web_policy/2024/10/202410-bunya15.html.
Kawasaka, Kazuyoshi. 2018. "Contradictory Discourses on Sexual Normality and National Identity in Japanese Modernity." *Sexuality & Culture* 22 (2): 593–613. https://doi.org/10.1007/s12119-017-9485-z.
Kawasaka, Kazuyoshi. 2023. "Queers and National Anxiety: Discourses on Gender and Sexuality from Anti-Gender Backlash Movements in Japan since the 2000s." In *Global Perspectives on Anti-feminism: Far-Right and Religious Attacks on Equality and Diversity*, edited by Stefanie Mayer and Judith Goetz, 182–20. Edinburgh University Press.
Kawasaka, Kazuyoshi. 2024. "The Progress of LGBT Rights in Japan in the 2010s." In *Beyond Diversity: Queer Politics, Activism, and Representation in Contemporary Japan*, edited by Kazuyoshi Kawasaka and Stefan Würrer, 21–38. Düsseldorf University Press. https://doi.org/10.1515/9783110767995-005.
Kawasaka, Kazuyoshi. 2025. "Human Rights and Affective Diplomacy: The Presence and Strategies of Foreign Embassies in LGBTQ rights Activism in Japan." *Sexualities*. Sage. https://doi.org/10.1177/13634607241304543.

Kawasaka, Kazuyoshi, and Stefan Würrer. 2024. "Introduction: A New Age of Visibility? LGBTQ+ Issues in Contemporary Japan." In *Beyond Diversity*, edited by Kazuyoshi Kawasaka and Stefan Würrer, 1–20. De Gruyter. https://doi.org/10.1515/9783110767995-004.

International Federation for Victory over Communism. 2022. "Dantai gaiyō: Kokusai Shōkyō Rengō to wa" [Overview: What is the IFVOC]. https://www.ifvoc.org/about_us/.

Law, David S. 2009. "The Anatomy of a Conservative Court: Judicial Review in Japan." In *Public Law in East Asia*, vol. 87, 1545–93.

Liberal Democratic Party of Japan. 2016. *Seiteki shikō / sei jinin no tayōna arikata o juyō suru shakai o mezasu tame no wagatō no kihontekina kangaekata* [Our Basic Views towards the Society Accepting the Diversity of Sexual Orientation and Sexual Identity]. https://www.jimin.jp/news/policy/132172.html.

Liberal Democratic Party of Japan. 2024. *Jimintō reiwa 6-nen seiken kōyaku* [The 2024 LDP Manufesto]. https://storage2.jimin.jp/pdf/pamphlet/202410_manifest.pdf.

Maree, Claire. 2004. "Same-Sex Partnerships in Japan: Bypasses and Other Alternatives." *Women's Studies* 33 (4): 541–49. https://doi.org/10.1080/00497870490464396.

Maree, Claire. 2020. "'LGBT Issues' and the 2020 Games." *The Asia-Pacific Journal Japan Focus* 18, 4–7. https://apjjf.org/2020/4/Maree.html.

Marriage for All. 2023. *Rikai Zōshin Hōan kishakaiken no hōkoku* [Report on the Press Conference for the Bill on LGBTQ+ Understanding Promotion]. June 16. https://www.marriageforall.jp/blog/20230616/.

Matsumoto, Tomoko. 2025. "How Party Manifestos Framed Political Distrust in the 2024 Election." In *Japan Decides 2024: The Japanese General Election*, edited by Kenneth M. McElwain, Robert J. Pekkanen, and Daniel M. Smith, 143–161. Palgrave Macmillan.

McLaughlin, Levi. 2025. "Perennial Fears, Novel Responses: The Unification Church in Japan after the Abe Assassination." In *Japan Decides 2024: The Japanese General Election*, edited by Kenneth M. McElwain, Robert J. Pekkanen, and Daniel M. Smith, 235–253. Palgrave Macmillan.

McLelland, Marc. 2005. *Queer Japan from the Pacific War to the Internet Age*. Rowman & Littlefield.

Nemoto, Kuniaki. 2025. "Reasons behind the LDP's Loss in the 2024 Election." In *Japan Decides 2024: The Japanese General Election*, edited by Kenneth M. McElwain, Robert J. Pekkanen, and Daniel M. Smith, 37–55. Palgrave Macmillan.

Nikaidō, Yuki. 2017. "Hyōryū suru LGBT hōan" [An Uncertain LGBT Rights Bill]. *Sekai*, vol. 5, 167–72.

Organisation for Economic Co-operation and Development. 2020. *Over the Rainbow? The Road to LGBTI Inclusion*. https://doi.org/10.1787/8d2fd1a8-en.

Reiwa. 2024. *Reiwa Shinsengumi manifesuto* [The Reiwa Manifesto]. https://shu50.reiwa-shinsengumi.com/wp-content/themes/shu50reiwa/assets/pdf/reiwa_2024_election_manifest.pdf.

Rich, Motoko, and Hikari Hida. 2023. "The Religious Right's Hidden Sway as Japan Trails Allies on Gay Rights." *The New York Times* (Online), May 17. https://www.nytimes.com/2023/05/17/world/asia/japan-same-sex-marriage.html.

Saikō Saibansho Hanketsu. 2023. *Reiwa 2nen (ku) dai 993-gō*. Saikōsai daihōtei.

Sakaguchi, Hirohiko, Chiharu Shibue, and Hiroyuki Tanaka. 2023. "Kyū Tōitsu Kyōkai 'han LGBTQ' 02-nen kara senmei" [Former Unification Church: "Anti-LGBTQ" Stance Clear Since 2002]. *Mainichi Shinbun* (Online), April 23. https://mainichi.jp/articles/20230422/k00/00m/040/145000c.

Sanseitō. 2024. *Sanseitō kōyaku 2024* [Sanseitō manifesto 2024]. https://www.sanseito.jp/50th_hore_policy/.

Social Democratic Party. 2024. *2024 shūgi'in sōsenkyo kōyaku* [Manifesto for 2024 General Election]. https://sdp.or.jp/2024-50-manifesto/.

Taniguchi, Masaki, Asano, Taka-aki, Ōmori, Shōko, and Shūsuke Takamiya. 2025. "Policy Positions of the Candidates." In *Japan Decides 2024: The Japanese General Election*, edited by Kenneth M. McElwain, Robert J. Pekkanen, and Daniel M. Smith, 125–142. Palgrave Macmillan.

Taniguchi, Hiroyuki. 2024. "LGBTQ Human Rights in Japanese Laws and Policies." In *Beyond Diversity: Queer Politics, Activism, and Representation in Contemporary Japan*, edited by Kazuyoshi Kawasaka and Stefan Würrer. Düsseldorf University Press. https://doi.org/10.1515/9783110767995-007.

Yamaguchi, Tomomi. 2014. "'Gender Free' Feminism in Japan: A Story of Mainstreaming and Backlash." *Feminist Studies* 40 (3): 541–72.

Yamaguchi, Tomomi, and Masami Saitō. 2023. *Shūkyō uha to feminizumu* [The Religious Right and Feminism]. Seikyūsha.

CHAPTER 17

Childcare Policy in the 2024 Election: Who Resonated with the Public Amid an Unprecedented Birthrate Decline?

Reiko Arami

CHILDCARE POLICY AS A WICKED PROBLEM IN JAPANESE POLITICS

This chapter clarifies the position of childcare policies in the 2024 election. Since the "1.57 Shock" in 1990, Japan has faced one of its most significant challenges: a declining birthrate and aging population, accompanied by a shrinking population. Japan's elderly population ratio stands at 29.3%, the highest in the world,[1] with projections for 2024 indicating a birthrate of 685,000, a total fertility rate of 1.15, and 475,000 marriages—all at record lows (*Nikkei Shinbun*, December 3, 2024).[2] Additionally, the trends toward remaining unmarried and marrying later

---

[1] Ministry of Internal Affairs and Communications, Statistics Bureau, "Population Estimates," 2024.
[2] Based on a survey by Japan Research Institute Research Eye No. 2024-075.

R. Arami (✉)
Nagoya University, Nagoya, Japan
e-mail: arami.reiko.s8@f.mail.nagoya-u.ac.jp

© The Author(s), under exclusive license to Springer Nature Switzerland AG 2025
K. M. McElwain et al. (eds.), *Japan Decides 2024*,
https://doi.org/10.1007/978-3-031-98797-7_17

in life are accelerating. The government has been unable to implement effective measures to halt the decline in birthrates. As a result, household structures are changing, with a significant decrease in the number of child-rearing households (18.1%, down from 46.2% in 1986) and an increase in single-person households (34.0%, up from 18.2% in 1986),[3] while the number of dual-income households is also increasing, the employment rate of mothers in households with children has increased from 56.7% in 2004 to 77.8% in 2023. As a result of these significant changes in societal structure, the "standard household" model of two married adults (one employed) and two children, which had served as the foundation for various systems, has become a minority group accounting for less than 5% of the population. This shift has also led to significant changes in people's attitudes toward child-rearing. According to a survey by the Nippon Foundation,[4] among those without children, 37.2% desire to have children, while 35.7% do not, with both groups accounting for approximately one-third of the population. The physical and mental costs of child-rearing and reproduction are increasing due to factors such as rising education and housing costs caused by the concentration of population in the Tokyo metropolitan area, long working hours that have not yet been sufficiently improved, and the still significant imbalance in the division of household and care work between men and women. These factors are no longer considered "normal."

The labor shortage caused by the declining birthrate and aging population, which began in the mid-2010s, has had an impact on the economy, and childcare policies have become an urgent policy issue that requires political action. However, childcare policies are a difficult issue for politicians in elections. First, it is not only a national issue but also varies in severity and type depending on regional population distributions. Second, it is difficult to achieve short-term results, making it hard to appeal to voters in elections. Third, while childcare policies require significant funding, the number of households with children—the narrowly defined beneficiaries—has been decreasing to less than 20%, making it challenging to appeal to other segments of the population. As exemplified by issues such as childcare facilities in NIMBY disputes and debates over "Entitled

---

[3] Ministry of Health, Labour and Welfare, Household Statistics Office, Overview of "Comprehensive Survey of Living Conditions" 2023 (Press release dated July 5, 2024).

[4] Nippon Foundation "Report on the Survey of Public Awareness Regarding the Declining Birthrate" (November 29, 2024).

Parents (*Komochi-sama*),"[5] demographic changes like declining birthrates and later marriages lead to greater diversity, accelerating social divisions and giving rise to both intergenerational and intra-generational conflicts. While opposition to such policies is generally difficult to justify in principle, disputes emerge when specific resource allocations are required.

In the 2024 general election, issues such as the economy, employment, price stabilization, social security, and political corruption stemming from the Liberal Democratic Party's slush fund scandal[6] became key points of contention (see Carlson 2025; Ko Maeda 2025; Umeda 2025), making childcare policies a lesser concern than in recent elections. What does this mean for Japanese politics, given that child-rearing households now account for less than one-fifth of the population? This chapter will clarify how childcare policies were positioned in the election strategies of each political party in 2024 and what kinds of childcare policies were supported. It also attempts to examine from a political perspective why Japan has been unable to implement effective low birthrate countermeasures.

The first section provides an overview of the childcare policies of the ruling party and changes in the circumstances and needs surrounding childcare, focusing on the period following the 2021 general election. The second section examines the childcare policies proposed by each political party in the 2024 general election, comparing them with previous policies and highlighting what changes have occurred. The third section then clarifies how the policy trends to date are related to the election strategies of each political party in 2024. The final section addresses the impact of these choices on the election results and presents our outlook on the direction of childcare policies and Japanese politics in the future.[7]

---

[5] This refers to criticism that employees with childcare responsibilities who are forced to take time off or leave early due to their children's illness or other reasons are receiving special treatment or consideration at work (*Yomiuri Shinbun*, May 11, 2024).

[6] Nippon Television *Yomiuri Shinbun* Exit Poll "What policies did you prioritize?" "Economic conditions and employment" was the top priority across many age groups (October 27, 2024, 11:16 PM) https://news.ntv.co.jp/category/politics/90998a8919d3 459cbf50ff71d1e0f78b (Last accessed April 17, 2025).

[7] In this paper, reflecting the reality that policies to address declining birthrates, childcare support policies, and childcare policies, which should be distinguished from a policy perspective, are largely indistinguishable in Japanese politics, the term "childcare policy" is used as a concept that encompasses all three.

Positioning Childcare Policy Within Japanese Politics Before the 2024 Election

Childcare policies became a major election issue in Japanese politics following the 2009 general election, when the Democratic Party of Japan (DPJ) came to power with a platform centered on the "child allowance (*Kodomo-Teate*)." Prior to that, the need to address the declining birthrate was recognized as an issue, but efforts were limited to measures supporting work-life balance, such as the expansion of childcare facilities and the introduction of parental leave systems, with limited financial investment. Until 2009, family-related social spending as a percentage of GDP remained below 1%.[8] Although the DPJ did not fully fulfill its initial campaign promises, it made progress in securing stable funding through the "integrated reform of social security and taxation," leading to the implementation of the "Child and Childcare Support System" in 2015.

This trend continued under the second Abe administration, with progress made on cash benefits, measures to reduce the number of children on waiting lists for childcare facilities, and the provision of free early childhood and higher education. Policies were linked to economic policies such as "revitalizing local communities" and "human resource development," leading to progress in expanding childcare facilities, promoting women's participation in the workforce, and improving childcare leave systems. In fiscal 2020, family-related social spending reached 2.01% of GDP. Furthermore, under the Suga administration, a "social security reform for all generations" was proposed, including measures such as insurance coverage for infertility treatment and the promotion of paternity leave. As a result of the continued expansion of policies by the LDP and Kōmeitō, childcare policies have come to occupy an important position as a political issue, and many politicians have highlighted them as electoral priorities since 2012. In particular, the 2016 blog post titled "Japan, where you can't get into a nursery school, is a place to die!" sparked public outrage and heightened awareness. As shown in Figs. 17.1 and 17.2, which uses the Political Leader data from the University of

---

[8] Cabinet Secretariat, All-Generations Social Security Construction Headquarters, Secretariat for the Future of Children and Childcare Strategy Meeting (1st Meeting), Document 5-3: "Strengthening Childcare and Child-Rearing Policies (Draft)" (Reference Materials) (April 7, 2023).

Tokyo and Asahi Survey (UTAS),[9] the percentage of candidates in HR and HC elections who selected "Education and Childcare" as a policy they prioritize consistently increased in past elections, and in recent years, more than half of all candidates have included it among their top three priorities.

The importance of childcare policies has expanded beyond national elections to local elections, with local governments implementing a variety of support measures, such as medical expense subsidies. Since the late 2010s, political parties have also begun to emphasize the "free provision" of education. In the 2017 HR election, the LDP proposed making early childhood and higher education free, making it a key campaign issue (see also Pekkanen et al. 2018). Prior to this shift, childcare policies had

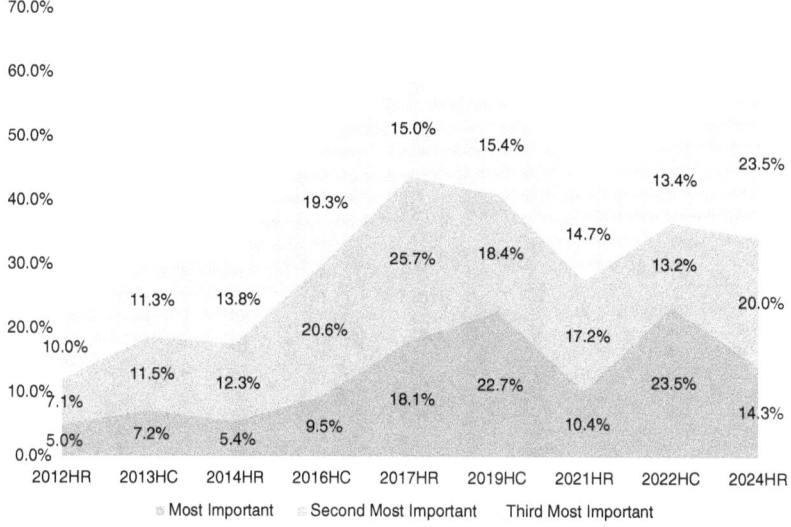

Fig. 17.1 Percentage of candidates who selected "Education and Childcare" as the policy they consider most important in this election (UTAS)

---

[9] Compiled by the author based on data from the University of Tokyo's Taniguchi Laboratory and *Asahi Shinbun* survey (UTAS). Since time-series data is available, the UTAS survey was used. Note that starting in 2022, one question was added (infection control measures in 2022 and digital policy in 2024), increasing the total number of questions from 16 to 17, so caution is required when making comparisons.

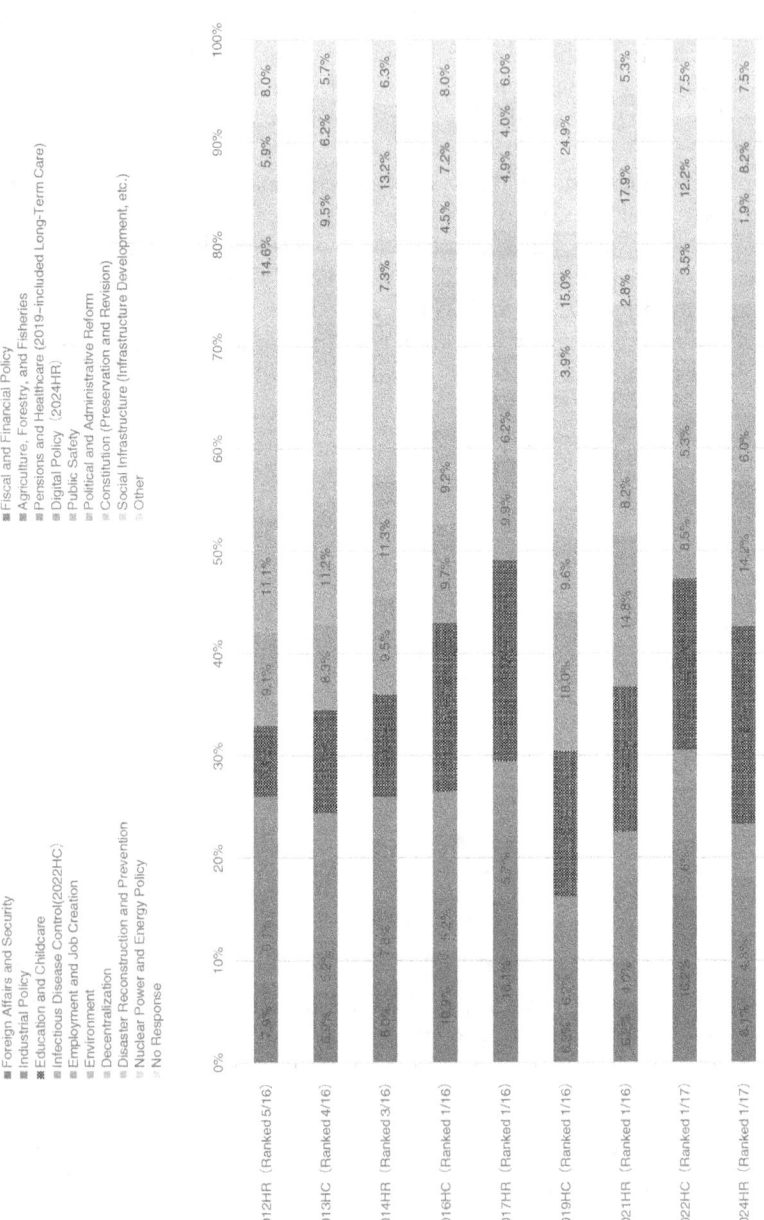

Fig. 17.2 Average percentage of candidates who selected the following policies as top-three priorities (UTAS)

focused on reducing the number of children on waiting lists for childcare facilities, expanding access to diverse childcare options, and improving the working conditions of childcare staff. However, the focus gradually shifted to a competition over "what to make free." By around 2021, some observers noted that the policies of various parties were beginning to converge.[10]

Under the Kishida administration, with the goal of reversing the declining birthrate trend by the 2030s, the Ministry for Children and Families (2023) and the Children's Future Strategy were established, and the Plan for Accelerating Support for Children and Childcare, with a focus on the period from 2024 to 2026, was launched. The pillars of the policy[11] are as follows:

1. **Strengthening economic support**: Expanding child allowances (removing income restrictions, extending payments to high school students, and increasing payments for third and subsequent children), providing economic support at the time of childbirth, raising temporary childbirth and childcare allowances and considering insurance coverage, providing housing support, and expanding scholarship programs.
2. **Support for all households**: Establishing a "childcare system for all children," revising childcare facility standards for 1-year-olds and 4- and 5-year-olds, improving childcare worker treatment, expanding after-school childcare clubs to break down the "first-grade barrier," strengthening support for children in poverty, abuse, and with disabilities, expanding child support allowances (raising the income ceiling), and removing income restrictions on support for assistive devices, etc.

---

[10] For example, "Promise Comparison... Free Education Competition" https://www.yomiuri.co.jp/election/shugiin/20211026-OYT8T50202/ (*Yomiuri Shinbun*, October 27, 2021).

[11] Ministry of Children and Families, "2024 Children's White Paper: Special Feature② Measures to Address the Different Dimensions of the Low Birthrate," pp. 54–62, https://www.cfa.go.jp/assets/contents/node/basic_page/field_ref_resources/0357b0f6-8b14-47fc-83eb-2654172c2803/6798e91e/20241009_resources_white-paper_r06_14.pdf. (Last accessed on April 18, 2025), Cabinet Secretariat, "Child and Future Strategy" (approved by the Cabinet on December 22, 2023) https://www.cas.go.jp/jp/seisaku/kodomo_mirai/index.html (Last accessed on April 18, 2025).

3. **Support for dual-income and co-parenting families**: Setting a target for raising the rate of men taking paternity leave to 85% by 2030, strengthening subsidies for small and medium-sized enterprises, ensuring full payment of paternity leave benefits, introducing benefits for shortened work hours during childcare leave and exemptions from national pension insurance premiums, and establishing a "parent-child flexible work system."

Through these measures, 3.6 trillion yen will be invested by fiscal year 2028, with the goal of increasing the ratio of family-related expenditures to GDP to 16% (on par with Sweden, which leads the OECD). Funding will be secured through a support grant system combined with medical insurance premiums, the issuance of special bonds, and the establishment of a special account. Additionally, local governments will be responsible for implementing these policies, and measures to address their fiscal burdens[12] have also been established. Table 17.1 summarizes the main policies and implementation schedules related to support for young carers.

CHILDCARE POLICY IN THE 2024 ELECTION CAMPAIGNS AND DETERMINING FACTORS FOR EACH PARTY'S STRATEGY

As the ruling coalition moved forward with major reforms in childcare and family policies, a central question in the 2024 general election was how each political party sought to differentiate itself.[13] The characteristics of each party's childcare-related policies in the election campaign can be

---

[12] Measures include allocating expenditures in local fiscal plans, implementing local government-specific projects in accordance with regional circumstances through tax allocation measures, and establishing a new calculation item for general tax allocation for "childcare and child-rearing expenses." Ministry of Internal Affairs and Communications (2024), "Part 3: Responses to Recent Issues in Local Finance 1. Strengthening Policies for Children and Childcare," "The State of Local Finance," pp. 119–120.

[13] Table 17.2 is based on each party's policy platforms, with summaries primarily drawn from NHK's election website for each election. Sanseitō and the Conservative Party of Japan are not included, because changes from 2021 were unclear and their childcare policies lacked distinctive features.

Table 17.1 Key measures of Acceleration Plan and implementation schedule for childcare policies

Effective Date	Revisions
Date of Promulgation October 1, 2024	· Strengthened support for young carers · Fundamental expansion of child allowance · Response to expiration of the temporary measure for free access to unlicensed childcare facilities not meeting standards · Issuance of special government bonds for child and child-rearing support
November 1, 2024	· Increase in additional amount of child-rearing allowance for third and subsequent children
April 1, 2025	· Introduction of support benefits for pregnant women and comprehensive consultation support programs · Institutionalization of the "Universal Access to Nursery Program" into regional child-rearing support services · Development of postpartum care service provision system (also positioned under regional child-rearing support) · Implementation of ongoing visualization of management information · Revision of contributions for child-rearing support · Introduction of benefits for postnatal leave and short-time work during child-rearing · Establishment of a special account for child-rearing support
April 1, 2026	· Formalization of the Universal Access to Nursery Program as a benefit · Establishment of a financial support system for child-rearing
October 1, 2026	· Introduction of national pension premium exemption during child-rearing period for Category I insured persons under the National Pension system

summarized as follows. (A broader overview of parties' policy pledges can be found in Taniguchi et al. 2025, and Matsumoto 2025.)

The LDP outlined a comprehensive policy, including the "Child Future Strategy" and a 3.6 trillion yen "Acceleration Plan," to expand child allowances, reduce higher education costs, significantly increase paternity leave uptake among men, improve working conditions for child-care workers, and develop a comprehensive childcare support system. This included the "Childcare for All" system and the expansion of after-school childcare clubs.

The Kōmeitō, building on its long-standing achievements in securing free preschool education, tuition-free private high schools, and grant-based scholarships through negotiations with the LDP, adopted the slogan "Children's Happiness First." Its campaign policies included tuition-free universities, the substantial elimination of childbirth-related expenses, promotion of pain-free childbirth, nationwide expansion of the "Childcare for All" system, flexible work arrangements and enhanced support for young caregivers, and the expansion of child allowance benefits. In addition, it advocated measures to respond to issues such as sexual violence and sexual crimes, risks related to social media use, and truancy and bullying. These proposals aimed to address the challenges faced by all households that had been underserved by existing government policies.

Ishin proposed "free education leading to free childcare," advocating for the constitutional enshrinement of free education for all educational programs and the reduction of hidden education costs, such as meal and textbook fees. The party also proposed its own "N-part N-article system" (household-based taxation), which included support for infertility treatment, assistance for children requiring medical care or living with disabilities, measures to address joint custody and child support issues, and the promotion of visitation rights. These policies aligned closely with the LDP's gender-conservative family policies. Ishin also stood out for its policies supporting private-sector education and care, including the provision of childbirth and childcare vouchers, tutoring vouchers, improvements in the working conditions of childcare workers, and tax cuts linked to the rate of male paternity leave uptake.

The Democratic Party for the People (DPP) declared that "building people is building the nation," and explicitly stated that it would abolish all income restrictions related to the free provision of childcare, education, medical care, school meals, and textbooks, while also expanding child allowances. In addition to increasing grant-based scholarships, the party also proposed reducing the repayment burden for existing scholarship recipients, including those from the "lost generation," reinstating the tax deduction for infertility treatment. It also advocated for "remittance deductions," "tutoring expense deductions," tax-exempt public benefits, free admission to public facilities, and other measures to reduce household financial burdens. The DPP further proposed the "Disposable Time Guarantee Act," support for gifted children and truant students, and the introduction of a child death verification system. These original policies aimed to address the detailed needs of the working generation and were designed to prevent divisions between child-rearing and working generations, enhancing their appeal.

The Constitutional Democratic Party (CDP) emphasized the free provision of school lunches at public elementary and middle schools, the elimination or reduction of university tuition fees, and the provision of a 15,000 yen child allowance. It also proposed improving teachers' working conditions, reducing class sizes, promoting free preschool education and childcare for children aged 0–2, abolishing income restrictions on high school tuition fees, allowing income tax deductions for loan-based scholarship repayments, providing scholarship repayment support, and establishing a Children's Commissioner. The party also focused on expanding child allowance payments and childcare leave systems for non-regular employees and freelancers, targeting groups not covered by the current administration.

The Japanese Communist Party (JCP) put "zero tuition fees" at the forefront of its platform, calling for an immediate 50% reduction in tuition fees and the elimination of entrance fees, the creation of grant-based scholarships, a 50% reduction in scholarship repayment, free medical care for children until high school graduation, free preschool education and childcare without income restrictions, and the elimination of school lunch and textbook fees as part of the national system. It also proposed improvements in the treatment of workers supporting children and the establishment of related systems. However, the JCP's policy platform did not include a separate section on "child-rearing."

Reiwa Shinsengumi, under the slogan "Ending the Parent Lottery," unveiled the boldest fiscal spending proposals, including a monthly child allowance of 30,000 yen until high school graduation without income restrictions, fully free childcare, school meals, medical care, and after-school programs, and free education up to graduate school. Its platform also featured a scholarship amnesty (waiving repayment), a doubling of salaries for childcare workers and teachers, full wage compensation during parental leave, and the restoration of the dependent deduction for young children, all of which aimed to completely eliminate the economic burden on families raising children.

The positions of each political party can be summarized as follows. First, in the 2024 general election, many political parties proposed the elimination of fees and the expansion of benefits for childcare and education policies, indicating a convergence in policy direction. Regarding the "Acceleration Plan," doubts about its effectiveness had been raised since its announcement,[14] but as in the 2021 election, while the policy direction of the ruling parties remained unchanged, there was an increase in policies that expand the scale of benefits. In particular, opposition parties identified the elimination of fees for higher education and school lunches, as well as the expansion of grant-based scholarships, as common priorities. Additionally, regarding in-kind benefits, housing support and rent subsidies were proposed by all parties, and there was also common ground in addressing the diverse support needs of children. Overall, there was a growing trend toward abolishing income restrictions, and there was a stronger emphasis on the role of the national government in addressing regional disparities.

Although the level of emphasis varied among the parties, many shared the same direction as the ruling coalition. Regarding childbirth expenses, while the government has announced policies to increase the childbirth allowance and apply insurance coverage, all parties except the DPP advocated insurance coverage, free services, and expanded support. As for seamless support from pregnancy through childbirth and childcare, the CDP, Ishin, and the DPP emphasized the enhancement of Neuvola[15] and consultation systems, while the JCP advocated for the nationalization of postpartum care programs. The DPP not only highlighted the free provision of postpartum care, but also free home visits for infants under one year old and free rest support services for parents caring for infants.

In terms of "hidden education costs" such as textbook fees, school supplies, and field trip expenses, all opposition parties except the Social Democratic Party (SDP) and Reiwa called for free provision. Many parties, excluding the Ishin and Reiwa, also advocated expanding child

---

[14] *Nikkei Shinbun*, December 14, 2023, "(Editorial) Can we have hope for the future with these measures to address the declining birthrate?" https://www.nikkei.com/article/DGKKZO77223430T21C23A2EA1000/ (last accessed on April 18, 2025).

[15] Neuvola refers to regional health checkup and counseling support centers targeting families with children from pregnancy to preschool age, which have developed in Finland (https://neuvola.com/), and the counseling support services provided by public health nurses and other professionals at these centers. In Japan, this system has been adopted to provide seamless support from pregnancy to childbirth and parenting. In 2017, the "Child-rearing Generation Comprehensive Support Center (Japanese version of Neuvola)" was established by law, and one-stop centers (Child-rearing Generation Comprehensive Support Centers) were established to provide seamless support from the prenatal period to the child-rearing period. However, the implementing entities are local governments, and there are currently differences in the content and quality of services provided depending on the local government.

allowance benefits. While improving the quality of childcare was a common policy goal, with a focus on improving the staffing and working conditions of childcare workers, Reiwa proposed making childcare workers public servants, while the JCP emphasized promoting the regularization of childcare workers' status. The CDP and Reiwa also presented specific wage increases.

Support for households with children of diverse backgrounds, such as childcare for sick children, medical care for children with special needs, and support for families with multiple births, as well as support for children living in poverty, children with developmental disabilities, and young caregivers, generally aligns with the direction of strengthening support. Support for children in need of social welfare, victims of child abuse, and the foster care system was a priority for the CDP, the Ishin, and Reiwa, though it was mentioned by nearly all political parties.

Regarding work-style reforms, while the government has decided to raise the parental leave allowance rate, introduce new allowances for reduced working hours, promote parental leave for men, and establish a flexible work style selection system, each party made additional proposals, such as the CDP's "Papa Quota," the DPP's mandatory parental leave, and the JCP, Ishin, and Reiwa parties' support measures for businesses.

Second, differences in direction were evident in individual policies. In early childhood education and childcare, the LDP focused on expanding the scope of the "childcare for all" program, while opposition parties converged on the common goal of abolishing income restrictions to achieve free childcare (except for the SDP). The CDP proposed expanding temporary childcare services. In childbirth-related policies, support for pain-free childbirth (Kōmeitō and Reiwa), infertility treatment support (Ishin, DPP, and JCP), and support for prenatal examination costs (CDP, DPP, JCP, and Reiwa) were among the key points.

Regarding scholarship repayment support, Kōmeitō, the CDP, the JCP, and the SDP advocated strengthening support, while the LDP and the Ishin made no mention of it. The DPP and Reiwa proposed policies to support those who had already received loans. While the government has indicated its intention to expand child allowances, there were differences among parties in the preferred amount based on the number and age of children. The CDP and the DPP proposed a uniform amount of 15,000 yen, while Reiwa proposed 30,000 yen. While the government has decided to expand both the quality and quantity of childcare services,

Ishin and the SDP made no mention of this. Responses varied, with the CDP and the JCP aiming to eliminate waiting lists for childcare, the CDP, the DPP, the JCP, and Reiwa focusing on improving staff treatment and quality, and the DPP and the JCP proposing to make after-school care and snack costs free.

Economic support for child-rearing households was also diverse, with Ishin proposing education vouchers and a household tax system, the DPP advocating tax deductions and tax-exempt grants, and the JCP and Reiwa parties prioritizing free medical care for children. There were also differences in in-kind benefits, such as smaller class sizes (CDP and Ishin) and air conditioner installation (Kōmeitō and DPP). Double care support was a priority for Kōmeitō, Ishin, and the DPP.

Regarding labor reform, there were two approaches: regulatory (the JCP's restrictions on transfers and overtime consent system) and supportive (Reiwa's 50% increase in overtime pay and the DPP's law to ensure disposable time). In family and gender policies, positions diverged on issues such as measures against sexual crimes and revisions to the custody system. For example, the Japanese version of the Disclosure and Barring Service (DBS) was promoted by Kōmeitō, the CDP, the DPP, and the JCP, while Ishin (promotion of joint custody) and Reiwa (revision of joint custody) mentioned related issues.

Finally, while each party proposed various free or cost-reducing policies, the issue of securing funding did not gain significant traction. The government planned to introduce a supplementary subsidy system for medical insurance, claiming that there would be no actual burden on taxpayers. In response, the CDP proposed transferring and utilizing the Bank of Japan's ETF holdings, Ishin suggested a GDP-linked budget framework, and the DPP proposed doubling education spending through the issuance of 5 trillion yen in education bonds annually. These reflect notable differences in fiscal strategy among parties.

The Determinants of Party Strategies and Their Electoral Impact

The strategies of each political party exhibited notable diversity, but their policy content can be broadly divided into two categories. First, there were policies that the government was already promoting and were believed to be popular among voters, such as expanding the scope of beneficiaries and increasing the amount of benefits. In particular, the abolition of income restrictions and support for diverse needs unrelated to children's attributes were advocated by most parties, often in the form of free services or expanded benefits to compensate for the ruling party's shortcomings. Second, regarding policies where the government's stance was not yet clear, responses diverged. This reflected differences between left- and right-wing parties on issues such as the extent to which parental responsibility for child-rearing should be emphasized (joint custody, sexual violence, child safety, etc.) and intervention policies related to reproductive rights. Measures for adults in disadvantaged situations, such as those of the "ice age generation" (scholarship repayment or exemption for existing borrowers), economic support for child-rearing households, views on public education (support for cram schools, etc.), and steps toward work-style reform, also reflected differences in economic philosophies between left-wing and right-wing parties. Furthermore, each party's unique childcare policy menu reflected which segments of the population they hoped to gain support from and whether coordination with support groups was necessary. This can be seen as a manifestation of the fact that childcare policies have progressed to a certain extent and now overlap with broader family policies, gender policies, and economic policies, rather than being limited to narrowly defined childcare policies and work-life balance support measures.

Did these strategies influence the election results? In this election, candidate surveys indicated that measures to address the declining birthrate and childcare and education policies were considered important issues. However, exit polls[16] conducted by Nippon Television and *Yomiuri Shinbun* after the election showed that population decline countermeasures ranked second out of 11 items among those in their 30s, third among those in their 20s and 40s, fourth among those in their teens and 50s, and ninth or lower among those in their 60s and 70s, indicating that even child-rearing generations prioritized the economy, employment, high prices, and politics and money.

The DPP and the Reiwa Shinsengumi significantly increased their seats in the proportional representation (PR) districts, but when examining the

---

[16] Nippon Television *Yomiuri Shinbun* Exit Poll "What policies do you prioritize?" "Economic Conditions and Employment" Dominates Across Many Generations (October 27, 2024, 11:16 PM) https://news.ntv.co.jp/category/politics/90998a8919d3459cbf50f f71d1e0f78b (Last accessed April 17, 2025).

voting preferences by age group in PR,[17] the DPP ranked first among voters in their 20s and 30s, second among those in their teens, and third among those in their 40s and 50s, while Reiwa ranked fourth among voters in their teens–50s. On child-rearing policies, the DPP and Reiwa espoused unique proposals not shared by other parties, such as a scholarship amnesty, the restoration of the dependent allowance for younger children, ensuring that wages during childcare leave are effectively 100% guaranteed, support for securing substitute staff for those on childcare leave, and clarifying regulations to prevent maternity leave and childcare leave from becoming obstacles to salary increases or promotions. These measures aimed to make it easier for people to take childcare leave in practice. Based solely on these results, it cannot be conclusively stated that the child-rearing generation prioritized measures to address the declining birthrate, child-rearing, and education policies, and that this led to the rise of these two parties. However, it cannot be denied that their emphasis on household support manifested in their child-rearing policies and garnered support.

On the other hand, does prioritizing childcare and education policies lead to more votes in each electoral district? We conducted a simple analysis using NHK's candidate survey,[18] voting results,[19] and data from the 2020 National Census.[20] We performed a regression analysis[21] with the vote share in single-member districts as the dependent variable and whether the candidate selected "childcare and education policies" as

---

[17] Nippon Television *Yomiuri Shinbun* Exit Poll and *Asahi Shinbun* Exit Poll: "Younger Voters Support Democratic Party for the People, Proportional Representation Sees Significant Increase" *Asahi Shinbun* Exit Poll: HR Election" (October 29, 2024, 5:00 AM) https://digital.asahi.com/articles/DA3S16070872.html (Last accessed on April 17, 2025) show similar rankings, though the percentages differ. In the 30s age group, the Reiwa Shinsengumi ranks 5th in the *Asahi Shinbun* survey.

[18] Data from questions 1, 10, and 11 of the NHK candidate questionnaire provided by Professor Miwa Hirofumi of Gakushuin University (https://www.nhk.or.jp/senkyo/database/shugiin/2024/survey/) (last accessed on April 18, 2025).

[19] Provided by Professor Yanai Yuki of Kochi Institute of Technology (last accessed on April 18, 2025).

[20] Provided by the Regional and Transportation Data Research Institute https://gtfs-gis.jp/senkyoku/ (last accessed on April 18, 2025).

[21] Since the interclass correlation for each single-member constituency was less than 0.01, a simple regression analysis was performed. The vif for this regression analysis was also less than 2 for all variables.

an area they wanted to focus on (Q1)[22] as the explanatory variable. We conducted an ordinary least squares (OLS) regression analysis with heteroskedasticity-robust (White) standard errors, controlling for candidates' gender, age, and party affiliation (represented by dummy variables for political parties that have demonstrated a proactive stance toward childcare policy—the Kōmeitō, the CDP, the DPP, and Reiwa). Additional control variables included dual candidacy, the proportion of the elderly population, and the percentage of residents who had lived in the constituency for less than five years (see Table 17.2).

As shown in Fig. 17.3, candidates who stated that they prioritized "childcare and education policies" had a negative effect on their vote share in the single-member district elections. As shown in Fig. 17.4, when other variables were fixed at their average values and the probability of vote share was calculated based on whether candidates prioritized "children and education policies," candidates who prioritized such policies had a 5.3% lower vote share compared to those who did not. In other words, at the candidate level in this election, the stance of prioritizing "children and education policies" cannot be said to have been sufficiently evaluated by voters.

THE FUTURE OF CHILDCARE POLICY AND POLITICS IN JAPAN

This chapter has shown that, although the issue of declining birthrates has been a policy issue for 30 years, it only became a major political issue under the DPJ administration, leading to the implementation of childcare policies with stable funding. Under the Abe administration, alongside policies to promote women's participation in the workforce, the government reframed measures to address declining birthrates and child-rearing support as economic policies under the banner of "regional revitalization," resulting in direct economic support for households. Since

---

[22] The questions are as follows. Q1: Areas you wish to focus on: Please select one area you would most like to focus on as a member of the HR. Answer: 1…Economic policy 2…Foreign affairs and security policy 3…Social security policy 4…Children and education policy 5…Agriculture, forestry, and fisheries policy 6…Energy and environmental policy 7…Administrative and fiscal reform 8…Political finance and political reform (issues concerning political funding and transparency) 9…Constitutional amendment 10…Disaster management and prevention 11…Regional Development 12…Other Issues 13…No Response. A dummy variable was created with 4 as 1.

Table 17.2 Childcare and education policy: descriptive statistics and variable definitions

Variable	Mean	SD	Min	Max	n	Source
Vote Share (%)	25.97	17.91	0.30	85.15	1113	2024 HR Election Results
Emphasis on Childcare/Education (1=yes)	0.17	0.37	0	1	1113	NHK Candidate Questionnaire
Gender (1=Female)	0.22	0.42	0	1	1113	2024 HR Election Results
age	54.23	11.85	25	84	1113	2024 HR Election Results
Candidate from Komeito	0.01	0.1	0	1	1113	2024 HR Election Results
Candidate from Reiwa	0.02	0.13	0	1	1113	2024 HR Election Results
Candidate from CDP	0.19	0.39	0	1	1113	2024 HR Election Results
Candidate from DPP	0.04	0.19	0	1	1113	2024 HR Election Results
Dual Candidacy (1=yes)	0.58	0.49	0	1	1113	2024 HR Election Results
% Population Over Age 65	0.28	0.05	0.17	0.42	1113	2020 National Census
% Residents < 5 Years	0.20	0.03	0.13	0.29	1113	2020 National Census

the second Abe administration, the political importance of childcare policies has consistently increased, and policies have been expanded. Amid the rapid decline in the birthrate and labor shortage, the Kishida administration adopted "fundamentally different measures to address the declining birthrate," and announced major policy reforms backed by the largest-ever budget allocation.

Although critical of the ruling parties' policies, in the 2024 HR election, the policies of the opposition parties became increasingly similar, with each party competing to offer free education to reduce the burden on households. While there were some innovative approaches to individual issues, the differences between the parties became less clear, and discussions on funding sources also failed to gain traction. As a result, the DPP and Reiwa, which successfully attracted child-rearing households by

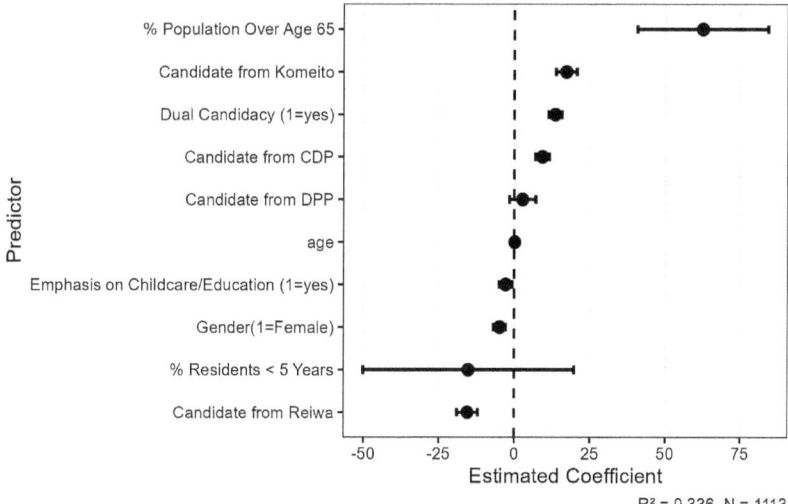

Fig. 17.3 Childcare and education policy emphasis and vote share: regression coefficient estimates with 95% CIs

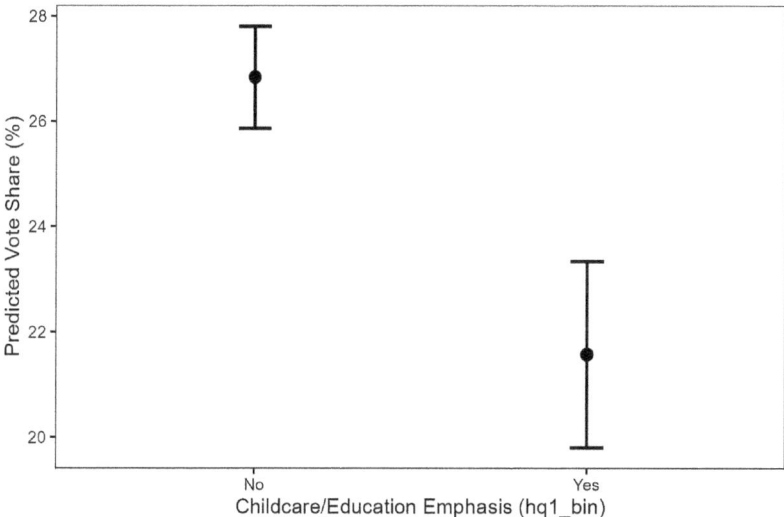

Fig. 17.4 Predicted vote share by "children and education emphasis (Yes = 1)"

incorporating unique policies, increased their votes in the proportional representation system. However, in the single-member districts, voters outside the child-rearing generation did not place much emphasis on childcare policies, and this did not translate into votes for individual candidates. As the number of child-rearing households continues to decline, a key question is how Japanese politics will address child-rearing policies, which may not necessarily deliver electoral gains.

These changes can be seen as part of a shift from the 20th-century welfare state to new social risks (Taylor-Goodby 2004), with advanced countries increasing spending on social investment policies (Hemerijcks 2015; Gingrich and Häusermann 2015; Garritzmann et al. 2018). However, Japan's characteristic feature is that its policies center on direct economic support for households rather than compensation policies (Beramendi et al. 2015).

Existing research on Japan's policies compares them with those of East Asian countries facing similar challenges of declining birthrates and mobilizing female labor, where the family-oriented regime is under strain. These studies argue that in Japan, due to the continuation of conservative government and lack of inter-party competition, the process of de-familialization of care has not progressed, leading to a return to policies based on traditional gender values through the guarantee of care costs (An and Peng 2016; Fleckenstein and Lee 2017, 2019). Alternatively, it has been argued that strong gender norms, conflicts between political leaders and bureaucrats (where the Kōmeitō may advocate for reforms but bureaucrats and the business community resist), the difficulty of raising taxes, and welfare provision dependent on corporate employment (such as housing allowances), all impede systemic reforms (Boling 2015).

Going forward, with the Liberal Democratic Party becoming a minority ruling party following the HR election, it is expected that policies advocated by the DPP and Ishin, which hold the casting vote, will be easier to implement. In fact, in addition to the Acceleration Plan, the LDP, Kōmeitō, and Ishin reached a three-party agreement in 2025 to make private high school education effectively free, abolish income restrictions, expand the "high school student scholarship grant" for low-income households to include middle-income households, and make elementary school meals free. Additionally, while policies where parties took different approaches in the election—such as Tokyo Governor Koike Yuriko's plan to eliminate childcare fees for the first child beginning in September 2025—are already being implemented locally, concerns about disparities between municipalities, particularly in neighboring prefectures, are growing. This is increasing pressure on the national government to address disparities, and it is expected that competition to implement free services will continue for some time, potentially leading to family-related expenditures on par with those in Nordic countries.

However, such policies have not separated measures to address the declining birthrate from childcare support, so while they do provide support to those who are currently able to have children, it is difficult to see how they will be effective in overcoming the "first-child barrier.[23]" To overcome gender norms (Brinton 2022) and respect reproductive rights—the right to make decisions about childbirth and marriage—it is essential to advance effective working reforms and measures to reduce long working hours promoted by the DPP and Reiwa during the recent HR election. The declining birthrate and demographic change are not only nationwide challenges in Japan but also issues of regional disparity (Matsuura 2024). Taking this into account, it is also necessary to secure adequate funding and to design and implement child-rearing policies that are both effective and comprehensible even to those without children. If this cannot be achieved, the public will lose interest in childcare policies, and Japan will have no choice but to shrink as a society.

Acknowledgements This work was supported by JSPS KAKENHI Grant Number 18K12700 and 23K22077. The author would like to express my sincere gratitude to Professor Hirofumi Miwa of Gakushuin University for providing the data related to the candidate survey, to Associate Professor Yuki Yanai of Kochi University of Technology for providing the 2024 election results, and to the Regional and Transportation Data Research Institute for providing the 2020 National Census data by single-member electoral district.

---

[23] The percentage of second and subsequent children in the total number of births is also increasing, and there is a view that there is a growing polarization between those who do not marry and have children and those who have two or more children. *Nihon Keizai Shinbun*, "Blind spots in measures to address the declining birthrate: How effective are child allowances? The 'First-Child Barrier' in Population Decline Countermeasures" (March 3, 2025, 11:00 AM), https://www.nikkei.com/article/DGXZQOUA073K00X 00C25A2000000/, last accessed April 18, 2025).

References

An, Mi Young, and Ito Peng. 2016. "Diverging Paths? A Comaprative Look at Childcare Policies in Japan, South Korea and Tiwan." *Social Policy and Administration* 50 (5): 540–558.
Beramendi, Pablo, Silja Häusermann, Herbert Kitschelt, and Hanspeter Kriesi, eds. 2015. *The Politics of Advanced Capitalism*. Cambridge University Press.
Boling, Patricia. 2015. *The Politics of Work-Family Policies: Comparing Japan, France, Germany and the United States*. Cambridge University Press.
Brinton, Mary C. 2022. *Shibarareru Nihonjin: Jinkō Genshō o Motarasu "Kihan" o Uchiyabureru ka*. Translated by Chiaki Ikemura. Tokyo: Chūō Kōron Shinsha.
Carlson, Matthew M. 2025. "Scandals During the Kishida Administration." In *Japan Decides 2024: The Japanese General Election*, edited by Kenneth M. McElwain, Robert J. Pekkanen, and Daniel M. Smith, 217–233. Palgrave Macmillan.
Fleckenstein, Timo, and Soohyun C. Lee. 2017. "The Politics of Investing in Families: Comparing Family Policy Expansion in Japan and South Korea." *Social Politics* 24 (1): 1–28.
Fleckenstein, Timo, and Soohyun C. Lee. 2019. "Roads and Barriers towards Social Investments: Comparing Labour Market and Family Policy Reforms in Europe and East Asia." *Policy and Society* 39 (2): 266–83.
Garritzmann, Julian L., Marius R. Busemeyer, and Erik Neimanns. (2018). "Public Demand for Social Investment: New Supporting Coalitions for Welfare State Reform in Western Europe?" *Journal of European Public Policy* 25 (6): 844–61.
Gingrich, Jane, and Silja Häusermann. 2015. "The Decline of the Working-Class Vote, the Reconfiguration of the Welfare Support Coalition and Consequences for the Welfare State." *Journal of European Social Policy* 25 (1): 50–75.
Hemerijck, Anton. 2015. "The Quiet Paradigm Revolution of Social Investment." *Social Politics: International Studies in Gender, State & Society* 22 (2): 242–256.
Maeda, Ko. 2025. "The 2024 Election Results: A Political Earthquake." In *Japan Decides 2024: The Japanese General Election*, edited by Kenneth M. McElwain, Robert J. Pekkanen, and Daniel M. Smith, 17–34. Palgrave Macmillan.
Matsumoto, Tomoko. 2025. "How Party Manifestos Framed Political Distrust in the 2024 Election." In *Japan Decides 2024: The Japanese General Election*, edited by Kenneth M. McElwain, Robert J. Pekkanen, and Daniel M. Smith, 143–161. Palgrave Macmillan.
Matsuura, Tsukasa. 2024. "Looking Back on 30 Years of Measures to Address the Declining Birthrate." *Japan Journal of Labor Studies* (768): 17–34.

Pekkanen, Robert J., Steven R. Reed, Ethan Scheiner and Daniel M. Smith, eds. 2018. *Japan Decides 2017: The Japanese General Election*. Palgrave Macmillan.

Takahata, Masayuki, Yasushi Kondo, Shigeru Sato, and Susumu Nishioka, eds. 2023. *The Shifting Middle Class and the Welfare State: Fiscal and Political Support for Welfare Provision*. Nakanishi Publishing.

Taniguchi, Masaki, Taka-aki Asano, Shōko Ōmori, and Shūsuke Takamiya. 2025. "Policy Positions of the Candidates." In *Japan Decides 2024: The Japanese General Election*, edited by Kenneth M. McElwain, Robert J. Pekkanen, and Daniel M. Smith, 125–142. Palgrave Macmillan.

Taylor-Goodby, Peter, ed. 2004. *New Risks, New Welfare: The Transformation of the European Welfare State*. Oxford University Press.

Umeda, Michio. 2025. "Electoral Campaigns in Japan's 2024 HR Election: Emerging Signs of Transformation." In *Japan Decides 2024: The Japanese General Election*, edited by Kenneth M. McElwain, Robert J. Pekkanen, and Daniel M. Smith, 109–124. Palgrave Macmillan.

CHAPTER 18

Election Under Inflation: LDP's Choice of Macroeconomic Policy

Kenya Amano and Saori N. Katada

INTRODUCTION

The economic bottom line affects voters' choices. The Japanese economy was facing a very different challenge at the time of the October 27 Lower House election in 2024, compared to its last election almost exactly 3 years earlier in 2021. Instead of facing a long deflationary environment that kept significantly accommodative monetary conditions by the Bank of Japan (BOJ), Japan was finally seeing serious inflation kicking in due to post-COVID-19 supply chain challenges and rising commodity prices on the heels of the wars in Ukraine and the Middle East. Inflation in other countries triggered their central banks to raise their policy rates since spring 2022, which weakened the yen and further pushed import prices up domestically.

K. Amano (✉)
Independent Scholar, New York, NY, USA
e-mail: kenya.amano@gmail.com

S. N. Katada
University of Southern California, Los Angeles, California, USA
e-mail: skatada@usc.edu

© The Author(s), under exclusive license to Springer Nature Switzerland AG 2025
K. M. McElwain et al. (eds.), *Japan Decides 2024*,
https://Doi.org/10.1007/978-3-031-98797-7_18

After almost a quarter century suffering from deflation, this is a brand-new challenge for Japanese leaders. Inflation aversion has long been well examined and documented (for example, Hibbs 1979), and the economic voting literature guides us to assess that inflation episodes have consistently had a negative impact on incumbents through "pocket-book voting."[1] As such, the incumbents' chances decrease quite significantly in an inflationary environment, especially when such inflation comes unexpectedly (Palmer and Whitten 1999). In fact, several incumbent governments from Italy, Iceland, the United Kingdom, Argentina, and the United States lost the election during the inflationary environment of 2022 to 2024. In Japan's case in 2024, after more than ten years under "bold monetary policy," the challenge is even more acute as the BOJ kept its extremely accommodative monetary policy, including a Negative Interest Rate Policy (NIRP) and Yield Curve Control (YCC), through its large purchases of Japanese Government Bonds (JGBs) to depress the cost of the government's borrowing so that it could widen the government's fiscal space (Buiter 2021). Reversing such a policy in the face of an inflation uptick will inevitably have fiscal implications. As such, political parties in Japan at the time of the 2024 Lower House election once again faced an economic policy trilemma among conventional growth strategy, distribution, and fiscal discipline (Amano and Katada 2024).[2] The pressure on the parties to respond to the people's *economic* needs in the face of inflation, especially through distributional measures, intensified in the last few years.

---

[1] The economic voting literature is vast. For a nice summary of different types of economic voting, see Afzal (2024).

[2] Our theory of trilemma emerges where the government can pursue only two of the following three goals. The first goal is economic growth capitalizing on the "old way of business," resorting to the supply-side of producers and large businesses and catering to vested economic interests and clientelism through public works such as infrastructure investment. The second goal puts the emphasis on distribution with various types of hand-out measures targeted towards the wider demography, as well as consumer-focused measures, such as time-limited suspension (or reduction) of the sales tax. Here, we define distribution policy as a resource allocation toward the demand side of the Japanese economy consisting of consumers and workers, where the typical policy menu is to implement a series of direct payments or reductions on income and sales tax. On the other hand, the supply-side growth strategy focuses on the producers, industries, and businesses where the government executes public expenditure programs to stimulate private investments and exploit regulations. The third and final goal is fiscal stability through the fiscal discipline of the central government.

In this chapter, we argue that Prime Minister Ishiba Shigeru's policy choice to adhere to fiscal discipline in the context of the economic policy trilemma narrowed the Liberal Democratic Party's policy space during the 2024 election. This challenge was exploited by smaller parties, such as the Democratic Party for the People (DPP) and Reiwa Shinsengumi (Reiwa), which emphasized distributive policies with fiscal expansion and gained significant electoral ground. As a result, the LDP lost significantly, which put it in the position of a minority party (see Ko Maeda 2025). Furthermore, we argue that Ishiba's policy choice also reflected intra-party struggles, as demonstrated by contrasting positions taken by the three candidates (Ishiba, Koizumi Shinjirō, and Takaichi Sanae) facing this trilemma at the time of the LDP presidential election only a month prior (see Nemoto 2025).

After discussing Japan's economic conditions from 2022 through 2024 before the country faced the Lower House election in October 2024, this chapter examines the respective macroeconomic policy stances of the LDP presidential candidates as reflected in their debates one month before the Lower House election. The chapter then covers Ishiba's strategy, focusing on his economic policy during the election, to analyze why it did not resonate with the public. We conclude with the shifting of Ishiba's economic policy choices as a minority government and the challenges Ishiba would face in the era of Trump 2.0.

Economic Conditions Before the Election

The primary economic issue in past elections in Japan was prolonged deflation, which had persisted since the late 1990s. After the LDP's defeat in 2009, former Prime Minister Abe Shinzō campaigned on an anti-deflation platform under the banner of Abenomics, which led to a landslide victory in the 2012 Lower House election (Tiberghien 2013; Amano and Park 2025). Since then, the implementation of Abenomics helped the LDP maintain electoral competitiveness by exploiting the macroeconomic policy space (Noble 2016; Katada and Cheung 2018; Hoshi and Lipscy 2021). However, the inflationary environment since 2022 shifted this political landscape. Inflation above 2% and a weakening yen forced political parties to prioritize fighting inflation—reversing their previous deflation-focused agendas.

Despite the BOJ's aggressive monetary easing, inflation remained below the 2% target for years, with the COVID-19 pandemic even causing negative price growth until the summer of 2021. At the 2021 election, inflation was not a key issue. Instead, the LDP-Kōmeitō coalition won by taking a straddling strategy between promoting distribution and supply-side growth policies while maintaining fiscal discipline at the debt level, which expanded due to the policy response to the COVID-19 pandemic (Katada and Amano 2023). However, while the COVID-19 pandemic initially caused a demand shock and deflation, it later disrupted global supply chains, raising production costs. The 2022 Russia-Ukraine war intensified inflationary pressures, as the war further disrupted energy and food supplies. Russia, a major exporter of oil and gas, was hit with sanctions, while Ukraine and Russia's grain exports were cut off, pushing food prices higher. These global shocks contributed directly to inflation in Japan. Moreover, while other central banks raised interest rates in response, the BOJ maintained its accommodative policy stance including NIRP, causing a widening interest rate gap and yen depreciation, which fueled import-driven inflation (See Fig. 18.1).

These economic developments significantly affected Japanese politics. Rising inflation eroded household purchasing power, especially with wage rises lagging behind. Opinion polls showed a shift in public concern from "economic recovery" to "inflation measures" between 2022 and

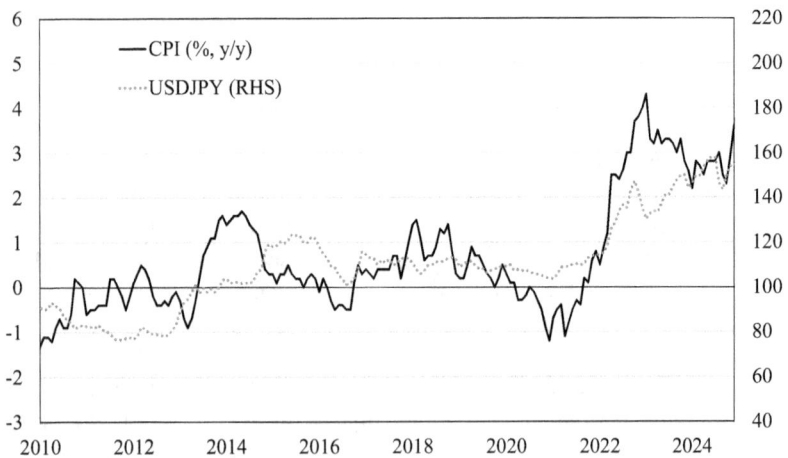

Fig. 18.1 Inflation and currency

2023 (Yukio Maeda 2025).[3] In response, the Kishida administration launched two fiscal packages: "Comprehensive Economic Measures for Overcoming Price Increases and Revitalizing the Economy" (October 2022) and "Comprehensive Economic Measures to Completely Overcome Deflation" (November 2023), including energy subsidies, cash handouts, and wage support. With these political efforts under inflationary environments, the "*Shuntō*" wage negotiation resulted in above 2% wage increases. Japanese unions achieved a 3.6% total wage increase in fiscal 2023 and a 5.1% total wage increase in 2024, which were the highest rates since 1991.

Meanwhile, Prime Minister Kishida Fumio intended to shift away from Abenomics by appointing Ueda Kazuo as BOJ governor in 2023 (Amano and Park 2025). After nearly a year, and following the positive wage data in March 2024, the BOJ made a historic policy shift on March 19 by ending YCC and NIRP—its first-rate hike since February 2007. This marked a step toward policy normalization, responding to sustained inflation above 2%.

LDP Presidential Election

Economic policy choice was a vital issue at the time of the 2024 LDP presidential election. Under the inflationary environment, Kishida and other politicians considered deviating from the course of Abenomics and ending the monetary and fiscal accommodation. On the other hand, others, especially those politicians in the former Abe faction, believed that the Japanese economy could fall back into deflation and thus needed more expansionary policy. The focus of this presidential election was also on whether to continue Abe's legacy in the non-economic policy sphere, because Prime Minister Kishida decided not to seek a second term with the party facing declining public approval stemming from a substantial slush fund scandal that implicated several prominent party factions (Carlson 2025; Umeda 2025). Kishida decided to dissolve the LDP factions, which led to an unusually volatile and unpredictable leadership election (Nemoto 2025). In addition, the impact of the assassination of former Prime Minister Abe in 2022 lingered in terms of concerns over

---

[3] For instance, see Public Opinion Survey on National Life by Cabinet Office at https://survey.gov-online.go.jp/ or Nikkei Public Opinion Survey by Nikkei at https://vdata.nikkei.com/newsgraphics/cabinet-approval-rating/

the LDP's ties to the Unification Church (McLaughlin 2025). Consequently, this presidential election exhibited a kind of judgment day to evaluate former Prime Minister Abe's cumulative legacy as the LDP faced a power vacuum. This resulted in a highly competitive race that ultimately saw a record number of nine candidates vying for the party's leadership.

The economic platforms presented by the candidates played a critical role in shaping the outcome of the election, and the economic policies proposed by the leading candidates in the 2024 LDP presidential election revealed distinct approaches to addressing Japan's economic challenges in the face of the economic policy trilemma. An analysis of their platforms highlights key differences in areas such as fiscal policy, monetary policy, and labor market regulation, the balance of which reflects distinct weights each candidate puts on the three corners of the trilemma: fiscal discipline, distribution, and supply-side growth. These distinct choices among the three top runners of the LDP presidential candidates demonstrated different approaches toward the economic policy trilemma (Table 18.1). Ishiba and Koizumi aimed to uphold fiscal discipline, while Takaichi followed the old Abenomics of monetary expansion, but also advocated for massive fiscal expansion. Meanwhile, Ishiba and Koizumi differed in their fiscal target: Ishiba focused on supply-side growth through clientelism, while Koizumi prioritized direct distribution.

Ishiba indicated a general alignment with the economic policies of the outgoing Prime Minister Kishida, emphasizing the concept of a "New Form of Capitalism" with his long-standing political agenda of "Regional Revitalization" (Yukio Maeda 2025). His focus was on achieving wage increases that would outpace inflation and stimulating consumer spending to create a positive economic cycle. Ishiba was guarded on fiscal expansion and supported the BOJ's monetary normalization process, while also signaling a greater emphasis on income distribution to workers compared to Kishida.[4] Notably, he expressed a willingness to consider increasing corporate taxes for certain companies and strengthening the taxation of financial income.

Takaichi presented an economic strategy closely following Abenomics, known as "Sanae-nomics," emphasizing investment as the primary driver of economic growth. Her overall economic approach was consistent with the policies of the Abe administration. In contrast to Ishiba, Takaichi

[4] Ishiba previously set a long-term goal of raising the national average minimum wage to JPY 1500 within the 2020s.

Table 18.1 Key economic policy differences of leading candidates

	Ishiba Shigeru	Takaichi Sanae	Koizumi Shinjirō
Final round of votes	215 (MP 189 + Region 26)	194 (MP 173 + Region 21)	–
First round of votes	154 (MP 108 + Supporter 46)	181 (MP 109 + Supporter 72)	136 (MP 75 + Supporter 61)
Fiscal policy	Willing to raise corporate and financial income taxes to secure fiscal discipline	Strategic fiscal expansion for food and energy security No need to increase taxes but increase government bond issuance for defense spending	Advocated for tax system reform (details not specified)
Monetary policy	Support BOJ's normalization policy stance of addressing inflation	Advocated caution in raising rates	Respect BOJ's independence and acquiesce to BOJ's normalization policy
Industry regulation	Strong interest in regional revitalization	Subsidies for farming, food industries, and energy sectors	Deregulation of regulated industries, such as opening ride share to the taxi industry
Distribution policy	Details not specified. Focus on the labor market	Details not specified	Following Kishida's policy, which distributes to low-income households
Labor market	Focus on wage increases and minimum wage	Opposed to deregulation of the labor market	Deregulation for easier hiring and firing, monetary compensation for dismissal

advocated for a cautious approach to raising interest rates. Instead, she did not hesitate to engage with advocates who supported Modern Monetary Theory, which promotes massive fiscal expansion. As Japan faced import-driven inflation in the face of a weakening yen with outstanding government debt, her approach raised concerns in some quarters.

Koizumi focused his economic proposals on distribution through labor market reforms and regulatory changes. A key element of his platform was the call for a relaxation of Japan's rigid labor rules to make it easier for businesses to hire and dismiss workers. He also proposed the establishment of a system of monetary compensation for dismissed employees as a means of resolving disputes and fostering greater flexibility in the labor market. Furthermore, Koizumi advocated for green policies, including the phasing out of coal power generation.

Nine candidates competed in the first round of the LDP presidential election, which combined LDP members of parliament (MPs) votes and LDP party supporters' votes. As indicated in Table 18.1, in the first round, Takaichi led with 181 votes, consisting of 72 votes from MPs and 109 from party supporters. Ishiba followed with 154 votes—46 from MPs and 108 from supporters. Koizumi came close with 136 votes, including a strong 75 from MPs but only 61 from supporters. Since no candidate secured a majority, a runoff was held between Takaichi and Ishiba. In the final round, Ishiba won with 215 total votes, composed of 189 MP votes and 26 regional supporter votes. Takaichi received 194 votes—173 from MPs and 21 from regional votes. Although Takaichi led the first round, a majority of LDP MPs ultimately swung their support to Ishiba in the final round, securing his victory and signaling a shift in party alignment from the former Abe faction to the coalition of former Prime Minister Kishida and Ishiba's factions.

In the immediate aftermath of his victory in the LDP presidential election, Ishiba was formally confirmed as the next Prime Minister of Japan by the National Diet on October 1, 2024, 4 days after the party leadership vote. Shortly after assuming office, Ishiba announced his intention to dissolve the Lower House of parliament and call a snap Lower House election, which was subsequently held on October 27. In terms of policy direction, Ishiba stated his commitment to continuing and accelerating the "New Form of Capitalism" advocated by his predecessor, Kishida, with a particular emphasis on achieving wage increases that outpace price increases and stimulating consumption to foster a positive economic cycle. In a move that signaled a degree of continuity and an eye towards the upcoming election, Ishiba appointed Koizumi, who had finished third in the presidential race, to head the party's election task force. His initial cabinet appointments included members from various factions within the LDP, but Takaichi refused the offer to be the Chairperson of the General Council of the LDP, suggesting that she and her supporters tried to maintain a distance from the Ishiba administration.

Macroeconomic Policies of Opposition Parties and Election Results

The snap Lower House election resulted in a significant erosion of LDP dominance, coupled with a surge in the opposition parties that supported fiscal expansion with distributional policies. Our assessment is that the LDP's strategic choice under Ishiba and his economic policy did not attract voters under conditions of rising inflation that had a significant impact on households.

As a politician who supported fiscal discipline, Prime Minister Ishiba did not propose a bold policy package in the election. Rather, his manifesto comprised of policies that were not particularly different from those of the Kishida administration (cf. Matsumoto 2025; Taniguchi et al. 2025). While advocating subsidies on energies and stressing his commitment to wage growth, other policies were more or less old-fashioned LDP supply-side growth measures under the name of Regional Revitalization. Meanwhile, the Constitutional Democratic Party of Japan (CDP) selected former Prime Minister Noda Yoshihiko as a new party leader in their presidential election in September 2024. Noda's economic policy was characterized as conservative as he had promoted fiscal discipline. As a social left party, CDP proposed to revive the "thick middle class" by boosting household finances and employment, revitalize consumption, and restore a "strong economy." But they were reluctant to cut taxes compared to other opposition parties. Also, as a part of its inflation measures, CDP proposed adjustments to the BOJ's inflation targets. Specifically, the party advocated for shifting the BOJ's inflation target from the existing 2% to a level "above 0%," suggesting a more flexible approach to raising the policy rate that was more hawkish on monetary policy than even the LDP. Thus, with respect to macroeconomic policy, Ishiba, as a fiscal conservative in a party on the right (LDP), and Noda, as a fiscal conservative in a party on the left (CDP), did not show significant differences from each other.

By contrast, the DPP, Ishin, and Reiwa advocated tax reduction. The DPP proposed a transitory cut of the consumption tax to 5% from 10%, Ishin also advocated for cutting the tax to 8%, and Reiwa argued for the abolition of the consumption taxes altogether. Moreover, the DPP's philosophy of macroeconomic policy was close to the policy that Takaichi and her supporters advocated. In their party manifesto, it constructed a typical reflationalist narrative, stating that "we will stabilize exchange rates and prices appropriately through a 'high pressure economy' boosted by aggressive fiscal and monetary expansion, thereby escaping from the wage deflation which causes economic stagnation." Furthermore, they proposed an income tax cut by increasing the tax exemption limits, issuing additional education bonds, and more aggressive subsidies on energy than the LDP proposed. Reiwa suggested a distribution of 100-thousand yen cash handouts to households, but they did not have a specific stance on monetary policy. While Ishin supported a consumption tax cut, they did not put forward any specific distribution policy. Rather, Ishin argued the need for structural reform toward a smaller government, which is the original basis of the party and the policy it has pursued (see Zenkyo 2025) (Table 18.2).

Although economic policy was not the only issue on which the 2024 Lower House election was fought over, we see a pattern of favorable electoral outcomes for the DPP, the biggest surprise winner (net seat gains of +21), and Reiwa (+6), which promoted both expansionary fiscal policy and massive distribution. The CDP, which was relatively conservative compared to these two parties, did gain 50 seats, while the LDP lost 56 seats and Kōmeitō 8. As a result, the incumbent two-party coalition was not able to maintain its Lower House majority. While the election results were also heavily influenced by the funding scandal and other social policies, if we look solely at economic policy, the LDP's loss could be attributed to the loss of the voter support base that agreed with Takaichi and the former Abe faction, as the party moved away from the expansionary monetary and fiscal policies advocated by this faction. Meanwhile, since the DPP, which had advocated almost the same policies as Takaichi, significantly increased its number of seats, it can be said that, from an economic policy perspective, some of the LDP's support base shifted their votes to the DPP (cf. Matsubayashi 2025). As a result, a minority government emerged, and for the LDP, political pressure for expansionary fiscal policy is expected to continue increasing in future elections.

Table 18.2 Key economic policy differences of political parties

	LDP	CDP	Ishin	DPP	Reiwa
Seats before the election	247	98	44	7	3
Seats after the election	191	148	38	28	9
Seat difference (rate)	−56 (-23%)	50 (51%)	−6 (−14%)	21 (300%)	6 (200%)
Trilemma	Fiscal discipline Less distribution More supply side	Fiscal discipline Less distribution More on social welfare	Fiscal expansion Less distribution Aggressive reform	Fiscal expansion Aggressive distribution Unclear/too broad	Fiscal expansion Aggressive distribution More on social welfare
Fiscal policy	Propose supplementary budgets within the current fiscal capacity	Propose economic measures within the current fiscal capacity Cautious on increasing defense spending	Cut income, corporate and consumption taxes with tax system reformation	New government bond issuance for education	Tax and social security fee cut for households with introduction of progressive taxation
Tax cut	Secure fiscal discipline	Secure fiscal discipline	Cut consumption tax to 8%	Temporarily cut consumption tax to 5% Raise income tax exemption threshold Cut gasoline tax	Abolish consumption tax
Monetary policy	Support BOJ's normalization policy stance of addressing inflation	Adjust the BOJ inflation target to "above 0%", and jointly set a real wage growth target	Details not specified	Advocate monetary expansion	Details not specified

(continued)

Table 18.2 (continued)

	LDP	CDP	Ishin	DPP	Reiwa
Distribution policy	Focus on wage increases and minimum wage Subsidize for energy costs	Progressive taxation, wealth redistribution, focus on fair contributions from the wealthy	Subsidize for Child-rearing households. Universal free education	Temporary consumption tax cut until wage increase, investment in growth sectors	Cash handouts as inflation measures and for child-rearing households Universal free education
Focus areas of expenditure	Future-ready industries (GX, DX), defense (planned increase)	Increase social welfare and economic development (prioritized over defense)	Education (universal free), technology	Growth sectors (semiconductors, AI, batteries)	Increase social welfare

Conclusion

The 2024 Lower House election took place under a rare economic circumstance in Japan's recent history, with noticeable inflation in the face of persistently low wages. After almost thirty years of low or negative inflation and very little growth, people felt price hikes on many essentials, from electricity, gas, to rice. This chapter has examined how such economic conditions influenced the dismal electoral outcome for the LDP under the brand-new Ishiba government. We argue that Prime Minister Ishiba's defense of fiscal health and his slow dole-out of distributional measures in the face of the economic policy trilemma constituted an essential variable to explaining the LDP's relative defeat to parties such as DPP or Reiwa, as these opposition parties capitalized on such distributional policies with significant tax reductions. Meanwhile, still tied to supply-side interests such as support for small and medium industries, Ishiba chose to neglect distributional measures at his peril.

With inflation and the weakening of the yen placing pressure on the BOJ's super-loose monetary policy that started with Abenomics in 2013, the economic policy trilemma among fiscal responsibility, distributional policy, and supply-side policy continues to limit what each political party can propose to the voters. Despite the proposal of a $1.34 trillion New Industrial Policy by Ishiba's economic advisory panel, the winning ticket so far centers around wealth distribution, including wage increases. With further pressures coming from the Trump 2.0 administration in both economics (e.g. 15% tariffs on almost all imported goods to the United States as of September 30, 2025) and defense (e.g. demands to spend up to 3% of Japan's GDP on defense to burden-share the security arrangement in the region), the Japanese economy and fiscal conditions continue to face a very tough environment. As such, the parties' choice of economic policies will have dire electoral consequences.

REFERENCES

Afzal, Muhammad Hassan Bin. 2024. "Pocketbook and Sociotropic Economic Voting: How Does Inflation Affect Voting Decisions?" ZBW – Leibniz Information Centre for Economics, Kiel, Hamburg. https://www.econstor.eu/bitstream/10419/300581/1/Full-Paper-MHB%20Afzal%20(7-30-2024).pdf.

Amano, Kenya, and Gene Park. 2025. "The Limits of Statutory Independence: The Bank of Japan and The Politics of Monetary Policy." *Wisconsin International Law Journal* 42 (2): 209–238.

Amano, Kenya, and Saori N. Katada. 2023. "Economic Policy Trilemma: Macroeconomic Politics in the 2021 Election." In *Japan Decides 2021: The Japanese General Election*, edited by Robert J. Pekkanen, Steven Reed, and Daniel Smith, 255–274. Palgrave Macmillan.

Amano, Kenya, and Saori N. Katada. 2024. "Economic Policy Trilemma and Longevity of a Political Party: A Study of Japan's Liberal Democratic Party in a Comparative Perspective." *unpublished manuscript.*

Buiter, Willem. 2021. *Central Banks as Fiscal Players: The Drivers of Fiscal and Monetary Policy Space.* Cambridge: Cambridge University Press.

Carlson, Matthew M. 2025. "Scandals During the Kishida Administration," In *Japan Decides 2024: The Japanese General Election,* edited by Kenneth M. McElwain, Robert J. Pekkanen, and Daniel M. Smith, 217–233. Palgrave Macmillan.

Hibbs Jr, Douglas A. 1979. "The Mass Public and Macroeconomic Performance: The Dynamics of Public Opinion toward Unemployment and Inflation." *American Journal of Political Science,* 23 (4), 705–731.

Hoshi, Takeo, and Phillip Y. Lipscy. 2021. "The Political Economy of the Abe Government." In *The Political Economy of the Abe Government and Abenomics Reforms,* edited by Takeo Hoshi and Phillip Y. Lipscy, 3–39. Cambridge University Press.

Katada, Saori N., and Gabrielle Cheung. 2018. "The First Two Arrows of Abenomics: Monetary and Fiscal Politics in the 2017 Snap Election." In *Japan Decides 2017: The Japanese General Election*, edited by Robert J. Pekkanen, Steven R. Reed, Ethan Scheiner, and Daniel M. Smith, 243–259. Palgrave Macmillan.

Maeda, Ko. 2025. "The 2024 Election Results: A Political Earthquake," In *Japan Decides 2024: The Japanese General Election*, edited by Kenneth M. McElwain, Robert J. Pekkanen, and Daniel M. Smith, 17–34. Palgrave Macmillan.

Maeda, Yukio. 2025. "Public Opinion and Scandals in Economic Hard Times." In *Japan Decides 2024: The Japanese General Election*, edited by Kenneth M. McElwain, Robert J. Pekkanen, and Daniel M. Smith, 163–179. Palgrave Macmillan.

Matsubayashi, Tetsuya. 2025. "Partisanship and Turnout in the 2024 General Election." In *Japan Decides 2024: The Japanese General Election*, edited by Kenneth M. McElwain, Robert J. Pekkanen, and Daniel M. Smith, 197–214. Palgrave Macmillan.

Matsumoto, Tomoko. 2025. "How Party Manifestos Framed Political Distrust in the 2024 Election." In *Japan Decides 2024: The Japanese General Election*, edited by Kenneth M. McElwain, Robert J. Pekkanen, and Daniel M. Smith, 143–161. Palgrave Macmillan.

McLaughlin, Levi. 2025. "Perennial Fears, Novel Responses: The Unification Church in Japan after the Abe Assassination." In *Japan Decides 2024: The Japanese General Election*, edited by Kenneth M. McElwain, Robert J. Pekkanen, and Daniel M. Smith, 235–253. Palgrave Macmillan.

Nemoto, Kuniaki. 2025. "Reasons Behind the LDP's Loss in the 2024 Election." In *Japan Decides 2024: The Japanese General Election*, edited by Kenneth M. McElwain, Robert J. Pekkanen, and Daniel M. Smith, 37–55. Palgrave Macmillan.

Noble, Gregory W. 2016. "Abenomics in the 2014 Election: Showing the Money (Supply) and Little Else." In *Japan Decides 2014: The Japanese General Election*, edited by Robert J. Pekkanen, Steven R. Reed, and Ethan Scheiner, 155–169. Palgrave Macmillan.

Palmer, Harvy D., and Whitten, Guy D. 1999. "The Electoral Impact of Unexpected Inflation and Economic Growth." *British Journal of Political Science* 29 (4): 623–639.

Taniguchi, Masaki, Taka-aki Asano, Shōko Ōmori, and Shūsuke Takamiya. 2025. "Policy Positions of the Candidates." In *Japan Decides 2024: The Japanese General Election*, edited by Kenneth M. McElwain, Robert J. Pekkanen, and Daniel M. Smith, 125–142. Palgrave Macmillan.

Tiberghien, Yves. 2013. "Election Surprise: Abenomics and Central Bank Independence Trump Nationalism and Fukushima." In *Japan Decides 2012: The*

Japanese General Election, edited by Robert Pekkanen, Steven R. Reed, and Ethan Scheiner, 195–200. Palgrave Macmillan.

Umeda, Michio. 2025. "Electoral Campaigns in Japan's 2024 HR Election: Emerging Signs of Transformation." In *Japan Decides 2024: The Japanese General Election,* edited by Kenneth M. McElwain, Robert J. Pekkanen, and Daniel M. Smith, 109–124. Palgrave Macmillan.

Zenkyo, Masahiro. 2025. "Why Did Public Support for the Japan Innovation Party Decline in the 2024 HR Election?." In *Japan Decides 2024: The Japanese General Election,* edited by Kenneth M. McElwain, Robert J. Pekkanen, and Daniel M. Smith, 91–105. Palgrave Macmillan.

CHAPTER 19

Japan Decides Its Role in the Global Economy: Trade and Economic Security in the 2024 Election

Kristin Vekasi

INTRODUCTION

Contemporary Japan is caught between the rock of economic integration and the hard place of increasing securitization of the same globalized economy. Over the past decade, Japan has upheld its commitment to economic globalization, not only in terms of private sector trade and investment patterns but also through institutional commitments such as regional and preferential trade agreements. At the same time, Japan has increasingly adopted policies that securitize elements of its economy, including the passage of the comprehensive Economic Security Promotion Act (ESPA) between the general elections of 2021 and 2024.

K. Vekasi (✉)
University of Montana, Missoula, MT, USA
e-mail: kristin.vekasi@mso.umt.edu

Achieving domestic economic prosperity while simultaneously managing security concerns stemming from complex economic interdependence creates tensions, sometimes acute. These tensions are evident in policy debates surrounding the 2024 general election. However, in 2024, the ruling coalition and primary opposition parties largely held consensus views on the economic security aspects, differing mainly on points of detail or implementation. While there was more discord on trade policy, these differences also centered on details of implementation, not on the fundamental question of Japan's status as a trading nation. On the other hand, the less mainstream opposition parties, both left- and right-wing, were more vocal in their opposition to the status quo. Ishin and the Japanese Communist Party, in particular, have been critical of the economic security approach, albeit from different perspectives, with Ishin more hawkish than the ruling coalition, and the Japanese Communist Party more generally critical of economic security.

The 2024 general election revealed that some of the contradictions at the heart of Japan's contemporary political economy are likely to persist for the foreseeable future as Japan navigates this rocky geopolitical moment. While a Japanese election where the Liberal Democratic Party-led coalition loses a majority is always momentous, the 2024 election did not bring significant changes to external economic policy and probably does not presage major shifts in the future. Rather, there seems to be a shared consensus on balancing industrial policy with the securitization of the economy, more generally, and maintaining Japan's position as a regional trading power.

This chapter unpacks the debates among political parties and actors regarding Japan's trade and economic security posture. It begins by describing the status quo of Japan's external economic policies, including industrial policies related to semiconductors and critical materials, and Japan's current stance on trade and economic institutions. The chapter then examines the political stances of parties in Japan on trade and economic security issues, largely drawing from party manifestos, speeches by party leaders, and some limited use of legacy media reporting. While not all political parties are included in the discussion, there is a sample across the right-left ideological spectrum. The chapter concludes with a discussion of post-election changes in trade and economic security policy and offers some predictions about the future.

Trade and Regional Economic Integration: The Status Quo

During the last general election in 2021, there was broad agreement across the political spectrum that the rise of China posed a concern for Japan, though differences existed over the precise nature of the threat and the appropriate response (Vekasi 2023). Japan's responses to China have taken two forms: continued economic engagement and hedging against vulnerability with economic security policy. In the 2024 election, the tensions between Japan's leadership in economic globalization and economic security policy defined the policy status quo.

On trade policy, Japan has taken a leadership role in regional trade integration, with trade agreements and a renewed commitment to cross-border trade and investment (Solis 2024; Katada 2020; Govella 2023). The Regional Comprehensive Economic Partnership (RCEP) and the Comprehensive and Progressive Agreement for Trans-Pacific Partnership (CPTPP) are two prominent examples. Japan has also negotiated an FTA with the European Union, as well as numerous smaller agreements. The CPTPP, originally known as the TPP or Trans-Pacific Partnership, was a U.S.-led initiative from the Obama era that was finalized under Japan's leadership after the United States withdrew under Donald Trump. This agreement notably did not include China, but it aimed to upgrade regional trade rules and architecture. Signatories anticipated that China would use the rewards of TPP membership as an incentive to improve its domestic economic governance. Indeed, China has made a bid to join the CPTPP, though the path to membership appears rocky. The RCEP, a large regional trade agreement involving fifteen Asian countries, includes China and other regional economic partners. Both institutions represent Japan's commitment to multilateral trade, involving both traditional security partners and regional partners viewed with more skepticism.

The Japanese government has largely fostered the regional trade framework because it leverages the strengths of its private sector. The Ministry of Economy, Trade, and Industry (METI) identified "niche sectors" such as advanced chip-making materials, smartphone components, and medical equipment, where Japan holds significant global market shares and is highly profitable (Ministry of Economy, Trade, and Industry 2019). This strategy (in part) responds to competition from China, with Japanese companies focusing on high-tech, hard-to-replicate products in specialized industries. As part of this "aggregate niche strategy," Japan aims to dominate global supply chains in areas where it holds a strong advantage, without withdrawing from globalization more generally (Schaede 2020). These products often integrate into cross-border supply chains, particularly with China and Southeast Asia, as Japan relies on its neighbors for raw materials, intermediate components, and assembly, focusing on high-value-added downstream production domestically (Vekasi 2023).

These two components—diplomatic and institutional commitment to trade alongside economic incentives for cross-border integration—cement Japan's status as a "trading nation" (Solís 2017). At the same time, recent shocks to the global economy, such as the US-China trade war, the COVID-19 pandemic, and the Russian invasion of Ukraine, have increased wariness about unrestrained globalization, pushing for more national security guardrails (Katada and Solis 2022; Igata and Glosserman 2021; Govella 2021). In 2021, Japan began massive state investments to revive a domestic semiconductor industry in response to pandemic-induced shortages and security concerns around supply chain bottlenecks (Negrine 2024). In conjunction with the Japan External Trade Organization (JETRO), the Ministry of Economy, Trade, and Industry concurrently began programs funding either the reshoring of industries to Japan or (more commonly) new Japanese investments in Southeast Asia (Solis 2021). In May 2022, these more piecemeal approaches were codified when Japan passed the Economic Security Promotion Act (ESPA) to formalize these concerns and the government's official response. With the passage of this legislation, Japanese national security priorities intruded into economic decision-making. The bill mandates that under certain conditions, the private sector must prioritize security over profitability, a substantial shift after decades of focusing on just-in-time efficiency gains and prioritizing complex cross-border supply chains.

The concept of economic security was also codified in three core strategic documents in late 2022: the National Security Strategy (NSS), the National Defense Strategy (NDS), and the Defense Buildup Program. Economic security is most heavily integrated into the NSS, but the "whole-of-government approach" that emphasizes "integrating Japan's national power—diplomatic, intelligence, economic, and technological—as well as systematically combining all policy means" is present in all of the documents (Japan Ministry of Defense 2022). Economic security, specifically the implementation of the ESPA, was explicitly written into the new National Security Strategy. Within the NSS, there is a clear turn towards more industrial policy to "curb excessive dependence on specific countries, carry forward next-generation semiconductor development and manufacturing bases, secure stable supply for critical goods including rare earths, and promote capital reinforcement for private enterprises with critical goods and technologies" (Cabinet Office of Japan 2022).

In summary, Japan's approach to trade policy and economic security reflects a balance between market-oriented engagement in globalization and state-oriented measures to safeguard national interests. These developments position Japan as a "trading nation" deeply integrated into global markets yet increasingly guarded against risks to its economic and national security. While seemingly at odds, these two goals are broadly reflected in the policies of most mainstream political parties even as they are pointedly critiqued by smaller opposition parties, as discussed in the next section.

The Politics of Trade and Economic Security in the 2024 Election

Since the previous general election, the economic security and trade debates in Japan have been relatively non-ideological. Both the ruling parties on the right and the opposition parties on the center-left have largely agreed on the need for economic security policies and, to some extent, even on the target sectors and best methods of implementation. There is broad agreement on the need to support emerging technologies and the raw materials needed for them, for pharmaceuticals and food security. There are disagreements about how state intervention in the economy should relate to more traditional defense issues, particularly related to increased defense spending, defense readiness, and military industries without clear dual-use applications. However, there is common ground on intervention in supply chains, focusing on resilience, and reducing vulnerabilities related to trade and economic dependence on China.

This section uses party manifestos to summarize and analyze the stances of different political groups on trade and economic security, elucidating their positions and identifying points of commonality and conflict (see Matsumoto 2025 for a general discussion of the history and role of election manifestos). Some parties had very limited discussion of external economic issues in their core platform for the election; in those cases, I relied on speeches or statements from party leaders or official party publications. In this volume, Taniguchi and co-authors also have a helpful broader analysis of differences within and between parties' policy positions (Taniguchi et al. 2025).

The Liberal Democratic Party and Kōmeitō

The LDP and Kōmeitō have been the ruling coalition since late 2012. While the economic security approach originated from the LDP's Policy Research Council, Kōmeitō also supported these efforts and the ESPA bill (Policy Research Council 2020). In their 2024 manifestos, both the LDP and Kōmeitō devoted substantial sections to economic security, with far less explicit attention given to trade or trade institutions (Liberal Democratic Party 2024; Kōmeitō 2024). Both parties emphasized strengthening domestic resilience and fostering international cooperation, though they somewhat diverged in prioritizing different sectors and implementation mechanisms.

Both the LDP and Kōmeitō prioritized implementing and enhancing the ESPA to ensure stability and reduce vulnerability in sectors like semiconductors, energy, and critical infrastructure. Both parties shared a focus on supply chain resilience not only for semiconductors but also for pharmaceuticals and raw materials. They highlighted artificial intelligence, quantum computing, and space technologies as additional priorities. However, Kōmeitō placed more emphasis on food and medicine security and support for small and medium-sized enterprises (SMEs), while the LDP concentrated more on institutionalizing economic security policies. This included advocating for the creation of a national-level economic security think tank, fostering large-scale public-private partnerships, and implementing statutory measures for semiconductor mass production.

Both parties also highlighted the overlap between trade, international collaboration, and economic security. They underscored the importance of working with partners, particularly within frameworks such as the G7, CPTPP member states, and the Indo-Pacific Economic Framework (IPEF), to strengthen a "rules-based international order" and build resilient supply chains. Kōmeitō additionally promoted engagement with initiatives like the World Bank-Japan Resilient and Inclusive Supply-Chain Enhancement (RISE) program, which focuses on green technology and global promotion of Japanese exports (World Bank 2024).

Kōmeitō devoted greater attention to trade-specific goals compared to the LDP, advocating for forming a Free Trade Area of the Asia-Pacific (FTAAP), an Asia-Pacific Economic Cooperation (APEC) initiative, alongside existing institutions such as RCEP, CPTPP, and IPEF (APEC Policy Support Unit 2024). Strengthening the World Trade Organization's dispute settlement framework was another key focus for the party.

The LDP, in contrast, did not campaign specifically on trade issues, indicating the dominance of the economic security narrative. For the LDP, economic security was not merely a subset of trade policy but the central philosophy underpinning various policy areas, including trade, international cooperation, energy, and technology. The LDP framed economic security as essential to safeguarding Japan's sovereignty and prosperity, stating that:

> Values such as freedom, democracy, and human rights, work[ing] with like-minded nations to establish a free and open international order based on the rule of law, and promote economic security policies to ensure our nation's survival, independence, and prosperity from an economic perspective. (Liberal Democratic Party 2024)

Economic security was also portrayed as integral to transforming economic growth into national power while protecting people's livelihoods. Kōmeitō echoed this sentiment, emphasizing the need for ESPA-like policies to ensure stability for citizens and economic activities (Kōmeitō 2024).

Ishin

Ishin also supported the ESPA, perhaps even more stridently than the LDP. In their 2024 manifesto, they addressed economic security and trade as one of their eight key "strategies" aimed at shaping the international order and protecting people's lives (Ishin 2024). Unlike the LDP and Kōmeitō, Ishin explicitly framed China as the primary driver of economic security policy and related reforms. In their 2022 statement on the ESPA, they emphasized the need to confront challenges posed by China, stating: "Achieving lasting security requires possessing national power comparable to China…it is essential to again recognize that resolute reforms and economic growth are fundamental" (Ishin 2022).

A key difference between Ishin and the ruling coalition was their stance on autonomy. Ishin argued that Japan cannot rely solely on the Japan-U.S. alliance for defense and needs to develop greater self-sufficiency in critical resources, technologies, and industries (Ishin 2022). This contrasts with the LDP-Kōmeitō coalition, which positioned economic security more within the alliance framework.

Ishin also expressed concerns about the potential inefficiencies of excessive national security-driven regulation, warning that such policies might stifle innovation and competitiveness. Industry groups, such as Keidanren, have voiced concerns about the ESPA's potential to prioritize security over profitability (Keidanren 2022). Ishin's critique focused on what we might call crony capitalism, or the use of national security as a pretext to protect vested interests or implement inefficient policies. At the same time, Ishin also advocates for more centralized power and the ability of the state to pursue economic security aims, which may be at odds with the efficiency concerns.

The Constitutional Democratic Party

The Constitutional Democratic Party (CDP), as the primary center-left opposition party, could have taken a more oppositional stance to the LDP's economic security approach. However, their 2024 policy platform closely resembled the status quo, with only minor differences in emphasis.

The CDP's policy platform emphasized commitments to globalization and private-sector-driven economic activity within a market economy. Like other parties, the CDP supported measures to strengthen supply chain resilience and promote public-private collaboration in next-generation technologies. However, compared to the LDP or Kōmeitō, the CDP placed greater emphasis on renewable energy and green technology (Constitutional Democratic Party 2024).

On trade, the CDP expressed clear support for regional economic integration and trade liberalization. Similar to Kōmeitō, the CDP advocated for regional organizations such as the CPTPP and RCEP and called for advancing a Free Trade Area of the Asia-Pacific. Additionally, the CDP supported finalizing the long-stalled trilateral Japan-China-South Korea FTA negotiations, an initiative under discussion for over a decade (Yeo 2024; Ministry of Foreign Affairs 2012).

New Perspectives from the Left: Reiwa and the Far Left

Since the passage of the ESPA, opposition from left-leaning parties such as the Japanese Communist Party (JCP), Social Democratic Party (SDP), and Reiwa has become more articulated. While their objections are not uniform, they generally fall into three categories: opposition to U.S. militarism, opposition to significant government intervention in the economy, and concerns about the distributional consequences of trade liberalization.

The JCP, while acknowledging concerns about China, criticized Japan for closely aligning with U.S. policy on economic security. In the 2024 general election, the JCP explicitly opposed the ESPA, stating that the "Economic Security Promotion Law and the Economic Secrets Protection Law should be decisively abolished" (Japanese Communist Party 2024).

In contrast, the SDP's 2024 manifesto did not explicitly address economic security, focusing instead on domestic inequalities resulting from globalization (Social Democratic Party 2024). However, SDP leaders had previously criticized the ESPA, echoing concerns raised by the JCP. For example, the SDP's magazine described the ESPA as aligning too closely with U.S. policy toward China and increasing state involvement in private-sector activities. They indicate the potential contradiction where in countering "China's economic system, in which the state is deeply involved in economic activities, the government is seeking to manage and increase its own involvement in private-sector activities" (Matsumoto 2022).

Both the JCP and SDP express concerns about state intervention in the private sector. These concerns center on heavy government regulation, state interference in economic activities, and possible collusion between state and business actors. The SDP, for example, is critical of "the government for its intervention in businesses, raising concerns that it could stifle free economic activities, foster collusion between politicians, bureaucrats, and industries" (Matsumoto 2022). Additionally, both parties critique a growing role of the military-industrial complex, aligning with traditional leftist criticisms of Japanese policy (Green 2023). However, some critiques, such as concerns about interference in research and limits on free enterprise, reflect more classically liberal positions that diverge from the Japanese left's typical stance, even as they still embrace the left's pacifist ideals.

Reiwa offered a unique perspective, blending environmentalism and economic nationalism. Their manifesto enthusiastically embraced certain aspects of the economic security approach, promoting domestic production, re-shoring industries, increasing wages, and emphasizing green technology. However, they also called for divestment from military-related products (Reiwa 2024).

Conclusion

While the 2024 general election revealed some emerging fault lines on economic security and trade, it also underscored a shared set of policy beliefs among Japan's political mainstream. Both the center-left and center-right largely agree on the need to balance economic security concerns with Japan's status as a trading nation. This consensus reflects the broader political economy dilemma at the heart of Japan's foreign economic policy: how to engage in economic globalization while safeguarding national security in an era of geopolitical uncertainty.

Japan's approach—emphasizing pragmatic engagement in global markets alongside targeted economic security measures—offers a potential model for other nations. As the United States continues to adopt increasingly protectionist policies, Japan's steadfast commitment to trade liberalization and multilateral cooperation could position it as a stabilizing force in the global economic order. By championing frameworks such as the CPTPP and RCEP while also forging new agreements, Japan demonstrates that economic security need not come at the expense of international collaboration.

This leadership role becomes even more significant if the United States retreats further from its historical role as a global economic leader. Japan, with its focus on rules-based trade and economic partnerships, could fill some of the resulting void by strengthening alliances in Asia and Europe. Recent initiatives, such as Japan's economic security consultations with Germany, underscore its growing influence beyond its traditional reliance on U.S.-centric frameworks (Ministry of Foreign Affairs 2024).

At the same time, there are risks and challenges inherent in this balancing act. Japan's economic security measures, if perceived as overly protectionist or nationalistic, could alienate key trading partners, particularly in Southeast Asia. Domestically, these policies could raise concerns about excessive state intervention in the private sector or stifle innovation if implemented without care.

In the lead-up to the election, Prime Minister Ishiba's selection of Kiuchi Minoru as Economic Security Minister signaled Japan's commitment to refining its economic security approach. Kiuchi, a former Ministry of Foreign Affairs official with expertise in Germany and experience as both an independent and an LDP member, brought a unique perspective to the role (*Nikkei Shinbun* 2024). Shortly after the election, Japan held its first economic security consultations with Germany, expanding its cooperation beyond its traditional ally, the United States (Ministry of Foreign Affairs 2024).

As the reelection of Donald Trump in the United States has heightened uncertainty over future U.S.-Japan economic cooperation, Japan has continued its strategy of "double hedging" between the United States and China (Harris 2025). This includes discussions of finalizing the long-delayed China-Japan-South Korea FTA as advocated in the CDP's manifesto. However, the fundamentals of Japan's tightrope walk between globalization and economic security remain unchanged. As Japan navigates these challenges, its approach will likely remain a balance between pragmatic engagement in global markets and safeguarding its economic sovereignty through targeted security measures. If the United States further retreats from its role as a global economic leader, Japan has an opportunity to step into a more prominent leadership position, shaping a resilient, rules-based international order that balances openness with security.

References

Amano, Kenya, and Saori N. Katada. 2025. "Election Under Inflation: LDP's Choice of Macroeconomic Policy." In *Japan Decides 2024: The Japanese General Election,* edited by Kenneth M. McElwain, Robert J. Pekkanen, and Daniel M. Smith, 317–331. Palgrave Macmillan.

APEC Policy Support Unit. 2024. "A New Look at the Free Trade Area of the Asia-Pacific (FTAAP): Review of APEC's Collective Progress." APEC, May 2024. https://www.apec.org/docs/default-source/publications/2024/5/224_psu_anew-look-at-the-ftaap.pdf?sfvrsn=232741b0_2.

Cabinet Office of Japan. 2022. "Japan National Security Strategy." December 2022. https://www.cas.go.jp/jp/siryou/221216anzenhoshou/nss-e.pdf.

Constitutional Democratic Party. 2024. "Constitutional Democratic Party Policies 2024 [Rikken Minshutō Seisakushū 2024]." 立憲民主党. October 10, 2024. https://cdp-japan.jp/visions/policies2024.

Govella, Kristi. 2021. "The Adaptation of Japanese Economic Statecraft: Trade, Aid, and Technology." *World Trade Review* 20 (2): 186–202. https://doi.org/10.1017/S1474745620000543.

Govella, Kristi. 2023. "From Trade Laggard to Trade Leader: Japan's Role in Countering the Backlash against Globalization." In *Non-Western Nations and the Liberal International Order*, 71–94. Routledge.

Green, Michael J. 2023. "Foreign Policy and Defense." In *Japan Decides 2021: The General Election*, edited by Robert J. Pekkanen, Steven R. Reed, and Daniel M. Smith, 347–359. Palgrave Macmillan.

Harris, Tobias. 2025. "The Double Hedge Revisited." Substack. *Observing Japan* (blog). January 13, 2025.

Igata, Akira, and Brad Glosserman. 2021. "Japan's New Economic Statecraft." *The Washington Quarterly* 44 (3): 25–42. https://doi.org/10.1080/0163660X.2021.1970334.

Ishin. 2022. "Recommendations on Economic Security [Keizai Anzen Hoshō Ni Kansuru Teigen 経済安全保障に関する提言]." https://o-ishin.jp/news/2022/images/f24ccf3613bda5c1151189aed7f467fac4877f57.pdf.

Ishin. 2024. "Ishin's Eight Policies: Break Away from Old Politics [Ishin Hassaku: Furui seiji o uchiyabure 維新八策:古い政治を打ち破れ]." https://o-ishin.jp/shuin2024/manifest/pdf/pamphlet.pdf.

Japan Ministry of Defense. 2022. "National Defense Strategy of Japan." https://www.mod.go.jp/j/approach/agenda/guideline/strategy/pdf/strategy_en.pdf.

Japanese Communist Party. 2024. "Economic Security [Keizai Anzen Hoshō経済安全保障]." Japanese Communist Party. October 2024. https://www.jcp.or.jp/web_policy/2024/10/202410-bunya35.html.

Katada, Saori N. 2020. "Japan's New Regional Reality." In *Japan's New Regional Reality*. Columbia University Press.

Katada, Saori N., and Mireya Solis. 2022. "Examining US-Japan Cooperation in the Economic Security Era." Nippon.Com. December 15, 2022. https://www.nippon.com/en/in-depth/d00864/.

Keidanren. 2022. "Keizai anzen hoshō suishin hōan no sōki seiritsu o motomeru [Call for the Early Passage of the Economic Security Promotion Bill]." https://www.keidanren.or.jp/policy/2022/025.html.

Kōmeitō. 2024. "Kōmeitō Manifesto 2024 [衆院選政策集]." October 2024. https://www.komei.or.jp/special/shuin50/manifesto/manifesto2024.pdf.

Liberal Democratic Party. 2024. "Manifesto / Policy Pamphlet | Key Policies [Kōyaku / Seisaku Panfuretto | Jūten Seisaku公約・政策パンフレット | 重点政策]." 自由民主党. 2024. https://www.jimin.jp/policy/pamphlet/.

Matsumoto, Takahiro. 2022. "Toward the Enactment of the Economic Security Act ~ Strengthening Government Intervention in Economic Activities [Keizai Anzen Hoshō-hō ga Seiritsu e ~ Keizai Katsudō e no Seifu Kainyū o Kyōka]."

社民党 *SDP Japan* (blog). April 18, 2022. https://sdp.or.jp/sdp-paper/eco nomic-security/.

Matsumoto, Tomoko. 2025. "How Party Manifestos Framed Political Distrust in the 2024 Election." In *Japan Decides 2024: The Japanese General Election*, edited by Kenneth M. McElwain, Robert J. Pekkanen, and Daniel M. Smith, 143–161. Palgrave Macmillan.

Ministry of Economy, Trade, and Industry. 2019. "Sekai No Naka de No Wagakuni Seizō-Gyō No Tachi Ichi to Kakkoku No Torikumi [Position of Japan's Manufacturing Industry in the World]." In *2019年版ものづくり白書*, 22–48. Tokyo, Japan: Japanese Ministry of Economy Trade and Industry. https://www.meti.go.jp/press/2019/06/20190611002/201 90611002_07.pdf.

Ministry of Foreign Affairs. 2012. "Announcement of the Launch of the FTA Negotiations among Japan, China and Korea." November 20, 2012. https:// www.mofa.go.jp/announce/announce/2012/11/1120_02.html.

Ministry of Foreign Affairs. 2024. "The First Meeting of the Japan-Germany Economic Security Consultations." Ministry of Foreign Affairs of Japan. November 22, 2024. https://www.mofa.go.jp/erp/c_see/de/pag eite_000001_00001.html.

Negrine, Joseph. 2024. "All That Glitters May Not Be Gold for Japan's Semiconductor Revival | East Asia Forum." November 5, 2024. https://eastasiaforum.org/2024/11/05/all-that-glitters-may-not-be-gold-for-japans-semiconductor-revival/.

Nikkei Shinbun. 2024. "Profile of Economic Security Ministry Kiuchi Minoru [Kiuchi Minoru Keizai Anzen Hoshō-Shō No Yokogao]." 日本経済新聞. October 1, 2024. https://www.nikkei.com/article/DGXZQOUA293TO0Z 20C24A9000000/.

Policy Research Council. 2020. "Recommendations Toward Developing Japans 'Economic Security Strategy.'" Strategic Headquarters on the Creation of a New International Order. Liberal Democratic Party of Japan. https://sto rage2.jimin.jp/pdf/news/policy/201021_5.pdf.

Reiwa. 2024. "Reiwa Shin-Sengumi House of Representatives Election 2024 [Reiwa Shin-Sengumi Shūin-sen 2024]." れいわ新選組 衆院選2024 #比例 はれいわ. 2024. https://shu50.reiwa-shinsengumi.com/.

Schaede, Ulrike. 2020. *The Business Reinvention of Japan: How to Make Sense of the New Japan and Why It Matters*. Stanford University Press.

Social Democratic Party. 2024. "Social Democratic Party Manifesto [Shakai Minshutō Sengen]." 社民党 *SDP Japan* (blog). 2024. https://sdp.or.jp/dec laration/.

Solís, Mireya. 2017. *Dilemmas of a Trading Nation: Japan and the United States in the Evolving Asia-Pacific Order*. Brookings Institution Press.

Solis, Mireya. 2021. "The Big Squeeze: Japanese Supply Chains and Great Power Competition." *Joint U.S.-Korea Academic Studies.*

Solis, Mireya. 2024. *Japan's Quiet Leadership: Reshaping the Indo-Pacific.* Washington, DC: Brookings Institution Press. https://rowman.com/ISBN/978 0815740261/Japan%27s-Quiet-Leadership-Reshaping-the-Indo-Pacific.

Taniguchi, Masaki, Taka-aki Asano, Shōko Ōmori, and Shūsuke Takamiya. 2025. "Policy Positions of the Candidates." In *Japan Decides 2024: The Japanese General Election,* edited by Kenneth M. McElwain, Robert J. Pekkanen, and Daniel M. Smith, 125–142. Palgrave Macmillan.

Vekasi, Kristin. 2023. "China in Japan's 2021 Elections." In Robert J. Pekkanen, Steven R. Reed and Daniel M. Smith, eds. *Japan Decides 2021: The Japanese General Election,* 361–373. Palgrave Macmillan.

Vekasi, Kristin. 2023. "Japan's Approach to Economic Security and Regional Integration." In *Strategic Asia: Reshaping Economic Interdependence in the Indo-Pacific,* edited by Ashley Tellis, Alison Szalwinski, and Michael Wills.

World Bank. 2024. "Resilient and Inclusive Supply-Chain Enhancement." World Bank. May 21, 2024. https://www.worldbank.org/en/programs/ egps/brief/resilient-and-inclusive-supply-chain-enhancement.

Yeo, Han-koo. 2024. "Economic Cooperation by Korea-Japan-China Trilateral Could Ease Tensions | PIIE." June 13, 2024. https://www.piie.com/blogs/ realtime-economics/2024/economic-cooperation-korea-japan-china-trilat eral-could-ease-tensions.

CHAPTER 20

Conclusion: The LDP Loses Trust and the Illusion of Invincibility

Kenneth M. McElwain, Robert J. Pekkanen, and Daniel M. Smith

INTRODUCTION

The October 27, 2024, general election for the House of Representatives (HR) was a disaster for the Liberal Democratic Party (LDP) and its coalition partner, Kōmeitō. The LDP failed to secure a majority for only the third time since its founding in 1955, marking its second-worst performance in 70 years—surpassed only by the 2009 election, when it was supplanted by the Democratic Party of Japan (DPJ) as the largest

---

K. M. McElwain
University of Tokyo, Tokyo, Japan
e-mail: mcelwain@iss.u-tokyo.ac.jp

R. J. Pekkanen (✉)
University of Washington, Seattle, WA, USA
e-mail: robert.pekkanen@gmail.com

D. M. Smith
University of Pennsylvania, Philadelphia, PA, USA
e-mail: dms2323@sas.upenn.edu

© The Author(s), under exclusive license to Springer Nature Switzerland AG 2025
K. M. McElwain et al. (eds.), *Japan Decides 2024*,
https://doi.org/10.1007/978-3-031-98797-7_20

party. The LDP won only 191 seats (41%), losing 56 from its pre-election total of 247. Its most dramatic losses occurred in single-member districts (SMDs), where it lost 55 seats despite facing a less coordinated opposition than in the 2021 election (Maeda 2025). With Kōmeitō's 24 seats (down from 32), the coalition came up short of the 233 needed for a majority, with only 215 seats. Following the election, Prime Minister Ishiba Shigeru, already in a weak position within the LDP, was forced to govern with an even more tenuous grip on power, leading the country in a minority government.

The rebuke from voters in 2024 is all the more noteworthy as it came on the heels of more than a decade of lopsided electoral victories for the LDP. Under former Prime Minister Abe Shinzō, the LDP won successive landslide elections in 2012, 2014, and 2017 (see Pekkanen et al. 2013, 2016, 2018). After Abe stepped down in 2020, Prime Minister Kishida Fumio also managed to lead the LDP to victory in 2021 in the immediate aftermath of the Abe era, and despite the challenges of the COVID-19 pandemic (Pekkanen et al. 2023). With Abe's assassination in 2022, the financial controversies and partial dismantlement of the LDP's factions, and the LDP–Kōmeitō coalition's poor electoral performance in 2024, it appears that the period of renewed LDP dominance since 2012 is nearing an end.

How did the LDP manage to squander its dominance in 2024? Drawing on the insights presented in this volume, we argue that one of the defining differences between the 2021 and 2024 general elections was the basis on which voters judged the ruling party. In 2021, the LDP was seen as competent, or at least as more capable of governing than the opposition. By 2024, this perception had eroded. The election was no longer about competence, but about integrity. Revelations of ties between LDP politicians and the Unification Church (UC), combined with the reemergence of factional slush fund scandals, painted a picture of a party unwilling or unable to reform. The sense that the LDP could no longer be trusted, on top of growing frustration with its policy direction, turned disaffection into rejection.

In this concluding chapter, we synthesize the key analytical takeaways from the chapters in the volume to offer a coherent narrative for understanding the election results. In the process, we underline the historical significance of the 2024 election for Japanese politics and place it into comparative context with other incumbent party defeats in democratic elections around the world. Finally, we assess the post-electoral situation of minority government, and what it might mean for Japanese politics moving forward.

Understanding the LDP's 2024 Loss of Seats

At first glance, the Japanese case may appear consistent with a broader global trend. In national elections held across advanced democracies in 2024, nearly all incumbent governments saw declines in vote share. Outside observers, such as John Burn-Murdoch of *The Financial Times*, characterized this pattern as part of a "global anti-incumbent wave," driven by widespread dissatisfaction with rising inflation and increased migration (Burn-Murdoch 2024).

While this explanation is not without merit, dissatisfaction with incumbents does not automatically lead to their defeat. The LDP has long governed without majority support from the electorate—indeed, it has not captured a majority of votes in a general election since 1963. Public dissatisfaction is a necessary, but not sufficient, condition for electoral change. For incumbents to be removed from power, voters must not only disapprove of the status quo but also conclude that the ruling party is incapable of addressing their concerns and that credible alternatives exist.

In 2024, multiple developments converged to erode the LDP's electoral appeal. Japan experienced its first sustained inflation in more than two decades, coupled with stagnant real wages, reinforcing a sense of economic unease. At the same time, revelations of deep and ongoing ties between LDP politicians and the UC, as well as the exposure of factional slush funds, undermined public trust in the party's integrity. While perceptions of competence had insulated the LDP during the 2021 election cycle, by 2024, these reputational advantages had significantly weakened. The party was unable to offer compelling policy responses to either the economic downturn or the scandals that dominated headlines.

The consequences were clear. Many habitual LDP voters pulled back, either abstaining or shifting their support. Meanwhile, opposition parties that offered sharper alternatives—most notably the Democratic Party for the People (DPP)—were able to capitalize on the shifting mood.

Importantly, the outcome of the 2024 election reflects more than just short-term voter dissatisfaction. It reveals deeper fractures in the LDP's political brand and a broader erosion of trust in Japan's ruling establishment. Public opinion research shows that the institutional and reputational foundations that have long sustained the LDP are increasingly fragile (e.g., Kuriwaki et al. 2025). Across multiple domains—economic management, scandal response, and generational alignment—the 2024 election exposed how changing patterns in political behavior are contributing to the ongoing fragmentation of Japan's party system. Reinforcing this trend, Asano (2022) finds that ideological extremists have become more politically active relative to centrists since 2012, further destabilizing mainstream party support. The 2024 election also signaled a rising demand for political reform and a growing receptiveness to alternative voices on the political periphery.

Economic Frustration

Persistent economic dissatisfaction provided the underlying conditions for voter frustration. Yukio Maeda notes that disapproval of the LDP's economic policy began rising in early 2022 and surpassed scandal-related disapproval by midyear (Maeda 2025). Kristin Vekasi (2025) further observes that while the LDP emphasized abstract themes like "economic security"—covering trade, energy, and technological autonomy—its messaging in the 2024 campaign failed to connect with voters' immediate concerns. The party largely avoided specific trade issues, and its economic platform did little to address stagnating wages or rising prices.

Poor macroeconomic performance is not new in Japan, but the LDP has historically mitigated its political costs through redistributive measures and targeted pork-barrel spending (e.g., Naoi 2015; Catalinac 2025). Kenya Amano and Saori N. Katada (2025) argue that this compensatory logic broke down in 2024. The party's limited fiscal maneuverability, driven by internal divisions and Ishiba's commitment to fiscal restraint, narrowed its policy options during the campaign. Even though Ishiba highlighted the importance of local rejuvenation (*chihō sōsei*) in the LDP's campaign, both Yukio Maeda (2025) and Michio Umeda (2025) note that this agenda failed to resonate with voters. The LDP's inability to pivot toward redistribution or tax relief reinforced perceptions of policy stagnation.

Political Scandals and Declining Trust

The erosion of trust in the LDP played a central role in the party's 2024 losses. Scholars of political trust have noted that it can encompass several meanings for voters, including benevolence, competence, and integrity (e.g., Devine et al. 2025). In each of these meanings, trust is often regarded as a key example of a "valence" issue in elections, in contrast to the policy positions of parties (e.g., Hetherington 1998; Clark 2013; Green and Jennings 2017).

In survey experiments conducted across the three most recent general elections, Kuriwaki et al. (2025) find that LDP support in 2017 and 2021 was driven largely by valence considerations—perceptions of competence and credibility. In 2021, for example, the party was viewed as competently handling the COVID-19 pandemic (Pekkanen et al. 2023). In 2024, in contrast, the LDP's valence advantage collapsed. The series of money-related scandals and ethical breaches leading up to the election resulted in many less ideologically committed voters abandoning the party.

Kuniaki Nemoto (2025) identifies three major scandal-related factors: revelations of widespread ties between LDP politicians and the UC, the exposure of illegal kickbacks through factional slush funds, and a lack of decisive leadership in response. Masaki Taniguchi et al. (2025) show that "political and administrative reform" was the most frequently cited campaign issue by candidates in the University of Tokyo and *Asahi Shinbun* (UTAS) survey, surpassing social welfare and education for the first time since UTAS began surveying candidates and voters in 2007. The prominence of this issue reflected public concern about institutional integrity and elite accountability.

Despite the visibility of these issues, none of the LDP presidential candidates in September 2024—including eventual winner Ishiba—offered meaningful reform proposals. Party manifestos revealed contrasting framings of political distrust. Tomoko Matsumoto (2025) shows that the LDP emphasized procedural responses, focusing on transparency and adherence to existing rules. Opposition parties—especially those on the left—stressed systemic corruption, citing collusion between government and business and the misuse of public funds.

These scandals had measurable electoral effects. Nemoto (2025) finds that candidates linked to the UC or implicated in underreporting political funds performed significantly worse at the polls. The resulting climate of distrust appears to have demobilized even some core LDP supporters. According to Tetsuya Matsubayashi (2025), many habitual LDP voters became disillusioned with the party's leadership and chose to abstain rather than shift their support, thereby amplifying LDP losses, particularly in SMDs.

A Fragmented Opposition and Strategic Gains

The 2024 election did not produce a wholesale realignment, but it did reveal important shifts within the opposition. Fumi Ikeda writes that the Constitutional Democratic Party (CDP) gained seats, particularly in urban areas, by distancing itself from the Japanese Communist Party (JCP) and targeting districts affected by LDP corruption scandals (Ikeda 2025). However, the CDP's vote share was roughly the same as in 2021. One limitation of the party's strategy was its shift toward the political center. Under the moderate leadership of former Prime Minister Noda Yoshihiko, the CDP moved closer to the LDP on key policy issues, including support for constitutional revision and strengthened defense policy—positions it shared not only with the ruling party but also with the newly formed Conservative Party of Japan (CPJ). As Ko Maeda (2025) notes, this repositioning under Noda failed to expand the party's appeal to centrist voters. The ideological gap between the CDP and the LDP narrowed, even as new parties with more polarizing messages gained visibility on both the left and right (Taniguchi et al. 2025).

Other opposition parties were even less successful. Nippon Ishin no Kai (Ishin), previously viewed as a rising third force in Japanese politics (Reed et al. 2013; Pekkanen and Reed 2023), underperformed in 2024. As Masahiro Zenkyo (2025) shows, the party suffered from inconsistent messaging and was seen as ineffective during Diet deliberations on political finance reform. These perceptions undercut its reformist image and limited its appeal beyond Osaka Prefecture.

By contrast, smaller parties with more targeted platforms were able to capitalize on voter dissatisfaction. The DPP campaigned on increasing take-home pay and lowering taxes, attracting strong support among voters under 40, particularly those in their twenties (Maeda 2025). Matsubayashi (2025) argues that these younger voters, traditionally less likely to turn out, were mobilized in part by the DPP's economic messaging and leadership appeal. As Matsumoto (2025) further highlights, the DPP's platform emphasized inclusivity and immediate economic benefits, while giving relatively little attention to older voters or long-term fiscal tradeoffs.

The DPP and Reiwa Shinsengumi also stood out for proposing distinctive policies—such as scholarship amnesties, full income compensation during childcare leave, and tailored tax relief—that helped differentiate them from more established parties. As Reiko Arami (2025) observes, while most parties emphasized support for childcare and education, the specificity and boldness of the DPP and Reiwa's proposals made them more electorally competitive, especially among younger cohorts. This generationally targeted strategy sharpened age-based divides in policy preferences and contributed to their relative success.

Shifting Electoral Terrain

The 2024 election also underscored gradual but important changes in the structure and style of electoral competition. Umeda (2025) and Matsumoto (2025) document how demographic shifts, urbanization, and the growing role of digital media are reshaping both the electorate and the methods used to reach it. Traditional forms of mobilization—such as street-level canvassing, postal flyers, and personal networks—are proving less effective among younger voters, who respond more readily to digital outreach. Robert A. Fahey (2025) highlights how the DPP, more than its rivals, leveraged social media to engage younger constituencies through targeted and responsive messaging, contrasting with the standardized approaches favored by established parties.

These evolving campaign practices also exposed the limits of older mobilization strategies. Kōmeitō, once a highly disciplined junior coalition partner, suffered one of its worst electoral outcomes since aligning with the LDP. Axel Klein and Levi McLaughlin (2025) attribute this decline to internal organizational challenges following the 2023 death of Sōka Gakkai's longtime leader Ikeda Daisaku and the aging of its core base. Its weakening coordination with the LDP further reduced its competitiveness, particularly in SMDs.

Alongside these strategic and demographic shifts, the ideological contours of party competition appear to be changing. Taniguchi et al. (2025) argue that the narrowing policy gap between the LDP and CDP created openings for smaller parties with more populist or outsider appeals. Though still peripheral, Reiwa, Sanseitō, and the CPJ drew attention by challenging the elite consensus and advocating for fiscal expansion. The platforms of these parties echo a broader skepticism—also identified by Vekasi (2025)—toward fiscal conservatism and technocratic policymaking. While framed differently across the political spectrum, these critiques reflect emerging cleavages in how economic governance and political legitimacy are contested in contemporary Japan.

The Post-Election Situation: A New Era of Uncertainty

The 2024 election ushered in an unusual political configuration: a minority government led by Prime Minister Ishiba. While minority governments are common in other parliamentary democracies (Field and Martin 2022), they remain rare in Japan, where LDP dominance (even if in coalition) has long been the norm. As defined by Cheibub et al. (2021, 351), a minority government is one where the parties holding ministerial portfolios do not control a majority of seats in the legislature. In the Japanese context, this development marks a significant departure from postwar political patterns.

The last instance of a minority government in Japan occurred under LDP Prime Minister Hashimoto Ryūtarō, following the 1996 general election. At that time, the LDP secured 239 out of 500 seats in the HR and governed as a single-party minority, relying on "confidence and supply" agreements with the Social Democratic Party (SDP) and New Party Sakigake. Although the three parties had formed a formal coalition prior to the election, the post-election arrangement functioned without full cabinet integration.

The conditions that political scientists associate with the emergence of minority governments may now apply to Japan. Strøm (1990) argues that such governments are more likely when parties expect future elections to be competitive and when opposition parties have sufficient strength to influence legislation in the interim. Both dynamics are visible in the post-2024 environment: the LDP has lost its dominant position, and opposition parties—while divided—have gained enough presence to shape key legislative debates, particularly around economic reform and political accountability.

Within this evolving landscape, the DPP has emerged as a potential pivotal player in future coalition-building. Taniguchi et al. (2025) observe that the DPP's gains have positioned it as a centrist force capable of playing a swing role in the more fragmented Diet. However, the DPP remains smaller than the CDP, both in total seat share and organizational depth. Its rise has also revealed new fault lines within the opposition. Both the DPP and CDP draw institutional support from Rengō, Japan's largest trade union federation, which has historically pushed for a unified center-left bloc. As Ikeda (2025) notes, Rengō's traditional base has become divided between two competing parties, complicating voter mobilization strategies in districts where both the DPP and CDP field candidates.

Despite its success in carving into the LDP's base, the DPP's long-term viability remains uncertain. As discussed earlier, the party's appeal in 2024 stemmed from targeted, issue-specific proposals that resonated with younger and economically frustrated voters. But it is still a relative newcomer to national politics, and it remains to be seen whether voters will continue to support the DPP as a credible alternative across the broader spectrum of policy challenges facing Japan. Its ability to institutionalize this support and build a durable centrist identity will be a key factor in shaping the next phase of party system development.

Broader Implications for Japanese Democracy

The 2024 election holds important implications for the future of Japanese democracy. Unlike many recent elections around the world, it was not bedeviled by widespread disinformation or political violence. Voter choices appeared to move Japan back toward the political center—a notable development following the rightward drift that characterized the era of former Prime Minister Abe, Japan's longest-serving leader.

However, there are also warning signs. The left-wing populist Reiwa secured nine seats, while the right-wing newcomer parties, Sanseitō and the CPJ, each won three. These numbers are modest, and it may be tempting to dismiss them as outliers. However, as experience from other democracies suggests, once such parties gain a foothold, they often persist and gradually expand their influence. Their emergence underscores growing voter frustration with the status quo and signals potential volatility in future contests.

Low turnout adds to this concern. Continuing a trend since 2014, participation in 2024 remained stagnant, at around 54%. Paired with the modest but noticeable gains of fringe parties, this suggests a broader disaffection with established political actors. As discussed earlier, dissatisfaction with the LDP's integrity was a central driver of electoral behavior in 2024, but it remains unclear whether mainstream parties can rebuild trust and reengage a disenchanted electorate.

This disillusionment extends to the internal workings of the ruling party itself. The future of factions within the LDP—long a central feature of its internal organization—has become increasingly uncertain. Widely viewed as contributing to the slush fund scandals, factions have fallen out of favor with voters, but they have historically played a key role in managing leadership succession and internal discipline (e.g., Krauss and Pekkanen 2011). If factions continue to weaken, it is unclear what will replace them as mechanisms of party cohesion and governance.

Despite these potentially worrying trends, it is important to recognize that the 2024 election also affirmed Japan's continued commitment to democratic norms. The contest was free, fair, and orderly, and conducted without disinformation campaigns, electoral violence, or disputes over legitimacy. In a global context where democratic institutions are under strain, Japan's relative political stability stands out. The country may now have an opportunity to assume a more prominent role in defending liberal democracy and supporting the rules-based international order. Without Abe, who positioned himself as a conduit to leaders like U.S. President Donald Trump, this role may be more difficult to define. Even so, Japan's steady democratic performance, despite domestic discontent and shifting party dynamics, offers a foundation for renewed leadership both at home and abroad.

References

Amano, Kenya, and Saori N. Katada. 2025. "Election Under Inflation: LDP's Choice of Macroeconomic Policy." In *Japan Decides 2024: The Japanese General Election,* edited by Kenneth M. McElwain, Robert J. Pekkanen, and Daniel M. Smith, 317–331. Palgrave Macmillan.

Arami, Reiko. 2025. "Childcare Policy in the 2024 Election: Who Resonated with the Public Amid an Unprecedented Birthrate Decline?" In *Japan Decides 2024: The Japanese General Election,* edited by Kenneth M. McElwain, Robert J. Pekkanen, and Daniel M. Smith, 293–315. Palgrave Macmillan.

Asano, Taka-aki. 2022. "Ideological Extremism and Political Participation in Japan." *Social Science Japan Journal* 25 (1): 125–140.

Burn-Murdoch, John. 2024. "Democrats join 2024's graveyard of incumbents." *The Financial Times,* November 6, 2024. https://www.ft.com/content/e8ac09ea-c300-4249-af7d-109003afb893.

Catalinac, Amy. 2025. *Dominance Through Division: Group-Based Clientelism in Japan.* Cambridge University Press.

Cheibub, José Antonio, Shane Martin, and Bjørn Erik Rasch. 2021. "Investiture Rules and Formation of Minority Governments in European Parliamentary Democracies." *Party Politics* 27 (2): 351–362.

Clark, Michael. 2013. "Understanding Parties' Policy Shifts in Western Europe: The Role of Valence, 1976–2003." *British Journal of Political Science* 44 (2): 261–286.

Devine, Daniel, Viktor Valgardsson, Will Jennings, Gerry Stoker, and Hannah Bunting. 2025. "The Causes of Perceived Government Trustworthiness." *European Journal of Political Research* 64 (3): 1394–1412.

Fahey, Robert A. 2025. "Social Media in the 2024 General Election." In *Japan Decides 2024: The Japanese General Election*, edited by Kenneth M. McElwain, Robert J. Pekkanen, and Daniel M. Smith, 181–195. Palgrave Macmillan.

Field, Bonnie N., and Shane Martin, eds. 2022. *Minority Governments in Comparative Perspective*. Oxford University Press.

Green, Jane, and Will Jennings. 2017. *The Politics of Competence: Parties, Public Opinion and Voters*. Cambridge University Press.

Hetherington, Marc J. 1998. "The Political Relevance of Political Trust." *American Political Science Review* 92 (4): 791–808.

Ikeda, Fumi. 2025. "The CDP in 2024: The Legacy of the Electoral Coalition with the JCP." In *Japan Decides 2024: The Japanese General Election*, edited by Kenneth M. McElwain, Robert J. Pekkanen, and Daniel M. Smith, 57–74. Palgrave Macmillan.

Klein, Axel, and Levi McLaughlin. 2025. "A Costly Coalition: Komeito's Enduring Partnership with the LDP." In *Japan Decides 2024: The Japanese General Election*, edited by Kenneth M. McElwain, Robert J. Pekkanen, and Daniel M. Smith, 75–90. Palgrave Macmillan.

Krauss, Ellis S., and Robert J. Pekkanen. 2011. *The Rise and Fall of Japan's LDP: Political Organizations as Historical Institutions*. Cornell University Press.

Kuriwaki, Shiro, Yusaku Horiuchi, and Daniel M. Smith. 2025. "Winning Elections with Unpopular Policies: Valence Advantage and Single-Party Dominance in Japan." *Quarterly Journal of Political Science*, 20 (4): 439–476.

Maeda, Ko. 2025. "The 2024 Election Results: A Political Earthquake." In *Japan Decides 2024: The Japanese General Election*, edited by Kenneth M. McElwain, Robert J. Pekkanen, and Daniel M. Smith, 17–34. Palgrave Macmillan.

Maeda, Yukio. 2025. "Public Opinion and Scandals in Economic Hard Times." In *Japan Decides 2024: The Japanese General Election*, edited by Kenneth M. McElwain, Robert J. Pekkanen, and Daniel M. Smith, 163–179. Palgrave Macmillan.

Matsubayashi, Tetsuya. 2025. "Partisanship and Turnout in the 2024 General Election." In *Japan Decides 2024: The Japanese General Election*, edited by Kenneth M. McElwain, Robert J. Pekkanen, and Daniel M. Smith, 197–214. Palgrave Macmillan.

Matsumoto, Tomoko. 2025. "How Party Manifestos Framed Political Distrust in the 2024 Election." In *Japan Decides 2024: The Japanese General Election*, edited by Kenneth M. McElwain, Robert J. Pekkanen, and Daniel M. Smith, 143–161. Palgrave Macmillan.

Naoi, Megumi. 2015. *Building Legislative Coalitions for Free Trade in Asia.* Cambridge University Press.

Nemoto, Kuniaki. 2025. "Reasons Behind the LDP's Loss in the 2024 Election." In *Japan Decides 2024: The Japanese General Election,* edited by Kenneth M. McElwain, Robert J. Pekkanen, and Daniel M. Smith, 37–55. Palgrave Macmillan.

Pekkanen, Robert J., and Steven R. Reed. 2023. "The Opposition in 2021: A Second Party and Third Force." In *Japan Decides 2021: The Japanese General Election,* edited by Robert J. Pekkanen, Steven R. Reed, and Daniel M. Smith, 59–69. Palgrave Macmillan.

Pekkanen, Robert, Steven R. Reed, and Ethan Scheiner, eds. 2013. *Japan Decides 2012: The Japanese General Election.* Palgrave Macmillan.

Pekkanen, Robert J., Steven R. Reed, and Ethan Scheiner, eds. 2016. *Japan Decides 2014: The Japanese General Election.* Palgrave Macmillan.

Pekkanen, Robert J., Steven R. Reed, Ethan Scheiner, and Daniel M. Smith. eds. 2018. *Japan Decides 2017: The Japanese General Election.* Palgrave Macmillan.

Pekkanen, Robert J., Steven R. Reed, and Daniel M. Smith, eds. 2023. *Japan Decides 2021: The Japanese General Election.* Palgrave Macmillan.

Reed, Steven R., Ethan Scheiner, Daniel M. Smith, and Michael Thies. 2013. "The 2012 Election Results: The LDP Wins Big by Default." In *Japan Decides 2012: The Japanese General Election,* edited by Robert Pekkanen, Steven R. Reed, and Ethan Scheiner, 34–46. Palgrave Macmillan.

Strøm, Kaare. 1990. *Minority Government and Majority Rule.* Cambridge University Press.

Taniguchi, Masaki, Taka-aki Asano, Shōko Ōmori, and Shūsuke Takamiya. 2025. "Policy Positions of the Candidates." In *Japan Decides 2024: The Japanese General Election,* edited by Kenneth M. McElwain, Robert J. Pekkanen, and Daniel M. Smith, 125–142. Palgrave Macmillan.

Umeda, Michio. 2025. "Electoral Campaigns in Japan's 2024 General Election: Emerging Signs of Transformation." In *Japan Decides 2024: The Japanese General Election,* edited by Kenneth M. McElwain, Robert J. Pekkanen, and Daniel M. Smith, 109–124. Palgrave Macmillan.

Vekasi, Kristin. 2025. "Japan Decides Its Role in the Global Economy: Trade and Economic Security in the 2024 Election." In *Japan Decides 2024: The Japanese General Election,* edited by Kenneth M. McElwain, Robert J. Pekkanen, and Daniel M. Smith, 333–346. Palgrave Macmillan.

Zenkyo, Masahiro. 2025. "Why Did Public Support for the Japan Innovation Party Decline in the 2024 HR Election?" In *Japan Decides 2024: The Japanese General Election,* edited by Kenneth M. McElwain, Robert J. Pekkanen, and Daniel M. Smith, 91–105. Palgrave Macmillan.

INDEX

A

Abenomics, 130, 132, 321, 323, 324, 330
Abe, Shinzō, 4, 5, 10, 11, 38–43, 46, 51, 77, 79, 81, 84, 111, 117, 119, 135, 165–167, 169, 173, 177, 186, 219, 221–223, 225, 228–231, 234, 237–246, 249, 251, 253, 259, 281–283, 298, 311, 321, 323, 324, 326, 328, 350, 357, 358
Age cohort, 114
Article 9, 128. *See also* Constitutional revision

B

Baba, Nobuyuki, 8, 27, 93, 95–99, 103, 104
Budget, 32, 88, 133, 142, 308, 312, 329

C

Cabinet, 6, 19, 22, 32, 39, 43, 45, 47, 83, 117, 146, 166–170, 186, 200, 206, 222, 225, 226, 228, 233, 240, 241, 326, 356
Campaign law. *See* Public Office Election Law
Childcare policy, 11, 12, 298, 302, 309, 311
Cohorts. *See* Age cohort
Collective self-defense, 84, 128
Comprehensive and Progressive Agreement for Trans-Pacific Partnership (CPTPP), 337, 340–342, 344
Constitutional amendment. *See* Constitutional revision
Conservative Party of Japan (CPJ, Nippon Hoshutō), 10, 19, 137, 149, 184, 260, 261, 283, 285, 354, 355
Constitutional Democratic Party of Japan (CDP, Rikken Minshutō),

37, 57, 91, 150, 260, 280, 286, 327
Constitutional revision, 9, 93, 354
Consumption tax, 327, 329, 330
COVID-19 (coronavirus), 4, 5, 166, 178, 179, 184, 188, 319, 321, 322, 338, 350, 353

D
Democratic Party for the People (DPP, Kokumin Minshutō), 4, 18, 58, 92, 110, 148, 184, 190, 260, 279, 287, 309, 321, 351
Democratic Party of Japan (DPJ, Minshutō), 29, 57, 114, 349
Demographic change, 123, 297

E
Economic security, 12, 336–345, 352
Edano, Yukio, 30, 58, 60, 61, 64–68, 71
Education policy, 311
Electoral coalition, 58–61, 71

G
Gender equality, 11, 244, 246, 258, 267, 283, 286, 287
Gender parity quota, 268, 269

H
Hashimoto, Ryūtarō, 356
Hope, Party of Hope (Kibō no Tō), 29
House of Councillors (HC)
 2013 election, 59, 115
 2016 election, 59, 71
 2019 election, 59
 2022 election, 19, 30, 45, 60, 91, 116, 166

House of Representatives (HR)
 2012 election, 3
 2014 election, 3
 2017 election, 3
 2021 election, 3

I
Immigration, 19, 283
Inequality, 12
Inflation, 12, 13, 116, 319–323, 325, 329, 330, 351
Ishiba, Shigeru, 4, 6, 8, 9, 12, 18, 19, 22, 25, 32, 37, 38, 46–48, 50, 51, 109–111, 116–120, 123, 146, 173–179, 186, 187, 231, 232, 251, 252, 259, 283, 321, 324, 326, 327, 330, 331, 345, 350, 352, 353, 356
Ishin, Japan Ishin no Kai (Nippon Ishin no Kai), 4, 7, 8, 18, 19, 22, 25–28, 31, 62, 64, 70, 81, 83, 87, 91–96, 98, 100–104, 110, 123, 134–136, 140, 141, 150, 154, 155, 157, 192, 201, 202, 208, 209, 212, 248, 260–262, 264, 265, 267, 268, 279, 280, 287–289, 304, 306–308, 314, 327–330, 336, 341, 342, 354

J
Japanese Communist Party (JCP, Nihon Kyōsantō), 8, 18, 41, 58, 110, 249, 260, 280, 286, 305, 336, 343, 354
Japan Innovation Party. *See* Ishin

K
Kishida, Fumio, 4–6, 10, 17, 19, 32, 42–47, 77, 79, 82, 109, 118, 144, 164–173, 175, 176, 179,

186, 187, 200, 222, 223, 225, 226, 228–231, 233, 238, 240, 241, 248, 250, 251, 279, 280, 283, 301, 312, 323–327, 350
Koike, Yuriko, 60, 116, 314
Koizumi, Shinjirō, 6, 46, 173, 174, 176, 259, 321, 324–326
Kōmeitō, 4, 5, 8, 13, 18–22, 27, 31, 37, 48–51, 75–85, 87, 88, 94, 103, 110, 113, 114, 116, 133–135, 140, 141, 150, 151, 153–155, 157, 232, 233, 248, 251, 260–262, 264, 268, 277, 285, 288, 298, 303, 307, 308, 314, 328, 340–342, 349, 350, 355

L
LGBTQ+ rights, 11, 246, 275–280, 282–286, 288, 289
Liberal Democratic Party (LDP) (Jiyū Minshutō), 4–13, 18, 22–26, 29–33, 37, 38, 40–45, 47–51, 57, 59, 62, 64, 65, 68, 70, 72, 75, 76, 79, 81–88, 92–95, 109–111, 113–119, 121–123, 128, 132–141, 145, 150, 151, 153–155, 157, 158, 165, 167, 169, 171, 173–177, 179, 186, 188, 189, 191, 192, 200–202, 204–206, 208, 209, 212, 214, 219–221, 223–233, 237, 238, 241, 245, 246, 248, 250–252, 258–263, 265, 267–270, 277–289, 297–299, 303, 304, 307, 314, 321, 323, 324, 326–330, 340–342, 345, 349–357

M
Manifesto, 9, 11, 61, 83, 85, 146, 148–155, 157–159, 275, 278, 284–289, 327, 336, 339, 341, 344, 345, 353
Matsuno, Hirokazu, 169
Minority government, 4, 76, 88, 195, 321, 328, 350, 351, 356
Monetary policy, 134, 320, 324, 325, 327–330

N
Noda Yoshihiko, 30, 37, 60, 140, 327, 354
Nomination, 6, 18, 37, 44, 47, 48, 58, 62, 109, 119, 122, 232, 261

O
Okada, Katsuya, 62, 64
Olympics, 278, 279
Ozawa, Ichirō, 60–62, 65, 187

P
Party competition, 33, 112, 314, 355
Political corruption, 297
Political Funds Control Law (PFCL), 51, 93, 134, 135
Political scandal, 7, 9, 13, 123, 145, 284, 352
Political trust, 9, 145, 146, 352
Prefectural assembly, 86, 224, 240
  Osaka, 87
  Tokyo, 194
Proportional representation (PR), 7, 11, 17, 19, 20, 22, 25, 26, 28, 30–32, 61, 68, 69, 76, 79, 85, 87, 88, 91, 92, 94, 101, 112–114, 116, 119, 121, 123, 138, 139, 176, 177, 201, 211, 232, 262–265, 270, 310

Public Office Election Law (POEL), 183
Public opinion, 9, 95, 145, 146, 177–179, 222, 277, 283, 351

R
Reiwa Shinsengumi, 9, 18, 110, 188, 241, 305, 309, 321, 354
Renho, 60, 116, 194
Rural districts, 110, 113, 118
Russia, 5, 278, 322

S
Saitō Tetsuo, 80, 82, 88
Sanseitō, 10, 18, 19, 110, 116, 133, 137, 138, 149–154, 184, 185, 191, 192, 260, 262, 266, 268, 283, 285, 355, 357
Scandal. *See* Political scandal
Self-Defense Forces (SDF), 5, 18, 84, 126, 148, 149, 152, 156, 258, 259, 266, 304, 305, 341
Single-member districts (SMDs), 7, 47, 49, 50, 61, 76, 82, 111–113, 119, 121, 138, 262, 310, 314, 350
Single-seat districts. *See* Single-member districts
Slush funds scandal, 168
Social Democratic Party (SDP, Shakai Minshutō), 18, 147, 278, 284, 341, 354
Social media, 7, 10, 30, 149, 183–186, 188–195, 221, 223, 240, 241, 304, 355
Sōka Gakkai, 8, 76, 77, 81–84, 87, 88, 114, 240, 246, 353
South Korea, 221, 244, 245, 277
Suga, Yoshihide, 4, 77, 79, 170, 186
Supply chain, 319, 322, 338–340, 342

Supreme Court, 113, 280, 281, 284–286, 288

T
Takaichi, Sanae, 6, 47, 117, 173–175, 186, 189, 231, 259, 321, 324, 326–328
Tamaki, Yūichirō, 29, 116, 141, 190–192, 194, 205
Taxation, 191, 298, 304, 324
Tokyo prefectural assembly. *See* Prefectural assembly, Tokyo
Trade policy, 336, 337, 339, 341
Trans-Pacific Partnership (TPP), 337
Trump, Donald, 195, 337, 345, 358
Trust. *See* Political trust
Turnout, 10, 19, 80, 114, 148, 199–204, 207–210, 212, 214, 357
Twitter. *See* X/Twitter

U
Ukraine, 5, 166, 168, 188, 319, 322, 338
Unification Church (UC), 5, 38, 49, 51, 57, 77–79, 81, 165, 219–221, 224, 226, 233, 238–246, 248, 249, 251, 252, 259, 269, 281, 282, 284, 324, 350
United States (United States of America), 195, 243, 247, 277, 320, 337, 344, 345
 alliance, 128, 129, 342
 Security treaty, 128, 129
University of Tokyo-Asahi Survey (UTAS), 9, 127, 133–136, 140, 141, 268, 269, 299, 353
Uragane. *See* slush funds scandal
Urban districts, 113

V
Voter turnout. *See* Turnout

W
Women's representation, 257, 260

X
X/Twitter, 116, 185, 189, 193

Y
Yamamoto, Tarō, 187, 188, 190, 191
YouTube, 115, 116, 123, 185, 189, 193

GPSR Compliance

The European Union's (EU) General Product Safety Regulation (GPSR) is a set of rules that requires consumer products to be safe and our obligations to ensure this.

If you have any concerns about our products, you can contact us on

ProductSafety@springernature.com

In case Publisher is established outside the EU, the EU authorized representative is:

Springer Nature Customer Service Center GmbH
Europaplatz 3
69115 Heidelberg, Germany

www.ingramcontent.com/pod-product-compliance
Lightning Source LLC
LaVergne TN
LVHW012032070526
838202LV00056B/5473